CliffsNotes®

CBEST®

CliffsNotes®

CBEST®

7TH EDITION

By
Jerry Bobrow, Ph.D.

Revised by
Joy Mondragon-Gilmore, M.S.
Paula Moseley, Ph.D.
Barbara Swovelin, M.A.
Jerry Swovelin, M.A.
Nadine Krystkowiak, B.S.

Contributing Authors

Peter Z. Orton, Ph.D.
William A. Covino, Ph.D.
Debbie Budesa, M.A.
Jean Eggenschwiler, M.A.
Allan Casson, Ph.D.
Ron Podrasky, M.S.
Bill Burns, M.A.

Houghton Mifflin Harcourt
Boston   New York

About the Authors

Dr. Jerry Bobrow, Ph.D., founded Bobrow Test Preparation Services, and his faculty and contributing authors have conducted the test preparation programs at over 25 California institutions for the past 30 years. Dr. Bobrow authored over 30 national best-selling test preparation books, and his books and programs have assisted over two million test-takers. Bobrow Test Preparation Services lectures to thousands of students on preparing for graduate, college, and teacher credentialing exams.

Editorial

Acquisitions Editor: Greg Tubach

Project Editor: Suzanne Snyder

Copy Editor: Marylouise Wiack

Technical Editors: Mary Jane Sterling

Composition

Proofreader: Penny Stuart

Wiley Publishing, Inc. Composition Services

CliffsNotes® CBEST® 7th Edition

Library of Congress Cataloging-in-Publication data is available from the publisher upon request.
ISBN: 978-0-470-45453-4

Printed in the United States of America
DOO 10 9 8
4500572257

For information about permission to reproduce selections from this book, please write
Permissions, Houghton Mifflin Harcourt Publishing Company,
215 Park Avenue South, New York, New York 10003.

www.hmhco.com

Dedication

This book is dedicated to the memory of Dr. Jerry Bobrow, award-winning author and educator. Dr. Bobrow passed prior to the publication of this book, after a valiant battle against cancer. Dr. Bobrow helped thousands of prospective teachers achieve their goal of becoming teachers. His lifelong commitment to helping others seek advancement through higher education continues with this preparation guide, *CliffsTestPrep® CBEST.* Dr. Bobrow believed that a person's highest potential is achieved through education and learning. Born in Rome, Italy, he is survived by his wife of thirty-three years, Susan; his three children, Jennifer, Adam, and Jonathan; and his parents, Abram and Julia Bobrow, both Holocaust survivors.

Acknowledgments

This book would not be possible without the collaboration of a team of professional educators and administrators at school districts throughout California. In addition, sincere thanks and appreciation are extended to Suzanne Snyder of Wiley Publishing, Inc., and Marylouise Wiack, for their dedication and careful attention to editing details; Cindy Hadash and Ann Rothstein for their assistance in assembling the manuscript; and Pitt Gilmore, Linnea Fredrickson, and Melinda Masson for proofreading the revised edition.

Table of Contents

PART I: ANALYSIS OF EXAM AREAS

PART II: MATHEMATICS REVIEW

PART III: PRACTICE-REVIEW-ANALYZE-PRACTICE

PART IV: FINAL PREPARATION

Preface

We know that getting a good score on the CBEST is important to you, and thorough preparation is the key to doing your best! This guide is designed to provide you with the information necessary for your comprehensive and successful preparation while reintroducing you to some basic skills and knowledge that you may not have used in many years. To help increase your understanding of the test, we have included a complete analysis of exam areas and question types, instructional problem-solving explanations, up-to-date examples, and extensive practice in **four full-length practice tests.**

In keeping with the fine tradition of CliffsNotes, this material was carefully researched and developed by leading test preparation experts and instructors. The strategies and time-saving techniques have been tested and evaluated in test preparation programs presently being used in CBEST preparation programs offered through California universities, colleges, and teachers' associations.

This guide is divided into an introduction and four parts:

- **Introduction to CBEST:** A general description of the paper-based and computer-based exams, recent format of the exams, questions commonly asked, basic overall strategies, and a tutorial for the computer-based exam.
- **Part I — Analysis of Exam Areas:** Focuses on ability tested for reading, math, and writing along with basic skills necessary, directions, analysis, suggested approaches with lots of samples, and additional tips.
- **Part II — Mathematics Review:** A short, intensive review of the basics of arithmetic, algebra, and measurement, starting with a diagnostic test in each area. Important terminology is also included.
- **Part III — Practice-Review-Analyze-Practice:** Four complete, full-length practice tests with answers and in-depth explanations.
- **Part IV — Final Preparation:** A list of last-minute test-taking tips.

The practice tests are followed by analysis charts to assist you in evaluating your progress. This guide is not meant to substitute for comprehensive courses, but if you follow the Study Guide Checklist (the next section) and study regularly, you'll get the best CBEST preparation possible.

Study Guide Checklist

❏ 1. Read the CBEST information materials available at the Testing Office, Counseling Center, or Credential Preparation Office at your undergraduate institution.

❏ 2. Become familiar with the paper- and computer-based test formats (see Format of the CBEST on page 1).

❏ 3. Computer-based test takers: Read the tutorial for the computer-based exam.

❏ 4. Read General Description and Questions Commonly Asked about the CBEST Examination, starting on pages 1 and 2, respectively.

❏ 5. Learn the techniques of Three Successful Approaches to the Multiple-Choice Questions, starting on page 4.

❏ 6. Carefully read Part I, Analysis of Exam Areas, starting on page 13.

❏ 7. Review Mathematical Terminology, starting on page 149.

❏ 8. Take the Arithmetic Diagnostic Test, starting on page 157, check your answers, and review the appropriate areas in the Arithmetic Review.

❏ 9. Take the Algebra Diagnostic Test, starting on page 173, check your answers, and review the appropriate areas in the Algebra Review.

❏ 10. Take the Measurement Diagnostic Test, starting on page 177, check your answers, and review the appropriate areas in the Measurement Review.

❏ 11. Strictly observing the time allotment, take Practice Test 1, starting on page 183.

❏ 12. Check your answers and analyze your Practice Test 1 results, starting on page 210.

❏ 13. Fill out the Tally Sheet for Questions Missed to pinpoint your mistakes, page 211.

❏ 14. Study *all* the Answers and Complete Explanations to Practice Test 1, starting on page 213.

❏ 15. Have a friend or English instructor read and evaluate your essays using the Essay Checklist, page 212.

❏ 16. Review weak areas as necessary.

❏ 17. Strictly observing the time allotment, take Practice Test 2, starting on page 227.

❏ 18. Check your answers and analyze your Practice Test 2 results, starting on page 256.

Follow the same procedures as for Practice Test 1: Fill out the Tally Sheet for Questions Missed; study *all* the Answers and Complete Explanations; have a friend or English instructor evaluate your essays using the Essay Checklists; review weak areas as necessary.

❏ 19. Strictly observing the time allotment, take Practice Test 3, starting on page 273.

Follow the same procedures as for Practice Tests 1 and 2: Fill out the Tally Sheet for Questions Missed; study *all* the Answers and Complete Explanations; have a friend or English instructor evaluate your essays using the Essay Checklists; review weak areas as necessary.

❏ 20. As time allows, take Practice Test 4, starting on page 321.

Follow the same procedures as for Practice Tests 1, 2 and 3: Fill out the Tally Sheet for Questions Missed; study *all* the Answers and Complete Explanations; have a friend or English instructor evaluate your essays using the Essay Checklists; review weak areas as necessary.

❏ 21. Carefully read Final Preparation: The Final Touches, page 368.

Introduction to the CBEST: California Basic Educational Skills Test

General Description

The CBEST measures your proficiency in three general areas: reading, mathematics, and writing. The test was developed to meet requirements related to credentialing and employment, and is based upon the theory that teachers should be able to use the same skills taught to students—skills essential to students both in the classroom and outside school. You should contact your university credentials preparation office, local school district, or state department of education for more information about testing requirements.

Format and Scoring of the CBEST

The CBEST is composed of two multiple-choice sections and one writing section:

Reading. This multiple-choice test determines your ability to read, comprehend, and evaluate passages, statements or tables and answer questions based upon the content of these passages. The reading passages are taken from a wide range of subject areas, but no prior knowledge of the topic is necessary to answer the questions. All questions are based upon the content of the passage provided.

Mathematics. This multiple-choice test requires a cumulative understanding of general math concepts and problem solving. Many of the math problems appear as word problem question types. Knowledge should include basics of math from elementary school to at least one year of high school and possibly one year of college.

Writing. This essay-writing section requires that you develop, organize, and write two essays. Knowledge should include your ability to plan and write a well-organized essay on an assigned topic.

All questions on both the paper-and-pencil and computer exams (except the essays in the Writing section) are multiple-choice with five answer choices for each question. Each of the three sections receives a score ranging from 20 to 80. The passing score for each section is 41; the total passing score for the CBEST is 123. If you score below the passing mark on one section (or even on two sections) but your total score is 123 or higher, you can still pass the exam, but *only* if your score in each section is 37 or above.

Note: Format and scoring are subject to change.

The following chart can give you some indication of your performance level:

Scoring	
Percent Right	**Performance Level**
90 to 100	Superior
80 to 90	Above Average
70 to 80	Average
60 to 70	Marginal
Below 60	Needs Improvement

You need to get about 70 percent of the questions right to receive a passing score.

Allotting Time on the CBEST

CBEST examinees have a four-hour test session to complete one, two, or all three sections of the test; the test can be taken by paper and pencil or by computer. Although you may divide your time among the three sections in any way you want, to be sure you have enough time to finish all sections, **we recommend that you budget your time approximately as follows:**

Time Allotment		
	Number of Questions	**Suggested Time**
Reading	50 Questions	75 Minutes
Mathematics	50 Questions	75 Minutes
Writing	2 Topics	60 Minutes
Time to check your work		30 Minutes
Total testing time		**4 hours**

Questions Commonly Asked about the CBEST Examination

Q: Who administers the CBEST?

A: The CBEST is administered by Evaluation Systems, a division of Pearson Education, with guidelines drawn up by the California Superintendent of Public Instruction with the assistance of the California Commission on Teacher Credentialing (CTC) and an advisory board. For further information regarding test administration, contact CBEST Program, Evaluation Systems, Pearson, P.O. Box 340880, Sacramento, CA 95834-0880, or call (916) 928-4001, or visit www.cbest.nesinc.com.

Q: Who needs to pass the CBEST?

A: The CBEST is typically required for initial issuance of a credential. It may also be required for issuance of a permit, certificate, authorization, administrative credential, or renewal of emergency credential. You may need to take the exam if you have not been employed in teaching for more than 39 months. It's important that you check with your state's department of education to see whether you must take the test.

Q: Do I need the CBEST for student teaching?

A: Most universities require it. Check with the appropriate department, credentials, or teacher preparation office.

Q: When and where is the CBEST given?

A: The paper-based CBEST is administered statewide six times each year. Computer-based testing is administered by appointment at locations throughout California and Oregon at Pearson Professional Centers. You can get dates and locations from www.cbest.nesinc.com or by contacting Pearson at www.pearsonvue.com/cbest. Computer-based test takers must wait 120 days before retaking the same section by computer, but the paper-based exam can be taken as often as the test is administered.

Q: Should I take the CBEST by paper and pencil or by computer?

A: There are several factors to consider when deciding if you should take the CBEST by the traditional paper-and-pencil method or by computer. Since both exams have the same level of difficulty, what matters most is that you are at ease with the method of test administration. For more information about the advantages of computer-based testing, read the section, "Taking the Computer-Based CBEST," on page 8 of this book.

Q: Do I have to pay again if I repeat the test?

A: You must pay the test fee each time you register to take the CBEST. In addition, if you register after the regular deadline but before the late registration deadline, an additional fee will be charged. If you are taking the test by computer, there is an additional charge. Check with Evaluation Systems to be sure of current fees.

Q: What materials should I take to the test?

A: Be sure to bring your admission ticket, some form of photo and signature identification, and a watch to help pace yourself during the exam. If you're taking the paper-based exam, then also take several Number 2 soft lead pencils with good erasers. No calculators or other aids are permitted in the test center.

Q: What is on the CBEST?

A: The exam consists of three areas: 50 multiple-choice reading comprehension questions, 50 multiple-choice math questions, and two essays.

Q: What is a passing score?

A: The total passing score, as established by the Superintendent of Public Instruction, is a total of 123 on all three sections combined and a minimum of 37 on each of the sections.

Q: When will I get my score report?

A: If you are taking the paper-based test, your test score will be mailed to you about three weeks after you take the exam. Check the CBEST registration bulletin for score reporting dates. You can also check the CBEST Web site for an "unofficial" score report about two weeks after the test date. If you register on the Internet, you can also have your scores sent to you by e-mail. Computer-administered test takers will receive an "unofficial" score report for the Reading and Math sections on the day of the test.

If you pass, you will also receive a Permanent Verification Card and two transcript copies of this card to use as may be required. No additional transcripts will be provided to school districts or universities. You may, however, receive additional sets of transcript copies for a small fee.

Q: May I take the CBEST more than once?

A: Yes, but remember, your plan is to pass on your first try.

Q: Do I need to take all three parts of the test?

A: Yes, you must take, and pass, all three parts of the test. If you have previously passed any part of the exam at one administration, you may retake that part to help you reach your overall passing score of 123. Sometimes it's more effective to retake a section that is your strength, rather than depending on a high score in a section that may be your weak subject. Thus, you do not have to pass all three sections in one examination. You can achieve a total passing score in separate administrations, but you must reach that magic total of 123 in all three parts combined and a minimum of 37 in each section in order to pass the CBEST.

Q: Should I guess on the test?

A: Yes! Since there is no penalty for guessing, guess if you have to. If possible, first try to eliminate some of the choices to increase your chances of choosing the right answer. But don't leave any of the answer spaces blank.

Q: Suppose I feel that I have performed poorly on the test. May I cancel my CBEST score?

A: Yes, you may cancel your CBEST score, but only if you notify the test supervisor before leaving the test center after you take the test. However, since no one will know your score except you, there is no reason to cancel — no refunds are given.

Q: May I write on the test?

A: Yes! If you are taking the paper-based test, you must do all of your work in the **test booklet**. Your **answer sheet**, however, must have NO marks on it other than your personal information (name, registration number, and so on) and your answers. Computer-based test takers are given scratch paper (or a writing board) on which to take notes.

Q: How should I prepare?

A: Understanding and practicing test-taking strategies can help a great deal. Subject matter review in arithmetic, simple algebra, and measurement is also invaluable. Some teachers' unions, school districts, and universities offer preparation programs to assist you in attaining a passing score. Check with them for further information.

Q: How do I get further information?

A: For questions about registration procedures, the admission ticket, or the score report, you should contact CBEST Program, Evaluation Systems, Pearson, P.O. Box 340880, Sacramento, CA 95834-0880, phone (916) 928-4001, or visit www.cbest.nesinc.com.

For late and emergency registration services, phone (916) 928-4001.

For Telecommunications Device for the Deaf (TDD), phone (916) 928-0430.

For questions about CBEST policies, contact the California Commission on Teacher Credentialing, P.O. Box 944270, Sacramento, CA 94244-2700, phone (888) 921-2682, or visit www.ctc.ca.gov; or contact the Oregon Teacher Standards and Practices Commission, 465 Commercial Street NE, Salem, OR 97301, phone (503) 378-3586, or visit www.tspc.state.or.us/.

Getting Started: Five Steps to Success on the CBEST

1. **Awareness.** Become familiar with the test—the test format, test directions, test material, and scoring—by visiting the CBEST Web site at www.cbest.nesinc.com.
2. **Basic Skills.** Review the basic abilities required on the test in reading, mathematics, and writing. Know what to expect on the exam. Review Part II: Analysis of Exam Areas to help you determine your strengths and weaknesses so that you can develop a study plan unique to your individual needs.
3. **Question Types.** Become familiar with the question types of each area on the test outlined in Part II: Analysis of Exam Areas so that you can practice different versions of the same types of questions.
4. **Strategies and Techniques.** Practice using the strategies outlined in the next section of this book and make a decision about what works best for you. Remember that if it takes you longer to recall a strategy than to solve the problem, it's probably not a good strategy for you to adopt. The goal in offering strategies is for you to be able to work easily, quickly, and efficiently. Remember not to get stuck on any one question. Taking time to answer the most difficult question on the test correctly but losing valuable test time won't get you the score you deserve. Most importantly, remember to answer every question, even if you answer with only an educated guess. There is no penalty for guessing, so it is to your advantage to answer all questions.
5. **Practice.** In addition to the sample practice problems in Part II: Analysis of Exam Areas, this book offers you four complete practice tests. Practice, practice, practice is the key to your success on the CBEST.

Three Successful Approaches to the Multiple-Choice Questions

The CBEST is offered in both paper-based and computer-administered formats. Although the test question types are identical in both versions, it is helpful to approach the test by using straightforward general test-taking strategies. This section will present overall test-taking approaches to help you prepare for success. Keep in mind that there is no right or wrong way to answer questions, but there are general strategies that can help you get your best possible score.

The "Plus-Minus" Approach

Paper-Based Strategy

Many people who take the CBEST don't get their best possible score because they spend too much time on difficult questions, leaving insufficient time to answer the easy questions. Don't let this happen to you. Since every question is worth the same amount, use the following system:

- **Solvable.** Answer easy questions immediately.
- **Possibly solvable** (+). When you come to a question that appears to be solvable but is overly time-consuming (a "time-consuming" question is a question that you estimate will take you more than several minutes to answer), mark a large plus sign ("+") next to that question in your test booklet and make an educated guess at the correct answer on your answer sheet. Then move on to the next question.
- **Difficult** (−). When you come to a question that seems impossible to answer, mark a large minus sign ("−") next to it on your test booklet. Then make a pure guess on your answer sheet and move on to the next question.

If you budget your time as suggested, you have just over a minute to a minute and a half per question. Don't waste time deciding whether a question is a "+" or a "−." Act quickly because the intent of this strategy is, in fact, to save you valuable time.

1. After working on all the easy questions, your booklet should look something like this:

1.

+2.

3.

−4.

+5.

and so on.

2. After answering all the questions that are possible to answer immediately (the easy ones), go back and work on your "+" problems. Change your "guess" on your answer sheet, if necessary, for those problems you are able to answer.

3. If you finish working on your "+" problems and still have time left, you can either:

A. Attempt those "−" questions—the ones that you considered impossible. Sometimes another problem will "trigger" your memory, and you'll be able to go back and answer one of the earlier "impossible" problems.

or

B. Don't bother with those "impossible" questions. Rather, spend your time reviewing your work to be sure you didn't make any careless mistakes on the questions you thought were easy to answer.

Remember: You don't have to erase the pluses and minuses you make on your question booklet. And be sure to fill in all your answer spaces—if necessary, with a guess. There is no penalty for wrong answers, so it makes no sense to leave an answer space blank.

Computer-Administered Strategy

The plus-minus system can also be used with the computerized test. By using scratch paper (or a writing board) provided by the test administrators, you can quickly identify three types of questions: solvable, possibly solvable (+), and difficult (–).

- **Solvable**. This type of question is answered with little difficulty.
- **Possibly solvable (+)**. This type of question leaves you feeling that it "may" be possible to answer, but doing so will require more time to think it through. If you continue to feel "stuck" when you return to this type of question, it's important that you make an "educated" guess and move on.
- **Difficult (–)**. The difficult question appears to be "impossible to solve." This is a question that you should come back to only if you have answered the first and second types of problems.

Don't spend too much valuable test time deciding whether or not a question is solvable. Since you have about one and a half minutes to answer each question, you must act quickly.

Follow these steps:

1. Use a sheet of paper to list those questions that may be solvable but will require more time. Draw two columns on the paper. Label the top of the first column with a plus symbol (+) and the top of the second column with a minus symbol (–).

   Your scratch paper should look like this:

   Reading

+	–
3. B or E	1. A or B, not C
11. A, not B	6. Not D or E
15. C	14. A

2. Answer easy questions immediately.
3. Remember that the computerized test allows you to go forward and backward, from question to question. For those questions that could not be answered immediately, quickly write down the problem number in the most appropriate of the two columns, including any notes to help trigger your memory when you go back to the question.
4. After you have solved all of the easier problems, and the problems in the "+" column, attempt to solve the impossible problems. For those problems you still cannot answer, pick one of the letter answer choices (A, B, C, D, or E) and use that letter on the remaining questions. Spend no more than a few minutes to mark all difficult problems that are left unanswered. Remember, there is no penalty for wrong answers, and statistically your chances are better if you pick one letter and use it on all unanswered questions.
5. Work on one section at a time (reading, math, or writing). Keep your mind focused on one subject at a time. Do not proceed to the next section without answering all questions within your section. DO NOT EXIT THE TEST UNTIL YOU HAVE ANSWERED ALL THE QUESTIONS. Once you exit, you cannot return.

The Elimination Approach

Using the elimination strategy can increase your odds of selecting the correct answer choice. For example, if you can eliminate one answer choice, your odds of selecting the correct answer choice is 25%, eliminating two choices = 33%, three choices = 50%, and 4 choices = 100%.

Paper-Based Strategy

Take advantage of being allowed to mark in your testing booklet. As you eliminate an answer choice from consideration, be sure to *mark it out in your question booklet* as follows:

A̶.
?B.
C̶.
D̶.
?E.

Notice that some choices are marked with question marks, signifying that they may be possible answers. This technique helps you avoid reconsidering those choices you have already eliminated. It also helps you narrow down your possible answers.

Again, the marks you make on your testing booklet do not need to be erased.

Computer-Administered Strategy

For computer-based testing, try to eliminate as many of the answer choices as possible, and then make an educated guess. On your scratch paper, you may find it helpful to quickly write the letters (with a diagonal line through them) of the answer choices you want to eliminate so that you don't keep reconsidering them.

The "Avoiding Misreads" Approach

This strategy is helpful for taking both the paper and computer-based tests.

Sometimes a question may have different answers, depending upon what is asked. *For example:*

If $6y + 3x = 14$, what is the value of y?

The question may instead have asked

"what is the value of x?"
or If $3x + x = 20$, what is the value of $x + 2$?

Notice that this question doesn't ask for the value of x, but rather the value of $x + 2$.

Be aware that the words *except* and *not* change a question significantly. *For example:*

All of the following statements are true except . . .

or

Which of the expressions used in the first paragraph does not help develop the main idea?

To avoid misreading a question (and therefore answering it incorrectly), simply *circle* or write down what you must answer in the question. For example, do you have to find x or $x + 2$? Are you looking for what is true or the *exception* to what is true? To help you avoid misreading the question, if you are taking a paper-based test, mark the questions in your test booklet in this way:

If $6y + 3x = 14$, what is the value of y?

If $3x + x = 20 + 4$, what is the value of $x + 2$?

All of the following statements are true except

Which of the expressions used in the first paragraph does not help develop the main idea?

And, once again, you don't have to erase the circles you make in your question booklet or on your scratch paper.

Taking the Computer-Based CBEST

The computer-based CBEST is offered at many locations throughout California and Oregon. Like the paper-and-pencil exam, the computer-administered exam contains questions that test your knowledge in reading, mathematics, and writing. All of the material covered in this book—subject matter reviews, the practice test questions and explanations, and the essay practice problems—will help to prepare you for both the computer-administered and paper-based tests. Here are some of the benefits of taking the CBEST by computer:

- Numerous test dates are available because appointments can be scheduled throughout the week (the paper-and-pencil test is administered about six times per year on specified dates).
- You are allowed time on the computer-administered exam to review a computer tutorial program.
- Your unofficial scores for reading and math are available immediately after the test (the score for the writing section is available after it is evaluated).
- Your answers are recorded electronically, which can often reduce the chance of human error in posting your written responses.

Computer-Administered Tutorial

Immediately before taking the computerized test, you will have the option of being led through a tutorial that will show you how to read and answer the questions for each section on the CBEST. You do not need advanced computer skills to take the computer-based exam. Basic computer skills are sufficient to operate the mouse, keyboard, and word processor. The types of questions given on the test are used in the tutorial. Remember that you are allowed enough time to work through a tutorial, so take advantage of this excellent opportunity to learn more about what you will encounter on the test. Here is an example of what you can expect to see on the computer screen. These illustrations are for informational purposes only; exact computer functions and specifications are subject to change.

Computer Screen Layout

The example provided is for informational purposes only. For updated information about the CBEST Computer-Administered Test, contact Evaluation Systems at www.cbest.nesinc.com. A computer-administered practice test is available at www.cbest.nesinc.com/ca_viewPT_opener.asp.

- **Time.** A digital time clock appears in the corner of your computer screen. You should regularly check the time remaining to help pace yourself.
- **Answer Sheet.** This function key allows you to view and check your selected answers for the section that you are working on.
- **Instruction Box.** Directions for each question are boxed at the top of each page of your computer screen.

- **Scroll Bar.** If a passage or information is too long to fit on the screen, a scroll bar will appear alongside the passage (on the right side of the screen). The scroll bar is used to move (scroll) the passage on the reading pane up and down to read the entire text.

- **Next and Previous.** The two computer functions, next and previous, allow you to move forward or backwards from question to question. You can change your answer by clicking the corresponding oval answer choice at any time during the exam administration.

- **Cut, Paste, and Delete.** (Writing section only.) The word processing program used in the writing section includes a few basic keyboard functions: cut, paste, and delete.

- **Quit (Test Finished) Test.** This function key will enable you to exit the test. A message will appear, asking you to confirm that you want to exit, but *once you exit the test, you cannot go back.* Only use this key if you're finished with the entire exam. If you want to go to a previous problem or another section on the test, use the next and previous keys.

Question Number

Time

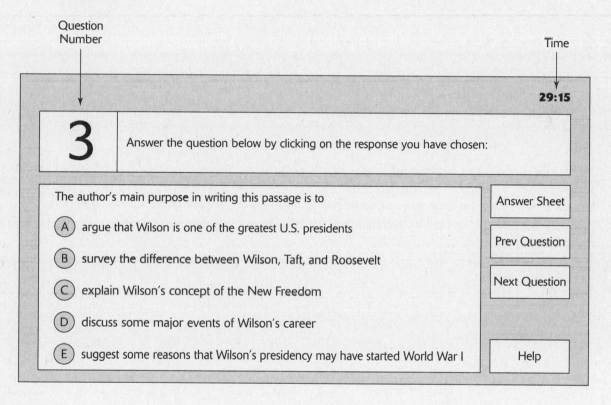

29:15

3 Answer the question below by clicking on the response you have chosen:

The author's main purpose in writing this passage is to

(A) argue that Wilson is one of the greatest U.S. presidents

(B) survey the difference between Wilson, Taft, and Roosevelt

(C) explain Wilson's concept of the New Freedom

(D) discuss some major events of Wilson's career

(E) suggest some reasons that Wilson's presidency may have started World War I

Answer Sheet

Prev Question

Next Question

Help

PART I

ANALYSIS OF EXAM AREAS

This part is designed to introduce you to each area of the CBEST by carefully reviewing

- Ability Tested
- Basic Skills Necessary
- Directions
- Analysis of Directions
- Suggested Approach with Samples

This part emphasizes important test-taking techniques and strategies and how to apply them to a variety of problem types. Sample essays are also included in this section as a guideline to assist you in evaluating your own essays and to point out some of the common errors in essay writing.

The Reading Section

Introduction

The reading section of the CBEST is designed to test your comprehension of a variety of written passages. The selections used for the passages frequently come from social studies, science, humanities, health, consumer affairs, and literature. Each passage, statement, graph, and so on, is followed by questions based on its content. There are 50 questions that comprise the reading section on the actual exam, and questions come from written material in the form of passages, outlines, indexes, charts, graphs, and tables consisting of:

- long passages (200 or more words)
- short passages (approximately 100 words)
- short statements (1 or 2 sentences)

Ability Tested

This section tests your ability to understand, interpret, and analyze passages. You will be asked to assess and respond to four different selections of reading passages:

- reading comprehension passages;
- reading comprehension passages with numbered sentences;
- fill-in-the-blank items; and
- interpretation of displays and graphs.

CBEST test takers should know that the assessment of these passages tests your ability to recognize two general skill areas of reading. Approximately 40 percent of the questions are drawn from *critical analysis and evaluation* skills, and about 60 percent of the questions require *comprehension* and *research* skills.

Critical Analysis and Evaluation Questions

- Identify reasons, details, or facts that *support the author's main idea*
- Distinguish between *fact and opinion*
- Evaluate *strengths and weaknesses* of an argument
- *Compare and contrast* information presented in the passage
- Make general *predictions* or logical *assumptions*
- Recognize the author's underlying *attitude, opinion, tone, or viewpoint*
- Recognize the *intended audience*

Comprehension and Context Questions

- Identify the *main idea* of the passage
- Identify the *purpose* of the passage (informative, descriptive, persuasive, or narrative)
- Identify the *meaning of a word or phrase* in context to the passage
- *Draw conclusions or generalizations*, or make *inferences* between people, ideas, or events in the passage
- Identify relationships between *general and specific ideas*
- *Make inferences and implications* based on information in the passage
- Determine the meanings of *figurative language*
- Determine the *sequence of events* in a passage

Research and Reference Skills Questions

- Understand the *organization* of the passage
- Understand how to *locate and use information* in a book (table of contents, indexes, chapters, paragraphs, reports, and so on)

Reading passages are from a broad spectrum of general-interest topics, but no outside knowledge of the topics is necessary to answer questions. All questions must be answered on the basis of what is stated or implied in the passage, or information given.

Basic Skills Necessary

The level of difficulty and complexity of selections varies among passages. Being able to comprehend what is specifically stated in the lines and what is "suggested or implied" between the lines are important skills. The test-taking techniques of active reading and marking a passage, described later in this chapter, are also helpful.

Directions

The directions given for the Reading Section are:

A question or number of questions follow each of the statements or passages in this section. Using only the *stated* or *implied* information given in the statement or passage, answer the question or questions by choosing the *best* answer from among the five choices given.

General Strategies for Answering Reading Questions

1. **Use your time wisely!** You should take about 70 minutes to complete 50 reading questions.
2. **Use only the information specifically stated or implied.** Do not use outside information or previous knowledge to answer the questions, even if it seems more accurate than the information in the passage.
3. **Answer all the questions for one passage** before moving on to the next passage.
4. **Do not spend too much time on any one question.** All the questions are of equal value. If you are taking the entire three sections of the CBEST in one day (reading, math, and writing), you have about a minute and a half to answer each question. This includes the time required to read, mark, or write down information from the passage. If you're stuck on a question, mark it (or write it down) and move on. There is no penalty for guessing wrong answers because your score is based upon your number of correct responses.
5. For paper-based test takers, **make sure your answers on the answer sheet correspond to the answer choices** in your answer booklet. Placing one answer in the incorrect choice can shift all your answers to incorrect spots! For computer-based test takers, **make sure you have clicked the correct answer choice** and that it is completely filled in before you proceed.
6. If a question takes you more than a minute and a half to answer, use the **elimination approach** described in the Introduction on page 7 and move on.

Four-Step Approach

1. Preread the questions.
2. Read and mark the passage.
3. Focus on stated or implied information.
4. Answer the question that is asked.

CBEST candidates who become comfortable using these strategies tend to score higher on reading tests than readers who do not use these strategies.

Step One: Preread the Questions

The technique of *prereading the questions* is an important skill that will help you remember specific information so that you'll know what to look for in the passage. It will also help you assess what type of question is being asked.

Circle, underline, or write down key words or phrases that may stand out in the question. Do not read the answer choices at this time. Just mark or write down the operative words or phrase in each question—that is, look for what you are being asked to answer.

Computer-based test takers can preread questions by using the *next* and *previous* buttons on the computer while taking notes on the scratch paper that is provided. Make sure that you are comfortable with this approach before the day of the exam.

Step Two: Read and Mark the Passage (Active Reading)

The technique of active reading involves steady concentration while reading the passage. As you become actively engaged and purposeful in your reading, you become actively in control of your reading experience. This is accomplished by marking, highlighting, underlining, circling, or writing down important words or phrases in the passage. Do not overmark or overwrite! Just give yourself a few reminders. A few marked or written phrases per paragraph help those ideas stand out. Don't worry if you're doing this incorrectly. As you practice this skill of gathering information while focusing your attention, you will become more efficient at quickly identifying important information in the passage.

As you read the passage, look for the writer's main idea. Do not memorize the passage. You can go back and review anything you need to later. Just look for the main point or think about how you might summarize the passage. Ask yourself, "What is the author's main point?"

Note important ideas and details. Pay special attention to information relevant to the question you have skimmed. When reading passages, it is important to identify facts and details that support the main idea of the passage. Look for facts, statistics, and details. Make note of quotes and words that are highlighted. Circle, underline, or write down definitions, places, numbers, and ideas. Be brief. Remember not to underline or write down too much, just a few details that stand out.

Computer-based test takers may find it useful to briefly write down key words or phrases, along with the line numbers (if available) on scratch paper to help trigger your memory for subsequent questions. Some passages contain numbered lines for reference to help you easily refer back to details of the passage. Longer passages may not fit on the computer screen, so you may need to scroll down to read the entire passage. Remember that you can move forward to the next question and back to a previous question at any time, but you should answer all the questions for one passage before moving on to the next passage. This helps you stay focused on one topic at a time. Note that you may be asked to refer back to the passage on a previous screen each time you answer a new question. It's an easy process, but make sure you are comfortable with this computer skill before the exam date.

Step Three: Focus on Stated or Implied Information

Answer the questions based only on the material in the passage. Assume that the information in each passage is accurate. Use the information that is *stated* or *implied*. Implied means that the answer is something *suggested* but not explicitly stated in the passage. These question-types test your understanding of the passage alone; they do not test the historical background of the passage, biography of the author, or previous familiarity with the work from which the passage is taken.

Step Four: Answer the Question That Is Asked

Identifying what is being asked may seem obvious, but make sure the answer you choose corresponds with the question being asked. As you read the question, circle, underline, or write down key words or phrases to help you recall what is being asked. Many of the questions on the CBEST may have more than one answer choice that is true. However, just because an answer is true does not mean it is the correct response if it does not answer the question! This type of answer choice is often on the test to "distract" you from the correct choice. Make sure you read all the answer choices before making your final selection.

Practice General Strategies Using the Four-Step Approach

Before specific strategies are introduced for the critical analysis, comprehension, and research question types, let's review and practice the general strategies in the four-step approach that will be useful on *all* types of reading questions:

1. Preread the questions.
2. Read and mark the passage.
3. Focus on stated or implied information.
4. Answer the question that is asked.

Sample for Step One: Preread the Questions

Prior to reading the passage, read each question (but don't spend time reading all the multiple-choice answers) and circle or write down the most important words or phrases.

---

1. The author's argument in favor of freedom of speech may be summarized in which of the following ways?

   A. If every speaker is not free, no speaker is.
   B. Speech keeps us free from the animal kingdom.
   C. As we think, so we speak.
   D. The Bill of Rights ensures free speech.
   E. Lunatic speeches are not free speeches.

The most *important* part is usually the most concrete and specific one. In this case, you might circle "freedom of speech." The question parts that you circle will be those you'll tend to remember when you read the passage. In this case, you would be likely to notice and pay close attention to "freedom of speech" when it occurs in the passage.

After prereading the questions, read and mark the passage. Always mark or write down those spots that contain information relevant to the questions you've read. In addition, you should mark other important ideas and details. In general, remember not to overmark; never make more than a few marks per paragraph in order to make those parts you mark stand out. More specific advice on marking follows, in reference to specific subareas of reading skills.

Sample for Step Two: Read and Mark the Passage

Directions: Use the passage that follows to answer the next two questions.

By the time a child starts school, he or she has mastered the major part of the rules of grammar. The child has managed to accomplish this remarkable feat in such a short time by experimenting with and generalizing the rules all alone. Each child, in effect, discovers language in the first few years of life.

When it comes to vocabulary growth, it's a different story. Unlike grammar, the chief means by which people learn vocabulary is memorization.

Some people have a hard time learning and remembering new words.

2. Although vocabulary growth involves memorization and grammar learning does not, which of the following can be concluded about both vocabulary and grammar?

    A.   Both make use of memorization.
    B.   Both make use of study skills.
    C.   Both make use of words.
    D.   Neither makes use of words.
    E.   Neither makes use of writing skills.

The correct answer is **C**. Sometimes it is useful to mark out and eliminate incorrect choices. You should eliminate choices **A**, **D**, and **E**. Choice **A** contradicts both the passage and the question. Choices **D** and **E** are not reasonable. Choice **B** is a possibility, but Choice **C** is better because grammar learning in young children does not necessarily involve study skills but does involve words. Remember to use the elimination strategy described on page 7.

Samples for Step Three: Focus on Stated or Implied Information

Use the passage provided above to answer the question that follows.

3. Which of the following is implied by the last sentence in the passage?

    A.   Some people have no trouble learning and remembering new words.
    B.   Some people have a hard time remembering new words.
    C.   Grammar does not involve remembering words.
    D.   Old words are not often remembered.
    E.   Learning and remembering are kinds of growth.

The correct answer is **A**. *Implies* tells you that the answer is something suggested but not explicitly stated in the passage. Choice **B** is explicitly stated in the passage, so you may eliminate it. But Choice **A** implies the opposite: If some people have a hard time, then it must be true that some people don't. Choices **C**, **D**, and **E** are altogether different from the meaning of the last sentence.

Directions: Read the passage below and answer the three questions that follow.

It sounds like such a simple thing to do: buy some new light bulbs, screw them in, save the planet.

But a lot of people these days are finding the new compact fluorescent bulbs anything but simple. Consumers who are trying them say they sometimes fail to work or wear out early. At best, people discover that using the bulbs requires learning a long list of do's and don'ts.

Take the case of Karen Zuercher and her husband in San Francisco. Inspired by watching the movie *An Inconvenient Truth*, they decided to swap out nearly every incandescent bulb in their home for energy-saving compact fluorescents. Instead of having a satisfying green moment, however, they wound up coping with a mess.

One of the 16 electric bulbs the Zuerchers bought at a local discount store did not work at all, they said, and three others died within hours. The bulbs were supposed to burn for 10,000 hours, meaning they should have lasted for years in normal use. "It's irritating," Mrs. Zuercher said.

Irritation seems to be rising as more consumers try compact fluorescent bulbs, which now occupy 11 percent of the nation's eligible sockets, with 330 million bulbs sold every year. Consumers are posting vociferous complaints on the Internet after trying the bulbs and finding them lacking.

Some experts who study the issue blame the government for the quality problems, saying an intensive federal push to lower the price essentially backfired by encouraging manufacturers to use cheap components.

"In pursuit of the holy grail, we stepped on the consumer," said Michael Siminovitch, director of a lighting center at the University of California, Davis.

"Somebody decides to save a little money somewhere," he said, "and suddenly we have hundreds of thousands of failures."

> 4. From the information in the above passage, it can be <u>inferred</u> that
>
>   **A.**   Karen Zuercher was inspired by the movie *An Inconvenient Truth*.
>   **B.**   The incandescent bulb is better than the new compact fluorescent bulbs.
>   **C.**   The bulbs purchased from the local discount store were all defective.
>   **D.**   Consumers should learn more about the new bulbs before using them.
>   **E.**   The new bulbs should burn for 10,000 hours.

The correct answer is **D.** Choices **A** and **E** are explicitly stated in the passage, so you can eliminate these choices. Remember that the answer must be clearly stated or implied in the passage, and there is no clear evidence in the passage to support choices **B** or **C.** Based on the information about the problems the Zuerchers are having with the new compact fluorescent light bulbs, and the author's comments, such as "instead of having a satisfying green moment…they wound up coping with a mess," it can be *inferred* or *implied* that the consumer should learn more before replacing all their bulbs.

Sample for Step Four: Answer the Question That Is Asked

> 5. According to the passage, what is (an advantage) of (using) the (new) compact fluorescent (bulbs)?
>
>   **A.**   You can purchase them from a discount store at a reduced price.
>   **B.**   The bulbs should burn for 10,000 hours.
>   **C.**   All consumers love using these new energy-saving bulbs.
>   **D.**   All the new compact fluorescent bulbs prove to be efficient and long lasting.
>   **E.**   The manufacturer has poor quality control.

The correct answer is **B.** You should have circled or marked the word *advantage* in the question. As you read through the answer choices to look for an advantage in using the new light bulbs, you should have eliminated Choice **D** immediately, since it is not true. There is no evidence in the passage to support choices **A** and **C,** so they can be eliminated. Although Choice **E** is not stated in the passage, it may be implied that there was poor quality control because some of the bulbs "did not work at all." Remember that you are looking for the *best* answer choice that "answers the question." Do not read beyond the scope of the question. It is directly stated in the passage that the "bulbs are supposed to burn for 10,000 hours." This is an advantage in purchasing the bulbs.

Look for the Author's Main Point

There are many ways to ask about the main point of the passage. What is the main idea? What is the best title? What is the author's purpose?

> 6. The author's (main idea) in this passage is to
>
>   **A.**   promote the use of the new compact fluorescent bulbs.
>   **B.**   get consumers to replace old bulbs with the new "green" bulbs.
>   **C.**   describe the problems consumers are having with the new bulbs.
>   **D.**   explain the amount of energy saved with the new bulbs.
>   **E.**   inspire us to see the movie *An Inconvenient Truth*.

The correct answer is **C.** Although choices **A** and **B** are popular ideas about saving energy while helping to prevent greenhouse gas emissions, they do not support the main idea of the passage. Choice **D** is mentioned in the passage, but is not the focus of the author's main point. *An Inconvenient Truth*, Choice **E,** is briefly discussed as an inspiration for purchasing new light bulbs. The main point of the passage is to "describe the problems consumers are having with the new bulbs," as illustrated by repeated criticisms of the new light bulbs throughout the passage. Choice **C** supports the overall main idea of the passage.

Directions: Read the passage below and answer the question that follows.

The fact that bacteria are capable of chemical communication first emerged from investigations into marine bacteria that are able to glow in the dark. Kenneth H. Nealson and John Woodland Hastings of Harvard University observed that luminous bacteria in culture do not glow at a constant intensity. In fact, they emit no light until the population reaches a high density.

Nealson and Hastings knew that the light resulted from chemical reactions catalyzed by the enzyme luciferase. They postulated that this enzyme was ultimately controlled not by some mechanism inside each bacterial cell, but by a molecular messenger that traveled between cells. Once inside target cells, the messenger, which the researchers called an autoinducer, could induce expression of the genes coding for luciferase and for the other proteins involved in light production; that is, the autoinducer could stimulate synthesis of the encoded proteins and, thus, of light. Their theory met with skepticism at first but has since been confirmed and expanded.

Read All the Choices to Look for the Best Answer

7. According to the passage, Nealson and Hasting's research was instrumental in indicating that

  A. bacteria communicate through molecular messengers that travel between cells.
  B. luminous bacteria glow not at a constant density but at various densities.
  C. bacteria are genetically coded by the autoinducer.
  D. the molecular messenger luciferase causes bacteria to glow at high densities.
  E. the autoinducer, not the enzyme luciferase as was previously believed, produces the luminosity of certain marine bacteria.

The correct answer is **A.** Although the research focused on marine bacteria that glow, its broader significance is that it shows the chemical communication between bacteria. Choice **B** is the observation that led to the theory but is not the best answer. Choice **C** is inaccurate; an autoinducer does not code genes but induces their expression. Choice **D** is also incorrect because the molecular messenger that causes bacteria to glow is not the enzyme luciferase. Choice **E** might seem correct at first reading, but although the autoinducer allows the expression of the light-producing enzymes such as luciferase, it doesn't produce light itself.

Practice Specific Strategies for Question Types

Now that we have covered *general* strategies that can apply to all reading question types, let's practice *specific* strategies and with sample questions from the three skill areas in the reading section:

- Critical Analysis and Evaluation
- Comprehension and Context
- Research and Reference Skills

Critical Analysis and Evaluation Questions

Critical analysis and evaluation draws on a specific set of reading skills that determine whether you can make general assumptions to evaluate and think about the meaning of the passage. These types of questions require you to use the context of the information to figure out the significance of the passage in order to make comparisons and predictions. You will be asked to analyze information and respond by:

- identifying reasons and details that support the main idea
- distinguishing between fact and opinion
- evaluating strengths and weaknesses of an argument
- comparing and contrasting
- making general predictions and logical assumptions
- recognizing the author's underlying attitude, opinion, or viewpoint
- recognizing the intended audience

> A note about passages with numbered sentences: Some of the passages in the critical analysis and evaluation section appear with numbered line references. These lined sentences allow you to focus your attention on specific phrases or words by directing your attention to a particular place in the passage. This is especially helpful for computer-based test takers. Always look back in the passage after reading the question to verify the sentence(s) that the test question references.

The following example will use numbered sentences to illustrate how critical analysis and evaluation skills may be assessed.

Passages with Numbered Sentences

Directions: Read the passage below and answer the five questions that follow.

[1]People who Googled anything on the first day of spring this year were met with a particularly charming version of the search engine's logo. [2]*The Very Hungry Caterpillar,* a beloved children's book character created by Eric Carle in 1969, crawled across the page, eating holes in letters brilliantly colored in characteristic collage style. [3]The only other children's literature icon the Internet giant has deemed recognizable enough to grace its opening search page is Dr. Seuss.

[4]No wonder. *The Very Hungry Caterpillar,* celebrating its 40th year in print, the same year its creator celebrates his 80th year, has sold 29 million copies in 45 languages. [5]Among the 70 or so books Carle has written and illustrated, it holds a special place. [6]Every 30 seconds, somewhere in the world, a copy of the book is sold, and its publisher, Penguin, crows.

[7]Crowing penguins are something you won't find in an Eric Carle book. [8]His stories combine scientific accuracy with emotional resonance, a winning combination for the preschool set.

Identify Details that Support the Main Idea

> 8. The author's main idea in the passage is to
>
>   **A.** describe the scientific accuracy of Carle's books.
>   **B.** describe the first day of spring.
>   **C.** describe why Carle's books are famous.
>   **D.** inform the reader about Carle's age.
>   **E.** persuade the reader to buy Carle's books.

The correct answer is **C.** Before reading the passage, you should have circled or written "main idea" in the question. "Scientific accuracy," Choice **A,** and "the first day of spring," Choice **B,** are only mentioned briefly in the passage, so you can immediately eliminate them as choices. Choice **D** is a fact about the age of the author, but it does not support the main idea of the passage. After reading this passage, some readers may be convinced to purchase *The Very Hungry Caterpillar,* but it is not the author's main intent, Choice **E.** Remember that critical evaluation questions ask you to "figure out" the answer based upon the information presented in the passage. The information presented "describes" why Carle's books are famous—"a beloved children's book…holds a special place."

Distinguish Fact from Opinion

> 9. In this passage, sentences [4] and [5] can be described as
>
>   **A.** opinions about Carle's work.
>   **B.** facts about *The Very Hungry Caterpillar*'s popularity.
>   **C.** persuasive techniques used to convince the reader.
>   **D.** descriptions of Carle's illustrations.
>   **E.** examples of figurative language.

The correct answer is **B**. As you read sentences [4] and [5], notice that most of the information consists of statistical facts. While "it holds a special place" is an opinion, it is of minor significance when compared to the specific details of the two sentences. Knowing that you're not looking for opinions, persuasive techniques, descriptions, or figurative language, you can eliminate choices **A, C, D,** and **E**.

---

10. Sentence [8] is an example of

    A. a fact.
    B. an opinion.
    C. a description.
    D. an idea.
    E. a grammatical error.

The correct answer is **B**. Everything in sentence [8] is an opinion, Choice **B**. Nothing in the passage supports the "scientific accuracy" of *The Very Hungry Caterpillar*. There is not any subjective proof of what qualities create a "winning combination" or "emotional resonance." Furthermore, there are not any facts (Choice **A**), descriptions (Choice **C**), or ideas (Choice **D**) expressed in the sentence. The grammatical error, Choice **E**, occurs in sentence [3].

Identify the Meaning of a Word or Phrase in the Context of the Passage

---

11. In the statement, "Every 30 seconds, somewhere in the world, a copy of the book is sold, and its publisher, Penguin, crows," the author uses the phrase "Penguin, crows" to mean

    A. the book has references to crows and penguins.
    B. the publisher, Penguin, is thrilled to have high sales.
    C. the publisher, Penguin, wants to sell more book copies around the world.
    D. crows are a frequent subject in Carle's books.
    E. books sold around the world are often published by Penguin.

The correct answer is **B**. This question asks you to identify the "meaning" of the phrase "Penguin, crows." To accomplish this, you must read the words in context to sentence [6]. The publisher, Penguin Books, is celebrating soaring book sales: "Every 30 seconds…a book is sold." With this information, you can eliminate choices **A** and **D**. The author of this passage is using figurative language to describe the publisher's enthusiasm for high book sales, Choice **B**. Choice **C** infers that the publisher would like to sell more books, but the question is about the "meaning" of the author's choice of words in the passage.

Evaluate Strengths and Weaknesses of an Argument

---

12. Which of the following numbered sentences provides strength to the writer's opinion that Carle is a prominent author?

    A. 1
    B. 2
    C. 4
    D. 5
    E. 7

On any reading comprehension test, be alert to the strengths and weaknesses of supporting evidence. Sentences [1] and [2] introduce the passage but do not add to the strength of the argument that Carle is a "prominent author," eliminating choices **A** and **B**. Sentences [5] and [7], choices **D** and **E**, do not address the fact that Carle is a well-known author. Sentence [4], Choice **C**, provides "facts" about the author's accomplishments—"40th year in print" and "sold 29 million copies"—confirming his notoriety and strengthening the writer's opinion of Carle. The correct answer is **C**.

Passages with Missing Words, Phrases, or Sentences

Directions: Read the passage below and answer the four questions that follow.

Paragraph I

As the 21st century begins, the coyote can be found in 49 of the 50 states. Thirty years ago, most of the coyote population was confined to the western United States, but now they prowl from Maine to Florida, and increasingly in urban areas. The coyote's range has extended north as far as Alaska and south through almost all of Central America.

Paragraph II

This population explosion has alarmed sheep ranchers in the western states, and they have responded with a new weapon: a collar worn by sheep that contains the fiercely toxic Compound 1080. Ranchers say the amount of deadly poison is so small that it does not present a threat to the environment. _____ the Environmental Protection Agency has approved the use of the collars in several sheep-raising states. _____ there is still opposition from many environmental groups. They point to the cruelty of the coyotes' death, which can last from three to twelve hours. They claim that Compound 1080 can kill innocent animals and poses a special threat to eagles. Because the collars may find their way into stream beds, they fear the widespread killing of fish and fish-eating birds and animals.

Understand the Author's Position

13. Which of the following best describes the position of the author of this passage on the use of poisoned collars to protect sheep?

    A. The author favors their use since the passage points out that they have been approved by the Environmental Protection Agency.
    B. The author disapproves of their use since the passage describes the poison as "fiercely toxic."
    C. The author presents the point of view of both sides without clearly taking sides.
    D. The author favors their use if they can be used without posing a threat to other wild animals.
    E. Though the author's position is never explicit, the author disapproves of the killing of any wild animals.

The correct answer is **C**. Before reading the passage, you should have marked "position of the author" and "use of poisoned collars" in the question. After reading the entire passage, notice that it's difficult to pinpoint the author's point of view. The author presents a perspective from both sides of the argument regarding the use of "poisoned collars," Choice **C**. The author does not commit to one side or the other. On the one hand, the author reports what the ranchers and the EPA have said in favor of the devices, Choice **A**. Yet he also reports the objections of the environmentalists, choices **B** and **E**.

In passages with missing words, phrases, or sentences, remember the following:

- ❏ Read the selection for the main point and the author's position.
- ❏ Imagine what should go in the blank spaces.
- ❏ Read each answer choice into the blank spaces in the passage to see what fits.
- ❏ Check that your answer is consistent with the style, content, and grammar of the passage.
- ❏ Watch for connecting words and phrases such as *also, therefore, futhermore, in other words,* etc. The content following these connectors should convey information *similar* to the content that precedes them. Watch also for contrasting words, such as *but, however, although, except,* etc. The content following these words should convey *opposite* information.

Understand the Function of Key Transition Indicators

> **14.** Which of the following words or phrases used respectively to fill in the blanks, would make paragraph 2 clearer?
>
> **A.** However; Also
> **B.** Thus; And
> **C.** But; On the other hand
> **D.** Furthermore; But
> **E.** Yet; However

The correct answer is **D.** This type of question requires that you "fill in the blanks" based upon the context of the passage. Start by making a prediction about possible word choices in the blank spaces. The first blank space requires a conjunctive adverb showing a *continuation* of the author's thought from the preceding sentence. The poison is not a threat and "thus" and "furthermore," as in choices **B** or **D,** support that opinion. Next, notice that the second blank space requires a *contrasting* conjunctive adverb, which expresses that an opposing opinion will follow. "On the other hand," "But," and "However" are all good choices, **C, D,** and **E.** The use of "Furthermore" makes it clear that the sentence about the EPA is part of the argument on one side. The "But" signals the shift to the opposition's point of view.

Identify the Passage Summary

> **15.** Which of the following most accurately represents the content of this passage?
>
> **A.** I. the coyote overpopulation problem
> II. the ranchers' solution to coyote expansion
> **B.** I. the expanding range of the coyote
> II. the case for and against poisoning the coyote
> **C.** I. coyotes in America today
> II. protecting sheep against coyote predation
> **D.** I. new data on the coyote population
> II. the dangers to the environment from Compound 1080
> **E.** I. the population increase of the coyote
> II. coyote overkill and the western environment

The correct answer is **B.** None of the summaries of the first paragraph are bad, although Choice **A,** unlike the passage, calls the coyote an "overpopulation problem." The best summary of the second paragraph should refer to the positions of both the ranchers and the environmentalists. It appears that the sheep are being used as bait for the coyote and not being protected, Choice **C.** Choice **D** is true because there is new data in paragraph I, but it is not as specific as Choice **B.**

Draw Conclusions from Material Presented in the Passage

> **16.** Which of the following is the most appropriate addition as a final sentence for the second paragraph?
>
> **A.** So you can see that there is no easy answer to the problem of the coyote versus the sheep rancher.
> **B.** Americans have been trying to eradicate the coyote for over one hundred years, but its population and range have relentlessly increased; there is no reason to be optimistic about the results of this latest battle in the coyote wars.
> **C.** I think that maybe we should try out the collar under restrictions which could prevent any accidents and make sure nothing goes wrong to hurt the environment.
> **D.** If the collar can save the sheep, don't you think it's a good idea?
> **E.** The rancher's battle with the coyote is part of a long war with nature, and the collar is a new device, like a James Bond gadget, that might bring victory.

The correct answer is **B**. Choice **B** is consistent with the style of the rest of the paragraph and relates the content of the second paragraph to the information about the coyote's range that began the first paragraph. Choice **A** is weak and, unlike the rest of the passage, directly addresses the reader. Choice **C** is ineffectual, and for the first and only time, uses the first person pronoun "I." Choice **D** surprisingly takes sides, and for the first time it uses a direct question. Choice **E** overuses figurative language and also takes sides.

Comprehension and Context Questions

Comprehension and context questions are straightforward questions used to determine if you comprehend the passage and its direct meaning. This type of question will often focus your attention on specific sentences, phrases, or words. This reading skill will test your ability to:

- identify the *main idea* of the passage.
- identify the *purpose* of the passage (informative, descriptive, persuasive, or narrative).
- identify the *meaning of a word or phrase* in the context of the passage.
- *draw conclusions or generalizations*, or make *inferences*.
- identify relationships between *general and specific ideas*.
- *make inferences and implications* based on information in the passage.
- determine the meanings of *figurative language*.
- determine the *sequence of events* in a passage.

The primary purpose of the passages is to be:

- **informative**, filled with facts while providing information throughout the passage to support these facts. This type of passage does not provide the author's opinion or biased views.
- **descriptive**, drawing a sensory picture or visual image for the reader.
- **persuasive**, attempting to sway the reader to agree with the opinion of the author.
- **narrative**, telling a story.

Directions: Read the passage below and answer the question that follows.

Pirates on the loose, North Koreans in pursuit of nukes, Depression-era economics, and on top of all that, tax day. No wonder we're all gaga over the first puppy. He's the cutest news out there. So curly, feisty, cute—in fact, we'll forgive his political correctness.

The president's pollsters couldn't have come up with a more perfect Obama dog. He's black *and* white, so no picking sides there. He comes from good immigrant stock (Portuguese), and yet he's steeped in Americana, a gift from the Kennedy clan and named after Rock and Roll Hall of Famer Bo Diddley. Born in Texas, he's registered with what you might call a Spanish surname—Amigo's New Hope. And although he wasn't a rescue, he was at least pre-owned. All of which amounts to 40 million Google hits and counting.

Bo joins a line of presidential dogs dating to George Washington's American foxhounds. Abraham Lincoln had Fido (origins unknown), and Franklin D. Roosevelt's Scottish terrier, Fala, was a movie star with his own press secretary. Harry S. Truman, who had a cocker spaniel named Feller, once said, "You want a friend in Washington? Get a dog." Presidents did, especially after the Nixon family's cocker spaniel, Checkers, saved his owner's political bacon. Gerald R. Ford named his pal Liberty, Ronald Reagan had Lucky, and George H. W. Bush had Millie, whose autobiography was ghostwritten by First Lady Barbara Bush. Bill Clinton found a friend in Buddy, and George W. Bush had Spot and Barney.

Like many of his predecessors, Bo will have access to the Oval Office. He is supposed to belong to the Obamas' daughters, Malia and Sasha, and to be a well-trained 6-month-old, but he certainly seemed to be leading a besotted president around by the leash at his press debut. We certainly don't begrudge President Obama a little puppy love. Another high-seas drama, a few more international crises, and the leader of the free world may need a pal to lick him behind the ears.

Recognize the Author's Main Purpose of the Passage

As you read the passage below, remember to ask:

❏ What is the author trying to say?

❏ What is the main idea?

❏ What is the purpose of the passage?

❏ What is a good title for the passage?

---

17. The author's main purpose in writing this passage is to

    A. inform the reader about former and current presidential pets.

    B. persuade the reader to buy a Portuguese Water Dog.

    C. tell a story about the president and his new dog.

    D. describe the Obama family's life in the White House.

    E. describe the world crises facing the president.

The correct answer is **A.** This type of passage is informative. It provides the reader with information about the history of pets in the White House. Choice **B** can be eliminated because it suggests that the passage is persuasive. Choice **C** suggests the passage is a narrative, and choices **D** and **E** suggest the passage is descriptive. Choice **A** is the best choice since it provides the reader with the purpose of writing the entire passage—to "inform the reader."

Directions: Read the passage below and answer the four questions that follow.

Urban legends are a form of modern folklore—a combination of fairy tales, parables, and information from the grapevine. Unlike fairy tales, however, urban legends are intended to be taken as truth, stories of real events happening to real people, even when the events seem not only unlikely but also bizarre or farcical. Usually urban legends are passed on in the form of "I heard it from a friend of a friend." The audience assumes that while the story isn't firsthand information, it comes from a source close enough to be verified, if one chose to verify it, which one seldom does. While some urban legends are elaborate stories filled with gruesome details, others are succinct. For example, the story that Mrs. O'Leary's cow caused the Chicago fire by knocking over an oil lamp is an urban legend captured in a single line.

With the advent of the Internet, cyberlegends are born every day and cover subjects ranging from massive governmental conspiracies to animals performing incredible feats to medical mishaps and miracles to tear-jerking stories of redemption. Some contain warnings about products (deodorant causes cancer, for example) or the end of the world. The Internet has become the backyard fence of the good old days, when gossip and stories were exchanged without the filter of facts and hardcore information.

Like every form of mythology and folklore, urban legends reveal aspects of human nature. A quick look at urban legends in today's world reveals both our fears and suspicions and our need to believe in miracles, as well as both our taste for shocking details and our need for a good cry.

Identify Logical Assumptions

---

18. Which of the following is an unstated assumption of the author expressed in the passage?

    A. Urban legends are part of an oral tradition.

    B. If a story is particularly bizarre, it is untrue.

    C. People will try to verify a story that is passed on to them by a friend.

    D. Urban legends are dangerous and cause serious misunderstandings.

    E. The story of Mrs. O'Leary's cow and the Chicago fire is unlikely but true.

The correct answer is **A**. The third sentence of the passage indicates that the author sees urban legends as part of an oral tradition. Choice **C** is directly contradicted in the passage, and although it is stated that urban legends are often bizarre, no assumption is made that "bizarre" is equal to "untrue," Choice **B**. Choice **E** is not indicated in the passage, nor does the passage make the judgment in Choice **D**.

Determine the Meaning of Figurative Language

19. In the second paragraph, the author uses the metaphor of the backyard fence to describe the Internet for which of the following reasons?

    A. Both can be sources of uncensored tales and information.
    B. Both are means by which uneducated people can communicate with each other.
    C. A backyard fence, like the Internet, has a definite purpose.
    D. The Internet, like the backyard fence, encourages casual friendships.
    E. Both are the result of urban existence.

The correct answer is **A**. According to the passage, both the backyard fence and the Internet are places where information is passed without the filter of facts. Choice **D** may be true, but it isn't the reason the metaphor is used. Choice **C** is vague, and Choice **E** is untrue. Nothing in the passage suggests that people who use the Internet and talk over the backyard fence are uneducated, Choice **B**.

Identify the Relationship between Two Specific Ideas

20. According to the passage, the difference between fairy tales and urban legends is that

    A. fairy tales have individual authors, whereas urban legends do not.
    B. urban legends are produced for adults, whereas fairy tales are for children.
    C. fairy tales don't deal with grotesque behavior, whereas urban legends often relish in bizarre details.
    D. the intention of urban legends is to cause people to change behavior, whereas the intention of fairy tales is to entertain.
    E. fairy tales are intended to be seen as fiction, whereas urban legends are intended to be seen as true.

The correct answer is **E**. The second sentence makes this point. Choices **A** and **B** are not supported, and Choice **C** is not true; fairy tales sometimes deal with grotesque behavior. Nothing in the passage indicates that the intention of urban legends is to change behavior; in fact, no intention whatsoever is suggested in Choice **D**.

Identify Accurate Summaries of Ideas

21. The author's intention in the last sentence of the passage is to

    A. contrast the modern world with an earlier age.
    B. summarize some of the main themes of modern urban legends.
    C. criticize the quality of urban legends passed on through the Internet.
    D. show that urban legends lack the charm of earlier legends and fairy tales.
    E. ridicule people's need to pass on stories that are not true.

The correct answer is **B**. The last sentence of the passage briefly touches on the main themes of urban legends. It doesn't contrast modern legends with those of the past to make a point about changes in the world, Choice **A**, nor does it make judgments, choices **C, D,** and **E**.

Directions: Read the selection below and answer the six questions that follow.

There are some things you never forget. Your first kiss. Your first fish.

I'll never forget the February day, just two months ago, when I took a peek at what I expected to be the vivid greenscape of Dodger Stadium and discovered instead a giant sandbox, 330 feet down the lines, 400 feet to center.

It was like catching Grandma in the arms of the postman, wrong on levels you didn't even know existed. Major League fields are supposed to be the sort of lush summer glens that inspire men to craft weepy movies about their fathers. The Dodgers in particular have always had perhaps the finest field of dreams in all baseball. In a *Sports Illustrated* survey, players named it their favorite playing surface.

But on this perfect February morning—a day that cried out for picnics and marriage proposals—Dodger Stadium was a lunar landscape, not a single blade of grass in sight. You call this a ball yard?

Turns out Eric Hansen, the head groundskeeper, is the one who's painted over the Picasso. Under his guidance, crews have peeled up all that beautiful turf. It looks to be the sort of thing you'd do in revenge, out of spite and anger.

But it's something the Dodgers do routinely every four or five years, beginning with a two-week makeover in late January, followed by careful nurturing over the next two months, just before fans show up for the April opener. They pull up the old carpet and put in the new. Fans never witness the upheaval; we just swoon over the finished product.

As with any major yard project, it takes different skill sets, big crews, and lots of heavy lifting. A lot of the real work goes on beneath the surface.

Step 1: The old grass comes out, along with about 2 inches of roots, seed and soil (dirt infield areas are left intact).

Step 2: New sand is brought in, about 400 tons, to replace most of the discarded stuff.

Step 3: Gypsum, the double-malt scotch of Southland lawns, is added to loosen the soil and keep it from compacting.

Step 4: The new and existing material are blended together to a depth of 6 or so inches, but not deep enough to disturb the Byzantine system of pipes, pumps and other irrigation devices beneath the field.

Step 5: Using laser guides, contractors smooth the field nearly flat, in preparation for the sod.

Step 6: A 12-man crew from West Coast Turf brings in 100,000 square feet of sod, in 42-inch widths nearly three times as wide as the turf you get at the corner nursery. Over a two-day period, they press and caress this new field into place, as if smoothing on a Band-Aid.

This is where the remake gets interesting.

The makeover that Hansen and his crew undertook this spring is necessary when, after several years, the rye adapts and refuses to go dormant during the summer, giving the field a scruffy appearance.

Recognize the Main Idea or Main Purpose of the Passage

> 22. The author's main purpose in writing this passage is to describe
>
> A. the process of resodding the old field and preparing a new baseball field for play.
> B. the head groundskeeper's responsibilities in Yankee Stadium this year.
> C. the important job of the groundskeeper of a major ballpark.
> D. the installation of the irrigation system used at Dodger Stadium.
> E. the reason the Dodgers needed to delay the start of the season.

The correct answer is **A**. You should have highlighted "author's main purpose," and "describe" in the question. Remember, a descriptive passage provides you with a visual image of the author's purpose. Choice **D** is a possibility, but the author mentions the irrigation system only at the end of the passage. Choice **A** is the only other choice that refers to describing something (the "process of resodding") that is mentioned throughout the passage. Choice **E** is irrelevant since it is not mentioned in the passage. Choice **B** provides inaccurate information, "Yankee Stadium." This passage is about the Dodger Stadium.

Determine the Meaning of Figurative Language in the Passage

> **23.** The title of this passage is *Blades of Glory*. This title refers to
>
>   **A.** swords.
>   **B.** tools.
>   **C.** glass.
>   **D.** grass.
>   **E.** carpet.

The correct answer is **D.** This is a descriptive passage. Authors will often use figurative language to enhance the meaning of a descriptive passage. To answer this question, look for the meaning of the title in the context of the passage. This passage is about grass on a baseball field; thus "blades" is a metaphor for grass, Choice **D.** Choices **A, B,** and **C** can be eliminated because these are not related to the baseball field. Choice **E** is another metaphor for grass and therefore incorrect.

Identify a Word or Meaning in the Context of the Passage

> **24.** As it is used in paragraph 6, "old carpet" refers to the aged
>
>   **A.** rug.
>   **B.** turf.
>   **C.** pitcher's mound.
>   **D.** dugout.
>   **E.** clay.

The correct answer is **B.** As you read paragraph 6, you will notice that "old carpet" is the author's use of figurative language for describing the turf on the baseball field, Choice **B.** Choice **A** can be eliminated since it is not related to baseball. All of the other answer choices are related to baseball, but only Choice **B** describes the relationship to the baseball field. The pitcher's mound, dugout, and clay are discussed later in the passage.

Recognize Language That Sets the Tone and Describes the Purpose of the Passage

> **25.** In the statement, "painted over the Picasso . . . the sort of thing you'd do in revenge, out of spite and anger," in paragraph 5, the author
>
>   **A.** wants the reader to understand how strongly he feels about the look of the field.
>   **B.** describes the recent destruction of a valuable painting by vandals.
>   **C.** describes the process Hansen used to replace the baseball field.
>   **D.** uses language to explain how the painter feels about having his painting destroyed.
>   **E.** discusses the injuries the players received during the season.

The correct answer is **A.** This is an example of a question that requires you to look for the author's tone in the passage. The author uses figurative language to help readers understand "how strongly he feels about the look of the field," Choice **A.** Choices **B** and **D** refer to visual art and can be eliminated. Choice **E** is not mentioned in the passage, and Choice **C** is the central (main) theme of the passage. The author is referring to the field in paragraph 5.

Make Inferences Based on Information from the Passage

26. According to the passage, which of the following statements best represents how the author feels about baseball?

    A. He loves the game of baseball.
    B. He is upset about the demise of baseball stadiums.
    C. He is a Yankees fan.
    D. He is a friend of the groundskeeper.
    E. He feels Americans need to support baseball.

The correct answer is **A.** As you read the passage, it is implied that the author is fond of baseball, as he takes great care in describing the process of replacing the "greenscape" field and expressing his sentiment that "we swoon over the finished product." Although in the beginning of the passage he appears to be upset with conditions in his beloved Dodger Stadium, there is no evidence to support this position, Choice **B.** Choices **C, D,** and **E** may be true, but they are not explicitly stated in the passage.

Determine the Sequence of Events

27. According to the passage, what process takes place immediately before the sod is put in place?

    A. The old and new soil are blended together.
    B. The sod is watered and flattened.
    C. Laser guides are used to smooth the field.
    D. The old grass is removed, and the roots are ground into the soil.
    E. The grass on the field is dug up and ground into mulch.

The correct answer is **C.** This question requires you to search for specific details in the passage and determine the sequence of events. This information is provided as the author refers to the step-by-step process of the field makeover. After skimming the answer choices, you will notice that Choice **B** is the last step in this process and therefore can be eliminated. Choice **D** is only partially correct and in sequence. Choice **A** is not done "immediately before the sod is put in place."

Directions: Read the passage below and answer the two questions that follow.

    Two important factors for a manufacturing company to consider before deciding to enter the global market are "Can we produce enough inventory to fill foreign orders?" and "Does our product meet local standards and regulations?" If enough product can't be produced to fill foreign orders efficiently, or if the product doesn't meet the local requirements and cannot be modified to meet these requirements, the result could be "channel frustration," which is defined as a situation in which the foreign market wants a product but can't buy it because of inadequate supply or because the product fails to meet local regulations. "Channel frustration" breeds unhappy customers and could lead to an exporter's retreat from the market.

Recognize Implications Based on Information from the Passage

28. The passage is most likely to appear in

    A. a magazine article profiling multinational corporations.
    B. a how-to book for new managers.
    C. a newspaper editorial on foreign trade barriers.
    D. a news article on standards for products marketed in the European Union.
    E. a general guide to companies interested in global marketing.

The correct answer is **E.** This passage is most likely to appear in a general guide for companies. It is unlikely that it would be in a how-to book for new managers, Choice **B,** or in a news article that specifically covered standards for the European Union, Choice **D.** It doesn't present an opinion and therefore would not appear in an editorial, Choice **C,** nor would it be appropriate in an article profiling multinational corporations, Choice **A.**

Make Inferences Based on Information from the Passage

29. From the passage it can be inferred that

    A. entering foreign markets is an important way to increase profit.
    B. modification of an existing product may be necessary if the product is going to be marketed in other countries.
    C. "channel frustration" is the most common problem for companies that want to enter foreign markets.
    D. elimination of foreign tariffs would be a positive step for successful global marketing.
    E. in general, small companies should not consider entering foreign markets.

The correct answer is **B.** The only inference that can be made is that in order to meet the requirements of local standards, the company would be required to make modifications to the product. Choices **A, C, D,** and **E** may or may not be true, but they cannot be inferred from information in the passage.

Research and Reference Skills Questions

Research and reference skills draw upon your knowledge of interpretation. As you work through these practice problems, read the headings and skim the subheadings, and notice how information is organized in the display. Look for specific facts and information in the display to help you answer the question. You will be asked to

- understand the organization of the passage.
- locate information in a table of contents, glossary, or index.
- explain a graph or display.

Table of Contents or Indexes

Directions: Use the excerpt from the table of contents below to answer the next three questions.

Notice How Information Is Organized

30. Which of the following best describes the organizational pattern used in dividing this book?

    A. By topic, alphabetically

    B. By category and subcategory

    C. By level of difficulty

    D. By length of section

    E. By importance of concepts

The correct answer is **B.** A careful review of the table of contents shows that the organizational pattern is by category and subcategory.

Understand How to Locate Specific Information

31. On what pages of a table of contents would one look to find information about subordinate clauses?

    A. Pages 30–32

    B. Pages 45–47

    C. Pages 27–28

    D. Pages 35–36

    E. Pages 44–45

The correct answer is **C**. As you skim the table of contents, you will notice that "Clauses" is a subheading listed under the heading of "Sentence Style." "Subordinate Clauses" should be included in this subheading on page 27.

Understand How to Locate Specific Information

---

32. According to this table of contents, where would one find information on plural subjects and verbs?

    A. Pages 30–32
    B. Pages 45–47
    C. Pages 25–26
    D. Pages 35–36
    E. Pages 49–51

The correct answer is **E**. This question requires you to decode headings and subheadings. At first glance you might choose pages 25–26, since "Multiple Subjects" is listed in "Sentence Style." However, verbs are not listed in this heading. Skim the table of contents to look for specific information related to "subjects" and "verbs." The best answer is on page 49, Choice **E**. This question requires you to be familiar with grammar, but even if you're not, look for recognizable words to find your answer. "Subject-Verb Agreement" is listed under "Grammar."

Directions: Use the graph below to answer the two questions that follow.

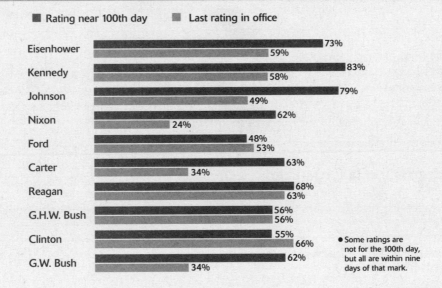

Identify and Compare Information in a Table or Graph

---

33. According to the graph above, which of the following presidents had the highest 100th-day approval rating?

    A. Eisenhower, Johnson, and Reagan
    B. Obama and Kennedy
    C. Johnson, Kennedy, and Eisenhower
    D. Reagan and Kennedy
    E. Eisenhower and Clinton

Graphs are often used to emphasize information, as they provide an organized picture of data to support the author's point of view. Be sure to understand the information that is given. Notice that the purpose of this bar graph is to compare 100th-day approval ratings of past presidents. The 100th-day rating is indicated in the darkened bar. Clinton and Reagan had low 100th-day ratings; therefore, choices **A**, **D**, and **E** can be eliminated.

Obama's approval ratings are not on the graph, eliminating Choice **B.** Kennedy had an 83% approval rating, Johnson a 79% approval rating, and Eisenhower a 73% approval rating, Choice **C.** The correct answer is **C.**

---

34. Which of the following presidents had better ratings when leaving office than in their first 100 days in office?

   A. George H. Bush and George W. Bush
   B. Reagan and George W. Bush
   C. Nixon and Carter
   D. Clinton and Ford
   E. Kennedy and Johnson

The correct answer is **D.** This question asks the reader to compare two bars for each president. Only Ford and Clinton had higher ratings when leaving office than in their first 100 days in office, Choice **D.** Notice that sometimes data remains the same, as with George H. Bush's ratings.

Five Key Questions for Understanding and Interpreting What You Read

Practice your reading skills daily. After you read a newspaper, magazine, or book, ask yourself the following questions:

1. **What is the main idea of the passage?** After reading any passage, try summarizing it in a brief sentence. To practice this very important skill, read the editorials in your local paper each day and write a brief sentence summarizing each one.

2. **What details support the main idea?** Usually such details are facts, statistics, experiences, and so on, that strengthen your understanding of and agreement with the main idea.

3. **What is the purpose of the passage?** Ask yourself what the author is trying to accomplish. The four most common general purposes are (1) to narrate (tell a story), (2) to describe, (3) to inform, and (4) to persuade.

4. **Are the style and tone of the passage objective or subjective?** In other words, is the author presenting things factually or from a personal point of view? If an author is subjective, you may want to pin down the nature of the subjectivity. Ask yourself, is the author optimistic? pessimistic? angry? humorous? serious?

5. **What are the difficult or unusual words in the passage?** Readers who do not mark words that are difficult or used in an unusual way in a passage often forget that the words occurred at all and have difficulty locating them if this becomes necessary. By calling your attention to difficult or unusual words, you increase your chances of defining them by understanding their meaning in context.

A PATTERNED PLAN OF ATTACK
Reading Section

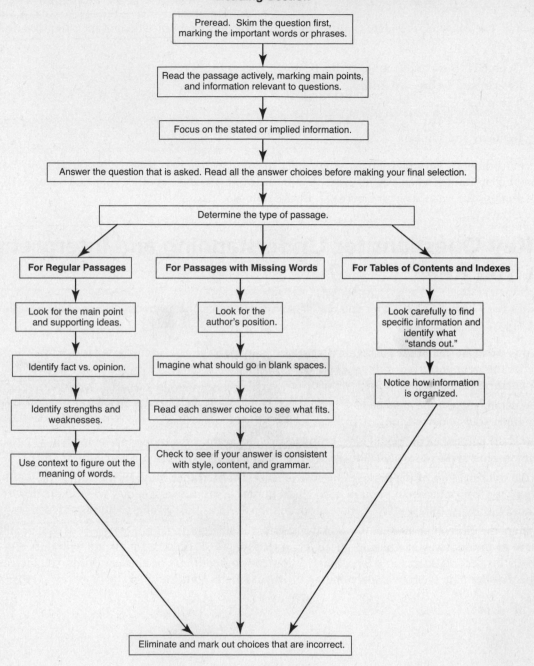

Preread. Skim the question first, marking the important words or phrases.

Read the passage actively, marking main points, and information relevant to questions.

Focus on the stated or implied information.

Answer the question that is asked. Read all the answer choices before making your final selection.

Determine the type of passage.

For Regular Passages

Look for the main point and supporting ideas.

Identify fact vs. opinion.

Identify strengths and weaknesses.

Use context to figure out the meaning of words.

For Passages with Missing Words

Look for the author's position.

Imagine what should go in blank spaces.

Read each answer choice to see what fits.

Check to see if your answer is consistent with style, content, and grammar.

For Tables of Contents and Indexes

Look carefully to find specific information and identify what "stands out."

Notice how information is organized.

Eliminate and mark out choices that are incorrect.

The Mathematics Section

Introduction

The Mathematics section of the test contains 50 questions. The questions are selected from different areas of mathematics, with questions on basic computation, measurement, ratios, percentages, probability, and reading and interpreting tables, graphs, charts, and standardized test scores (for example, stanine scores). *Complex computations are not required,* and most of the terms used are general, commonly encountered mathematical expressions (for example: *perimeter, integer,* and *prime number*). Most questions are presented as word problems and the use of calculators is prohibited.

Ability Tested

This part of the exam tests your ability to use your cumulative knowledge of mathematics and your reasoning ability. Computation is minimal; you are not required to have many specific formulas or equations memorized. What's most important is that you demonstrate a working understanding of general math concepts that *any* teacher may need. These basic math skills are necessary for teachers to average grades, read charts and graphs, understand diagrams, interpret test results, and so on.

The test is composed of the following content areas with *approximate* questions and percentages.

Test Format		
Skill Factor	**Number of Questions**	**Approximate Percentage**
Estimation, Measurement and Statistical Principles	15 questions	30%
Computation and Problem Solving	17 questions	35%
Numerical and Graphic Relationships	18 questions	35%

Estimation and Measurement: Recognize and make use of U.S. measurement systems (units of length, temperature, weight); demonstrate ability to measure length and perimeter; understand and use estimates of time; and estimate problem results prior to computing (addition, subtraction, multiplication, division).

Statistical Principles: Basic statistical arithmetic operations associated with test scores (average, proportions, probability, ratios, and percentiles); make simple predictions of an outcome based on statistical data (e.g. what is the probability of occurrence); interpret and compare the results of student test scores (e.g. stanine scores or percentiles).

Computation and Problem Solving: Simple arithmetic operations and computation (add, subtract, multiply, and divide) with whole numbers (positive and negative), fractions, decimals, and percentages; simple algebra equations (identifying facts in a problem); and identify alternative methods for solving math problems.

Numerical and Graphic Relationships: Identify relationships in data and in the position of numbers (less than, greater than, equal to); identify numbers and formulas for math expressions that are the same (e.g. $\frac{3}{6} = \frac{1}{2}$ or $\frac{1}{4} = 25\%$); identify "rounding off" rules; apply the understanding of logical connectives (such as *and, or, if-then*), and quantifiers (*some, all,* or *none*); understand and interpret tables and graphs (bar, circles, lines, total, subtotal).

Basic Skills Necessary

A cumulative knowledge of mathematics is necessary for this section of the CBEST—math from elementary grades through at least one year of high school, and possibly one year of college. Thus, no single math course can prepare you specifically for this part of the test.

The math topics covered include those in the following areas.

Arithmetic

You need to be able to:

- Use operations involving whole numbers and fractions, decimals and percents.
- Apply arithmetic operations to practical math, such as invoices, unit cost, totals.
- Understand basic statistics and averages.
- Work with ratios and proportions.
- Determine percents, including percent increase, decrease, and change.
- Compare fractions, decimals, and positive and negative numbers.
- Approximate values and round-off numbers.
- Estimate results of addition, subtraction, multiplication, and division prior to actual computation.
- Understand basic principles of probability and predict likely outcomes.

Basic Algebra

You need to be able to:

- Set up simple equations.
- Solve equations with one variable.
- Understand problem-solving terminology:
  - Logical connectives, such as *if-then, and,* and *or*
  - Quantifiers, such as *some, all, few,* and *none*
- Recognize different methods of solving a problem.
- Identify important facts in a problem.
- Determine whether enough information is given to solve a problem.

Measurement

You need to be able to:

- Understand and use standard units in the U.S. measurement and metric systems, including length, temperature, weight, and capacity.
- Measure length and perimeter.
- Convert from one measurement unit to another.
- Interpret the meaning of standardized test scores.

Graphs, Charts, and Tables

You need to be able to:

- Understand data entry and information given.
- Find missing information.
- Use numerical information to solve math problems.
- Work with line, bar, and circle graphs.

See page 67 for a complete review of graphs, charts, and tables.

Directions

Each of the questions in this section is followed by five choices. Select the best answer for each question. *Paper-based test takers,* fill in the corresponding lettered space on the answer sheet and make sure you mark your answers for this section on the Mathematics section of your answer sheet. *Computer-based examinees,* click on the oval to the left of your selection to fill in your identified answer choice.

Analysis of Directions

- **Pace Your Time:** You should spend about 75 minutes to do the 50 problems. This averages to a minute and a half per problem, so keep that in mind as you attack each problem. If you know that you can work a problem but that it will take you far, far longer than a minute and a half, skip it and return to it later if you have time. Keep in mind that it's important to finish all math problems before proceeding to the next section. This will allow you to remain focused on one subject at a time.
- **Work Easy Problems First:** Remember, you want to do all the easy, quick problems first, before spending valuable time on the others.
- **Answer Every Question:** There is no penalty for guessing, so don't leave any blanks. If you do not know the answer to a problem but you can size it up to get a general range for your answer, you may be able to eliminate one or more of the answer choices, thus increasing your odds of guessing the correct answer. But even if you cannot eliminate any of the choices, take an educated guess because there is no penalty for wrong answers.
- **Mark the Correct Answer Choice:** *Paper-based test takers,* be sure that your answers on your answer sheet correspond to the numbers on your question sheet. Placing one answer in the incorrect number on the answer sheet may shift *all* your answers to the incorrect spots. Also check that the oval you have chosen is completely filled in before proceeding to the next question. And above all, double-check to make sure that you mark your answers to math questions on the Mathematics section of your answer sheet. *Computer-based test takers,* check to make sure that you have clicked on the correct oval.
- **Calculating Problems:** Remember that the use of a calculator is prohibited on the exam, but complex computations are not required. *Computer-based test takers,* be sure to take advantage of the scratch paper provided to help you visualize and work out problems.

Suggested Approaches with Samples

A number of different approaches can be helpful in attacking many types of mathematics problems. Of course, the strategies in this section don't work on *all* the problems, but if you become familiar with them, you will find them helpful in answering quite a few questions.

Mark Key Words

- **Paper-based test takers:** Circling and/or underlining key words in each question is an effective test-taking technique. You can easily be misled if you overlook a key word in a problem, so take advantage of this opportunity to focus your attention. By circling or underlining these key words, you help yourself focus on what you are being asked to find. Keep in mind that you are allowed to mark and write on your testing booklet. **37**

- **Computer-based test takers:** You will be given scratch paper or a dry-erase board to write down important key words. Remember to write down just one or two key words; any more than that will waste valuable testing time.

Samples

1. In the following number, which digit is in the thousandths place?

   6574.12398

   A. 2
   B. 3
   C. 5
   D. 6
   E. 9

The key word here is *thousandths*. By circling or writing down *thousandths,* you pay closer attention to it. This is the kind of question which, under the pressures of time and testing, you may misread. You may easily misread it as *thousands* place. Hopefully, circling the important words minimizes misreading. For paper-based test takers, your completed question may look like this after you mark the important words or terms:

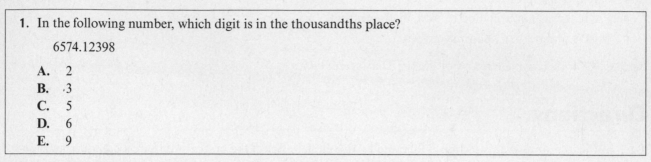

1. In the following number, which (digit) is in the (thousandths) place?

   6574.12(3)98

   A. 2
   (B. 3)
   C. 5
   D. 6
   E. 9

The correct answer is **B.**

2. If 3 yards of ribbon cost $2.97, what price is the price per foot?

   A. $ .33
   B. $ .99
   C. $2.94
   D. $3.00
   E. $8.91

The correct answer is **A.**

The key word here is *foot*. Dividing $2.97 by 3 will tell you only the price per yard, and, of course, that price is Choice **B**—$.99. Therefore, it would be very helpful to circle or write down the words *price per foot* in the problem. You must still divide by 3 (because there are 3 feet per yard) to find the cost per foot: $.99, divided by 3 is $.33.

3. If $3x + 1 = 16$, what is the value of $x - 4$?

   A. 19
   B. 16
   C. 5
   D. 1
   E. −1

The correct answer choice is **D.**

The key here is *what is the value of* $x - 4$? Therefore circle "$x - 4$." Note that solving the original equation gives you only the value of x.

$$3x + 1 = 16$$
$$\underline{-1 \quad -1}$$
$$\frac{3x}{3} = \frac{15}{3}$$
$$x = 5$$

Here again notice that 5 is one of the choices, **C.** But the question asks for the value of $x - 4$, not just x. To continue, replace x with 5 and solve:

$$x - 4 = ?$$
$$5 - 4 = 1$$

---

4. Together a bat and glove cost $110. The bat costs $40 more than the glove. What is the cost of the bat?

   A. $35.00
   B. $40.00
   C. $70.00
   D. $75.00
   E. $110.00

The correct answer is **D.**

The key words here are *cost of the bat,* so mark or write down these words. Solving this algebraically:

Let x = cost of the glove

$x + 40$ = cost of the bat (cost is $40 more than the glove)

Together they cost $110

$$x + (x + 40) = 110$$
$$2x + 40 = 110$$
$$\underline{-40 \quad -40}$$
$$2x = 70$$
$$\frac{2x}{2} = \frac{70}{2}$$
$$x = 35$$

Notice that x is the cost of the glove and $35 is one of the choices, **A.** Since x = $35, then the cost of the bat is $x + 40$ = $75. *Always answer the question that is being asked.* Circling, marking, or writing down the key words can help you do that.

---

5. Tia is trying to round the number 4,547 to the nearest hundred. If she gets the right answer, she receives extra credit. What answer must Tia get to receive extra credit?

   A. 5,000
   B. 4,600
   C. 4,550
   D. 4,500
   E. 4,540

The correct answer is **D.** To round to the nearest hundred, you must check to see whether the number in the tens place is 5 or more. If it is less than 5, which it is in this case, let the hundreds place stand as is and put zeros in the tens and ones place, respectively—4,500.

Pull Out Information

Pulling information out of the wording of a word problem can make the problem more workable and give you additional insight into the problem. Pull out the given facts and identify which of those facts will help you work the problem. Not all facts will always be needed!

Samples

6. If a mixture is $\frac{3}{7}$ alcohol by volume and $\frac{4}{7}$ water by volume, what is the ratio of the volume of alcohol to the volume of water in this mixture?

   A. $\frac{3}{7}$

   B. $\frac{4}{7}$

   C. $\frac{3}{4}$

   D. $\frac{4}{3}$

   E. $\frac{7}{4}$

The correct answer is **C.**

The first bit of information to pull out is what you're looking for: *ratio of the volume of alcohol to the volume of water.* You should have circled, marked or written this information in the question.

Rewrite the question as *A* (alcohol): *W* (water) and then put this ratio into working form:

$$\frac{A}{W}$$

Next, pull out the volumes of each:

$$A = \frac{3}{7} \text{ and } W = \frac{4}{7}$$

Now, you can figure out the answer easily by inspection or substitution using $\dfrac{\frac{3}{7}}{\frac{4}{7}}$. Invert the bottom fraction and

multiply to get $\dfrac{3}{\cancel{7}_1} \times \dfrac{\cancel{7}^1}{4} = \dfrac{3}{4}$. The ratio of the volume of alcohol to the volume of water is 3 to 4.

> When pulling out information, actually write the numbers and/or letters to put them into a helpful form and eliminate some of the wording.

7. If the ratio of boys to girls in a drama class is 2 to 1, which of the following is a possible number of students in the class?
   A. 10
   B. 16
   C. 19
   D. 25
   E. 30

The correct answer is **E.**

First mark or write down the words *possible number of students*. Pulling out this information gives you the following:

b:g = 2:1

Because the ratio of boys to girls is 2:1, the possible total number of students in the class must be a multiple of 2 + 1 (boys plus girls), or 3. The multiples of 3 are 3, 6, 9, 12, 15 and so on. Only 30 is a multiple of 3.

---

8. An employee's annual salary was increased $15,000. If her new annual salary now equals $90,000, what was the percent increase?

   A.   15%

   B. $16\frac{2}{3}\%$

   C.   20%

   D.   22%

   E.   24%

The correct answer is **C**.

Mark or write down what you are looking for. In this case, *percent increase*.

$$\text{Percent increase} = \frac{\text{change}}{\text{starting point}}$$

Now pull out information.

If the employee's salary was increased by $15,000 to $90,000, then the starting salary was $90,000 – $15,000 = $75,000.

Therefore, $\frac{15,000}{75,000} = \frac{1}{5} = 20\%$.

Identify the Facts Needed

Not all the facts given are always needed to work out the problem. Pull out the given facts and identify which of those facts help you work the problem.

Samples

---

9. Jason is 10 years older than his sister. If Jason was 25 years of age in 2008, in what year could he have been born?

   A.   1973

   B.   1984

   C.   1983

   D.   1988

   E.   1993

The correct answer is **C**.

The key words here are *in what year* and *could he have been born*. Thus, the solution is simple: 2008 – 25 = 1983. Notice that you should pull out the information *25 years of age* and *in 2008*. Jason's age in comparison to his sister's age is not relevant, and therefore, should not be pulled out.

10. Dan is 18 years old. He works for his father for $\frac{3}{4}$ of the year, and he works for his brother for the rest of the year. What is the ratio of the time per year that Dan spends working for his brother to the time he spends working for his father?

  A. $\frac{1}{4}$

  B. $\frac{1}{3}$

  C. $\frac{3}{4}$

  D. $\frac{4}{3}$

  E. $\frac{4}{1}$

The correct answer is **B.**

The key word *rest* points to the answer:

$$1 - \frac{3}{4} = ?$$

$$\frac{4}{4} - \frac{3}{4} = \frac{1}{4} \text{ (the part of the year that Dan works for his brother)}$$

A key idea is the way you write the ratio. The problem becomes that of finding the ratio of $\frac{1}{4}$ to $\frac{3}{4}$.

$$\frac{\frac{1}{4}}{\frac{3}{4}} = \frac{1}{4} \div \frac{3}{4} = \frac{1}{{}_1\cancel{4}} \times \frac{\cancel{4}^1}{3} = \frac{1}{3}$$

Note that you don't need Dan's age to solve the problem.

Recognize When Not Enough Information Is Given

Sometimes you may not have sufficient information to solve the problem. Focus on what information is needed to get the answer.

Sample

11. A woman purchased several books at $15 each plus one more for $12. What was the average price of each book?

  A. $12
  B. $13
  C. $14
  D. $15
  E. not enough information given

The correct answer is **E.**

To calculate an average, you must have the total amount and then divide by the number of items. The difficulty here, however, is that *several books at $15* does not specify exactly *how many* books were purchased at $15 each. Does *several* mean two? Or does it mean three? *Several* is not a precise mathematical term. Therefore, there is not enough information to pull out to calculate an average.

Work Forward

If you immediately recognize the method or proper formula to solve the problem, then go ahead and do the work. Work forward.

Samples

> **12.** Which of the following numbers is between $\frac{1}{4}$ and $\frac{1}{3}$?
>
> A. .45
> B. .35
> C. .29
> D. .22
> E. .20

The correct answer is **C.**

First underline, circle, or write down "between $\frac{1}{4}$ and $\frac{1}{3}$." If you know that $\frac{1}{4}$ is .25 and $\frac{1}{3}$ is .333..., you have insight into the problem and should be able to work it forward. Because .29 is the only number between .25 and .333..., it is the correct answer. A quick peek at the answer choices tips you off that you should work in decimals.

> **13.** What is the final cost of a watch that sells for $49.00 if the sales tax is 7%?
>
> A. $49.07
> B. $49.70
> C. $52.00
> D. $52.43
> E. $56.00

The correct answer is **D.**

Because the sales tax is 7% of $49.00,

$$7\% \text{ of } \$49.00 = (.07)(\$49.00)$$
$$= \$3.43$$

The total cost of the watch is therefore:

$$\$49.00 + \$3.43 = \$52.43$$

Use the information below to answer the question that follows.

Price List	
Top sirloin	$4.99 per pound or 2 pounds for $9.00
Filet mignon	$8.99 per pound
London broil	$3.89 per pound or 3 pounds for $10.00

14. Randy owns and manages Randy's Steakhouse. He needs to buy the following meats in order to have enough for the weekend: 9 pounds of top sirloin, 8 pounds of filet mignon, and 7 pounds of London broil. What is the least amount Randy can spend to buy the meat he needs for the weekend business?

   A. $144.06
   B. $136.80
   C. $127.92
   D. $ 57.92
   E. $ 17.87

The correct answer is **B**.

   top sirloin: 8 pounds + 1 pound
   $= (4 \times \$9.00) + \$4.99 (1)$ (*Note:* 2 pounds for $9.00)
   $= \$36.00 + \$4.99$
   $= \$40.99$
   filet mignon: 8 pounds
   $= 8 \times \$8.99$
   $= \$71.92$
   London broil: 6 pounds + 1 pound
   $= (2 \times \$10) + \$3.89 (1)$ (*Note:* 3 pounds for $10.00)
   $= \$20.00 + \$3.89$
   $= \$23.89$

Add to find the total: $\$40.99 + \$71.92 + \$23.89 = \$136.80$

Work Backward from the Answers

If you don't immediately recognize a method or formula, or if using the method or formula would take a great deal of time, try working backward—from the answers. Because the answers are usually given in ascending or descending order, always start by plugging in Choice **C** first. Then you know whether to go up or down with your next try. (In some cases, you may want to plug in the simplest answer first.)

Samples

15. If $\frac{x}{2} + \frac{3}{4} = 1\frac{1}{4}$, what is the value of x?

   A. −2
   B. −1
   C. 0
   D. 1
   E. 2

The correct answer is **D.** You should first underline, circle or write down *value of x.* If you've forgotten how to solve this kind of equation, work backward by plugging in answers. Start with Choice **C** and plug in 0:

$$\frac{0}{2} + \frac{3}{4} \stackrel{?}{=} 1\frac{1}{4}$$

Because this answer is too small, try Choice **D,** a larger number. Plugging in 1 gives you:

$$\frac{1}{2} + \frac{3}{4} \stackrel{?}{=} 1\frac{1}{4}$$

$$\frac{2}{4} + \frac{3}{4} \stackrel{?}{=} 1\frac{1}{4}$$

$$\frac{5}{4} = 1\frac{1}{4}$$

This answer is true. Working from the answers is a valuable technique.

16. Find the counting number that is less than 15, and when divided by 3 has a remainder of 1, but when divided by 4 has a remainder of 2.

    A. 5
    B. 8
    C. 10
    D. 12
    E. 13

The correct answer is **C.** By working from the answers, you can eliminate wrong answer choices. For example, you can eliminate choices **B** and **D** immediately because they are divisible by 4, leaving no remainder. Choices **A** and **E** can also be eliminated because they each leave a remainder of 1 when divided by 4. Therefore, 10 leaves a remainder of 1 when divided by 3 and a remainder of 2 when divided by 4.

17. What is the *greatest* common factor of the numbers 18, 24, and 30?

    A.   2
    B.   3
    C.   4
    D.   6
    E. 12

The correct answer is **D.**

$$18 = 2 \times 3 \times 3$$
$$24 = 2 \times 2 \times 2 \times 3 \qquad 2 \times 3 \text{ are common factors}$$
$$30 = 2 \times 3 \times 5$$

You can work from the answers, but here you should start with the largest answer choice, because you're looking for the "greatest" common factor. The largest number which divides evenly into 18, 24, and 30 is 6.

Plug In Simple Numbers

Substituting numbers for variables can often help you understand a problem. Remember to plug in *simple, small* numbers, because you have to do the work.

Samples

18. If r represents an even integer, then an odd integer is represented by which of the following?

   A. $3r$
   B. $2r + 1$
   C. $3r + 2$
   D. $4r - 2$
   E. $5r - 4$

Because the question says that *r represents an even integer,* substitute 2 for r. You should make note of *an odd integer* because that's what you're looking for. So as you substitute 2 into each choice, you can stop when you get an odd integer.

   A. $3r = 3(2) = 6$
   B. $2r + 1 = 2(2) + 1 = 5$

Notice 5 is an odd integer; therefore, the correct answer is **B.**

19. If x is a positive integer in the equation $2x = y$, then what must y be?

   A.   a positive even integer
   B.   a negative even integer
   C.   zero
   D.   a positive odd integer
   E.   a negative odd integer

At first glance, this problem appears quite complex. But let's plug in other numbers and see what happens. For instance, first plug in 1 (the simplest positive integer) for x.

$$2x = y$$
$$2(1) = y$$
$$2 = y$$

Now try 2:

$$2x = y$$
$$2(2) = y$$
$$4 = y$$

Try it again. No matter what positive integer is plugged in for x, y is always positive and even. Therefore, the correct answer is **A.**

20. If $x > 1$, which of the following decreases as x decreases?

   I. $x + x^2$
   II. $2x^2 - x$
   III. $\dfrac{1}{x+1}$

   A.   I only
   B.   II only
   C.   III only
   D.   I and II only
   E.   II and III only

The correct answer is **D**. You can solve this problem most easily by taking each situation and substituting simple numbers.

However, in the first situation—I. $x + x^2$—you should recognize that this expression will decrease as x decreases.

Trying $x = 2$ produces $2 + (2)^2$, which equals 6.

Trying $x = 3$ gives you $3 + (3)^2 = 12$.

Notice that choices **B, C,** and **E** are already eliminated because they do not contain I. You should also realize that now you need to try only the values in II—because III is not paired with I as an answer choice, III cannot be one of the answers.

Trying $x = 2$ in the expression $2x^2 - x$ gives you $2(2)^2 - 2$, or $2(4) - 2$, which leaves 6.

Trying $x = 3$ gives you $2(3)^2 - 3$, or $2(9) - 3 = 18 - 3 = 15$. This expression also decreases as x decreases. Notice that III was not even attempted because it was not one of the possible choices.

Be sure to make logical substitutions. Use the appropriate type of number—a positive number, a negative number, zero, and so on, to get the full picture.

Use 10 or 100

Some problems may deal with percent or percent change. If you don't see a simple method for working the problem, try using values of 10 or 100 and see what you get.

Samples

21. If 40% of the students in a class have brown eyes and 20% of those with brown eyes have brown hair, then what percent of the original total number have brown hair and brown eyes?

    A.   4%
    B.   8%
    C.   16%
    D.   20%
    E.   32%

The correct answer is **B**. First, make note of "percent of the original total number," "brown hair," and "brown eyes." In this problem, if you don't identify a simple method, start with 100 students in the class. Because 40% of the students have brown eyes, then 40 students have brown eyes. Now, the problem says that 20% of those students with brown eyes have brown hair. So take 20% of 40, which gives you:

$$.20 \times 40 = 8.0$$

Because the question asks what percent of the original total number have brown eyes and brown hair, and because you started with 100 students, the answer is 8 out of 100, or 8%.

22. A corporation triples its annual bonus to 50 of its employees. What percent of the employees' new bonus is the increase?

    A.   50%
    B. $66\frac{2}{3}\%$
    C.   100%
    D.   200%
    E.   300%

The correct answer is **B.** Use $100 for the normal bonus. If the annual bonus was normally $100, tripled it is now $300. Therefore the increase, $200, must be placed over the new bonus of $300:

$$\frac{\$200}{\$300} = \frac{2}{3}$$

$$\frac{2}{3} = 66\frac{2}{3}\%$$

Approximate

If it appears that you need to do extensive calculations to solve a problem, check to see how far apart the choices are and then approximate. The reason for checking the answers first is to give you a guide to see how freely you can approximate.

Samples

23. What is the value of $\frac{(.889 \times 55)}{9.97}$ to the nearest tenth?

    A.   49.1
    B.   17.7
    C.   4.9
    D.   4.63
    E.   .5

The correct answer is **C.** First underline or write down what you are looking for: *nearest tenth.* Before starting any computations, take a glance at the answers to see how far apart they are. Notice that the only close choices are **C** and **D,** but **D** is not a possible choice because it is to the nearest hundredth, not tenth. Now, make some quick approximations— $.889 \approx 1$ and $9.97 \approx 10$—leaves the problem in this form:

$$\frac{1 \times 55}{10} = \frac{55}{10} = 5.5$$

Notice that choices **A** and **E** are not reasonable. The closest answer is 4.9.

24. If 2,100 people work in a factory, and 21% of them work only the night shift, approximately how many people work the other shifts?

    A.   400
    B.   800
    C. 1,100
    D. 1,600
    E. 2,000

The correct answer is **D.** First underline or circle *approximately how many people* and *other shifts.* Remember, you're looking for *other shifts.* Notice that the answers are spread out.

Now, approximate 21% as 20%. Next, approximate 2,100 people as 2,000 people. So, 20% of 2,000 is $.20 \times 2,000 = 400$.

But be careful; 400 is the number of those who work only on the night shift, and you want the number of people who work the other shifts. So subtract 400 from 2,000, leaving 1,600. Another method is to approximate, then subtract 20% from 100%, to get 80%, which is the percent of other workers. Multiply 80% times 2,000 and you get 1,600.

Simplify the Problem

Sometimes combining terms, performing simple operations, or simplifying the problem in some other way gives you insight and makes the problem easier to solve.

Samples

> **25.** Which of the following is between $\frac{1}{4}$ and 0.375?
>
>   **A.**   0.0094
>   **B.**   0.291
>   **C.**   0.38
>   **D.**   0.4
>   **E.**   0.51

The correct answer is **B**. First underline or write down the word "between." Next, simplify $\frac{1}{4}$ to .25. A quick glance at the choices is valuable because it tips you off that you are working in decimals. Simply check which decimal is between .250 and .375. The correct answer .291 is between .250 and .375. Notice that changing .25 to .250 makes the problem even easier. (Adding or eliminating zeros to the far right of a decimal doesn't change the value of the number.)

> **26.** Which of the following is equal to $\frac{1}{5}$ of 0.02 percent?
>
>   **A.**   0.4
>   **B.**   0.04
>   **C.**   0.004
>   **D.**   0.0004
>   **E.**   0.00004

The correct answer is **E**. Simplifying this problem first means changing $\frac{1}{5}$ to .2. Next change 0.02 percent to 0.0002 (that is .02 × .01 = 0.0002).

Now that you have simplified the problem, multiply .2 × 0.0002 which gives 0.00004.

Simplifying can make a problem much easier to solve.

Make Comparisons

At times, questions require you to compare the sizes of several decimals, or several fractions. If you're comparing decimals, make sure that the numbers you compare have the same number of digits. (Remember: You can insert or eliminate zeros to the far right of a decimal point without changing the value of the number.)

Samples

> **27.** Which one of the answer choices places these decimal fractions in order from smallest to largest .6, .16, $.66\frac{2}{3}$, .58?
>
>   **A.**   .6, .16, $.66\frac{2}{3}$, .58
>
>   **B.**   .58, .16, .6, $.66\frac{2}{3}$
>
>   **C.**   .16, .58, .6, $.66\frac{2}{3}$
>
>   **D.** $.66\frac{2}{3}$, .6, .58, .16
>
>   **E.**   .58, .6, $.66\frac{2}{3}$, .16

The correct answer is **C**. Rewrite .6 as .60 so that all the decimals have the same number of digits: .60, .16, .66$\frac{2}{3}$, .58. Treating these as though the decimal point were not there (you can do this only when all the numbers have the same number of digits to the right of the decimal), the order is as follows: .16, .58, .60, .66$\frac{2}{3}$. Remember to circle or write down "smallest to largest" in the question.

---

28. Which of the following answer choices places the fractions $\frac{5}{8}, \frac{3}{4}, \frac{2}{3}$, in order from smallest to largest?

   A. $\frac{2}{3}, \frac{3}{4}, \frac{5}{8}$

   B. $\frac{2}{3}, \frac{5}{8}, \frac{3}{4}$

   C. $\frac{5}{8}, \frac{2}{3}, \frac{3}{4}$

   D. $\frac{3}{4}, \frac{5}{8}, \frac{2}{3}$

   E. $\frac{3}{4}, \frac{2}{3}, \frac{5}{8}$

The correct answer is **C**.

Find the common denominator: $\frac{5}{8} = \frac{15}{24}, \frac{3}{4} = \frac{18}{24}, \frac{2}{3} = \frac{16}{24}$.

Therefore the order becomes $\frac{5}{8}, \frac{2}{3}, \frac{3}{4}$, or you can use decimal equivalents:

$$\frac{5}{8} = .625$$

$$\frac{3}{4} = .75 \text{ or } .750$$

$$\frac{2}{3} = .66\frac{2}{3} \text{ or } .666\frac{2}{3}$$

The order again becomes $\frac{5}{8}, \frac{2}{3}, \frac{3}{4}$.

Mark Diagrams

When a figure is included with the problem, mark or draw the given facts on the diagram. This helps you visualize all the facts given.

Samples

Use the figure to answer the question that follows.

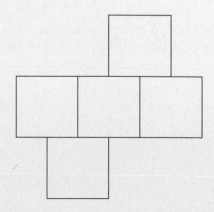

29. If each square in the figure has a side of length 1, what is the perimeter?

A. 8
B. 12
C. 14
D. 16
E. 20

The correct answer is **B.** Mark or draw the known facts:

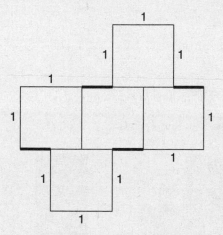

Now you have a calculation for the perimeter: 10 *plus* the darkened parts. Now look carefully at the top two darkened parts. They add up to 1. (Notice that sliding the top square over illustrates this fact.)

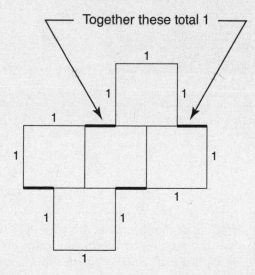

The same is true for the bottom darkened parts. They add to 1. Thus, the total perimeter is 10 + 2, or 12.

All of the squares are identical in size. To check your work, move the top and bottom squares to form the figure below:

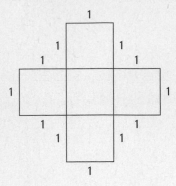

Each side has a length of 1, the perimeter becomes 12 groups of 1, or 12.

Use the figure below to answer the question that follows.

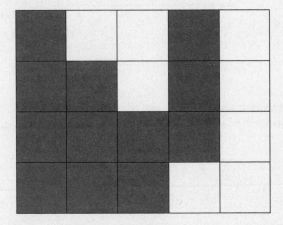

30. In the preceding figure, if each small square is 2 inches in length, what is the perimeter of the shaded area?

    A.   20 inches
    B.   24 inches
    C.   40 inches
    D.   48 inches
    E.   60 inches

The correct answer is **C.** Mark in the diagram as you start counting from the lower left-hand corner. As you go around the outside of the shaded region, your markings can help you make sure that you don't miss a side. You should have 20 numbered sides in the perimeter. But remember, each side is 2 inches long, so multiply $20 \times 2 = 40$ inches.

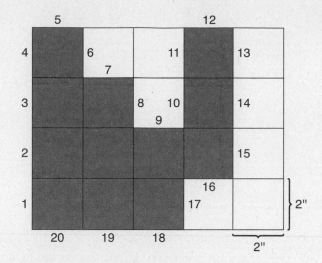

Draw a Diagram If None Is Given

Drawing diagrams to meet the conditions set by the word problem can often make the problem easier for you to work. Being able to *see* the facts is more helpful than just reading the words.

Samples

> **31.** What is the maximum number of pieces of birthday cake of size 4" by 4" that can be cut from a cake 20" by 20"?
>
> **A.** 5
> **B.** 10
> **C.** 16
> **D.** 20
> **E.** 25

The correct answer is **E.** Sketching the cake and marking it as follows makes this a fairly simple problem.

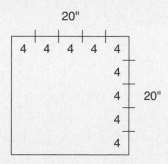

Notice that five pieces of cake will fit along each side; therefore, $5 \times 5 = 25$. Finding the total area of the cake and dividing it by the area of one of the 4×4 pieces also gives you the correct answer, but beware of this method because it may not work if the pieces do not fit evenly into the original area.

Finding Probability Combinations

Some questions involve probability and possible combinations. *Probability* is the numerical measure of the chance of an outcome or event occurring. When all outcomes are equally likely to occur, the probability of the occurrence of a given outcome can be found by using the following formula:

$$\text{probability} = \frac{\text{number of favorable outcomes}}{\text{total number of possible outcomes}}$$

Samples

---

32. What is the probability of throwing two dice in one toss so that they total 11?

   A. $\frac{1}{6}$

   B. $\frac{1}{11}$

   C. $\frac{1}{18}$

   D. $\frac{1}{20}$

   E. $\frac{1}{36}$

The correct answer is **C.** You can simply list all the possible combinations resulting in 11, (5 + 6 and 6 + 5), and realize that the total possibilities are 36, (6 × 6). Thus the probability equals:

$$\frac{\text{possibilities totalling 11}}{\text{total possibilities}} = \frac{2}{36} = \frac{1}{18}$$

---

33. What is the probability of tossing a penny twice so that both times it lands heads up?

   A. $\frac{1}{8}$

   B. $\frac{1}{4}$

   C. $\frac{1}{3}$

   D. $\frac{1}{2}$

   E. $\frac{2}{3}$

The correct answer is **B.**

The probability of throwing a head in one throw is

$$\frac{\text{chances of a head}}{\text{total chances (1 head + 1 tail)}} = \frac{1}{2}$$

Because you're trying to throw a head *twice,* multiply the probability for the first toss $\left(\frac{1}{2}\right)$ times the probability for the second toss (again $\frac{1}{2}$). Thus, $\frac{1}{2} \times \frac{1}{2} = \frac{1}{4}$, and $\frac{1}{4}$ is the probability of throwing heads twice in two tosses. Another way of approaching this problem is to look at the total number of possible outcomes:

First Toss	Second Toss
H	H
H	T
T	H
T	T

There are four different possible outcomes and only one way to throw two heads in two tosses. Thus, the probability of tossing two heads in two tosses is 1 out of 4 total outcomes, or $\frac{1}{4}$.

Use the figure below to answer the question that follows.

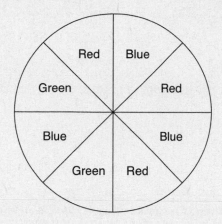

34. In the preceding spinner, all sections are equal. What is the probability of getting a blue on the first spin?

A. $\frac{1}{8}$

B. $\frac{1}{4}$

C. $\frac{3}{8}$

D. $\frac{3}{5}$

E. $\frac{5}{8}$

The correct answer is **C.**

Because there are 3 favorable (blue) outcomes out of 8 total possible outcomes, the probability is $\frac{3}{8}$:

$$\frac{\text{blue possibilities}}{\text{total possibilities}} = \frac{3}{8}$$

Read the information below and answer the three questions that follow.

Tom is pulling marbles out of a hat. There are 6 red marbles, 4 green marbles, and 2 yellow marbles. There are no other marbles in the hat.

35. What is the probability that Tom will pull a green marble on his first pull?

A. $\frac{1}{4}$

B. $\frac{1}{3}$

C. $\frac{2}{5}$

D. $\frac{1}{2}$

E. $\frac{2}{3}$

The correct answer is **B.**

Because there are 12 total marbles and 4 green marbles, the probability is

$$\frac{\text{green possibilities}}{\text{total possibilities}} = \frac{4}{12} = \frac{1}{3}$$

---

36. What is the least number of marbles that Tom can pull to ensure that he gets at least one of each color?

    A.   3
    B.   4
    C.   5
    D.   7
    E. 11

The correct answer is **E.** To ensure getting at least one of each color, Tom must pull 11 marbles. He could pull 6 reds and then 4 greens, so he would have pulled 10 marbles, and still only have two different colors. But on his next pull he would have to get a yellow because only yellow marbles would be left.

---

37. If Tom pulls a green marble first, and doesn't put it back in the hat, what is the probability that his next pull will be another green marble?

    A. $\frac{1}{12}$

    B. $\frac{1}{11}$

    C. $\frac{1}{4}$

    D. $\frac{3}{11}$

    E. $\frac{1}{3}$

The correct answer is **D.** When the first green marble is pulled and not put back, it leaves 3 greens, 6 reds, and 2 yellows. So the probability of pulling another green marble is

$$\frac{\text{green possibilities}}{\text{total possibilities}} = \frac{3}{11}$$

Corey charts the hair color of the students in her drama class. The chart gives the following information:

Hair Color	Number of Students
Black hair	12
Brown hair	18
Red hair	4
Blonde hair	6

38. From the information given in the preceding chart, if the teacher randomly picks a student to read a passage, what is the probability of the teacher selecting a student with black hair or red hair?

    A. $\dfrac{2}{5}$

    B. $\dfrac{3}{10}$

    C. $\dfrac{1}{5}$

    D. $\dfrac{3}{20}$

    E. $\dfrac{1}{10}$

The correct answer is **A.** Because you're looking for a probability of selecting a student with black hair or red hair to read a passage, you must first add:

black hair + red hair =

    12 + 4 = 16

Then get the total number of students in the class:

    12 + 18 + 4 + 6 = 40

And finally set up the fraction $\dfrac{16}{40}$, which reduces to $\dfrac{2}{5}$.

39. How many combinations of outfits are possible if a person has 4 sports jackets, 5 shirts, and 3 pairs of slacks?

    A. 4
    B. 5
    C. 12
    D. 60
    E. 120

The correct answer is **D.** Because each of the 4 sports jackets may be worn with 5 different shirts, there are 20 possible combinations. These 20 combinations may be worn with each of the 3 pairs of slacks for a total of 60 possible combinations. Stated simply, $4 \times 5 \times 3 = 60$ possible combinations.

Be Reasonable

Make sure that your answer is reasonable. That is, if you read it back into the problem, does it make sense? Is it a possible answer?

Sample

40. Robert works at a clothing store. He spends Monday and Tuesday folding shirts. On Monday, he folds 22 more shirts than he folds on Tuesday. If Robert folded a total of 88 shirts on the two days, how many shirts did he fold on Tuesday?

    A. 22
    B. 33
    C. 66
    D. 99
    E. 110

The correct answer is **B.**

First circle or underline *how many shirts did he fold on Tuesday.* Notice that answer choices **D** and **E** are greater than the total for both days. Those choices are not reasonable and can be eliminated. If you work the problem and come up with Choice **C,** you again have an unreasonable answer, because if Robert folds 66 shirts on Tuesday, and 22 more than the 66 on Monday, that is 88 shirts on Monday alone, which equals the total for the two days.

To solve the problem, let x be the number of shirts Robert folds on Tuesday; then $x + 22$ is the number of shirts he folds on Monday. So the equation looks like this:

Tuesday	Monday	Total
$x +$	$(x + 22)$	$= 88$

Solving gives you:

$$2x + 22 = 88$$

Subtract 22 from each side:

$$2x + 22 = 88$$
$$\underline{-22 \quad -22}$$
$$2x \quad = 66$$

Dividing by 2 leaves:

$$\frac{2x}{2} = \frac{66}{2}$$
$$x = 33$$

So the correct answer is **B.** Is this reasonable? Well, if Robert folds 33 shirts on Tuesday, and 22 more than 33 on Monday, he folded 55 shirts on Monday. So the total of Monday and Tuesday is 33 + 55 = 88. Yes, it is reasonable. It checks.

Glance at the Choices

Glance at the choices on procedure problems. Some problems may not ask you to solve for a numerical answer or even an answer including variables. Rather, you may be asked to set up the equation or expression without doing any solving. A quick glance at the answer choices can help you know what is expected.

Samples

41. 51×6 could be quickly mentally calculated by

    A. $50 \times 6 + 1$
    B. $51 + 51 + 51 + 51 + 51 + 51$
    C. $(50 \times 6) + (1 \times 6)$
    D. $(50 \times 6) + \frac{1}{6}$
    E. adding 51 sixes

The correct answer is **C.** The quickest method of calculating 51×6 is to first multiply 50×6 (resulting in 300), then multiplying 1×6 (resulting in 6), and adding the products together 300 + 6 = 306. Answer choices **B** and **E** give the correct answer (306) as well, but neither is the best way to quickly calculate the answer.

Sometimes, however, actually working the problem can be helpful, as the next sample demonstrates.

42. The fastest method to solve $\frac{7}{48} \times \frac{6}{7}$ is to

    A. invert the second fraction and then multiply.
    B. multiply each column across and then reduce to lowest terms.
    C. find the common denominator and then multiply across.
    D. divide 7 into the numerator and denominator, divide 6 into the numerator and denominator, and then multiply across.
    E. reduce the first fraction to lowest terms and then multiply across.

The correct answer is **D**. In this problem, the way to determine the fastest procedure may be to actually work the problem as you would if you were working toward an answer. Then see whether that procedure is listed among the choices. You should then compare it to the other methods listed. Is one of the other *correct* methods faster than the one you used? If so, select the fastest.

These types of problems are not constructed to test your knowledge of obscure ways to solve mathematical equations. Rather, they test your knowledge of common procedures used in standard mathematical equations. Thus, the fastest way to solve this sample problem is to first divide 7 into the numerator and denominator:

$$\frac{\overset{1}{\cancel{7}}}{48} \times \frac{6}{\underset{1}{\cancel{7}}} =$$

Then divide 6 into the numerator and denominator:

$$\frac{\overset{1}{\cancel{7}}}{\underset{8}{\cancel{48}}} \times \frac{\overset{1}{\cancel{6}}}{\underset{1}{\cancel{7}}} =$$

Then multiply across:

$$\frac{\overset{1}{\cancel{7}}}{\underset{8}{\cancel{48}}} \times \frac{\overset{1}{\cancel{6}}}{\underset{1}{\cancel{7}}} = \frac{1}{8}$$

43. Which equation can be used to find the perimeter, P, of a rectangle that has a length of 18 feet and a width of 15 feet?

    A. $P = (18)(15)$
    B. $P = 18 + 15$
    C. $P = 2(15)(18)$
    D. $P = (2)15 + 18$
    E. $P = 2(15 + 18)$

The correct answer is **E**. The perimeter of a rectangle can be found by adding the length to the width and doubling this sum: $P = 2(15 + 18)$.

Read the Question First

If information is given that is needed to answer a question, *read the question first* (usually below the information); then read the information.

Samples

Use the information below to answer the question that follows.

Celia travels $4\frac{1}{2}$ miles. She runs most of the way, but walks the last 1 mile. Lillian travels $2\frac{1}{4}$ miles, but runs all the way.

44. From the preceding information, which of the following methods could be used to find out how many total miles Celia and Lillian ran?

A. $\left(4\frac{1}{2}-1\right)-2\frac{1}{4}$

B. $4\frac{1}{2}-2\frac{1}{4}$

C. $\left(4\frac{1}{2}+1\right)-2\frac{1}{4}$

D. $\left(4\frac{1}{2}-1\right)+2\frac{1}{4}$

E. $4\frac{1}{2}+2\frac{1}{4}$

The correct answer is **D**. To find the total distance run by Celia and Lillian, you need to first find out how many miles Celia ran, which is $\left(4\frac{1}{2}-1\right)$. Add that to how many miles Lillian ran, which is $2\frac{1}{4}$.

Read the information below and answer the question that follows.

Rick is three times as old as Maria, and Maria is four years older than Leah.

45. If Leah is z years old, what is Rick's age in terms of z?

A. $3z+4$
B. $3z-12$
C. $3z+12$
D. $\dfrac{(z+4)}{3}$
E. $\dfrac{(z-4)}{3}$

The correct answer is **C**. Because:

$$z = \text{Leah's age}$$
$$z + 4 = \text{Maria's age}$$
$$3(z + 4) = \text{Rick's age, or}$$
$$3z + 12 = \text{Rick's age}$$

Review Information Carefully

Some problems may ask you to use mathematical or logical reasoning. Review the information carefully before you work the problem. Write in given values and mark diagrams to help you see the reasoning involved.

Samples

Use the figure below to answer the question that follows.

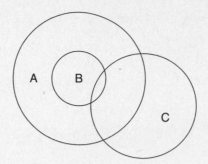

46. What conclusion can be drawn from the preceding diagram?

    A. Circles A and B have nothing in common.
    B. Circles A and C have nothing in common.
    C. Circles B and C have nothing in common.
    D. Circle C has something in common with circles A and B.
    E. Not enough information is given to draw a conclusion.

The correct answer is **D**. Because circle C intersects (overlaps) with circles A and B, it must have something in common with A and B, as the shaded area in the following figure shows.

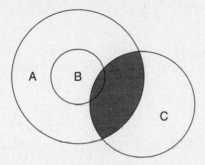

Use the information below to answer the question that follows.

If Spencer's class starts at noon, then he will leave the house at 10 a.m.

If Spencer's class starts at 2 p.m., then he will leave the house between 11 a.m. and noon.

If Spencer's class starts at 3 p.m., then he will leave the house before 1 p.m.

47. If Spencer leaves the house at 11:30 a.m., which of the following must be true?

    A. His class starts at 10 a.m.
    B. His class starts at 2 p.m.
    C. His class starts at 3 p.m.
    D. His class starts after 1 p.m.
    E. His class starts before 3 p.m.

The correct answer is **D**. Since Spencer leaves the house at 11:30 a.m., he may be going to either a 2 p.m. or 3 p.m. class. From the choices, all that you know for certain is that the class must start after 1 p.m.

Use the figure below to answer the question that follows.

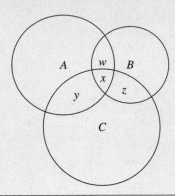

Circle A is composed of multiples of 3, circle B is composed of multiples of 5, and circle C is composed of multiples of 2.

48. From the preceding information and diagram, which of the following is a possible value for x?

  A.   5
  B.   6
  C.   10
  D.   15
  E.   30

The correct answer is **E.** All the circles intersect at x, so x must be a multiple of 2, 3, and 5, as shown in the following figure.

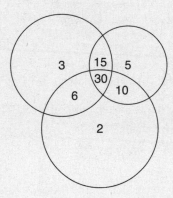

From the diagram, you can see that the answer is 30, which is a multiple of 2, 3, and 5, because $2 \times 3 \times 5 = 30$.

Watch for Missing Information

Some questions require you to fill in missing information in a chart or table. Be careful to focus on what is given and how you can use it to obtain what is needed.

Sample

Use the information given below to answer the question that follows.

> Hillary's lunch bill was as follows:
>
> | | |
> |---|---|
> | Salad | $2.95 |
> | Sandwich | $4.95 |
> | Soft Drink | $??.?? |
> | Subtotal | <u>$8.65</u> |
> | Tax | $.61 |
> | Tip | <u>$1.50</u> |
> | TOTAL | $10.76 |
>
> **49.** From the preceding information, what was the cost of Hillary's soft drink?
>
> A. $1.75
> B. $1.25
> C. $1.00
> D. $ .95
> E. $ .75

The correct answer is **E**. To answer this question, simply add the cost of the salad and the sandwich and then subtract that total from the subtotal to find the cost of the soft drink.

Salad	$2.95
Sandwich	<u>$4.95</u>
TOTAL	$7.90

Now subtract that total from the subtotal of $8.65:

$8.65
<u>$7.90</u>
$ .75

Analyzing Basic Statistical Data

The following table shows Maristella's scores on her first-semester Psychology exams.

Date	Score
September 27	90%
October 6	80%
October 12	90%
November 2	86%
November 14	83%
November 21	91%
December 4	88%
December 13	96%

50. What is her mean score on the Psychology exams?

    A. 87
    B. 88
    C. 89
    D. 90
    E. 91

    See pages 153–156 for a review of basic statistics.

The correct answer is **B.** To find the mean, add up the sum of all of Maristella's scores.

$$80 + 83 + 86 + 88 + 90 + 90 + 91 + 96 = 704$$

Next, divide the total sum of her scores (704) by the number of scores (8) to find her average score.

$$704 \text{ divided by } 8 = 88$$

Know How to Read Percentile Scores

51. Kelsey took a standardized math test, and her grade report showed that her score was in the 89th percentile. Which of the following is the best interpretation of the meaning of this percentile?

    A. She got 89% of the problems correct.
    B. Eighty-nine percent of all those taking the exam had scores below Kelsey's score.
    C. Eighty-nine percent of all those taking the exam had scores above Kelsey's score.
    D. Only 89% of those taking the exam received passing scores.
    E. There was an 89% probability that her score was above the mean on the exam.

The correct answer is **B.** The percentile associated with a score represents how many whole percent of all scores lie below that score. Therefore, if a score is in the 89th percentile, this means that 89% of all other scores are below that score.

Know How to Read Stanine Test Scores

A sixth-grade English teacher notices that one of her students, Lydia, is struggling in English. The teacher reviews Lydia's English standardized test results to determine intervention and placement strategies.

Use the table below to answer the question that follows.

Raw Score	Percentile	Stanine
55	45	5

52. Which of the following is a true statement regarding Lydia's stanine test scores?

   A.   Lydia answered 45% of the questions correctly.
   B.   Lydia's raw score and percentile show that she scored above-average.
   C.   Lydia achieved a score that is higher than 55% of other students who took the test.
   D.   Lydia's performance was at the same level as other students who took the test.
   E.   Lydia answered 55% of the questions correctly.

Only Choice **D** shows the correct meaning of *stanine scores*. Choice **A** is incorrect because answering 45% of the questions correctly makes an assumption that there were a total of 100 questions. The test could have consisted of any number of questions. Choice **B** is incorrect since raw scores and percentile scores are different, and this question is about stanine scores. Choice **C** is incorrect because Lydia achieved a (percentile) score that is higher than 45% of the other students who took the test. Choice **E** is incorrect because we don't know the percentage of correctly answered questions. A stanine test score of 4, 5, or 6 shows that her score is average and that she performed at the same level of other students who took the test.

A PATTERNED PLAN OF ATTACK
Math Ability

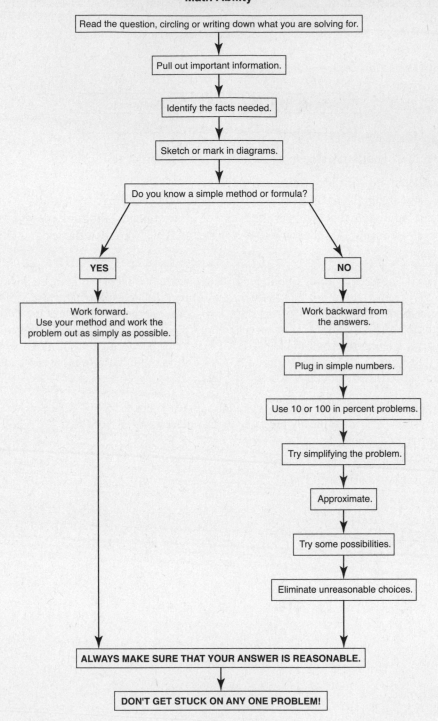

Read the question, circling or writing down what you are solving for.

Pull out important information.

Identify the facts needed.

Sketch or mark in diagrams.

Do you know a simple method or formula?

YES

Work forward.
Use your method and work the problem out as simply as possible.

NO

Work backward from the answers.

Plug in simple numbers.

Use 10 or 100 in percent problems.

Try simplifying the problem.

Approximate.

Try some possibilities.

Eliminate unreasonable choices.

ALWAYS MAKE SURE THAT YOUR ANSWER IS REASONABLE.

DON'T GET STUCK ON ANY ONE PROBLEM!

Introduction to Graphs, Charts, and Tables

Some questions on the CBEST require you to understand and use information given in charts, graphs, and tables.

What to Expect from CBEST's Graphs, Charts, and Tables

Following is some general information regarding the use of graphs, charts, and tables in the CBEST:

Ability Tested

You need to be able to understand and derive information from graphs, charts, and tables. Many of the problems require brief calculations based on the data, so your mathematical ability is also tested.

Basic Skills Necessary

When a graph, chart, or table appears in the Reading section, typically you are asked to read or interpret it. When a graph, chart, or table appears in the Mathematics section, you are asked not only to read and interpret, but also to do some mathematical computations. Your familiarity with a wide range of chart and graph types will help you feel comfortable with these problems and read the data accurately.

Directions

The directions for graph, chart, and table questions are the same as those for the Reading or Mathematics sections. However, the graph or chart is typically preceded by a statement similar to: "Use the graph or chart below to answer the question(s) that follow."

Description

You are given data represented in chart, graph, or table form. Following each set of data are one, two, or three questions based on that data. You are to select the best answer to each question by referring to the appropriate chart or graph, or the appropriate part of the chart or graph. To determine your answer, use only the information given or implied.

Suggested Approach with Samples

This section contains some helpful strategies for extracting accurate information, followed by some sample graph questions.

- Unless you are told otherwise, use only the information given in the chart or graph to answer the question.
- Skim the question and quickly examine the whole graph before starting to work on the problem; this sort of pre-reading tells you what to look for.
- Sometimes the answer to a question is available in the supplementary information given with a graph (headings, scale factors, legends, and so on); be sure to read this information.
- Look for the obvious—dramatic trends, high points, low points, tendencies, and so on. Obvious information often leads directly to an answer.
- There are three main types of graphs on the CBEST: bar graph, line graph, and circle graph (pie chart).
- In a circle graph showing percentages, the amounts always total 100 percent. The amounts written as money or in numerical form on a circle graph always add to the *total amount* being referred to.

Charts and Tables

Often, charts and tables are used to give an organized picture of information or data. Be sure that you understand *what is given*. Column headings and line items give the important information. These titles give the numbers meaning.

Pay special attention to what information is given in the chart. The following chart shows the number of burger sales for the week of August 8–14. The days of the week are along the left side of the chart. The number of *hamburgers* for each day is given in the first column and the number of *veggie burgers* in the second column.

Samples

Use the table below to answer the three questions that follow.

Burger Sales for the Week of August 8–14		
Day	Hamburgers	Veggie Burgers
Sunday	120	92
Monday	85	80
Tuesday	77	70
Wednesday	74	71
Thursday	75	72
Friday	91	88
Saturday	111	112

1. On which day were the most burgers sold (hamburgers and veggie burgers)?

   A. Sunday
   B. Monday
   C. Friday
   D. Saturday
   E. Tuesday

The correct answer is **D.** To answer this question, you must understand the chart and do some simple computation. Working from the answers is probably the easiest method.

   A. Sunday: 120 + 92 = 212
   B. Monday: 85 + 80 = 165
   C. Friday: 91 + 88 = 179
   D. Saturday: 111 + 112 = 223
   E. Tuesday: 77 + 70 = 147

Another method is to *approximate* the answers.

2. On how many days were more hamburgers sold than veggie burgers?

   A. 7
   B. 6
   C. 5
   D. 4
   E. 3

The correct answer is **B**. To answer this question, you must compare the sales for each day. Hamburgers outsold veggie burgers every day except Saturday.

---

3. If the pattern of sales continues,

    A. the weekend days will have the fewest number of burger sales next week.
    B. the veggie burgers will outsell hamburgers next week.
    C. generally, when hamburger sales go up, veggie burger sales will go up.
    D. hamburgers will be less expensive than veggie burgers.
    E. more customers will buy hamburgers than veggie burgers next Saturday.

The correct answer is **C**. To answer this question, you must notice one of the trends. Most days that hamburger sales go up, veggie burger sales go up (with the exception of Saturday and Sunday). If you cannot recognize what the correct answer is, see if you can eliminate some choices. Since weekend days had greater sales than weekdays, Choice **A** would be incorrect. Since veggie burgers only outsold hamburgers once during the week, Choice **B** would be incorrect. Since the chart made no indication of how expensive either type of burger is, Choice **D** would be incorrect.

Graphs

Graph displays may appear in several forms. The three basic types of graphs on the CBEST are bar graphs, line graphs, and circle graphs (or pie charts).

Bar Graphs

Bar graphs convert the information in a chart into separate bars or columns. Some graphs list numbers along one edge, and places, dates, people, or things (individual categories) along another edge. Always try to determine the *relationship* between the columns in a graph or chart.

Samples

Use the graph below to answer the three questions that follow.

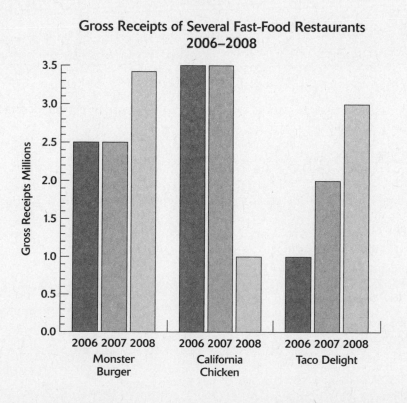

Gross Receipts of Several Fast-Food Restaurants 2006–2008

---

4. The 2006–08 gross receipts of Monster Burger exceeded those of Taco Delight by approximately how much?

    A.   0.2 million
    B.   2 million
    C.   8.2 million
    D.   8.4 million
    E.   17 million

The correct answer is **B.**

In this graph, multiple bars represent each fast-food restaurant; each single bar represents the receipts from a single year.

You may be tempted to write the numbers as you do your arithmetic (3.5 million = 3,500,000), but this is unnecessary since it is often on graphs that use large numbers. Because all the measurements are in millions, adding zeros does not add precision to the numbers.

Referring to the Monster Burger bars, you can see that gross receipts are as follows: 2006 = 2.5 million, 2007 = 2.5 million, 2008 = 3.4 million (if you have trouble seeing how the bars line up with the numbers, you can use your answer sheet as a straightedge to determine a number such as this last one). Totaling the receipts for all three years, you get 8.4 million.

Referring to the Taco Delight bars, you can see that gross receipts are as follows: 2006 = 1 million, 2007 = 2 million, 2008 = 3 million (don't designate numbers beyond the nearest tenth, because the graph numbers and the answer choices prescribe no greater accuracy than this). Totaling the receipts for all three years, you get 6 million.

So Monster Burger exceeds Taco Delight by 2 million. The answer that best approximates this figure is 2 million.

---

5. From 2007 to 2008, the percent increase in receipts for Taco Delight exceeded the percent increase for Monster Burger by approximately how much?

    A.   0%
    B.   2%
    C.   10%
    D.   15%
    E.   43%

The correct answer is **D.**

Graph questions on the CBEST may ask you to calculate percent increase or percent decrease. The formula for figuring either of these is the same:

$$\frac{\text{amount of the change}}{\text{the starting amount (follows the word "from")}}$$

In this case, you may first calculate the percent increase for Monster Burger:

    Gross receipts in 2007 = 2.5 million
    Gross receipts in 2008 = 3.4 million
    Amount of the change = 0.9 million

The 2007 amount is the "starting" or "from" amount:

$$\frac{\text{amount of the change}}{\text{starting amount}} = \frac{0.9}{2.5} = 0.36 = 36\%$$

Percent increase for Taco Delight:

> Gross receipts in 2007 = 2 million
>
> Gross receipts in 2008 = 3 million
>
> Amount of the change = 1 million
>
> $\dfrac{\text{amount of the change}}{\text{starting amount}} = \dfrac{1}{2} = 50\%$

So, Taco Delight exceeds Monster Burger by 14% (50% – 36%). The answer that best approximates this figure is 15%.

---

6. The 2008 decline in California Chicken's receipts may be attributed to the following:

    A.   An increase in the popularity of burgers.

    B.   An increase in the popularity of tacos.

    C.   A decrease in the demand for chicken.

    D.   A predictable slump attributed to a sluggish economy.

    E.   It cannot be determined from the information given.

The correct answer is **E**. Never use information that is not given. In this case, the multiple factors that could cause a decline in receipts are not represented by the graph. All choices except **E** require you to speculate beyond the information given.

Line Graphs

Line graphs convert data into points on a grid. Notice the slopes of lines connecting the points. These lines will show increases and decreases. The *steeper the line slants upward towards the right,* the greater the *increase.* The *steeper the line slants downward towards the right*, the greater the *decrease.* Line graphs can show trends, or changes in data over a period of time.

Samples

Use the graph below to answer the two questions that follow.

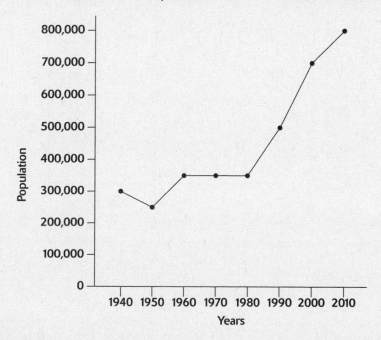

American Indian Population in the United States from 1940 to 2010

7. In which of the following years were there about 500,000 Native Americans?

   A. 1970
   B. 1980
   C. 1990
   D. 2000
   E. 2010

The correct answer is **C.** To answer this question, you must be able to read the graph. The information along the left side of the graph shows the number of Native Americans in increments of 100,000. The bottom of the graph shows the years from 1940 to 2010. Notice that in 1990 there were about 500,000 Native Americans in the United States. Using the edge of your answer sheet as a straightedge can help you see that the dot representing 1990 lines up with 500,000.

8. During which of the following time periods was there a decrease in the Native American population?

   A. 1940 to 1950
   B. 1950 to 1960
   C. 1960 to 1970
   D. 1990 to 2000
   E. 2000 to 2010

The correct answer is **A.** Since what is being asked involves a decrease, you need to find segments joining points that slant down as they go to the right. The segments that join the points for 1940 to 1950 slant down as they go to the right.

Use the graph below to answer the three questions that follow.

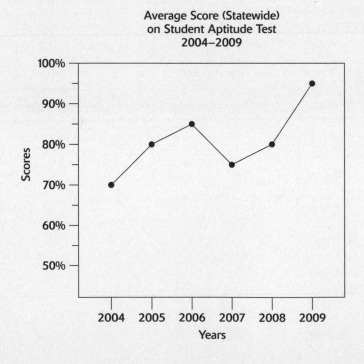

Average Score (Statewide)
on Student Aptitude Test
2004–2009

9. Between which two years was there the greatest rise in average test scores?

   A. 2004 and 2005
   B. 2005 and 2006
   C. 2006 and 2007
   D. 2007 and 2008
   E. 2008 and 2009

The correct answer is **E.** The most efficient way to compute the greatest rise is to locate the *steepest* upward slope on the chart. Note that the steepest climb is between 2008 and 2009. Therefore, 2008–2009 indicates the greatest rise in average test scores.

10. In which year was the average score approximately 85%?

    A. 2004
    B. 2005
    C. 2006
    D. 2007
    E. 2008

The correct answer is **C.** According to the graph, the average test score was approximately 85% in 2006. In such cases, when you must read the graph for a precise measurement, remember that it may be helpful to use your answer sheet as a straightedge to more accurately compare points with the grid marks along the side.

11. Approximately what was the highest score achieved statewide on the test?

    A. 80%
    B. 85%
    C. 90%
    D. 97%
    E. This cannot be determined from the information given.

The correct answer is **E.** The first thing to do when confronted with a graph or chart is to read its title to understand what the graph is telling you. In this case, the graph is relating information about average scores. It tells you nothing about the *highest* score achieved.

Circle Graphs (Pie Charts)

A circle graph, or pie chart, shows the relationship between the whole circle (100%) and the various slices that represent portions of that 100%. The larger the slice, the higher the percentage.

Samples

Use the graph below to answer the three questions that follow.

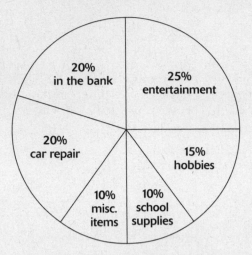

How Matt Spends His Weekly Paycheck

12. Matt puts $\frac{1}{4}$ of his weekly paycheck toward

    A.   his hobby.
    B.   car and bike repairs.
    C.   entertainment.
    D.   school supplies.
    E.   the bank.

The correct answer is **C.** To answer this question, you must be able to read the graph and apply some simple math. Notice how the information is given in the circle graph (pie chart). The graph shows percentages and the question shows a fraction.

To change a fraction to a percent:

1. Multiply by 100.
2. Divide by the denominator (bottom part of the fraction).
3. Insert a percent sign.

$$\frac{1}{4} = \frac{1}{4} \times 100 = \frac{100}{4} = 25\%$$

One-quarter is the same as 25%, so entertainment is the answer you are looking for.

13. If Matt receives $1,000 per weekly paycheck, how much money does he put in the bank?

    A. $20
    B. $200
    C. $350
    D. $800
    E. $1,000

The correct answer is **B.** To answer this question, you must again read the graph carefully and apply some simple math. Matt puts 20% of his income in the bank, and 20% of $1,000 is $200. To solve this: 20% (1,000) = .20 (1,000) = 200.

Matt, thus, puts $200 in the bank.

Remember, when changing a percent to a decimal, eliminate the percent sign and move the decimal point two places to the left; for example, 20% becomes .20 or 0.2.

14. The ratio of the amount of money Matt spends on his hobby to the amount he puts in the bank is

A. $\frac{1}{6}$

B. $\frac{1}{2}$

C. $\frac{2}{3}$

D. $\frac{3}{4}$

E. $\frac{5}{8}$

The correct answer is **D.** To answer this question, you must use the information in the graph to make a ratio.

$$\frac{\text{his hobby}}{\text{in the bank}} = \frac{15\%}{20\%} = \frac{15}{20} = \frac{3}{4}$$

Notice that the ratio of 15% : 20% reduces to $\frac{3}{4}$.

A PATTERNED PLAN OF ATTACK
Graphs and Charts

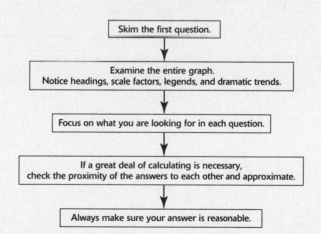

Skim the first question.

Examine the entire graph.
Notice headings, scale factors, legends, and dramatic trends.

Focus on what you are looking for in each question.

If a great deal of calculating is necessary,
check the proximity of the answers to each other and approximate.

Always make sure your answer is reasonable.

The Writing Section

Introduction

The Writing portion of the CBEST is designed to measure the basic skills necessary for elementary school teachers to effectively communicate in standard written English form. As a future educator, you must be able to convey and support your thoughts and ideas in writing with students, parents, colleagues and school administrators. This chapter will lead you through step-by-step guidelines to help you plan and compose a well-written essay.

Types of Essay Questions

The Writing section contains two essay questions. One essay requires a *descriptive* or *narrative* response relating to a personal experience, and the other essay requires an *analytical* or *expository* response, in which you analyze a situation or statement. You are asked to draw upon your personal experience and observations for information, provide examples, and support with generalizations. In some cases, you may need to use your imagination. Fiction is acceptable!

Ability Tested

This section tests your ability to read an essay prompt carefully, analyze what is required, organize your ideas, and write a college-level essay with clarity and precision. Approaching the writing of an essay using a step-by-step process will help you present an organized response. In this section you will see a variety of prewriting techniques and formulas that will help you organize your response, answer all parts of the question, and stay on the topic while writing.

Basic Skills Necessary

The Writing section requires a basic college-level writing background. Papers are scored on the basis of the writer's ability to achieve the following: comprehension of the assigned topic; organization and logical development of the central idea with supporting evidence or specific examples; skillful use of language; and correctness of mechanics (e.g., spelling, punctuation, and capitalization), usage, and paragraphing; and the ability to appropriately address the topic for the intended audience.

Directions

The following instructions will appear in the Writing section of your CBEST. If you are taking the entire CBEST in one day (reading, math, and writing), spend about 30 minutes on each writing topic, since both are equally weighted. Both paper-based and computer-administered test takers will have space for prewriting notes. You are urged to use this space to organize your thoughts. For the paper-based test, double-check how much space you have in which to write your essay.

> **Directions:** In the Writing section, you will plan and write two essays, one for each topic given. Read each topic carefully to make sure you are properly addressing the issue or situation. **You must write on the specified topic. An essay on another topic will not be acceptable.** Plan your time wisely. Each essay is equally weighted. Plan to spend the same amount of time on each essay.
>
> The two essay questions are designed to give you an opportunity to write clearly and effectively. Use specific examples whenever appropriate to aid in supporting your ideas. Keep in mind that the quality of your writing is much more important than the length of your essay.

Paper-based test takers write essay responses using a pencil and lined answer sheets provided in the test booklet. You may use the bottom of the topic page in your test booklet to organize and plan your essay before you begin writing. Before you begin writing your essay, look to see how much space is provided to write your essay. Your writing should be neat and legible. If your handwriting is particularly difficult to read, consider taking the computer version of the CBEST. Because you have only a limited amount of space in which to write, do *not* skip lines, do *not* write excessively large, and do *not* leave wide margins. Plan to write 250 to 400 words to adequately answer the question.

Computer-administered test takers write essay responses using a computer. The computer screen appears split horizontally. Your essay topic appears on the top part of the screen, and in the lower part, you have space to type your essay response. You can request scratch paper (or a writing board) for your prewriting activities. The word processing program has three editing tools to help with changes and revisions. These tools are *cut, paste,* and *undo.* Plan to write 250 to 400 words to adequately answer the question.

Scoring the CBEST Essays

Each essay is rated by two readers. Each reader assigns a score of 1 to 4 for each essay based on the CBEST rubric, or scoring guide. CBEST essays are scored holistically. This means that the readers look at the *overall quality* of the work. Each essay is scored on a scale of 1 to 4 as follows:

4 = pass

3 = marginal pass

2 = marginal fail

1 = fail

Since each essay is scored by two readers, the total possible raw score you can receive is outlined in the following table:

	Possible Raw Score Reader One	Possible Raw Score Reader Two	Total Score from Both Readers
Essay 1 Descriptive or Narrative	1 to 4 plus	1 to 4	2 to 8
Essay 2 Analytical or Expository	1 to 4 plus	1 to 4	2 to 8
Total Possible Raw Score			4 to 16
Raw scores are converted to a scaled score of approximately 20 to 80.			

Your final score is based on a combination of four scores. A raw score of approximately 12 should be a passing score. Focus on the components of a good essay. CBEST test takers who achieve a top score submit an essay that

- presents a clear thesis statement on the topic and stays well focused on the main idea throughout the essay.

- develops the essay in an organized, logical sequence.

- uses smooth transitions that flow from one paragraph to another.

- supports the main idea with relevant supporting evidence, details, and examples.

- responds to all parts of the essay question.

- shows clear handwriting and is legible.

- uses the correct mechanics of writing—including spelling, sentence structure, punctuation, and word usage.

Spell-check or grammar checking features are not available to either paper-based or computer-administered test-takers! Multiple errors will lower your score, especially if they interfere with the reader's ability to understand your essay. If you're unsure of the spelling of a difficult word, use basic words instead. That is, use a "25¢ word" if you are unsure of the spelling of the "50¢ word." Remember that the readers are professional graders, so avoid using trendy words, clichés, and jargon.

Some General Tips

If you are taking the CBEST in the paper-and-pencil format, some of your test-taking strategies will be slightly different from those who use the computer-administered format. The test-taking strategies are similar, but the format requires a few special considerations. Before you begin the writing process, here are some general tips that, unless otherwise indicated, apply to both formats of the test.

Use your own words. You may wish to rephrase the topic or question in your own words. This often helps you understand what is required.

Prewriting. Use a form of prewriting *before* you begin writing your actual essay. Prewriting can consist of brainstorming, clustering, outlining, and so on. These techniques are discussed in the next section.

Three *don'ts* of paper-based writing. Paper-based test takers should not use excessively large handwriting, leave wide margins, or skip any lines. Double-check the amount of space you have in which to write each essay.

Timing. If you are taking all sections of the test in one day, spend approximately one hour on the two essays (30 minutes each), using these guidelines:

2–3 minutes. Read the topic carefully two or three times, if necessary, before writing. Circle, underline, or write down key words. This helps you focus on the assigned task.

5–6 minutes. Organize your thoughts. A poorly written essay is often the result of inadequate planning. Choose the prewriting technique you're most comfortable with that you want to use for this essay. Prewriting techniques are described in the next section.

20 minutes. Write. Let your thoughts flow onto the paper or the computer screen. Answer all parts of the question. Follow your prewriting outline. Stay on topic. Use adequate details. Don't let spelling slow down your writing. Keep the flow of your writing going, and correct spelling and grammar errors later.

3–4 minutes. Reread, edit, and correct your essay. Don't make extensive changes when you reread—just correct spelling, grammar, and punctuation. Erase, line out, or delete errors, and insert the corrections neatly. Keep your paper legible.

The Three-Step Essay Writing Process

There are a number of strategies you can use to write a successful essay, but if you are able to understand the stages of the writing process, it will help you gain control over any method you choose. As you work through the steps of the writing process—*prewriting, writing, and editing*—take note of which strategies work best for you and use them to develop your own preferred writing style.

Step One: Prewriting

Prewriting is the initial step in which the writer gathers ideas and examples. The purpose of the prewriting process is to organize your thoughts and plan the order in which you will present points, examples, arguments, and so on. Organizing your thoughts in a few minutes can be difficult unless you are ready with an effective technique. Using one of the prewriting techniques discussed in this section will help you organize your thoughts before you begin writing.

There are four types of prewriting techniques you can use: *brainstorming, creating lists, clustering,* and *outlining.* Choose the prewriting technique that works best for you! Remember to spend 5 to 6 minutes on prewriting.

Brainstorming

You can brainstorm when you are having difficulty answering the question and need to capture some unedited ideas on paper. Brainstorming is a discovery process. Your "imaginings" will help you compile words, thoughts, and ideas about the essay topic. Do not edit your thoughts during brainstorming; just write down any ideas that come to mind. All ideas are acceptable during brainstorming—just let your stream of consciousness flow with prompting related to your topic. You can form and organize your thoughts later. Here is an example of brainstorming on an expository writing topic.

TOPIC

Political candidates have both advocates and foes. Write an essay describing your views as to why or why not Hillary Clinton would make a good presidential candidate.

Creating Lists

Creating lists helps you focus and capture your thoughts regarding your topic. On a small section of your scratch paper, draw two columns that help you compare thoughts and ideas. This prewriting technique is valuable for questions that ask you to compare and contrast a topic. You can label column headings *pro* and *con, positive* and *negative, like* and *dislike,* and so on. This technique helps you create a template with lists of ideas regarding your topic. It is especially helpful to use when you're asked to choose sides on a topic to support your position. The resulting list will help you think about examples that can support or weaken your standpoint.

Pro	Con

Clustering or Webbing

Clustering is a popular method for initial organizing of your thoughts. Take a few moments to think about all the elements of the topic and connect them to a central theme. Clustering, or webbing, provides a way to put all your thoughts down on paper before you write, so you can quickly see the structure of the whole paper. The connections of ideas are placed near one another and appear as *connected bubbles.* After you select a topic or main idea, start by writing it down and drawing a circle around it.

For a few moments, think of all the elements of that topic and connect them to the central topic cluster. Related ideas are written in groups, and their circles are connected to the main idea with lines. A sample cluster might look like this:

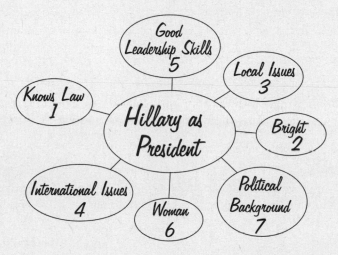

You can also number the parts of the cluster to give an order to your thoughts. You don't have to use all the elements in your cluster.

Outlining

Outlining is the most formal and traditional form of organizing. The main advantage of outlining is that it clearly organizes each main idea into headings and subheadings. Outlining visually displays the difference between main ideas (identified by Roman numerals), supporting ideas (identified by capital letters), and minor points (identified by numbers).

    I. Introduction/Main Idea/Thesis
       A. Subordinate Idea
       B. Subordinate Idea
   II. Expand Main Idea
  III. Expand Main Idea
       A. Subordinate Idea
       B. Subordinate Idea
          1. Example
          2. Example

A simple outline may look something like this:

Course: Music 101— How Mozart Impacted My Life

    I. Caused me to change my major
       A. Hated economics but never knew it
       B. Music raised my spirits—new outlook on life

   II. Broadened my life

      A. Began attending concerts—became more social

      B. Got out of the house

      C. Appreciation for a new art form—now more open about other things as well

  III. Developed new skills

      A. Learned how to listen better

      B. Began learning to play French horn

         1. Made new friends in community orchestra

         2. Met my present husband, who played first chair French horn in community orchestra

Organizing an outline like the preceding one (it need not be this formal) can help you write a well-structured, well-planned essay.

Whichever way you choose to prewrite—by brainstorming, creating lists, clustering, or outlining—the important thing is that you think and plan before you actually begin writing your essay.

Step Two: Writing

After completing your prewriting, you are ready to begin writing your essay. The body of your essay should have three main sections: an introduction, body, and conclusion. The content of each section is described below.

Introduction

A strong opening paragraph is essential. An effective first paragraph tells the reader what to expect in the body of the essay. Present your main idea, purpose, or thesis in the introduction. Let the reader know your position and understand what you are about to say. The first sentence is a general description of your essay's purpose. The next sentences focus on the topic of your essay, providing the subordinate topics or reasons you will discuss. The remaining sentences cover what you intend to discuss in the essay.

Body

The body of your essay explains the main points you outlined in your introduction. In the body, give the details and examples that relate to what you introduced in the first paragraph. Use several paragraphs to explain your points, support your statements, and give examples. Each paragraph has a topic sentence in which the main idea of the paragraph is stated. In the rest of the paragraph, give supporting details and examples that relate to the points you made in the first paragraph.

You can use several paragraphs to accomplish this, but make sure that each paragraph

- has at least three sentences.
- stays on topic.
- does not ramble.
- follows your prewritten notes.

Conclusion

It is often thought that a conclusion is merely a summary of what was previously written, but a conclusion should instead *complete your response* to the question. An effective conclusion

- sums up your main point and supporting ideas.
- makes a prediction or recommendation.
- contains a relevant quote.
- points to the future.
- adds information not mentioned earlier.

Step Three: Proofreading (Editing)

Always allow a few minutes to proofread your essay for errors in grammar, usage, and spelling. If you detect an error, either erase it cleanly or simply line it out carefully and insert the correction neatly. Keep in mind, both while you are writing and while you are correcting, that your handwriting must be legible.

Types of Essays

Now that we have covered the three basic steps in the essay-writing process—prewriting, writing, and proofreading—this section will provide you with the types of essays to write, practice topics, and sample essays. The two types of essays that appear in the CBEST writing section are:

Descriptive or Narrative Essays. This type of essay topic draws on your personal life experiences and asks you to show (describe) and tell about (narrate) a significant event in your life.

Analytical or Expository Essays. This type of essay topic requires you to explain and analyze an issue, problem, or quote. You may be asked to agree or disagree, and support your opinion with specific examples.

The descriptive or narrative essay is described below. The analytical or expository essay is described on page 94.

The Descriptive or Narrative Essay

The descriptive or narrative essay emphasizes a written reaction that expresses your personal thoughts or feelings about a situation, person, memory, or experience. Responses are vividly described through the writer's own personal perspective. The writer often tells a story that paints a sensory picture for the reader through the senses—seeing, smelling, tasting, hearing, feeling. The events in this type of essay are usually in chronological order. For example, let's look at this sample descriptive/narrative essay:

> Students can look back on their years in school and pinpoint one particular course or one particular teacher that was most instrumental in shaping their lives. Reflect on your own school years and focus on one such instructor or course. Describe the conditions or qualities that made that particular experience or teacher special.

Keep in mind that the test is concerned with your writing ability, not your personal experiences. Therefore, it may be helpful for you to use your imagination to describe qualities of a fictional character or experience. Your imagination will provide you with unlimited resources to help you write a descriptive or narrative essay.

Try making up information or a fictional character at least once when you practice writing an essay. This can help you in the event that you get stuck trying to recall a person or situation on the actual test.

Three Approaches to Essay Writing

Using one of three different essay formats will help you respond to certain types of questions. The three types are the *Story Essay,* the *Why Essay,* and the *Compare and Contrast Essay*. The Story Essay is discussed below, and the Why Essay and Compare and Contrast Essay are discussed on pages 94 and 103.

The Story Essay

The Story Essay is a good way to approach a question that requires you to describe an experience. The Story Essay allows you to describe one experience in detail while keeping a unifying theme throughout your essay. With this format, the writer provides:

- **Setting:** The location of the story.
- **Main characters:** The people in the story.
- **Plot:** The problem in the story or the crisis to be overcome.

- **Climax:** The turning point in the story.
- **Resolution:** The ending, or how you are now as a result of the experience.

The story formula allows you to describe one experience in detail, using clear transitions, while keeping a unifying theme throughout your essay.

The essay structure follows this format:

Paragraph 1: Introduce the setting/location, time, and main characters of the story.

- Where
- When
- What
- Who

Paragraph 2: Write about the plot, problem, or crisis to be overcome. Build up the conflict.

Paragraph 3: Describe the climax or catalyst.

Final Paragraph: Provide the resolution to the problem.

The Finished Descriptive or Narrative Essay

A finished essay using the story formula follows. The writer used clustering to organize the essay's elements. Topic Prompt is on page 84.

Ten years ago, I was twenty-one and a junior at California State University at Long Beach. My schooling had been quite traditional, and because of this I regarded my college experience as a necessary means to an end and rarely educational. Shortly after I began my second semester in the Education Department, however, I took a course in abnormal psychology that became most instrumental in shaping my life.

On a cold blustery winter day, as I drove to my part-time job at the neuropsychiatric hospital, I had a nagging feeling that the psychology class I enrolled in was slowly changing my point of view. As I drove onto the damp parking lot and walked in the doorway to the children's unit, my professor's words haunted me: "The challenge of the new psychology is to look beyond the 'labels' given to people and to see for onself the human being that is there." I mulled over in my mind whether this day would bring me any closer to that goal.

That day a new patient arrived. He was a four-year old, child pinned tightly with the label "autistic." His name was Gregory, and in him I saw immediately all that I had previously only read about. He had all of the usual behaviors of a child who was autistic. He would not respond to touch or affection, engaged in constant finger flicking and hand gazing, and seemed to withdraw into his own world.

In the days that passed I spent much time with Gregory, involving him in whatever I was doing, always maintaining some physical contact with him. It was not until the fourteenth day that I dropped my ever-so-precious label.

Gregory and I frequently engaged in games, but his favorite game was entitled "Up." In this game I was to ~~tife~~ lift Gregory into the air as he gleefully shouted out, "up, up!" After several times my arms grew weary, and instead of putting him down, I held Gregory in my arms. There we stood in an embrace of trust—an opening to a place beyond his label. Tears flowed freely from my eyes as he calmly touched each one with his fingers, smiling as their wetness served to cement our relationship. Somehow, in that moment, all of what I had read mattered little compared to what I now know. As my professor had warned us in class, "The labels only serve to make things easy—it is up to you to discover the truth."

Each day I went to the neuropsychiatric institute filled with joy I had never known, yet in one sharp moment it was all shattered. One December 26, 1972, Gregory was transferred to a state mental institution. Over the advice of the staff and the doctors, Gregory was taken to a place where he ~~would~~ wear his label ~~forever~~.

The next few weeks at the hospital seemed empty to me. A challenge by a professor to see through the labels and the willingness and trust of a four-year old child enabled me to learn a lesson I shall never forget. For the first time a college course provided me with a real learning experience; all of the course work that I had taken never touched me as deeply as this one course.

A Second Look at the Finished Essay (with Comments)

Essay 1

Ten years ago, I was twenty-one and a junior at California State University at Long Beach. My schooling had been quite traditional, and because of this I regarded my college experience as a necessary means to an end and rarely educational. Shortly after I began my second semester in the Education Department, however, **I took a course in abnormal psychology that became most instrumental in shaping my life.**

> *Interesting introduction, giving some background with the last sentence giving the direction and focus of the essay.*

On a cold blustery winter day, as I drove to my part-time job in the neuropsychiatric hospital, I had a **nagging feeling** that the **psychology class** I enrolled in was slowly **changing my point of view.** As I drove onto the damp parking lot and walked in the doorway to the children's unit, my professor's words haunted me: **"The challenge of the new psychology is to look beyond the 'labels'** given to people and to see for oneself the human being that is there." I mulled over in my mind whether this day would bring me any closer to that goal.

> *Good specific information setting up the story.*

> *Notice the setting.*

> *Adds information about the psychology class.*

That day a new patient arrived. He was a four-year-old,* **child pinned tightly with the label of "autistic." His name was Gregory,** and in him I saw immediately all that I had previously only read about. He had all of the usual behavior of a child who was autistic. He would not respond to touch or affection, engaged in constant finger flicking and hand gazing, and seemed to withdraw into his own world.

> *Gives a specific example of "labels."*
> *Actually introduces another main character and plot here.*

> **Note minor comma error.** *Remember that the essay is graded holistically, minor flaws are okay.*

In the days that passed I spent much time with Gregory, involving him in whatever I was doing, always maintaining some physical contact with him. It was not until the fourteenth day that I dropped my ever-so-precious label.

> *Nice transition into how the label was dropped.*

Gregory and I frequently engaged in games, but his favorite game was entitled "Up." In this game I was to lift Gregory into the air as he gleefully shouted, "up, up!" After several times my arms grew weary, and instead of putting him down, I held Gregory in my arms. There we stood in an embrace of trust—**an opening to a place beyond his label.** Tears flowed freely from my eyes as he calmly touched each one with his fingers, smiling as their wetness served to cement our relationship. Somehow, in that moment, **all of what I had read mattered little compared to what I now know. As my professor had warned us in class, "The labels only serve to make things easy—it is up to you to discover the truth."**

> *Paragraph gives good specific detail reinforcing the "label" issue and ties back very cleanly to the psychology class.*

Each day I went to the neuropsychiatric institute filled me with a joy I had never known, yet in **one sharp moment it was all shattered.** On December 26, 1972, Gregory was transferred to the state mental institution. Over the advice of the staff and the doctors, Gregory was taken to a place where **he would wear his label forever.**

> *Notice the turning point or climax. Again the "label" is mentioned.*

The next few weeks at the hospital seemed empty to me. A challenge by a professor to see through the labels and the willingness and trust of a four-year-old child enabled me to learn a lesson that I shall never forget. **For the first time a college course provided me with a real learning experience; all of the coursework that I had taken never touched me as deeply as this one course.**

> *A strong ending, explaining the result of the experience.*

Two Additional Finished Essays

Following are two more attempts using the same topic. Both essays are evaluated in some detail. Analyze each essay's strengths and weaknesses.

A Well-Written Essay

Essay 2

Orienting the reader to the writer's background and experience.

By the time I was a junior in college, I had developed criteria for good teaching and bad teaching, criteria based on my experiences during those first two college years. **The good teachers were always (1) models of enthusiasm and curiosity about their subject, (2) interested in students' fulfilling their own potential and not trying to please the instructor, and (3) friendly as well as scholarly.** Of the few good teachers I enjoyed, **Bob Lincoln** (a professor of English) **was the best.** Four times a week, **sluggish and yawning from listening to my classics professor drone endlessly in a muffled monotone about Zeus and the Olympians,** I slumped into Dr. Lincoln's class on the Victorian novel. And always he would lift my spirits with his own spirited approach; **his was a remarkable talent for making connections between the experiences of Jane Eyre, Becky Sharp, and Adam Bede, and very modern problems of repression, alienation, and greed. He showed that good teachers make their subjects part of their own life and time and that literature can help us understand ourselves.**

Designating the points to be discussed; focusing the essay.

Restricting the discussion appropriately.

Balanced, contrasting sentence addressing point (1) from first paragraph. Able to control syntax, reference to specific details, orderly phrasing.

Vivid portrait of a bad teacher and the effects of bad teaching.

Thesis sentence, highlighting the significance of this paragraph.

But Dr. Lincoln never imposed his viewpoints on us. **The importance of the literature was ours to decide.** We kept journals in which we wrote about how instances in the novels were like those in our own experience, and by sharing those responses in class we learned how many different viewpoints a novel can provoke and learned to respect each other's differences. **All this came about because Dr. Lincoln was more interested in what the subject meant to us than what it meant to him.**

Effective transition (*but*), reference to point (2).

Clear, brief sentence; interesting contrast with longer ones.

Specific supporting details, logical parallel structure.

Summary sentence, reinforcing the overall point of the paragraph.

Reference to point (3) of the opening paragraph.

Specific supporting detail.

His attention to our learning didn't stop at the end of a class meeting. Always willing to make himself available for further discussion, **Dr. Lincoln even invited us to his home at times.** These uncommon occasions, sharing the professor's "natural habitat," helped us to learn that teachers are people, too, and that the best teachers are those who transform their students into a community, not just a bunch of anonymous paper pushers.

Additional information, fluency, and humor; clearly states the significance of the experience and its relationship to the general topic.

Ties the past into the present gracefully.

Each day of my own training in education and practice in teaching, I try to remember what Dr. Lincoln taught me. Good teaching takes energy, commitment, and good humor; it is a product of people, not merely of books and papers.

Summary conclusion that does more than simply restate what has already been said.

A Poorly Written Essay

Essay 3

Fragment sentence, which states information irrelevant to the topic and already known to the audience.

Seemingly irrelevant point. Paragraph as a whole lacks focus and clarity.

Faulty logic.

Run-on sentences, full of vague cliches, missing verb preceding the word "in," spelling error; in general a crazy quilt of undeveloped ideas.

Restatement of part of the question, disguised attempt to focus the conclusion, inappropriate verb (*doing*).

Vague pronoun reference.

As a person who would like to be a full-time teacher and who is right now student teaching until I pass my courses and this test, so that I can apply for promising positions. I can say that my best teachers throughout elementary, secondary school and higher was always on my side and very much a sense of humor. As long as we had the assignment read, he would discuss it with us.

Good teaching makes you want to know more, especially for tests since they are how we learn. I remember one day I have studied extremely complete, and then the test was not what I expected. This is what I mean by good teaching.

And then another time I enjoyed the class so much that when it came time to "show what you know" I was ready, willing and able, with so many of the lectures in an interesting fashion, to show me that if the teacher likes his job, than there is nothing to worry about.

How many times have you looked for the teacher and he doesn't answer the phone or even make an effort to be their. Giving of yourself is when you take extra time to make sure that students know how they got the answers.

The conditions or qualities that made the particular experience special, in conclusion, were what I find myself doing whenever I think about teaching and try to do something out of the ordinary. And it works.

Faulty parallelism, subject-verb disagreement, missing verb, vague sentence structure and diction.

Example of unclear relevance, ungrammatical verb, adjective-adverb confusion.

Vague pronoun reference, vague sentence in general. Paragraph lacks a clear thesis.

Faulty logic, missing question mark, misspelling.

Vague sentence.

In general, the response is disunified, lacks relevant and specific details, does not address only *one* instructor or experience, lacks planning and organization, and displays a number of mechanical errors.

Another Poorly Written Essay (What *Not* to Do)

Essay 4

This sample essay contains major faults in the writing. The essay lacks unity, focus, and a clear description of one experience. The essay also contains many flaws in grammar and usage.

One course I had in college which was instrumental in shaping my life was a college speech course. I was not a talkative person. During classroom discussions, my teacher made me participate and that was something I had not done in a long time.

This particular subject was a coed class and I had to discuss the current issues of today. There were only three females in a class of forty men.

After the semester was over, I was quite a different person than before the speech class.

I am now employed by the Over the Rainbow School District as a kindorgotten teacher in an area where people don't speak good. I feel happy to see the children grow up with the kind of experiences I can give them.

This essay rushes to the conclusion (resolution) without giving the reader an experience that caused a change. Simply enrolling in a class does not cause one to change. The writer left out a description of any experience that caused this change.

The essay has only a brief description that gives the reader a hint of the setting and early experiences.

The essay lacks a unified, clear focus without a described experience and fails to go beyond a general discussion. The final sentence doesn't seem to fit because it doesn't clarify why this course was special and how it helped this person in his or her job as a teacher.

One More Descriptive/Narrative Topic

> You are preparing a speech to be given to a group of educated adults. Select a person who has had a major influence in shaping your life and formulating or reaching your goals. Give specific details or examples in your speech.

Read the topic two or three times and circle or underline **key** words or phrases. This helps you to stay focused. Use the key words in your essay to reinforce staying on topic.

Often many different people help us shape our lives and formulate or reach our goals. You are preparing a speech to be given to a group of educated adults. Select a person who has had a major influence in shaping your life and formulating or reaching your goals. Give specific details or examples in your speech.

Begin by using **key words** to frame your introductory paragraph and point to the body of your essay.

- **Introduction:** The person who shaped your life goals.
- **Body:** Who the person was and how he or she did it.
- **Conclusion:** Summary of introduction and body.

Another Well-Written Essay

Essay 5

The body sets the stage, then provides a flowing narrative of what took place.

Many people have had an effect on my life. But the **person who had the greatest influence** in helping me formulate and reach my goals was **my senior English teacher, Mrs. Simpson.** It was her sound advice that **helped me choose the career path** that has served me well.

Nice intro.
• Brief, but to the point.
• Sets focus for body of essay.
• Points the way to body without going too far: Who is Mrs. Simpson? What was sound advice? How did she help me choose my career?

As a young rebellious teenager I had dreams of making great waves on this planet. **I thought that the field of law was the one where I could make my mark.** I decided to enter college as a pre-law major, and I went to Mrs. Simpson to share my decision with her and seek her advice.

Gives specific examples of how Mrs. Simpson worked at "shaping lives."

Mrs. Simpson was one of those teachers with that special gift. **She would always listen, smile, ask a few questions and suddenly the person who had come to her would find their own answer.** Mrs. Simpson rarely said "you should," rather she would offer a "well, if I were in your shoes I might..." **And in this crafty way she would offer a few options** that were soundly based upon her knowledge and personal experience.

Good detail of how Mrs. Simpson helped.

Doesn't get too specific. Stays in general overview.

I don't remember exactly how our conversation went on that particular day when I sought her counsel. I only remember that she agreed with me. She was well aware of my **verbal and acting skills** and thought that I would make an **excellent lawyer.** She went on to say that my final career decision was a long way off, and that I might find myself later choosing to be a **journalist, a doctor or some other professional.** She advised me that **instead of majoring in pre-law** it might be better to major in **English.** She explained that an **English major would lead to a BA and offer courses in critical reading, thinking and writing.** These were **skills,** she said, **that could be used in any field.** This way I wouldn't be boxed into one specific area and could choose the specifics later when I was in graduate school.

Remember: This is a speech. Write as though you are speaking to *an educated adult audience.*

Clear examples.

Variety of sentence structures.

I took her advice and entered college as an English major. My goal was still that of becoming a lawyer, but I could take my time. Mrs. Simpson's manner and **advice were so sound that years later I realized it wasn't the field of law that really interested me.** During my undergraduate years I decided to become a teacher. **Mrs. Simpson certainly helped shape my life and formulate my goals.**

Nice summary/conclusion.

Shows Mrs. Simpson's influence on the writer's life.

Nice, tight reminder to audience of main focus of speech.

Repeats the topic's key words: "formulate" and "reach goals."

The Analytical or Expository Essay

Analytical and expository essays require that you analyze, evaluate, or expound upon an issue. When writing your essay, you should create a clear, concise, logical response that helps to support your position. Expository writing is meant to "expose" information for the purpose of informing the reader. You are asked to agree or disagree and support your opinion with specific examples. For example, let's look at this sample analytical/expository essay topic:

> When school districts face budget constraints, district proposals often surface as movements in education to teach only fundamental disciplines. To attach an air of sophistication to the proposal, supporters label it "Back to Basics." Its proponents argue that the curriculum should concentrate only on reading, writing, and mathematics skills and completely ignore such courses as sociology, art appreciation, music, and drama.
>
> Imagine that you are a school principal faced with the task of making policy for your school with severe budget cuts. Present your arguments either for or against the issue of adopting a "Back to Basics" educational movement.

Preparing to Write

The following diagram shows what the prewriting technique of clustering might look like for this topic:

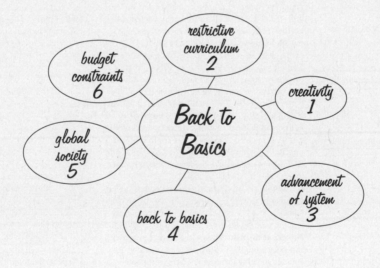

The Why Essay

One good way to approach a question that asks you to explain, analyze, or evaluate is to use a Why Essay format. A *Why Essay* is built around a thesis sentence. The thesis sentence begins with your opinion followed by the word *because* and then a list of the most important reasons why the opinion is valid, reasonable, or well-founded.

For example, in the following sample Analytical/Expository essay, the thesis statement is:

> I am against the "Back to Basics" movement because it inhibits creativity, fails to recognize the importance of the arts, and restricts the curriculum.

The thesis statement comes at the end of the introductory paragraph and is followed by paragraphs that explain each supporting point. The paper ends with a summary of the reasons and a restatement of the thesis sentence. Each paragraph should contain approximately three to five sentences.

The introduction invites the reader to read on. The following reasons (three are usually sufficient) should give supporting examples or evidence. Your concluding paragraph summarizes your reasons and restates the thesis statement.

The Why Essay format begins with your opinion followed by a list of the most important reasons your opinion is valid and reasonable. It looks like the following table in outline form:

Paragraph 1	Introduction—Write your thesis statement or opinion and reasons.
Paragraph 2	Use the first reason from your introduction as the topic sentence and provide relevant examples.
Paragraph 3	Use the second reason from your introduction as the topic sentence of this paragraph.
Paragraph 4	Use the third reason from your introduction as the topic sentence of this paragraph.
Paragraph 5	Conclusion—Write a summary, recommendation, or prediction.

The Finished Analytical or Expository Essay

As principal of your school, I have seen many educational movements come and go. Some are worthy of the attention given to them, and others should be ignored because of their devastating effect on the educational system. One such movement that falls into the latter category is the "Back to Basics" movement. Its proponents argue that education should concentrate on reading, writing, and mathematics skills and completely ignore such courses as drama, art appreciation, and sociology. I am against the "Back to Basics" movement because it inhibits creativity, fails to recognize the importance of the arts, and restricts the curriculum.

The enhancement of creative thinking is primal to the advancement of any educational system. To create, to invent, or to discover, one needs not only to have freedom of thought but that exposure and application of that creativity to all areas of the curriculum. To concentrate on only reading, writing, and mathematics would restrict thinking to a narrow focus. The future needs thinkers who can create in the widest spectrum so as to be able to meet the challenge of a global society.

The "Back to Basics" proponents also fail to see that a restrictive curriculum of only mathematics, reading, and writing fails to support the many advancements made in our culture by those whose first exposures to art, drama, or sociology took place in the schools. The great artists who have changed the way people see; the great dramatists who have told their stories worldwide; and the great sociologists who have helped us to understand social relations, organizations, and changes in our culture have all been products of an education that included the arts as basic to a well-rounded education.

Finally, the "Back to Basics" supporters fail to see their narrow view of education that the basics include art, drama, and sociology as well as music, dance, and computer literacy. "Basics," by definition, means that knowledge which is needed by children in our society in order to compete and simply survive in that society. The "Back to Basics" movement is an attempt to take education back to a time that has long since passed. The narrow focus of the movement also overlooks the integrative value of reading, writing, and mathematics throughout all curriculum areas and especially in the arts.

The "Back to Basics" issue is a sad attempt to restrict the information that children need for their future. It will stifle creativity in those knowledge areas upon which our society is dependent. So, as your principal, I hope that you on the school board continue to support an education for the future -- an education that defines the "basics" as those curriculum areas beyond the courses of reading, writing, and mathematics. We must meet the future with an education that includes art, drama, and sociology.

A Second Look at the Finished Essay (with Comments)

Essay 6

Clear introduction. Nice lead-in to thesis statement.

As **principal** of your school, **I have seen many educational movements come up and go. Some are worthy** of the attention given to them, and **others should be ignored because of their devastating effect on the educational system.** One such movement that falls into the latter category is the "Back to Basics" movement. Its proponents argue that education should concentrate on reading, writing, and mathematics skills and completely ignore such courses as drama, art appreciation, and sociology. **I am against the "Back to Basics" movement because it inhibits creativity, fails to recognize the importance of the arts, and restricts the curriculum.**

Thesis statement at end of first paragraph gives direction and focus.

Three clear reasons.

Starts paragraph with support of reason 1, "inhibits creativity."

The enhancement of creative thinking is primal to the advancement of any educational system. To create, to invent, or to discover, one needs not only have freedom of thought but the **exposure and application of that creativity to all areas of the curriculum.** To concentrate on only reading, writing, and mathematics would **restrict thinking to a narrow focus. The future needs thinkers who can create** in the widest spectrum so as to be able to meet the challenges of a global society.

Additional support and clarification is given.

Reason 2, "fails to realize the importance" is discussed and supported with specifics.

The "Back to Basics" **proponents also fail to see that a restrictive curriculum** of only mathematics, reading, and writing fails to support the many great advancements made in our culture by those whose first exposures to art, drama, or sociology took place in the schools. **The great artists who** have changed the way people see; **the great dramatists who** have told their stories worldwide; and **the great sociologists who** have helped us to understand social relations, organization, and changes in our culture have **all been products of an education that included the arts as basic to a well-rounded education.**

Strong last sentence.

Finally, the "Back to Basics" supporters **fail to see *their narrow view** of education that the basics include art, drama, and sociology as well as music, dance, and computer literacy. "Basics" by definition, means that knowledge which is needed by children in our society in order to compete and simply survive in that society. The "Back to Basics" movement is an attempt to take education back to a time that has long since passed. **The narrow focus** of the movement **also overlooks the integrative value of reading, writing, and mathematics throughout all curriculum areas and especially in the arts.**

This paragraph addresses reason 3, "restricts curriculum," and ends with a strong supporting sentence.

*The word *in* is missing. But this is only a minor flaw in the complete picture of this well-written essay.

Restates thesis statement using clear wording and an effective closing sentence.

The "Back to Basics" issue is a **sad attempt to restrict the information** that children need for their future. It will stifle creativity in those knowledge areas upon which our society is dependent. So, as your principal, I hope that you on the school board continue to **support an education for the future**—an education that defines the "basics" as **those curriculum areas beyond the courses of reading, writing, and mathematics. We must meet the future with an education that *includes* art, drama, and sociology.**

Reviews reasons using strong language— "sad attempt to restrict."

A Poorly Written Essay
Essay 7

Back to Basics is wrong for the schools. I don't like it. For one thing what are we going to do with all of the extra teachers when they fire all of the others. I will probably lose my job cause I have only been teaching for four years.

This essay has major flaws in organization, development, and grammar. It does not have a clear beginning, middle and end. Nowhere in the paper is there a clear thesis statement; reasons are merely scattered throughout the paper.
The paper contains many basic grammar and usage errors.

People get bored with the same thing day after day and the children will come to hate school and that is not good. I love to teach art and drama in my classroom. I have not taught sociology yet though. I know the children in my class could not stand to have only reading, writing and mathematics. All the time without ever a break. Behavior problems would increase because the children would be so board that I would have to be very strict to have any control. Those people in the back to basics movement probably have never taught and are just mad at schools because they have to pay taxes to the schools and they are mad. Being a teacher I don't like the back to basics movement and don't want to see it.

In this essay, the author fails to choose the two or three most important reasons and develop them fully, giving examples or evidence. The sentence beginning "Behavior problems..." hints at a possible example; yet this thought is not well developed with examples or evidence.

One More Analytical or Expository Topic

> Some parents encourage their high school students to get an after-school or weekend job. Other parents cite the importance of getting good grades, discouraging their high school students from getting after-school or weekend jobs.
>
> What is your opinion or viewpoint on this subject? Use specific supporting details from your own observations, experience, or reading as you write your response.

A few reminders:

- Read the topic two or three times.
- Underline key words or phrases.
- Restate the topic information in your own words. (In this case, part-time jobs in school versus good grades and no jobs.)
- This is a position paper—you need to pick **one** side and write in support of **that one side** only!
- It doesn't matter which side you choose. Usually, it's best to select the side you can most comfortably write about—even if you personally disagree with the position. Select the easiest position to write on and support it with observations and experiences. Keep in mind that these observations and experiences can be fictional, since this section of the exam is testing your writing ability, not your opinions.

Two Well-Written Essays (with Comments)

Essay 8

Introduction is focused and states position *clearly* and *immediately*.

Some parents want their high school aged children to work part-time, while other parents prefer their children not work and instead concentrate on studies. **I agree with the parents who want their children to get good grades, although I believe that after school work, sports or other activities are helpful in establishing good study habits** and creating a well-rounded, successful student.

Notice how it uses words from the counter-argument, "good grades," to support the position that part-time jobs are good because they lead to good grades.

The second paragraph supports the main position of the introduction—again supports the position that jobs can lead to good grades.

Life is not all study any more than it is all play. Students need to learn how to manage their time. They need to learn the organizational skills necessary to do a lot of different tasks in a timely manner. Work, sports, and other activities are necessary to provide a break from continual studying. **They also provide experiences that are essential to education and can lead to understanding and, hence, better grades.**

Since I was responsible for paying for my own college education, it was necessary for me to work part-time throughout my college years. I had to organize my work hours around my class and study hours, therefore I found **a job in a grocery store** as this afforded me the greatest flexibility. I organized my time and was able to work and keep up my grades.

The third paragraph gives supporting details from *experience* as asked for — personal experience *supports* the *position*.

The fourth paragraph shows that not working in part-time jobs doesn't mean that good grades will necessarily follow. Notice the supporting example from the experience and observation of the writer.

Many of my college classmates came from wealthier backgrounds than I did. **They didn't have to work and were able to concentrate full-time on their studies and their grades.** A lot of these kids took study breaks for coffee or beers or just chatting, and didn't organize their time well. **Some did quite poorly in school even though their parents did all they could to help them focus on grades.**

From my own observations and experience **I do not feel that after-school or weekend jobs hinder a student from getting good grades.** I feel that these activities can be more helpful than harmful by providing the student with the opportunity to organize their life activities. Whether in high school or in college **a student should be encouraged to engage in a multiplicity of activities and to organize their time so they can succeed in all they do. Interviews with today's successful people show that the busier and more involved people are the ones who rise to the top of their field.**

The conclusion:
• again restates the essay topic;
• uses support from observations to again support original restated position;
• uses observation of successful business people to support main thesis.

Note: Since the question is "what is your opinion," it is quite permissible to write in the first person (I) and give your opinion without saying "in my opinion" or "I believe" or "my viewpoint is." Be personal and invent supporting examples!

Another Well-Written Essay

Essay 9

This is a good first paragraph. It clearly states the writer's position, and by suggesting that work can develop nonacademic skills, it prepares for the arguments of the next three paragraphs.

Note how the repetition of the word "skills" links the second paragraph with the first.

Paragraph three moves on to another advantage (development of a work ethic). The second sentence explains fully what the writer understands a "work ethic" to be.

The last paragraph is the weakest paragraph of this essay. The writer has argued forcefully in favor of after-school work. There is no reason to weaken the argument with the trite suggestion that it will depend on the individual. What doesn't? In an argument essay like this, it is not necessary (and is usually a waste of time) to pay lip service to the opposing point of view.

There is a great deal of controversy among parents as to whether or not their children should hold a paying job while in high school. Some parents believe that working while in school is a valuable experience; others believe that the importance of good grades **superceeds** any value that a job might offer. **I think that working while in school can be very beneficial to students and provide them with skills that might enhance their "formal" education.**

One of the **skills** is time management. Learning how to balance your activities and obligations is essential as an adult. It is invaluable to know what you can handle and when you are taking on too much. **When I got a job in high school, I began to realize the importance of using my time wisely since I had less of it to throw around.** I think that I gained a lot from having to make those decisions as well as earning my own money.

Another benefit is that students can **develop a work ethic** which can be applied to their academic schooling or any task that they choose to take on. **Understanding the importance of working hard, doing a good job and being responsible are skills that are assets to any endeavor.** Students often develop **confidence** from being counted on to get something done and then rising to that challenge. **Additionally, learning to take pride in your work is really important.** When you care about something your performance often reflects that. Academic success largely depends upon this same kind of pride and confidence.

Ultimately, I believe that whether a child should work while in school **depends on the child.** Some children feel that they can't handle the responsibility while others are willing to try. I think **that students stand to gain a lot from working**, but should be able to **make that choice for themselves** in the end.

A well-chosen word, but misspelled. It should be "supersede."

The writer supports her argument (that part-time work develops the ability to manage time efficiently) by referring to personal experience.

The move to a second point in this paragraph (increased confidence) would be clearer with the addition of a transitional word or phrase (such as "Further" or "Also") to begin the sentence. But, the writer rightly does include a transitional word ("Additionally") at the beginning of the next sentence.

Compare and Contrast Essay

In the compare and contrast essay you are asked to recognize and discuss the similarities and differences of a topic. In other words, you will be comparing the qualities of a topic that are *alike* and contrasting the qualities of a topic that are *different*. You may find it helpful to draw a visual graph (i.e. Venn diagram) depicting the overlapping similarities and differences. Once you have discussed the similarities and differences, your conclusion should include a basis for your analysis of comparisons. The following outline illustrates this process.

> Compare a time in your life when a teacher helped you and a time when a teacher hindered you. Explain **which** teacher you learned the most from as a result of these experiences.

When writing an essay on a question that asks you to compare or contrast two things, you can use this framework as a basic outline for your paper:

Paragraph 1: Introduction

1. Introduce the reader to the topic.
2. Restate the question and state your opinion and reasons (thesis).

Paragraph 2: Body

1. Describe one teacher and his or her attributes.
2. Tell how the teacher helped you.
3. Include your feelings about the experience.

Paragraph 3: Body

1. Describe the second teacher and his or her attributes.
2. Tell how this teacher hindered you.
3. Include your feelings about the experience.

Paragraph 4: Conclusion

1. Tell how and why one teacher was the better one for you.
2. Restate your thesis.

Important Terms Used in Essay Questions

Writing topics often include words asking you to perform specific tasks. Pay close attention to how the essay question is phrased. Are you being asked to compare and contrast, or simply to describe? It is very important to focus on the exact assigned task; if you don't answer the question that is being asked, you will receive little credit for your work.

As a CBEST test taker, you should be familiar with the following terms that may appear in your topic question.

Analyze. Separate into parts and examine critically.

Argue. Take only one point of view (either pro or con) and substantiate that position. Don't be concerned about taking the *right* or *wrong* position. That doesn't matter. What matters is that whichever position you take, you support it soundly and clearly.

Cite Evidence. Give examples. Present support or proof. Illustrate.

Compare and Contrast. Examine. Note similarities and differences between two or more items.

Convince. Persuade. Argue the case.

Criticize. Decide the merits and faults.

Describe. Narrate. Present a mental picture for your reader.

Discuss. Take a more open-ended approach and write on a broader range of possibilities or approaches.

Evaluate. Determine. Appraise. Set the value.

Explain. Make it clear and give reasons that strengthen an argument. Answer the question, "why?"

Summarize. State your ideas in a concise form. Condense.

In most essay questions, regardless of type (compare, describe, or explain), you need to use examples to support your thoughts. Thinking in terms of examples is also helpful in planning your writing.

A PATTERNED PLAN OF ATTACK
Writing

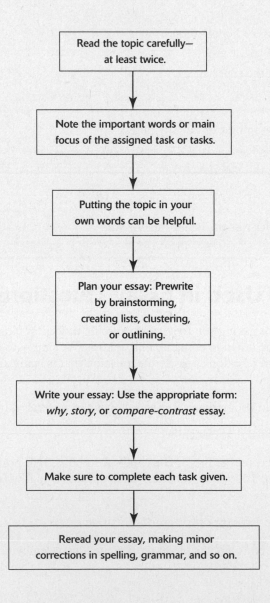

Read the topic carefully— at least twice.

↓

Note the important words or main focus of the assigned task or tasks.

↓

Putting the topic in your own words can be helpful.

↓

Plan your essay: Prewrite by brainstorming, creating lists, clustering, or outlining.

↓

Write your essay: Use the appropriate form: *why*, *story*, or *compare-contrast* essay.

↓

Make sure to complete each task given.

↓

Reread your essay, making minor corrections in spelling, grammar, and so on.

Practice Essay Topics

Use the techniques discussed on the previous pages to practice writing CBEST-type essays.

Following are topics to use for practice. Allow about 30 minutes to plan and write each essay on the two blank sheets of lined paper provided. Prepare to pre-write and write an essay under the same conditions you will use for the test. Write an essay every time you take a practice test. Then, upon completion of each essay, evaluate—or have a friend evaluate—your writing using the essay analysis sheet following each essay topic. Remember, you should try writing one Descriptive/Narrative Essay using a fictional character or situation.

Topic 1

Should there be any restriction on how many years a teacher may teach the same subject or grade level? Explain your answer. Support your opinion with specific examples.

CBEST Essay Analysis Sheet

How well does the writer **present the central idea or point of view?**

(4)	(3)	(2)	(1)
clearly presents	adequately presents	poorly presents	fails to present

Is the **focus** of the topic **maintained?**

(4)	(3)	(2)	(1)
yes, well focused	generally clear focus	sometimes loses focus	no, unfocused

How is the **reasoning** in the response?

(4)	(3)	(2)	(1)
well reasoned	adequately reasoned	simplistically reasoned	lacks reason

How are the **ideas or points organized?**

(4)	(3)	(2)	(1)
logically arranged	generally clear	some order evident	disorganized

How well is the **response supported?**

(4)	(3)	(2)	(1)
well supported with specific examples	adequately supported with some examples	partially supported, lacking detail	unsupported, no details

How good is the **choice of words** in the essay?

(4)	(3)	(2)	(1)
precise, careful, accurate choice of words	adequate choice of words	generally imprecise choice of words	poor choice of words

How well is the **topic addressed?**

(4)	(3)	(2)	(1)
completely addressed	adequately, but not fully addressed	incompletely addressed	not addressed

Does the essay use **language and style appropriate** to the given audience?

(4)	(3)	(2)	(1)
yes, appropriate language and style	fairly appropriate language and style	inadequately appropriate language and style	inappropriate language and style

To what extent is the writing **free from grammatical and mechanical errors?**

(4)	(3)	(2)	(1)
only a few minor flaws	some errors, but not serious	distracting errors	numerous errors

How is the **writing sample formed?**

(4)	(3)	(2)	(1)
well formed	adequately formed	partially formed	inadequately formed

How well is the **message communicated?**

(4)	(3)	(2)	(1)
effectively communicated	adequately communicated	effort made to communicate	not communicated

Topic 2

Describe a particular time in your life when you had difficulty making an important decision. Identify the situation and explain whether you were able to resolve the problem. If it was resolved, then how? If not, then why not—what happened?

CBEST Essay Analysis Sheet

How well does the writer **present the central idea or point of view?**

(4)	(3)	(2)	(1)
clearly presents	adequately presents	poorly presents	fails to present

Is the **focus** of the topic **maintained?**

(4)	(3)	(2)	(1)
yes, well focused	generally clear focus	sometimes loses focus	no, unfocused

How is the **reasoning** in the response?

(4)	(3)	(2)	(1)
well reasoned	adequately reasoned	simplistically reasoned	lacks reason

How are the **ideas or points organized?**

(4)	(3)	(2)	(1)
logically arranged	generally clear	some order evident	disorganized

How well is the **response supported?**

(4)	(3)	(2)	(1)
well supported with specific examples	adequately supported with some examples	partially supported, lacking detail	unsupported, no details

How good is the **choice of words** in the essay?

(4)	(3)	(2)	(1)
precise, careful, accurate choice of words	adequate choice of words	generally imprecise choice of words	poor choice of words

How well is the **topic addressed?**

(4)	(3)	(2)	(1)
completely addressed	adequately, but not fully addressed	incompletely addressed	not addressed

Does the essay use **language and style appropriate** to the given audience?

(4)	(3)	(2)	(1)
yes, appropriate language and style	fairly appropriate language and style	inadequately appropriate language and style	inappropriate language and style

To what extent is the writing **free from grammatical and mechanical errors?**

(4)	(3)	(2)	(1)
only a few minor flaws	some errors, but not serious	distracting errors	numerous errors

How is the **writing sample formed?**

(4)	(3)	(2)	(1)
well formed	adequately formed	partially formed	inadequately formed

How well is the **message communicated?**

(4)	(3)	(2)	(1)
effectively communicated	adequately communicated	effort made to communicate	not communicated

Topic 3

Every year, more and more computers are used for instruction. Is this good or bad? Discuss and explain your opinions on the growing use of computer-assisted instruction in the classroom. Support your opinions with specific examples from your personal experience, readings, or general knowledge.

CBEST Essay Analysis Sheet

How well does the writer **present the central idea or point of view?**

(4)	(3)	(2)	(1)
clearly presents	adequately presents	poorly presents	fails to present

Is the **focus** of the topic **maintained?**

(4)	(3)	(2)	(1)
yes, well focused	generally clear focus	sometimes loses focus	no, unfocused

How is the **reasoning** in the response?

(4)	(3)	(2)	(1)
well reasoned	adequately reasoned	simplistically reasoned	lacks reason

How are the **ideas or points organized?**

(4)	(3)	(2)	(1)
logically arranged	generally clear	some order evident	disorganized

How well is the **response supported?**

(4)	(3)	(2)	(1)
well supported with specific examples	adequately supported with some examples	partially supported, lacking detail	unsupported, no details

How good is the **choice of words** in the essay?

(4)	(3)	(2)	(1)
precise, careful, accurate choice of words	adequate choice of words	generally imprecise choice of words	poor choice of words

How well is the **topic addressed?**

(4)	(3)	(2)	(1)
completely addressed	adequately, but not fully addressed	incompletely addressed	not addressed

Does the essay use **language and style appropriate** to the given audience?

(4)	(3)	(2)	(1)
yes, appropriate language and style	fairly appropriate language and style	inadequately appropriate language and style	inappropriate language and style

To what extent is the writing **free from grammatical and mechanical errors?**

(4)	(3)	(2)	(1)
only a few minor flaws	some errors, but not serious	distracting errors	numerous errors

How is the **writing sample formed?**

(4)	(3)	(2)	(1)
well formed	adequately formed	partially formed	inadequately formed

How well is the **message communicated?**

(4)	(3)	(2)	(1)
effectively communicated	adequately communicated	effort made to communicate	not communicated

Topic 4

Some have argued that occupations that focus on creative expression (artists, poets, musicians) are not as important as occupations that emphasize analytical expression (lawyers, doctors, engineers). To what extent do you agree or disagree with this argument? Support your opinion with specific examples.

CBEST Essay Analysis Sheet

How well does the writer **present the central idea or point of view?**

(4)	(3)	(2)	(1)
clearly presents	adequately presents	poorly presents	fails to present

Is the **focus** of the topic **maintained?**

(4)	(3)	(2)	(1)
yes, well focused	generally clear focus	sometimes loses focus	no, unfocused

How is the **reasoning** in the response?

(4)	(3)	(2)	(1)
well reasoned	adequately reasoned	simplistically reasoned	lacks reason

How are the **ideas or points organized?**

(4)	(3)	(2)	(1)
logically arranged	generally clear	some order evident	disorganized

How well is the **response supported?**

(4)	(3)	(2)	(1)
well supported with specific examples	adequately supported with some examples	partially supported, lacking detail	unsupported, no details

How good is the **choice of words** in the essay?

(4)	(3)	(2)	(1)
precise, careful, accurate choice of words	adequate choice of words	generally imprecise choice of words	poor choice of words

How well is the **topic addressed?**

(4)	(3)	(2)	(1)
completely addressed	adequately, but not fully addressed	incompletely addressed	not addressed

Does the essay use **language and style appropriate** to the given audience?

(4)	(3)	(2)	(1)
yes, appropriate language and style	fairly appropriate language and style	inadequately appropriate language and style	inappropriate language and style

To what extent is the writing **free from grammatical and mechanical errors?**

(4)	(3)	(2)	(1)
only a few minor flaws	some errors, but not serious	distracting errors	numerous errors

How is the **writing sample formed?**

(4)	(3)	(2)	(1)
well formed	adequately formed	partially formed	inadequately formed

How well is the **message communicated?**

(4)	(3)	(2)	(1)
effectively communicated	adequately communicated	effort made to communicate	not communicated

Topic 5

You have met many people throughout your life. Choose one particular person you would call the most unforgettable and describe why he or she is so unforgettable.

CBEST Essay Analysis Sheet

How well does the writer **present the central idea or point of view?**

(4)	(3)	(2)	(1)
clearly presents	adequately presents	poorly presents	fails to present

Is the **focus** of the topic **maintained?**

(4)	(3)	(2)	(1)
yes, well focused	generally clear focus	sometimes loses focus	no, unfocused

How is the **reasoning** in the response?

(4)	(3)	(2)	(1)
well reasoned	adequately reasoned	simplistically reasoned	lacks reason

How are the **ideas or points organized?**

(4)	(3)	(2)	(1)
logically arranged	generally clear	some order evident	disorganized

How well is the **response supported?**

(4)	(3)	(2)	(1)
well supported with specific examples	adequately supported with some examples	partially supported, lacking detail	unsupported, no details

How good is the **choice of words** in the essay?

(4)	(3)	(2)	(1)
precise, careful, accurate choice of words	adequate choice of words	generally imprecise choice of words	poor choice of words

How well is the **topic addressed?**

(4)	(3)	(2)	(1)
completely addressed	adequately, but not fully addressed	incompletely addressed	not addressed

Does the essay use **language and style appropriate** to the given audience?

(4)	(3)	(2)	(1)
yes, appropriate language and style	fairly appropriate language and style	inadequately appropriate language and style	inappropriate language and style

To what extent is the writing **free from grammatical and mechanical errors?**

(4)	(3)	(2)	(1)
only a few minor flaws	some errors, but not serious	distracting errors	numerous errors

129

How is the **writing sample formed?**

(4)	(3)	(2)	(1)
well formed	adequately formed	partially formed	inadequately formed

How well is the **message communicated?**

(4)	(3)	(2)	(1)
effectively communicated	adequately communicated	effort made to communicate	not communicated

Topic 6

Many recent high school graduates discover that, despite possessing a high school diploma, they have no specific skills to enable them to obtain employment. Explain your feelings about introducing a *vocational skills program* as an alternative choice to the academic high school curriculum.

CBEST Essay Analysis Sheet

How well does the writer **present the central idea or point of view?**

(4)	(3)	(2)	(1)
clearly presents	adequately presents	poorly presents	fails to present

Is the **focus** of the topic **maintained?**

(4)	(3)	(2)	(1)
yes, well focused	generally clear focus	sometimes loses focus	no, unfocused

How is the **reasoning** in the response?

(4)	(3)	(2)	(1)
well reasoned	adequately reasoned	simplistically reasoned	lacks reason

How are the **ideas or points organized?**

(4)	(3)	(2)	(1)
logically arranged	generally clear	some order evident	disorganized

How well is the **response supported?**

(4)	(3)	(2)	(1)
well supported with specific examples	adequately supported with some examples	partially supported, lacking detail	unsupported, no details

How good is the **choice of words** in the essay?

(4)	(3)	(2)	(1)
precise, careful, accurate choice of words	adequate choice of words	generally imprecise choice of words	poor choice of words

How well is the **topic addressed?**

(4)	(3)	(2)	(1)
completely addressed	adequately, but not fully addressed	incompletely addressed	not addressed

Does the essay use **language and style appropriate** to the given audience?

(4)	(3)	(2)	(1)
yes, appropriate language and style	fairly appropriate language and style	inadequately appropriate language and style	inappropriate language and style

To what extent is the writing **free from grammatical and mechanical errors?**

(4)	(3)	(2)	(1)
only a few minor flaws	some errors, but not serious	distracting errors	numerous errors

134

How is the **writing sample formed?**

(4)	(3)	(2)	(1)
well formed	adequately formed	partially formed	inadequately formed

How well is the **message communicated?**

(4)	(3)	(2)	(1)
effectively communicated	adequately communicated	effort made to communicate	not communicated

Topic 7

Some educational experiments have included ungraded classrooms, which consist of students grouped by level of achievement rather than by age. Imagine that such an ungraded classroom system is suggested for your school. As a parent, write a strong argument (either pro or con) to be read at the next meeting of the Board of Education.

CBEST Essay Analysis Sheet

How well does the writer **present the central idea or point of view?**

(4)	(3)	(2)	(1)
clearly presents	adequately presents	poorly presents	fails to present

Is the **focus** of the topic **maintained?**

(4)	(3)	(2)	(1)
yes, well focused	generally clear focus	sometimes loses focus	no, unfocused

How is the **reasoning** in the response?

(4)	(3)	(2)	(1)
well reasoned	adequately reasoned	simplistically reasoned	lacks reason

How are the **ideas or points organized?**

(4)	(3)	(2)	(1)
logically arranged	generally clear	some order evident	disorganized

How well is the **response supported?**

(4)	(3)	(2)	(1)
well supported with specific examples	adequately supported with some examples	partially supported, lacking detail	unsupported, no details

How good is the **choice of words** in the essay?

(4)	(3)	(2)	(1)
precise, careful, accurate choice of words	adequate choice of words	generally imprecise choice of words	poor choice of words

How well is the **topic addressed?**

(4)	(3)	(2)	(1)
completely addressed	adequately, but not fully addressed	incompletely addressed	not addressed

Does the essay use **language and style appropriate** to the given audience?

(4)	(3)	(2)	(1)
yes, appropriate language and style	fairly appropriate language and style	inadequately appropriate language and style	inappropriate language and style

To what extent is the writing **free from grammatical and mechanical errors?**

(4)	(3)	(2)	(1)
only a few minor flaws	some errors, but not serious	distracting errors	numerous errors

How is the **writing sample formed?**

(4)	(3)	(2)	(1)
well formed	adequately formed	partially formed	inadequately formed

How well is the **message communicated?**

(4)	(3)	(2)	(1)
effectively communicated	adequately communicated	effort made to communicate	not communicated

Topic 8

Our lives have high points and low points. Choose one particular high point or low point in your life and describe why it had such an impact on you. Explain what you gained from the situation.

CBEST Essay Analysis Sheet

How well does the writer **present the central idea or point of view?**

(4)	(3)	(2)	(1)
clearly presents	adequately presents	poorly presents	fails to present

Is the **focus** of the topic **maintained?**

(4)	(3)	(2)	(1)
yes, well focused	generally clear focus	sometimes loses focus	no, unfocused

How is the **reasoning** in the response?

(4)	(3)	(2)	(1)
well reasoned	adequately reasoned	simplistically reasoned	lacks reason

How are the **ideas or points organized?**

(4)	(3)	(2)	(1)
logically arranged	generally clear	some order evident	disorganized

How well is the **response supported?**

(4)	(3)	(2)	(1)
well supported with specific examples	adequately supported with some examples	partially supported, lacking detail	unsupported, no details

How good is the **choice of words** in the essay?

(4)	(3)	(2)	(1)
precise, careful, accurate choice of words	adequate choice of words	generally imprecise choice of words	poor choice of words

How well is the **topic addressed?**

(4)	(3)	(2)	(1)
completely addressed	adequately, but not fully addressed	incompletely addressed	not addressed

Does the essay use **language and style appropriate** to the given audience?

(4)	(3)	(2)	(1)
yes, appropriate language and style	fairly appropriate language and style	inadequately appropriate language and style	inappropriate language and style

To what extent is the writing **free from grammatical and mechanical errors?**

(4)	(3)	(2)	(1)
only a few minor flaws	some errors, but not serious	distracting errors	numerous errors

144

How is the **writing sample formed?**

(4)	(3)	(2)	(1)
well formed	adequately formed	partially formed	inadequately formed

How well is the **message communicated?**

(4)	(3)	(2)	(1)
effectively communicated	adequately communicated	effort made to communicate	not communicated

PART II

MATHEMATICS REVIEW

The following pages are designed to give you an intensive review of the basic skills you need to use on the CBEST Mathematics section. Arithmetic, basic algebra, measurement, properties of numbers, terms, and simple statistics and probability are covered. Before you begin the diagnostic review tests, it would be wise to become familiar with basic mathematical terminology, simple formulas, and general mathematical information—a review that begins on the following page. Next, proceed to the arithmetic diagnostic test, which you should take to help spot your weak areas. Then use the arithmetic review that follows to strengthen those areas.

After reviewing the arithmetic, take the algebra diagnostic test and once again use the review that follows to strengthen your weak areas. Next, take the measurement diagnostic test and carefully read and complete the measurement review.

Even if you are strong in arithmetic, algebra, and measurement, you may want to skim the topic headings in each area to refresh your memory. If you are weak in math, read through the complete review. This is a good basis for starting your practice testing. Recent CBESTs have emphasized arithmetic, procedure, and word-type problems. The practice tests give good examples of each problem type.

Symbols, Terminology, Formulas, and General Mathematical Information

Common Math Symbols and Terms

Symbol References			
Symbol	**Meaning**	**Symbol**	**Meaning**
=	is equal to	≠	is not equal to
>	is greater than	<	is less than
≥	is greater than or equal to	≤	is less than or equal to
‖	is parallel to	⊥	is perpendicular to
≈	is approximately equal to	≅	is congruent to

Terms

Natural numbers—the counting numbers: 1, 2, 3, . . .

Whole numbers—the counting numbers beginning with zero: 0, 1, 2, 3, . . .

Integers—positive and negative whole numbers and zero—notice that words match the position of the integer:

$$. . . -3, -2, -1, \quad 0, \quad 1, 2, 3 . . .$$
$$\text{negative} \qquad \text{zero} \qquad \text{positive}$$

Odd numbers—numbers not divisible by 2: 1, 3, 5, 7, . . .

Even numbers—numbers divisible by 2: 2, 4, 6, . . .

Prime number—number divisible only by 1 and itself: 2, 3, 5, 7, 11, 13, . . .

Composite number—number divisible by more than just 1 and itself: 4, 6, 8, 9, 10, 12, 14, 15, . . .

Squares—the result when numbers are multiplied by themselves, $(2 \cdot 2 = 4)$, $(3 \cdot 3 = 9)$: 1, 4, 9, 16, 25, 36, . . .

Cubes—the result when numbers are multiplied by themselves twice, $(2 \cdot 2 \cdot 2 = 8)$, $(3 \cdot 3 \cdot 3 = 27)$: 1, 8, 27, . . .

Math Perimeter Formulas

Add the length of all sides to get the perimeter.

Shape	Illustration	Perimeter
Square		$P = a + a + a + a$
Rectangle		$P = 2b + 2h$ or $P = 2(b + h)$
Parallelogram		$P = 2a + 2b$ or $P = 2(a + b)$
Triangle		$P = a + b + c$

Important Equivalents

$\dfrac{1}{100} = .01 = 1\%$

$\dfrac{1}{10} = .1 = 10\%$

$\dfrac{1}{5} = \dfrac{2}{10} = .2 = .20 = 20\%$

$\dfrac{3}{10} = .3 = .30 = 30\%$

$\dfrac{2}{5} = \dfrac{4}{10} = .4 = .40 = 40\%$

$\dfrac{1}{2} = \dfrac{5}{10} = .5 = .50 = 50\%$

$\dfrac{3}{5} = \dfrac{6}{10} = .6 = .60 = 60\%$

$\dfrac{7}{10} = .7 = .70 = 70\%$

$\dfrac{4}{5} = \dfrac{8}{10} = .8 = .80 = 80\%$

$\dfrac{9}{10} = .9 = .90 = 90\%$

$\dfrac{1}{4} = \dfrac{25}{100} = .25 = 25\%$

$\dfrac{3}{4} = \dfrac{75}{100} = .75 = 75\%$

$\dfrac{1}{3} = .33\dfrac{1}{3} = 33\dfrac{1}{3}\%$

$\dfrac{2}{3} = .66\dfrac{2}{3} = 66\dfrac{2}{3}\%$

$\dfrac{1}{8} = .125 = 12\dfrac{1}{2} = 12\dfrac{1}{2}\%$

$\dfrac{3}{8} = .375 = .37\dfrac{1}{2} = 37\dfrac{1}{2}\%$

$\dfrac{5}{8} = .625 = .62\dfrac{1}{2} = 62\dfrac{1}{2}\%$

$\dfrac{7}{8} = .875 = 87\dfrac{1}{2} = 87\dfrac{1}{2}\%$

$\dfrac{1}{6} = .16\dfrac{2}{3} = 16\dfrac{2}{3}\%$

$\dfrac{5}{6} = .83\dfrac{1}{3} = 83\dfrac{1}{3}\%$

$1 = 1.00 = 100\%$

$2 = 2.00 = 200\%$

$3\dfrac{1}{2} = 3.5 = 3.50 = 350\%$

Math Words and Phrases

Many CBEST math questions are presented as word-type problems. The following key words help you understand the relationships between the words and phrases that give you clues as to how the problem should be solved.

Words That Signal an Operation			
Addition	**Subtraction**	**Multiplication**	**Division**
Addition The team needed the addition of three new players . . .	**Difference** What is the difference between 8 and 5 . . .	**Product** The product of 3 and 6 is . . .	**Quotient** The final quotient is . . .
Sum The sum of 5, 6, and 8 . . .	**Fewer** There were ten fewer girls than boys . . .	**Of** One-half of the people in the room . . .	**Divided by** Some number divided by 5 Is . . .
Total The total of the last two games . . .	**Remainder** What is the remainder when . . . or How many are left when . . .	**Times** Six times as many men as women . . .	**Divided into** The coins were divided into groups of . . .
Plus Three chairs plus five chairs . . .	**Less** A number is six less than another number . . .	**At** The cost of five yards of material at $9 a yard is . . .	**Ratio** What is the ratio of . . .
Increase Her pay was increased by $30 . . .	**Reduced** His allowance was reduced by $5 . . .	**Twice** Twice the value of some number . . . (multiply by 2)	**Half** Half of the cards were . . . (divide by 2)
More than Four more than a number . . .	**Decreased** His score decreased by 4 points . . .		**Each** How much did each pencil cost?
Greater than Her income was $100 greater than . . .	**Minus** Seven minus some number is . . .		
	Have left How many are left when . . .		

As you practice solving word problems, you will discover more key words and phrases that give you insight into the problem-solving process.

Mathematical Properties

Some Properties (Axioms) of Addition

- *Commutative* means that the *order* does not make any difference.

  $2 + 3 = 3 + 2$

  $a + b = b + a$

  Note: Commutative does *not* hold for subtraction.

  $3 - 1 \neq 1 - 3$

  $a - b \neq b - a$

- *Associative* means that the *grouping* does not make any difference.

  $(2 + 3) + 4 = 2 + (3 + 4)$

  $(a + b) + c = a + (b + c)$

  The grouping has changed (the parentheses moved), but the sides are still equal.

  Note: Associative does *not* hold for subtraction.

  $4 - (3 - 2) \neq (4 - 3) - 2$

  $a - (b - c) \neq (a - b) - c$

- The *identity element* for addition is 0. Adding any number to 0 gives the original number.

  $3 + 0 = 3$

  $a + 0 = a$

- The *additive inverse* is the opposite (negative) of the number. Any number plus its additive inverse equals 0 (the identity element).

  $3 + (-3) = 0$; therefore 3 and –3 are inverses

  $-2 + 2 = 0$; therefore –2 and 2 are inverses

  $a + (-a) = 0$; therefore a and $-a$ are inverses

Some Properties (Axioms) of Multiplication

- *Commutative* means that the *order* does not make any difference.

  $2 \times 3 = 3 \times 2$

  $a \times b = b \times a$

  Note: Commutative does *not* hold for division.

  $2 \div 4 \neq 4 \div 2$

- *Associative* means that the *grouping* does not make any difference.

  $(2 \times 3) \times 4 = 2 \times (3 \times 4)$

  $(a \times b) \times c = a \times (b \times c)$

  The grouping has changed (the parentheses moved), but the sides are still equal.

  Note: Associative does *not* hold for division.

  $(8 \div 4) \div 2 \neq 8 \div (4 \div 2)$

- The *identity element* for multiplication is 1. Multiplying any number by 1 gives the original number.

  $3 \times 1 = 3$

  $a \times 1 = a$

- The *multiplicative inverse* is the reciprocal of the number. Any number multiplied by its reciprocal equals 1.

  $2 \times \frac{1}{2} = 1$; therefore 2 and $\frac{1}{2}$ are inverses

  $a \times \frac{1}{a} = 1$; therefore a and $\frac{1}{a}$ are inverses

  Also, $a \neq 0$.

A Property of Two Operations

- The *distributive property* is the process of distributing the number on the outside of the parentheses to each number on the inside.

  - $2(3 + 4) = 2(3) + 2(4)$

  - $a(b + c) = a(b) + a(c)$

  Note: You cannot use the distributive property with only one operation.

  - $3(4 \times 5 \times 6) \neq 3(4) \times 3(5) \times 3(6)$

  - $a(bcd) \neq a(b) \times a(c) \times a(d)$ or $a(bcd) \neq (ab)(ac)(ad)$

Basic Statistics

These are just a few statistical concepts that may appear on the CBEST.

Mean

The *mean* is the sum of all the numbers divided by the amount of numbers. It is often referred to as the *average*. To find the arithmetic *mean*, simply total the numbers and divide by the number of data values.

To find the *average* of a group of numbers:

1. Add them up.
2. Divide by the number of items you added.

For example:

What is the average of 10, 20, 35, 40, and 45?

$$10 + 20 + 35 + 40 + 45 = 150$$
$$150 \div 5 = 30$$

The average is 30.

What is the average of 0, 12, 18, 20, 31, and 45?

$$0 + 12 + 18 + 20 + 31 + 45 = 126$$
$$126 \div 6 = 21$$

The average is 21.

What is the average of 25, 27, 27, and 27?

$$25 + 27 + 27 + 27 = 106$$
$$106 \div 4 = 26\frac{1}{2}$$

The average is $26\frac{1}{2}$.

Median

A *median* is simply the middle number of a list of numbers after it has been written in order. To find the *median,* arrange the scores or numbers in order from greatest to least. Then find the middle score or number.

Find the median of these scores: 2, 5, 7, 3, 6.

First, arrange them in order by size: 7, 6, 5, 3, 2. Then find the middle score.
The middle score is 5; therefore the median is 5.

If the number of scores is even, take the average of the two middle scores.

Find the median of these scores: 2, 5, 7, 4, 3, 6.

First, arrange them in order by size: 7, 6, 5, 4, 3, 2.
The two middle numbers are 4 and 5; therefore the median is $4\frac{1}{2}$.

Mode

The *mode* is simply the number most frequently listed in a group of numbers. For example, in the following list—5, 9, 7, 3, 9, 4, 6, 9, 7, 9, 2—the mode is 9 because it appears more often than any other number. It is possible to have more than one mode. For example, in the following list—7, 12, 8, 7, 12, 9, 7, 12, 3, 7, 12—the modes are 7 and 12 because they both appear equally more than any other numbers. It is also possible to not have a mode. For example, in the following list—18, 22, 7, 3, 19, 18, 22, 7, 3, 19—there is not a mode because no number appears more often than any other number.

Range

A *range* is the difference between the largest data value and the smallest data value. To calculate the *range* of a group of scores or numbers, subtract the smallest from the largest (range = maximum – minimum).

Find the range of the scores 3, 2, 7, 9, 12. The range is 12 – 2 = 10.

Probability

Probability is the numerical measure of the chance of an outcome or event occurring. *When all outcomes are equally likely to occur,* find the probability of the occurrence of a given outcome by using the following formula:

$$\text{probability} = \frac{\text{number of favorable outcomes}}{\text{number of possible outcomes}}$$

For example: Using the spinner shown below, what is the probability of spinning a 6 in one spin?

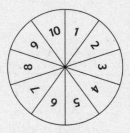

Because there is only *one* 6 on the spinner out of *ten* numbers and all the numbers are equally spaced, the probability is $\frac{1}{10}$.

What is the probability of tossing heads three consecutive times with a two-sided fair coin?

Since each toss is independent and the odds are $\frac{1}{2}$ for each toss, the probability is

$$\frac{1}{2} \times \frac{1}{2} \times \frac{1}{2} = \frac{1}{8}$$

For example: Three green marbles, two blue marbles, and five yellow marbles are placed in a jar. What is the probability of selecting at random a green marble on the first draw?

Since there are ten marbles (total possible outcomes) and three green marbles (favorable outcomes), the probability is $\frac{3}{10}$.

Counting Principles

If there are a *number of successive choices* to make and the choices are *independent of each other* (order makes no difference), the total number of possible choices (*arrangements*) is the product of each of the choices at each stage.

For example: How many possible arrangements of shirts and ties are there if there are five different color shirts and three different color ties?

To find the total number of possible arrangements, simply multiply the number of shirts times the number of ties.

$5 \times 3 = 15$

Simple Permutations

If there are a *number of successive choices* to make and the choices are *affected by the previous choice or choices* (dependent upon order), then *permutations* are involved.

For example: How many ways can you arrange the letters S, T, O, P in a row?

Number of choices for first letter (S)		Number of choices for second letter (T)		Number of choices for third letter (O)		Number of choices for fourth letter (P)
4	×	3	×	2	×	1

$$4! = 4 \times 3 \times 2 \times 1 = 24$$

The product $4 \times 3 \times 2 \times 1$ can be written *4!* (read *4 factorial* or *factorial 4*). Thus, there are 24 different ways to arrange four different letters.

Interpreting Standardized Test Scores

CBEST test takers should have a basic knowledge of analyzing standardized test scores. Standardized tests are designed to measure an individual student's performance compared to a large group of students.

Although interpreting test scores may appear like a challenging task, the primary focus of the CBEST is to use a few commonly used terms that help primary grade school teachers read and understand test results. Recognizing the format of standardized test reports will help you assess student performance. Terms you should know are: *raw score, percent score, percentile score,* and *stanine score.*

Raw Score: The raw score is simply the number of correct answers on a given test. For example, if a student answers 80 problems correctly out of 100 possible questions, the raw score is 80. If the student answers 80 problems correctly out of 85 possible questions, the raw score is still 80.

Percent Score: The percent score is the number of questions answered correctly compared to the total number of questions. For example, if a student answers 80 questions correctly out of a possible 100 questions, the student's percent score is 80 %. If the student answers 80 questions correct out of 85 possible questions, the student's percent score is 94 %.

Percentile Score: The percentile score is based upon the student's "standing" in a group. The percentile score is ascertained from the percentage of test takers who score the same or below the student's score. For example, if an exam is taken by 100 students, has 200 questions, and the student answers 100 questions correctly, the student will have a raw score of 100 and a percent score of 50%. If 85 of the 100 students have a percent score of 50% or below, then the student will have a score better than or equal to 85% of the test takers and will have scored in the 85th percentile.

Stanine Score: Stanine scores are based on a simple method that compares a student's performance to other students at the same grade level. The term *stanine* is a contraction of "standard nine." Stanine scores convert percentile scores into a single digit number from 1 to 9. The lowest score is 1 and the highest score is 9. For example, a stanine score of 5 is the middle or "average" score.

Rank	Percentile	Stanine
High	96–99	9
	89–95	8
	77–88	7
Average	60–76	6
	41–59	5
	24–40	4
Low	12–23	3
	5–11	2
	1–4	1

Arithmetic

Arithmetic Diagnostic Test

Questions

1. $6 = \frac{?}{4}$

2. Change $5\frac{3}{4}$ to an improper fraction.

3. Change $\frac{32}{6}$ to a whole number or mixed number in lowest terms.

4. $\frac{2}{5} + \frac{3}{5} =$

5. $\frac{1}{3} + \frac{1}{4} + \frac{1}{2} =$

6. $1\frac{3}{8} + 2\frac{5}{6} =$

7. $\frac{7}{9} - \frac{5}{9} =$

8. $11 - \frac{2}{3} =$

9. $6\frac{1}{4} - 3\frac{3}{4} =$

10. $\frac{1}{6} \times \frac{1}{6} =$

11. $2\frac{3}{8} \times 1\frac{5}{6} =$

12. $\frac{1}{4} \div \frac{3}{2} =$

13. $2\frac{3}{7} \div 1\frac{1}{4} =$

14. $.07 + 1.2 + .471 =$

15. $.45 - .003 =$

16. $\$78.24 - \$31.68 =$

17. $.5 \times .5 =$

18. $8.001 \times 2.3 =$

19. $.7\overline{)\ .147}$ =

20. $.002\overline{)\ 12}$ =

21. $\frac{1}{3}$ of $7.20 =

22. Circle the larger number: 43.051 or 043.0089

23. Change 4% to a decimal.

24. 46% of 58 =

25. Change .009 to a percent.

26. Change 12.5% to a fraction.

27. Change $\frac{3}{8}$ to a percent.

28. Is 93 prime?

29. What is the percent increase of a rise in temperature from 80° to 100°?

30. Average 0, 8, and 10.

31. 8^2 =

Answers

1. 24
2. $\frac{23}{4}$
3. $5\frac{1}{3}$
4. $\frac{5}{5}$ or 1
5. $\frac{13}{12}$ or $1\frac{1}{12}$
6. $4\frac{5}{24}$
7. $\frac{2}{9}$
8. $10\frac{1}{3}$
9. $2\frac{2}{4}$ or $2\frac{1}{2}$
10. $\frac{1}{36}$
11. $\frac{209}{48}$ or $4\frac{17}{48}$
12. $\frac{1}{6}$
13. $\frac{68}{35}$ or $1\frac{33}{35}$
14. 1.741

15. .447
16. $46.56
17. .25
18. 18.4023
19. .21
20. 6,000
21. $2.40
22. 43.051
23. .04
24. 26.68
25. .9% or $\frac{9}{10}$%
26. $\frac{125}{1000}$ or $\frac{1}{8}$
27. 37.5% or $37\frac{1}{2}$%
28. No
29. 25%
30. 6
31. 64

Rounding Off

To round off any number:

1. Underline the place value to which you're rounding off.
2. Look to the immediate right (one place) of your underlined place value.
3. Identify the number to the right. If it is 5 or higher, round your underlined place value up 1. If the number to the right is 4 or less, leave your underlined place value as it is and change all the other numbers to its right to zeros. *For example:*

Round to the nearest thousand:

34<u>5</u>,678 becomes 346,000
92<u>8</u>,499 becomes 928,000

This works with decimals as well. Round to the nearest hundredth:

3.4<u>6</u>78 becomes 3.47
298,435.0<u>8</u>3 becomes 298,435.08

Place Value

Each position in any number has a *place value*. For instance, in the number 485, 4 is in the hundreds place, 8 is in the tens place, and 5 is in the ones place. Thus, place value is as follows:

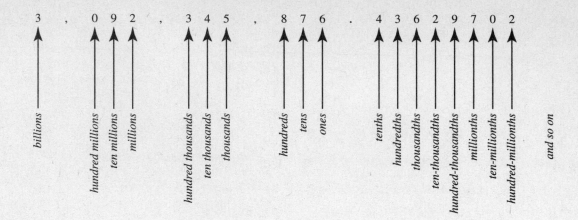

Estimating Sums, Differences, Products, and Quotients

Estimating Sums

Use rounded numbers to estimate sums. *For example:*

Give an estimate for the sum $3{,}741 + 5{,}021$ rounded to the nearest thousand.

$3{,}741 + 5{,}021$

$\downarrow \qquad \downarrow$

$4{,}000 + 5{,}000 = 9{,}000$

So $3{,}741 + 5{,}021 \approx 9{,}000$

(The symbol $\approx$ means *is approximately equal to.*)

Estimating Differences

Use rounded numbers to estimate differences. *For example:*

Give an estimate for the difference $317{,}753 - 115{,}522$ rounded to the nearest hundred thousand.

$317{,}753 - 115{,}522$

$\downarrow \qquad\quad \downarrow$

$300{,}000 - 100{,}000 = 200{,}000$

So $317{,}753 - 115{,}522 \approx 200{,}000$

Estimating Products

Use rounded numbers to estimate products. *For example:*

Estimate the product of 722×489 by rounding to the nearest hundred.

722×489

$\downarrow \quad \downarrow$

$700 \times 500 = 350{,}000$

So $722 \times 489 \approx 350{,}000$

If both multipliers end in 50, or are halfway numbers, then rounding one number up and one number down gives you a better estimate of the product. *For example:*

Estimate the product of 650×350 by rounding to the nearest hundred. Round one number up and one down.

650×350

$\downarrow \quad \downarrow$

$700 \times 300 = 210,000$

So $650 \times 350 \approx 210,000$

You can also round the first number down and the second number up to get this estimate.

650×350

$\downarrow \quad \downarrow$

$600 \times 400 = 240,000$

So $650 \times 350 \approx 240,000$

Rounding one number up and one number down gives you a closer approximation than rounding both numbers up, which is the standard rule.

Estimating Quotients

Use rounded numbers to estimate quotients. *For example:*

Estimate the quotient of $891 \div 288$ by rounding to the nearest hundred.

$891 \div 288$

$\downarrow \quad \downarrow$

$900 \div 300 = 3$

So $891 \div 288 \approx 3$

Fractions

Fractions consist of two numbers: a *numerator* (which is above the line) and a *denominator* (which is below the line).

$$\frac{1 \text{ numerator}}{2 \text{ denominator}} \quad \text{or} \quad \text{numerator } 1\!\!\Big/\!\!2 \text{ denominator}$$

The denominator indicates the number of equal parts into which something is divided. The numerator indicates how many of these equal parts are contained in the fraction. Thus, if the fraction is $\frac{3}{5}$ of a pie, then the denominator 5 indicates that the pie is divided into 5 equal parts, of which 3 (numerator) are in the fraction.

Sometimes it helps to think of the dividing line (in the middle of a fraction) as meaning "out of." In other words, $\frac{3}{5}$ also means 3 "out of" 5 equal pieces from the whole pie.

Common Fractions and Improper Fractions

A fraction whose numerator is smaller than its denominator is called a *common fraction*. All common fractions have a value that is less than one. The fraction $\frac{3}{5}$ is an example of a common fraction. A fraction whose numerator is the same or more than the denominator is called an *improper fraction*. All improper fractions have values equal to one or more than one. The fraction $\frac{6}{6}$ and the fraction $\frac{5}{4}$ are examples of improper fractions. $\frac{6}{6} = 1$ and $\frac{5}{4} = 1\frac{1}{4}$.

Mixed Numbers

When a term contains both a whole number (such as 3, 5, 8, 25, and so on) and a fraction (such as $\frac{1}{2}, \frac{1}{4}, \frac{3}{4}$, and so on), it is called a *mixed number*. For instance, $5\frac{1}{4}$ and $290\frac{3}{4}$ are both mixed numbers.

To change an improper fraction to a mixed number, divide the denominator into the numerator. *For example*:

$$\frac{18}{5} = 3\frac{3}{5} \qquad 5\overline{)18}^{\,3} \qquad \frac{-15}{3}$$

To change a mixed number to an improper fraction, multiply the denominator times the whole number, add in the numerator, and put the total over the original denominator. *For example:*

$$4\frac{1}{2} = \frac{9}{2} \qquad 2 \times 4 + 1 = 9$$

Reducing Fractions

A fraction must be reduced to *lowest terms*. Do this by dividing the numerator and denominator by the largest number that divides evenly into both. *For example:*

Reduce $\frac{14}{16}$ by dividing both terms by 2 to get $\frac{7}{8}$. Likewise, reduce $\frac{20}{25}$ to $\frac{4}{5}$ by dividing both numerator and denominator by 5.

Adding Fractions

To add fractions, you must first change all denominators to their *least common multiple* (LCM) which is also called the *lowest common denominator* (LCD)—the lowest number that can be divided evenly by all the denominators in the problem. When you make all the denominators the same, you can add fractions by simply adding the numerators (the denominator remains the same).

One way to find this value is to make a list of the multiples for the values involved and then find the least common one. *For example:*

Find the LCM for 24 and 36.

Multiples of 24	Multiples of 36
24	36
48	72
72	108
96	144
120	180
144	216

Notice that 72 and 144 are both common multiples, but that 72 is the least common multiple.

Now apply this to the adding of fractions. *For example:*

$\frac{5}{24} + \frac{7}{36} = ?$ As we saw above, the (LCD) for 24 and 36 is 72.

$+\frac{5}{24} = \frac{15}{72}$ Since 24 is multiplied by 3 to get 72, the 5 is also multiplied by 3.

$+\frac{7}{36} = \frac{14}{72}$ Since 36 is multiplied by 2 to get 72, the 7 is also multiplied by 2.

$= \frac{29}{72}$ Now that the denominators are the same, add the numerators and keep the denominator.

Of course, if the denominators are already the same, keep that denominator, and simply add the numerators.

For example: $\frac{6}{11} + \frac{3}{11} = \frac{9}{11}$

Adding Mixed Numbers

To add mixed numbers, the same rule (find the LCD) applies, but make sure that you always add the whole numbers to get your final answer. *For example:*

$$2\frac{1}{2} = 2\frac{2}{4} \longleftarrow \begin{cases} \text{change one-half} \\ \text{to two-fourths} \end{cases}$$
$$+ 3\frac{1}{4} = 3\frac{1}{4}$$
$$\overline{\qquad 5\frac{3}{4}}$$
$$\longleftarrow \begin{cases} \text{remember to add} \\ \text{the whole numbers} \end{cases}$$

Subtracting Fractions

To subtract fractions, the same rule (find the LCD) applies, except that you subtract the numerators. *For example:*

$$\frac{7}{8} = \frac{7}{8} \qquad\qquad \frac{3}{4} = \frac{9}{12}$$
$$-\frac{1}{4} = \frac{2}{8} \qquad\qquad -\frac{1}{3} = \frac{4}{12}$$
$$\overline{\quad\frac{5}{8}\quad} \qquad\qquad \overline{\quad\frac{5}{12}\quad}$$

Subtracting Mixed Numbers

When you subtract mixed numbers, sometimes you may have to "borrow" from the whole number, just like you sometimes borrow from the next column when subtracting ordinary numbers. *For example:*

$$6\overset{4\ \ 11}{\cancel{5}\cancel{1}} \qquad\qquad \overset{3\frac{7}{6}}{\cancel{4\frac{1}{6}}}$$
$$-\ 129 \qquad\qquad -\ 2\frac{5}{6}$$
$$\overline{\quad 522 \quad} \qquad\qquad \overline{\quad 1\frac{2}{6} = 1\frac{1}{3}}$$

you borrow 1 from
the 10s column

you borrow one, in
the form $\frac{6}{6}$, from
the 1s column

To subtract a mixed number from a whole number, you have to "borrow" from the whole number. *For example:*

$$6 = 5\tfrac{5}{5} \longleftarrow \begin{cases} \text{borrow 1 in the form of} \\ \tfrac{5}{5} \text{ from the 6} \end{cases}$$
$$\underline{-3\tfrac{1}{5} = 3\tfrac{1}{5}}$$
$$2\tfrac{4}{5}$$
$$\longleftarrow \begin{cases} \text{remember to subtract the} \\ \text{remaining whole numbers} \end{cases}$$

Multiplying Fractions

Simply multiply the numerators, then multiply the denominators. Reduce to lowest terms if necessary. *For example:*

$$\frac{2}{3} \times \frac{5}{12} = \frac{10}{36} \text{ reduce } \frac{10}{36} \text{ to } \frac{5}{18}.$$

This answer had to be reduced as it wasn't in lowest terms.

Canceling when multiplying fractions: You can first "cancel" the fractions. That eliminates the need to reduce your answer. To cancel, find a number that divides evenly into one numerator and one denominator. In this case, 2 divides evenly into 2 in the numerator (it goes in one time) and into 12 in the denominator (it goes in 6 times). *Thus:*

$$\frac{\overset{1}{\cancel{2}}}{3} \times \frac{5}{\underset{6}{\cancel{12}}} = \qquad \text{After you cancel, you can multiply out as you did before.}$$

$$\frac{\overset{1}{\cancel{2}}}{3} \times \frac{5}{\underset{6}{\cancel{12}}} = \frac{5}{18} \qquad \text{Remember, you may cancel only when } multiplying \text{ fractions.}$$

Multiplying Mixed Numbers

To multiply mixed numbers, first change any mixed number to an improper fraction. Then multiply as shown in the preceding section. To change mixed numbers to improper fractions:

1. Multiply the whole number by the denominator of the fraction.
2. Add this to the numerator of the fraction.
3. This is now your numerator.
4. The denominator remains the same.

$$3\frac{1}{3} \times 2\frac{1}{4} = \frac{10}{3} \times \frac{9}{4} = \frac{90}{12} = 7\frac{6}{12} = 7\frac{1}{2}$$

Then change the answer, if in improper fraction form, back to a mixed number and reduce if necessary.

Dividing Fractions

To divide fractions, invert (turn upside down) the second fraction and multiply. Then reduce if necessary. *For example:*

$$\frac{1}{6} \div \frac{1}{5} = \frac{1}{6} \times \frac{5}{1} = \frac{5}{6}$$

$$\frac{1}{6} \div \frac{1}{3} = \frac{1}{6} \times \frac{3}{1} = \frac{3}{6} = \frac{1}{2}$$

Simplifying Fractions

If either numerator or denominator consists of several numbers, combine them into one number. Then reduce if necessary. *For example:*

$$\frac{28+14}{26+17} = \frac{42}{43}$$

or

$$\frac{\frac{1}{4}+\frac{1}{2}}{\frac{1}{3}+\frac{1}{4}} = \frac{\frac{1}{4}+\frac{2}{4}}{\frac{4}{12}+\frac{3}{12}} = \frac{\frac{3}{4}}{\frac{7}{12}} = \frac{3}{4} \times \frac{12}{7} = \frac{36}{28} = \frac{9}{7} = 1\frac{2}{7}$$

Decimals

You can write fractions in decimal form by using a symbol called a *decimal point*. All numbers to the left of the decimal point are whole numbers. All numbers to the right of the decimal point are fractions with denominators of only 10, 100, 1,000, 10,000, and so on, as follows:

$$.6 = \frac{6}{10} = \frac{3}{5}$$

$$.7 = \frac{7}{10}$$

$$.07 = \frac{7}{100}$$

$$.007 = \frac{7}{1,000}$$

$$.0007 = \frac{7}{10,000}$$

$$.00007 = \frac{7}{100,000}$$

$$.25 = \frac{25}{100} = \frac{1}{4}$$

Adding and Subtracting Decimals

To add or subtract decimals, just line up the decimal points and then add or subtract in the same manner you would add or subtract regular numbers. *For example:*

$$
\begin{array}{r}
23.6 + 1.75 + 300.02 = 23.6 \\
1.75 \\
+300.02 \\
\hline
325.37
\end{array}
$$

Adding in zeros can make the problem easier to work:

$$
\begin{array}{r}
23.600 \\
1.750 \\
\underline{300.002} \\
325.352
\end{array}
$$

and
$$54.26 - 1.1 = \begin{array}{r} 54.26 \\ \underline{-1.10} \\ 53.16 \end{array}$$

and
$$78.9 - 37.43 = \begin{array}{r} 78.90 \\ \underline{-37.43} \\ 41.47 \end{array}$$

You can add decimal places to the right of whole numbers. *For example:*

$$17 - 8.43 = 1\cancel{7}^{\,6}.\cancel{0}^{\,10}\,\cancel{0}^{\,10}$$

$$
\begin{array}{r}
-8 \;\; .4 \;\;\; 3 \\
\hline
8 \;\; .5 \;\;\; 7
\end{array}
$$

Multiplying Decimals

To multiply decimals, just multiply as usual. Then count the total number of digits above the line and to the right of all decimal points. Place the decimal point in your answer so that there are the same number of digits to the right of it as there are above the line. *For example:*

$$
\begin{array}{r}
40.012 \;\; \leftarrow 3 \text{ digits} \\
\times \quad\; 3.1 \;\; \leftarrow 1 \text{ digit} \\
\hline
40012 \\
\underline{120036} \quad\;\; \\
124.0372 \;\; \leftarrow 4 \text{ digits}
\end{array}
$$

$\begin{cases} \text{total of 4 digits above the line} \\ \text{to the right of the decimal point} \end{cases}$

$\begin{cases} \text{decimal point placed so there are} \\ \text{the same number of digits to the} \\ \text{right of the decimal point} \end{cases}$

Dividing Decimals

Dividing decimals is the same as dividing other numbers, except that if the divisor (the number you're dividing by) has a decimal, you move it to the right as many places as necessary until it is a whole number. Then move the decimal point in the dividend (the number being divided into) the same number of places. Sometimes you may have to add zeros to the dividend (the number inside the division sign).

$$1.25 \overline{)5.} = 125 \overline{)\,\overset{4.}{500.}}$$

or

$$.002 \overline{)26} = 2 \overline{)\,\overset{13,000.}{26,000.}}$$

Changing Decimals to Percents

To change decimals to percents:

1. Move the decimal point two places to the right.
2. Insert a percent sign.

.75 = 75%
.05 = 5%

Changing Percents to Decimals

To change percents to decimals:

1. Eliminate the percent sign.
2. Move the decimal point two places to the left (sometimes adding zeros is necessary).

75% = .75   5% = .05
23% = .23   .2% = .002

Changing Fractions to Percents

To change a fraction to a percent:

1. Multiply by 100.
2. Divide by denominator.
3. Insert a percent sign.

$$\frac{1}{2} = \frac{1}{2} \times 100 = \frac{100}{2} = 50\%$$

$$\frac{2}{5} = \frac{2}{5} \times 100 = \frac{200}{5} = 40\%$$

Changing Percents to Fractions

To change percents to fractions:

1. Eliminate the percent sign.
2. Place the number without the percent sign over 100. (i.e., divide the percent by 100).
3. Reduce if necessary.

$$60\% = \frac{60}{100} = \frac{3}{5} \qquad 13\% = \frac{13}{100}$$

Changing Fractions to Decimals

To change a fraction to a decimal, simply do what the operation says. In other words, $\frac{13}{20}$ means 13 divided by 20, so do just that (insert decimal points and zeros accordingly):

$$20\overline{)13.00} = .65 \qquad \frac{5}{8} = 8\overline{)5.000} = .625$$

where the first quotient is $.65$ and the second is $.625$.

Changing Decimals to Fractions

To change a decimal to a fraction:

1. Read it: 0.8 (eight-tenths)
2. Write it: $\frac{8}{10}$ or
3. Reduce it: $\frac{4}{5}$

1. Read it: 0.028 (twenty-eight thousands)
2. Write it: $\frac{28}{1000}$
3. Reduce it: $\frac{7}{250}$

Finding a Percent of a Number

To determine a percent of a number, change the percent to a fraction or decimal (whichever is easier for you) and multiply. Remember, the word "of" means multiply. *For example:*

What is 20% of 80?

$$\frac{20}{100} \times 80 = \frac{1600}{100} = 16 \text{ or } .20 \times 80 = 16.00 = 16$$

What is 12% of 50?

$$\frac{12}{100} \times 50 = \frac{600}{100} = 6 \text{ or } .12 \times 50 = 6.00 = 6$$

What is $\frac{1}{2}$% of 18?

$$\frac{\frac{1}{2}}{100} \times 18 = \frac{1}{200} \times 18 \text{ or } \frac{18}{200} = \frac{9}{100} \text{ or } .005 \times 18 = .09$$

Other Applications of Percent

Turn the question word-for-word into an equation. For "what" substitute x; for "is" substitute an *equal sign;* for "of" substitute a *multiplication sign.* Change percents to decimals or fractions, whichever you find easier. Then solve the equation. *For example:*

18 is what percent of 90?

$$18 = x(90)$$
$$\frac{18}{90} = x$$
$$\frac{1}{5} = x$$
$$20\% = x$$

10 is 50% of what number?

$$10 = .50(x)$$
$$\frac{10}{.50} = x$$
$$20 = x$$

What is 15% of 60?

$$x = \frac{15}{100} \times 60 = \frac{90}{10} = 9 \text{ or } .15(60) = 9$$

Finding Percentage Increase or Percentage Decrease

To find the *percentage change* (increase or decrease), use this formula:

$$\frac{\text{change}}{\text{starting point}} \times 100 = \text{percentage change}$$

For example:

What is the percentage decrease of a $500 item on sale for $400?

Change: $500 - 400 = 100$

$$\frac{\text{change}}{\text{starting point}} \times 100 = \frac{100}{500} \times 100 = \frac{1}{5} \times 100 = 20\% \text{ decrease}$$

What is the percentage increase of Jon's salary if it went from $150 a month to $200 a month?

Change: $200 - 150 = 50$

$$\frac{\text{change}}{\text{starting point}} \times 100 = \frac{50}{150} \times 100 = \frac{1}{3} \times 100 = 33\frac{1}{3}\% \text{ increase}$$

Prime Numbers

A *prime number* is a number that can be evenly divided by only itself and one. For example, 19 is a prime number because it can be evenly divided only by 19 and 1, but 21 is not a prime number because 21 can be evenly divided by other numbers (3 and 7).

The only even prime number is 2; thereafter any even number can be divided evenly by 2. Zero and 1 are *not* prime numbers. The first ten prime numbers are 2, 3, 5, 7, 11, 13, 17, 19, 23, and 29.

Squares

To *square* a number, just multiply it by itself. For example, 6 squared (written 6^2) is 36. 36 is called a *perfect square* (the square of a whole number). Any exponent means multiply by itself that many times. *For example:*

$5^2 = 5 \times 5 = 25$
$8^2 = 8 \times 8 = 64$

Remember, $x^1 = x$ and $x^0 = 1$ when x is any number (other than 0).

Following is a list of perfect squares:

$1^2 = 1$
$2^2 = 4$
$3^2 = 9$
$4^2 = 16$
$5^2 = 25$
$6^2 = 36$

$7^2 = 49$
$8^2 = 64$
$9^2 = 81$
$10^2 = 100$
$11^2 = 121$
$12^2 = 144$

Signed Numbers (Positive Numbers and Negative Numbers)

On a number line, numbers to the right of 0 are positive. Numbers to the left of 0 are negative, as follows:

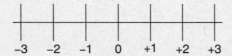

and so on, and so on

Given any two numbers on a number line, the one on the right is always larger, regardless of its sign (positive or negative).

Addition of Signed Numbers

When adding two numbers with the same sign (either both positive or both negative), add the numbers and keep the same sign. *For example:*

$$\begin{array}{r} +5 \\ \underline{++7} \\ +12 \end{array} \qquad \begin{array}{r} -8 \\ \underline{+-3} \\ -11 \end{array}$$

When adding two numbers with different signs (one positive and one negative), subtract the numbers and keep the sign from the larger one. *For example:*

$$\begin{array}{r} +5 \\ \underline{+-7} \\ -2 \end{array} \qquad \begin{array}{r} -59 \\ \underline{++72} \\ +13 \end{array}$$

Subtraction of Signed Numbers

To subtract positive and/or negative numbers, just change the sign of the number being subtracted and then add. *For example:*

$$\begin{array}{r} +12 \\ \underline{-+4} \\ \end{array} \begin{array}{r} +12 \\ \underline{+-4} \\ +8 \end{array} \qquad\qquad \begin{array}{r} -19 \\ \underline{-+6} \\ \end{array} \begin{array}{r} -19 \\ \underline{+-6} \\ -25 \end{array}$$

$$\begin{array}{r} -14 \\ \underline{--4} \\ \end{array} \begin{array}{r} -14 \\ \underline{++4} \\ -10 \end{array} \qquad\qquad \begin{array}{r} +20 \\ \underline{--3} \\ \end{array} \begin{array}{r} +20 \\ \underline{++3} \\ +23 \end{array}$$

Multiplying and Dividing Signed Numbers

To multiply or divide signed numbers, treat them just like regular numbers, but remember this rule: An *odd* number of negative signs produces a negative answer. An *even* number of negative signs produces a positive answer. *For example:*

$$(-3)(+8)(-5)(-1)(-2) = +240$$
$$(-3)(+8)(-1)(-2) = -48$$
$$\frac{-64}{-2} = +32$$
$$\frac{-64}{+2} = -32$$

Parentheses

Parentheses are used to group numbers. Everything inside parentheses must be done before any other operations. *For example:*

$$50\,(2 + 6) = 50\,(8) = 400$$

When a parenthesis is preceded by a minus sign, change the minus to a plus by changing all the signs in front of each term inside the parentheses. Then remove the parentheses. *For example:*

$$6 - (-3 + a - 2b + c) =$$
$$6 + (+3 - a + 2b - c) =$$
$$6 + 3 - a + 2b - c = 9 - a + 2b - c$$

Order of Operations

There is an order in which the operations on numbers must be done so that everyone doing a problem involving several operations and parentheses will get the same results. The order of operations is:

Order of Operations		
Step	**Operation**	**Procedure**
Step 1	Parentheses	Changing signs to their opposites. Simplify (if possible) all expressions in parentheses
Step 2	Exponents	Apply exponents to their appropriate bases
Step 3	Multiplication or Division	Do the multiplication or division in the order it appears as you read the problem left to right
Step 4	Addition or Subtraction	Do the addition or subtraction in the order it appears as you read the problem left to right

For example:

$$10 - 3 \times 6 + 10^2 + \underline{(6 + 12)} \div \underline{(4 - 7)} \qquad \text{parentheses first}$$

$$10 - 3 \times 6 + \underline{10^2} + (18) \div (-3) \qquad \text{exponents next}$$

$$10 - \underline{3 \times 6} + 100 + (18) \div (-3) \qquad \text{multiplication or division in order from left to right}$$

$$10 - 18 + 100 + \underline{(18) \div (-3)} \qquad \text{multiplication or division in order from left to right}$$

$$\underline{10 - 18} + 100 + (-6) \qquad \text{addition or subtraction in order from left to right}$$

$$\underline{-8 + 100} + (-6) \qquad \text{addition or subtraction in order from left to right}$$

$$\underline{92 + (-6)} \qquad \text{addition or subtraction in order from left to right}$$

$$86 \qquad \text{This is the answer}$$

An easy way to remember the order of operations is **PEMDAS**, or **Please Excuse My Dear Aunt Sally** (parentheses, exponents, multiply or divide, add or subtract).

Algebra

Algebra Diagnostic Test

Questions

1. Solve for x: $x + 5 = 17$

2. Solve for x: $4x + 9 = 21$

3. Solve for x: $5x + 7 = 3x - 9$

4. Solve for y: $\dfrac{3}{7} = \dfrac{y}{8}$

5. Evaluate: $3x^2 + 5y + 7$ if $x = 2$ and $y = 3$

6. Simplify: $(5x + 2z) + (3x - 4z)$

7. Simplify: $(4x - 7z) - (3x - 4z)$

8. Solve for x: $2x + 3 \leq 11$

9. Solve for x: $3x + 4 \geq 5x - 8$

Answers

1. $x = 12$

2. $x = 3$

3. $x = -8$

4. $y = \dfrac{24}{7} = 3\dfrac{3}{7}$

5. 34

6. $8x - 2z$

7. $x - 3z$

8. $x \le 4$

9. $x \le 6$

Algebra Review

Equations

An *equation* is a relationship between numbers and/or symbols. It helps to remember that an equation is like a balance scale, with the equal sign (=) serving as the fulcrum, or center. Thus, if you do the *same thing on both sides* of the equal sign (say, add 5 to each side), the equation stays balanced. To solve the equation $x - 5 = 23$, you must get x by itself on one side; therefore, add 5 to both sides:

$$
\begin{array}{r}
x - 5 = 23 \\
\underline{+5 \ \ +5} \\
x = 28
\end{array}
$$

In the same manner, you may subtract, multiply, or divide *both* sides of an equation by the same (nonzero) number, and the equation will not change. Sometimes you may have to use more than one step to solve for an unknown. *For example:*

$$3x + 4 = 19$$

Subtract 4 from both sides to get $3x$ by itself on one side:

$$
\begin{array}{r}
3x + 4 = 19 \\
\underline{-4 \ \ -4} \\
3x = 15
\end{array}
$$

Then divide both sides by 3 to get x:

$$\frac{3x}{3} = \frac{15}{3}; \ x = 5$$

Remember: When solving an equation, the goal is to get the variable "x" on one side of the equation by itself. Inverse (opposite) operations "undo" each other to get the variable "x" alone. (This applies to addition, subtraction, multiplication, division, and so on.)

Representations of Multiplication

When two or more letters, or a number and letters, are written next to each other, they are understood to be *multiplied*. Thus, $8x$ means 8 times x. Or ab means a times b. Or $18ab$ means 18 times a times b.

Parentheses also represent multiplication. Thus $(a)b$ means a times b. A raised dot also means multiplication. Thus, $6 \cdot 5$ means 6 times 5.

Proportions

Proportions are two equivalent ratios or fractions. Proportions are quickly solved by *cross-multiplying*.

Examples:

Solve for x:

$\frac{3}{x} = \frac{5}{7}$ Using the cross-multiplying technique, you get

$5x = 21$ Dividing each side of the equation by 5, you get

$x = \frac{21}{5}$ or $4\frac{1}{5}$

This problem could also have been presented in written form as "3 is to x as 5 is to 7; find the value of x."

Solve for x:

$\frac{p}{q} = \frac{x}{y}$ Using the cross-multiplying technique, you get

$xq = py$ Dividing each side of the equation by q, you get

$x = \frac{py}{q}$

Evaluating Expressions

To *evaluate* an expression, evaluate, replace, or substitute the numerical value in the variable and simplify the expression using *order of operations*. *For example:*

Evaluate: $2x^2 + 3y + 6$ if $x = 2$ and $y = 9$

$2(2^2) + 3(9) + 6 =$

$2(4) + 27 + 6 =$

$8 + 27 + 6 = 41$

Monomials and Polynomials

A *monomial* is an algebraic expression that consists of only one term. For instance, $9x$, $4a^2$, and $3xz^2$ are all monomials.

A *polynomial* consists of two or more terms: $x + y$, $y^2 - x^2$, and $15x^2 + 3x + 5y^2$ are all polynomials.

Adding and Subtracting Monomials

To *add* or *subtract monomials*, follow the same rules as with regular signed numbers, provided that the *terms are alike:*

$$3x + 2x = 5x$$

$$\begin{array}{r} 15x^2yz \\ -18x^2yz \\ \hline -3x^2yz \end{array}$$

Inequalities

An *inequality* is a statement in which the relationships are not equal. Instead of using an equal sign (=) as in an equation, an inequality uses > (greater than) and < (less than), or ≥ (greater than or equal to) and ≤ (less than or equal to).

When working with inequalities, treat them exactly like equations, *except:* If you multiply or divide both sides by a negative number, you must *reverse* the direction of the sign. *For example:*

Solve for x: $2x + 4 > 6$

$$\begin{array}{r} 2x + 4 > 6 \\ -4 \quad -4 \\ \hline 2x > 2 \end{array}$$

$$\frac{2x}{2} > \frac{2}{2}$$

$$x > 1$$

Solve for x: $-7x > 14$ (divide by -7 and reverse the sign)

$$\frac{-7x}{-7} < \frac{14}{-7}$$

$$x < -2$$

$3x + 2 \geq 5x - 10$ becomes $-2x \geq -12$ by opposite operations. Divide both sides by -2 and reverse the sign.

$$\frac{-2x}{-2} \leq \frac{-12}{-2}$$

$$x \leq 6$$

Measurement

Measurement Diagnostic Test

Questions

1. How many inches are in 1 yard?

2. How many feet are in 1 mile?

3. How many ounces are in 1 pound?

4. How many pounds are in 1 ton?

5. How many pints are in 1 quart?

6. How many quarts are in 1 gallon?

7. How many weeks are in 1 year?

8. How many years are in 1 decade?

9. What is the name of a polygon with four equal sides and four equal angles?

10. What is the name of a polygon with three sides?

11. What is the name of a quadrilateral with two sets of parallel sides?

12. What is the name of a quadrilateral with two sets of parallel sides and all right angles?

13. What is the perimeter of the figure?

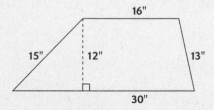

14. What is the perimeter of the parallelogram?

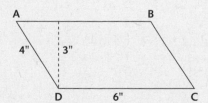

Answers

1. 36 inches = 1 yard

2. 5,280 feet = 1 mile

3. 16 ounces = 1 pound

4. 2,000 pounds = 1 ton

5. 2 pints = 1 quart

6. 4 quarts = 1 gallon

7. 52 weeks = 1 year

8. 10 years = 1 decade

9. a square

10. a triangle

11. a parallelogram, square, rectangle, or rhombus

12. a rectangle or square

13. perimeter = 16 + 13 + 30 + 15 = 74 inches

14. perimeter = 6 + 4 + 6 + 4 = 20 inches

Measurement Review

Measurement Systems

The *English customary system* of measurement is used throughout the United States, although the metric system is being phased in as well. You should be familiar with some basic measurements of the English system. It would be valuable to memorize most of these.

Length

- 12 inches (in.) = 1 foot (ft.)
- 3 feet = 1 yard (yd.)
- 36 inches = 1 yard
- 1,760 yards = 1 mile (mi.)
- 5,280 feet = 1 mile

Weight

- 16 ounces (oz.) = 1 pound (lb.)
- 2,000 pounds = 1 ton (T.)

Capacity

- 2 cups = 1 pint (pt.)
- 2 pints = 1 quart (qt.)
- 4 quarts = 1 gallon (gal.)
- 4 pecks = 1 bushel

Time

- 365 days = 1 year
- 52 weeks = 1 year
- 10 years = 1 decade
- 100 years = 1 century

Converting Units of Measure

For example: If 36 inches equal 1 yard, then 3 yards equal how many inches?

Intuitively, $3 \times 36 = 108$ in.

By proportion, using yards over inches:

$$\frac{3}{x} = \frac{1}{36}$$

Remember to place the same units across from each other—inches across from inches, and feet across feet. Then solve by cross-multiplying:

$$\frac{3}{x} = \frac{1}{36}$$

$$x = 108 \text{ in.}$$

For example: Change 3 decades into weeks.

Since 1 decade equals 10 years, and 1 year equals 52 weeks, then 3 decades equal 30 years.

30 years × 52 weeks = 1,560 weeks in 30 years, or 3 decades

Notice that this was converted step by step. It can be done in one step:

$3 \times 10 \times 52 = 1,560$ weeks

If 1,760 yards equal 1 mile, how many yards are in 5 miles?

$1,760 \times 5 = 8,800$ yards in 5 miles

Calculating Perimeter

Measurements for some basic figures, such as squares, rectangles, parallelograms, and triangles, are not difficult to calculate if the necessary information is given and the proper formula is used. You should first be familiar with the formula of perimeter.

Perimeter (P) means the total distance all the way around the outside of any polygon. The perimeter of any polygon can be determined by adding up the lengths of all the sides. The total distance around will be the sum of all sides of the polygon.

No special formulas are really necessary, although two are commonly seen.

perimeter (P) of a square = $4s$ (s = length of side)
perimeter (P) of a parallelogram (rectangle and rhombus) = $2l + 2w$ or $2(l + w)$ (l = length, w = width)

PRACTICE-REVIEW-ANALYZE-PRACTICE

Four Full-Length Practice Tests

This section contains four full-length simulation CBESTs. The practice tests are followed by complete answers, explanations, and analysis techniques. Each practice test also includes an example of a good, average, and poorly written essay response. The format, levels of difficulty, question structures, and number of questions are similar to those on the actual CBEST. The actual CBEST is copyrighted and may not be duplicated, and these questions are not taken directly from the actual tests.

When taking these exams, try to simulate the test conditions. Remember, the *total testing time for each practice test is four hours.* Although you may divide your time among the three sections in any way you wish, in order to be sure that you have enough time to finish all sections, budget your time approximately as follows:

- Reading, 70 minutes
- Mathematics, 75 minutes
- Writing, 65 minutes
- Checking your work, 30 minutes

Practice Test 1

Answer Sheet for Practice Test 1

(Remove This Sheet and Use It to Mark Your Answers)

Section I: Reading

1 Ⓐ Ⓑ Ⓒ Ⓓ Ⓔ		26 Ⓐ Ⓑ Ⓒ Ⓓ Ⓔ
2 Ⓐ Ⓑ Ⓒ Ⓓ Ⓔ		27 Ⓐ Ⓑ Ⓒ Ⓓ Ⓔ
3 Ⓐ Ⓑ Ⓒ Ⓓ Ⓔ		28 Ⓐ Ⓑ Ⓒ Ⓓ Ⓔ
4 Ⓐ Ⓑ Ⓒ Ⓓ Ⓔ		29 Ⓐ Ⓑ Ⓒ Ⓓ Ⓔ
5 Ⓐ Ⓑ Ⓒ Ⓓ Ⓔ		30 Ⓐ Ⓑ Ⓒ Ⓓ Ⓔ
6 Ⓐ Ⓑ Ⓒ Ⓓ Ⓔ		31 Ⓐ Ⓑ Ⓒ Ⓓ Ⓔ
7 Ⓐ Ⓑ Ⓒ Ⓓ Ⓔ		32 Ⓐ Ⓑ Ⓒ Ⓓ Ⓔ
8 Ⓐ Ⓑ Ⓒ Ⓓ Ⓔ		33 Ⓐ Ⓑ Ⓒ Ⓓ Ⓔ
9 Ⓐ Ⓑ Ⓒ Ⓓ Ⓔ		34 Ⓐ Ⓑ Ⓒ Ⓓ Ⓔ
10 Ⓐ Ⓑ Ⓒ Ⓓ Ⓔ		35 Ⓐ Ⓑ Ⓒ Ⓓ Ⓔ
11 Ⓐ Ⓑ Ⓒ Ⓓ Ⓔ		36 Ⓐ Ⓑ Ⓒ Ⓓ Ⓔ
12 Ⓐ Ⓑ Ⓒ Ⓓ Ⓔ		37 Ⓐ Ⓑ Ⓒ Ⓓ Ⓔ
13 Ⓐ Ⓑ Ⓒ Ⓓ Ⓔ		38 Ⓐ Ⓑ Ⓒ Ⓓ Ⓔ
14 Ⓐ Ⓑ Ⓒ Ⓓ Ⓔ		39 Ⓐ Ⓑ Ⓒ Ⓓ Ⓔ
15 Ⓐ Ⓑ Ⓒ Ⓓ Ⓔ		40 Ⓐ Ⓑ Ⓒ Ⓓ Ⓔ
16 Ⓐ Ⓑ Ⓒ Ⓓ Ⓔ		41 Ⓐ Ⓑ Ⓒ Ⓓ Ⓔ
17 Ⓐ Ⓑ Ⓒ Ⓓ Ⓔ		42 Ⓐ Ⓑ Ⓒ Ⓓ Ⓔ
18 Ⓐ Ⓑ Ⓒ Ⓓ Ⓔ		43 Ⓐ Ⓑ Ⓒ Ⓓ Ⓔ
19 Ⓐ Ⓑ Ⓒ Ⓓ Ⓔ		44 Ⓐ Ⓑ Ⓒ Ⓓ Ⓔ
20 Ⓐ Ⓑ Ⓒ Ⓓ Ⓔ		45 Ⓐ Ⓑ Ⓒ Ⓓ Ⓔ
21 Ⓐ Ⓑ Ⓒ Ⓓ Ⓔ		46 Ⓐ Ⓑ Ⓒ Ⓓ Ⓔ
22 Ⓐ Ⓑ Ⓒ Ⓓ Ⓔ		47 Ⓐ Ⓑ Ⓒ Ⓓ Ⓔ
23 Ⓐ Ⓑ Ⓒ Ⓓ Ⓔ		48 Ⓐ Ⓑ Ⓒ Ⓓ Ⓔ
24 Ⓐ Ⓑ Ⓒ Ⓓ Ⓔ		49 Ⓐ Ⓑ Ⓒ Ⓓ Ⓔ
25 Ⓐ Ⓑ Ⓒ Ⓓ Ⓔ		50 Ⓐ Ⓑ Ⓒ Ⓓ Ⓔ

Section II: Mathematics

1 Ⓐ Ⓑ Ⓒ Ⓓ Ⓔ	26 Ⓐ Ⓑ Ⓒ Ⓓ Ⓔ
2 Ⓐ Ⓑ Ⓒ Ⓓ Ⓔ	27 Ⓐ Ⓑ Ⓒ Ⓓ Ⓔ
3 Ⓐ Ⓑ Ⓒ Ⓓ Ⓔ	28 Ⓐ Ⓑ Ⓒ Ⓓ Ⓔ
4 Ⓐ Ⓑ Ⓒ Ⓓ Ⓔ	29 Ⓐ Ⓑ Ⓒ Ⓓ Ⓔ
5 Ⓐ Ⓑ Ⓒ Ⓓ Ⓔ	30 Ⓐ Ⓑ Ⓒ Ⓓ Ⓔ
6 Ⓐ Ⓑ Ⓒ Ⓓ Ⓔ	31 Ⓐ Ⓑ Ⓒ Ⓓ Ⓔ
7 Ⓐ Ⓑ Ⓒ Ⓓ Ⓔ	32 Ⓐ Ⓑ Ⓒ Ⓓ Ⓔ
8 Ⓐ Ⓑ Ⓒ Ⓓ Ⓔ	33 Ⓐ Ⓑ Ⓒ Ⓓ Ⓔ
9 Ⓐ Ⓑ Ⓒ Ⓓ Ⓔ	34 Ⓐ Ⓑ Ⓒ Ⓓ Ⓔ
10 Ⓐ Ⓑ Ⓒ Ⓓ Ⓔ	35 Ⓐ Ⓑ Ⓒ Ⓓ Ⓔ
11 Ⓐ Ⓑ Ⓒ Ⓓ Ⓔ	36 Ⓐ Ⓑ Ⓒ Ⓓ Ⓔ
12 Ⓐ Ⓑ Ⓒ Ⓓ Ⓔ	37 Ⓐ Ⓑ Ⓒ Ⓓ Ⓔ
13 Ⓐ Ⓑ Ⓒ Ⓓ Ⓔ	38 Ⓐ Ⓑ Ⓒ Ⓓ Ⓔ
14 Ⓐ Ⓑ Ⓒ Ⓓ Ⓔ	39 Ⓐ Ⓑ Ⓒ Ⓓ Ⓔ
15 Ⓐ Ⓑ Ⓒ Ⓓ Ⓔ	40 Ⓐ Ⓑ Ⓒ Ⓓ Ⓔ
16 Ⓐ Ⓑ Ⓒ Ⓓ Ⓔ	41 Ⓐ Ⓑ Ⓒ Ⓓ Ⓔ
17 Ⓐ Ⓑ Ⓒ Ⓓ Ⓔ	42 Ⓐ Ⓑ Ⓒ Ⓓ Ⓔ
18 Ⓐ Ⓑ Ⓒ Ⓓ Ⓔ	43 Ⓐ Ⓑ Ⓒ Ⓓ Ⓔ
19 Ⓐ Ⓑ Ⓒ Ⓓ Ⓔ	44 Ⓐ Ⓑ Ⓒ Ⓓ Ⓔ
20 Ⓐ Ⓑ Ⓒ Ⓓ Ⓔ	45 Ⓐ Ⓑ Ⓒ Ⓓ Ⓔ
21 Ⓐ Ⓑ Ⓒ Ⓓ Ⓔ	46 Ⓐ Ⓑ Ⓒ Ⓓ Ⓔ
22 Ⓐ Ⓑ Ⓒ Ⓓ Ⓔ	47 Ⓐ Ⓑ Ⓒ Ⓓ Ⓔ
23 Ⓐ Ⓑ Ⓒ Ⓓ Ⓔ	48 Ⓐ Ⓑ Ⓒ Ⓓ Ⓔ
24 Ⓐ Ⓑ Ⓒ Ⓓ Ⓔ	49 Ⓐ Ⓑ Ⓒ Ⓓ Ⓔ
25 Ⓐ Ⓑ Ⓒ Ⓓ Ⓔ	50 Ⓐ Ⓑ Ⓒ Ⓓ Ⓔ

CUT HERE

The total testing time is four hours. You may work on any section of the exam during this time period.

Section I: Reading—50 Questions

Section II: Mathematics—50 Questions

Section III: Writing—2 Essays

Section I: Reading

50 Questions

Directions: A question or number of questions follow each of the statements or passages in this section. Using only the *stated* or *implied* information given in the statement or passage, answer the question or questions by choosing the *best* answer from among the five choices given. Make sure to mark your answers for this section on the Reading section of the answer sheet.

Use this excerpt from an index to answer the two questions that follow.

Comparative degree of adjectives and adverbs, 255–256; double, 301

Comparison of adjectives, 255–256, 301–302; of adverbs, 256; illogical, 347–348; pronoun case in, 294

Comparison theme based on, 54–57

Complement, 186–198; intransitive verb, 187–188; objective, 194–195; subjective, with linking verb, 188–190; pronoun as, 290–291; of verbal, 245

Complex sentence, 216–220

Compound-complex sentence, 217

Compound sentence, 214–216; ineffective clause in, 355

Compound subject of sentence, 184–186; subject-verb agreement with, 275–277

Conclusion of theme, 92–98

1. On which pages should one look for information about subjective complements?

   A. 184–186
   B. 186–198
   C. 187–188
   D. 188–190
   E. 214–216

2. On which pages should one look to find information about organizing an essay about the similarities and differences of Mars and the Earth?

   A. 54–57
   B. 92–98
   C. 186–198
   D. 255–256
   E. 347–348

Read the passage below and answer the three questions that follow.

Despite his enormous ability, Jackie Robinson did not begin to play Major League baseball until he was twenty-eight. In 1947, he joined the Brooklyn Dodgers as the first black player. He promptly won the Rookie of the Year award, and within three years became the batting champion and the Most Valuable Player in the National League. He was, observers agree, the most <u>versatile</u> player of his era.

When his baseball career was over, Robinson entered the business world and rose to the vice presidency of a large coffee company. In addition, he wrote a sports column for a New York newspaper, appeared on a weekly radio program, and was active in the NAAPC. _____ He was, however, a leader of two of the earliest civil rights marches and an ally of Martin Luther King. Robinson's baseball achievements were never forgotten. In 1962, he was elected to the Baseball Hall of Fame.

3. Which of the following is the best definition of the word <u>versatile</u> as it is used in the first paragraph of this passage?

   A. famous
   B. fiercely competitive
   C. accomplished in many areas
   D. opportunistic and insightful
   E. victimized and courageous

GO ON TO THE NEXT PAGE

4. Which sentence, if inserted into the blank space in the second paragraph, would be most consistent with the writer's purpose and intended audience?

   A. When I was growing up, I was a Dodger fan, but when Robinson retired, I began to lose interest in baseball.

   B. Many expected he would one day enter politics, but he never really became an important political figure.

   C. If you lived in New York at this time, you probably read his column in the newspaper or heard his radio broadcasts.

   D. This was in the days when the NAACP was about to become a big deal in the campaign for civil rights.

   E. Informed opinion hypothesized that Robinson would become a political potentate, but this sanguine expectation proved to be erroneous.

5. Which of the following best describes the principles of organization used in this passage?

   A. The first paragraph is contrasted with the second, using the opposition of youthful success versus the decline of old age.

   B. The passage is organized chronologically, with the first paragraph on Robinson's baseball career and the second on his years after leaving baseball.

   C. In the first paragraph, the passage uses specific details from Robinson's baseball career, while the second paragraph uses generalizations derived from these details.

   D. The passage opposes factual reporting and speculation, presenting the facts in paragraph 1 and the speculations in paragraph 2.

   E. The first paragraph gives a subjective account of Robinson's life as a baseball player, and the second gives an objective report of his later life.

Read the passage below and answer the four questions that follow.

The ancient Greeks named the constellations of the Northern Hemisphere after the gods, goddesses, beasts, and heroes of their myths. _____, many of the stars of the Southern Hemisphere, which were not named until much later, reflect more modern notions such as instruments or geometric figures. _____, the rocks on Mars that have acquired names in the

1990s are named after late twentieth-century phenomena like the cartoon characters Calvin and Hobbes.

(1) As we begin the twenty-first century, many people expect a significant planetary event, as if the idea of the millennium had some important meaning throughout the universe. (2) They fail to see that any point we name in time is <u>arbitrary</u>, and has no special significance in the universe or the natural world. (3) The whole idea of time is human-constructed. (4) All any date can tell us is the position of the Earth in relation to the Sun. (5) Like the names of the stars, numbers are useful fictions that men have created to make relationships easier to grasp or to remember.

6. Which words or phrases, if inserted *in order* into the blanks in the first paragraph, would help the reader understand the writer's ideas?

   A. Thus; On the other hand

   B. Perhaps; Therefore

   C. Meanwhile; Consequently

   D. Although; Yet

   E. However; Similarly

7. Which of the following is the best definition of the word <u>arbitrary</u> as it is used in the second paragraph?

   A. based on whim; capricious

   B. lacking in judgment; foolish

   C. conveying a truth; informative

   D. of no practical value; useless

   E. having two meanings; ambiguous

8. Which of the following phrases from the second paragraph makes most clear the connection of the ideas of the first paragraph to those of the second?

   A. Sentence 1: "Many people expect a significant planetary event."

   B. Sentence 2: "Any point we name in time is arbitrary."

   C. Sentence 3: "The whole idea of time is human-constructed."

   D. Sentence 4: "All any date can tell us is the position of the Earth in relation to the Sun."

   E. Sentence 5: "Like the names of the stars, numbers are useful fictions that men have created."

9. Which of the following inferences about the beliefs of the author may be drawn from the information that this passage presents?

   A. The author believes in astrology, since he or she has an interest in the names of the stars.
   B. The author is skeptical about the claims of astrologers.
   C. The author expects the new century to be marked by unusually powerful earthquakes and volcanic eruptions.
   D. The author disapproves of reading comics and cartoons.
   E. The author believes that humans have no influence on the events of the natural world.

Use the chart below to answer the question that follows.

This chart presents the percentages of students majoring in the subjects offered in the three divisions of the college: Natural Sciences, Humanities, and Social Sciences.

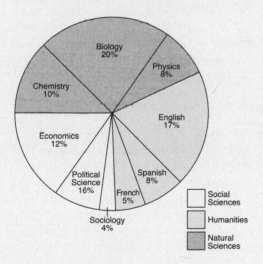

10. In which subject in each of the three divisions were the enrollments lowest?

    A. Physics, French, and Economics
    B. Chemistry, English, and Sociology
    C. Biology, Spanish, and Political Science
    D. Physics, French, and Sociology
    E. Spanish, Economics, and Physics

Read the passage below and answer the question that follows.

The major function of social psychology as a behavioral science, and therefore as a discipline that can contribute to the solution of many social problems, is its investigation of the psychology of the individual in society. Thus, the scientist's main objective is to attempt to determine the influences of the social environment on the personal behavior of individuals.

11. Which of the following best summarizes the passage?

    A. Social psychology is a science in which the behavior of the scientist in the social environment is a major function.
    B. The social environment influences the behavior of individuals.
    C. Social psychology studies the ways in which people in society are affected by their surroundings.
    D. Understanding human behavior, through the help of social psychology, leads to the eventual betterment of society.
    E. A minor objective of social society is the solution to social problems.

Read the passage below and answer the question that follows.

The quiet child is one of our concerns today. Our philosophy about children and speaking in the classroom has flip-flopped. Today we are interested in what Ruth Strickland implies when she refers to the idea of "freeing the child to talk."

12. Which of the following is implied by this passage?

    A. Teachers in the past have preferred quiet and reticent students.
    B. The behavior of children in the classroom is a trivial concern that can change abruptly.
    C. Whether or not a child is quiet determines the quality of his or her education.
    D. Ruth Strickland never explicitly stated her opinions about children and speaking in the classroom.
    E. There are fewer quiet children today than in the past.

GO ON TO THE NEXT PAGE

Read the passage below and answer the question that follows.

For some, the term *creative writing* seems to imply <u>precious</u> writing, useless writing, imaginative writing, or writing that is self-indulgent rather than a necessity, something that is produced during leisure or as a hobby.

13. By <u>precious</u>, the author of this passage means

    A. immature.
    B. costly.
    C. dainty.
    D. unfinished.
    E. affected.

Read the passage below and answer the question that follows.

No matter how significant the speaker's message, and no matter how strongly he or she feels about it, it will be lost unless the listeners attend to it. Attention and perception are key concepts in communication.

14. The primary purpose of the statement is to

    A. imply that some speakers without strong feelings find an attentive audience.
    B. note that some very important messages fall on deaf ears.
    C. stress the critical role of listening in oral communication.
    D. urge readers to listen more carefully to spoken language.
    E. argue that attention and perception are unimportant concepts in communication.

Read the passage below and answer the two questions that follow.

In future decades, what is actually required is the development of a new type of citizen—an individual who possesses confidence in his or her own potential, a person who is not intimidated by the prospect of actively pursuing a career after the age of 45, and an individual who comprehends that technology can produce an easier world but that only mankind can produce a better one.

15. Which of the following is an unstated assumption made by the author of this passage?

    A. Technology is the unrecognized key to a better future.
    B. Present citizens are intimidated by the prospect of ending their careers in middle age.
    C. Present citizens do not have limitless potentials.
    D. Many people in the future will pursue at least two careers in the course of a lifetime.
    E. An easier world is not necessarily a safer one.

16. The author of the passage would disagree with which of the following statements?

    A. The new type of citizen described in the passage does not presently exist.
    B. Future decades may bring about a change in the existing types of citizens.
    C. A new type of citizen will become necessary in future decades.
    D. Technology should be regarded as a source of a better life.
    E. Human potential is not limited, and we should be especially careful not to think of our potential as limited.

Read the passage below and answer the three questions that follow.

If we must have evaluation, at least do it without grades. Grades are not good indicators of intellectual ability; we must abolish them. Then we will have students who are motivated by factors such as interest, factors more important than a letter on a transcript. And the abolition of grades will encourage us to concentrate less on evaluation and more on instruction.

17. In order to agree with this author's argument, one must presume that

    A. wherever grades exist, instruction is poor.
    B. there are indicators of intellectual ability that are better than grades.
    C. graded students are not good students.
    D. intellectual ability can be measured only in a school situation.
    E. grades are the remaining hindrance to effective education.

18. A reader of this passage might conclude that the author feels that graded students are not motivated by

    A. the prospect of a high grade-point average.
    B. interest in the subject matter of their course.
    C. the evaluation criteria established by their instructors.
    D. a thoroughly prepared instructor.
    E. the practicality of academic disciplines.

19. This passage is most probably directed at which of the following audiences?

    A. politicians
    B. parents
    C. students
    D. teachers
    E. civic leaders

Read the passage below and answer the three questions that follow.

We should spend more time enjoying life than preparing for its challenges, but sometimes we don't. For example, toward the end of every semester, all students at the university are tired and irritable because they have spent long nights preparing for final exams. Consequently, they rarely look back on college as a time spent enjoying good fellowship and extracurricular activities.

20. To agree with this author, you must accept which of the following implications of his or her argument?

    A. It is only worthwhile to prepare for enjoyment.
    B. School examinations do not require preparation.
    C. Preparation is inappropriate only toward the end of the semester.
    D. The result of preparation for exams is fatigue.
    E. College students study too much.

21. According to this writer, the most memorable characteristic of college life should be

    A. social interaction.
    B. academic fastidiousness.
    C. the value of sleep.
    D. more efficient exam preparation.
    E. a pleasant attitude.

22. The author might have strengthened the argument without abandoning it by

    A. changing *all* to *some*.
    B. advancing arguments in favor of studying all night.
    C. acknowledging that being irritable is not necessarily related to fatigue.
    D. choosing a different example to illustrate the initial point.
    E. focusing the argument more explicitly on a particular audience.

Read the passage below and answer the question that follows.

When asked by his students to comment on the value of steroids for increasing muscle size, the physical education teacher said, "Steroids can be very dangerous. Many bodybuilders use them for a short period before a contest. However, the long-term use of steroids might possibly cause severe damage in body organs, including the reproductive system, while it helps to build a muscular body."

23. In this statement, the teacher is

    A. categorically against the use of steroids.
    B. an advocate of steroids but not of reproduction.
    C. recommending the short-term use of steroids.
    D. trying not to condemn steroids.
    E. preferring muscle definition to muscle size.

Read the passage below and answer the five questions that follow.

Creative writing may serve many purposes for the writer. Above all, it is a means of self-expression. It is the individual's way of saying, "These are my thoughts and they are uniquely experienced by me." But creative writing can also serve as a safety valve for dormant tensions. This implies that a period of time has evolved in which the child gave an idea some deep thought and that the message on paper is revealing of this deep, inner thought. Finally, a worthwhile by-product of creative writing is the stimulus it gives students to do further reading and experimentation in their areas of interest. A child may be an ardent reader of good literature in order to satisfy an appetite whetted by a creative writing endeavor.

GO ON TO THE NEXT PAGE

24. The primary purpose of the author of this passage is

   A. to call attention to a widespread lack of self-expression.
   B. to address the increasing anxiety that plagues many individuals.
   C. to stress the value of good literature, both amateur and professional.
   D. to encourage the reader to try some creative writing.
   E. to discuss some positive purposes and effects of creative writing.

25. The content of the passage indicates that the passage would be least likely to appear in which of the following?

   A. *Journal of English Teaching Techniques*
   B. *Psychology Today*
   C. *Journal of Technical Writing*
   D. *Teaching English Today*
   E. *The Creative Writer*

26. According to the passage, creative writing can help release dormant tensions because

   A. the writer will usually write something autobiographical.
   B. understanding literature means understanding the tensions of the characters.
   C. creative writing can express what the writer has long held within.
   D. tensions are a by-product of writer's block.
   E. self-expression is never tense.

27. All of the following are probably important to the ability to write creatively *except*

   A. deep thought.
   B. time to think and ponder.
   C. spelling.
   D. reading.
   E. good literature.

28. According to the passage, creative writing is most of all a

   A. stimulus for further reading.
   B. release valve for dormant tensions.
   C. way of expressing one's feelings and thoughts.
   D. chance to let off steam.
   E. by-product of reading.

Read the passage below and answer the six questions that follow.

Throughout human history, predictions of future events have found receptive audiences: during the thirteenth century, the English scientist Roger Bacon discussed the development of such things as optical instruments and motor boats; in the fifteenth century, Leonardo da Vinci wrote about tanks and helicopters; in the nineteenth century, Jules Verne described trips to the moon. Mankind has always been interested in where they are going. Since humanity's continued existence is dependent upon making intelligent decisions about the future, such fascination has taken on a very practical dimension. Along with the changes in social mores and attitudes, greater numbers of people are demanding a role in planning the future. The social studies curriculum must provide students with an understanding of how significant future challenges will be with regard to our national survival, social problems, religion, marriage, and family life, and in our political processes.

It is vital that social studies teachers immerse themselves in the new field of futuristics—the study of future prospects and possibilities affecting the human condition. Futuristics, as an academic area, is already being taught at many major universities for the purpose of encouraging students to achieve an awareness that they can contribute to the development of a much better national and global society than they ever dreamed of. The perspective of futurism is very important for today's students, since they know they can do nothing about the past.

29. Which of the following is the intended audience for the passage?

   A. Students planning which courses to take in high school.
   B. Teachers considering changing or enriching the curriculum.
   C. Historians interested in the ways that the past reflects the future.
   D. Politicians drafting future legislation that addresses present social problems.
   E. Parents concerned about what their children should be learning.

30. In order to show that "humans have always been interested in where they are going," the author provides which of the following types of facts?

   A. Unfounded
   B. Extraterrestrial
   C. Political
   D. Historical
   E. Scientific

31. Which of the following is an assumption of the passage but is not explicitly stated?

   A. Futuristic studies should take precedence over all other school studies.
   B. Today's students know little about the past and less about the future.
   C. Many social studies curriculums do not adequately acknowledge the importance of futurism.
   D. Some figures in the past have been the equivalent of modern fortune-tellers.
   E. Social studies gives little thought to the future.

32. In the passage, the intended meaning of global society is which of the following?

   A. A society well aware of the contributions of Bacon, da Vinci, and Verne.
   B. A society whose students have had courses in international relations.
   C. A society able to communicate with other societies around the globe.
   D. A society including the globes of other solar systems.
   E. A society including all the nations of earth.

33. Which of the following statements, if true, would most weaken the author's argument?

   A. Figures other than Bacon, da Vinci, and Verne might have been mentioned as well.
   B. Apart from Bacon, da Vinci, and Verne, many others who have tried to "see into" the future have voiced prospects and possibilities that did not come true.
   C. Those major universities not offering courses in futuristics are considering them.
   D. Futuristics has been the nonacademic interest of great numbers of people for many centuries.
   E. Futuristic predictions are the stock-in-trade of many sincere politicians trying to urge the passage of significant legislation.

34. The author of this passage would most likely be

   A. a historian.
   B. a traditionalist.
   C. a scientist.
   D. an educator.
   E. a pacifist.

Read the passage below and answer the five questions that follow.

Possibly everyone at some point has been in a classroom where he or she didn't dare express an idea for fear that it would be chopped off. And if it was expressed, it was chopped off and no further ideas came forth. Perhaps everyone at some time has been in a student group when a participant started to express an insight but was nipped in the bud by a teacher who corrected the student's usage. Perhaps some have been in a classroom where a child was groping for just the right way to express a thought only to have the teacher or another child supply the words. And some have wondered why a certain child was so talkative at age five and so reticent at sixteen.

35. The author implies which of the following in the passage?

   A. Wondering about human inhibitions will do little to solve the problem.
   B. Only certain children are either uninhibited at age five or inhibited at age sixteen.
   C. Sixteen-year-olds should spend more time in the classroom with five-year-olds.
   D. Attending school may cause children to become inhibited.
   E. Inhibitions go along with maturity.

36. Which of the following terms is an appropriate substitute for chopped off?

   A. put out
   B. removed
   C. severely criticized
   D. misunderstood
   E. cut back

GO ON TO THE NEXT PAGE

37. Which of the following techniques is the author using to make the point that classroom situations can be very undesirable?

   A. An appeal to the personal experiences of the readers
   B. Disguised references to recent educational theory
   C. Unsubstantiated and illogical anecdotes
   D. A story
   E. References to his or her own experiences as a teacher

38. The author's attitude may be described as being

   A. supportive.
   B. critical.
   C. skeptical.
   D. favorable.
   E. affected.

39. The author would probably most strongly agree with which of the following statements?

   A. Students should think carefully before expressing ideas in class.
   B. Teachers should be critical of students' expressions.
   C. Talkative students should be tactfully silenced.
   D. Teachers should be careful not to inhibit students' expressions.
   E. Teachers should assist students in completing their expressions.

Read the passage below and answer the six questions that follow.

Learning disabilities are among the most frequently occurring of all childhood disorders. It is estimated that eight million children in the United States can be classified as learning disabled, and many more function ineffectually *throughout their entire lives* due to learning disabilities. The Department of Health, Education, and Welfare's National Advisory Committee on Dyslexia and Related Reading Disorders estimates that 15 percent of children in public schools experience difficulty in learning to read. The majority of children identified as being learning disabled are so diagnosed because of difficulties in mastering the process of reading.

It is apparent that reading requires a number of intact auditory processing skills. All levels of auditory processing also require an intact sensorimotor system. In language acquisition, the child must be able to receive acoustical messages that make up the individual language system being acquired. In addition to requiring an adequate auditory mechanism, auditory processing involves a complex series of behaviors, including but not limited to the ability to focus attention on the content and the source of the message; the ability to detect and identify the selected message; the ability to transmit and conduct the message to the brain for analysis; the ability to store and retain the message by sorting out the appropriate perceptual or cognitive level; and the ability to retrieve and restore the message.

40. According to the preceding passage, the number of people who function ineffectually throughout their entire lives because of learning disabilities

   A. can never be estimated.
   B. has never been estimated.
   C. has been estimated at less than eight million.
   D. has been estimated at just over eight million.
   E. has been estimated at much greater than eight million.

41. The content indicates that the passage would be most likely to appear in which of the following?

   A. An article about successful classroom techniques for teaching reading
   B. A book on the history of linguistic research in the United States
   C. A budget report by the Department of Education
   D. A book on auditory processing and learning disabilities
   E. A technical manual for practicing audiologists

42. The author of the passage would agree with which of the following statements?

   A. Auditory processing may be either simple or complex.
   B. Those children who have difficulty reading probably have an adequately functioning sensorimotor system.
   C. For fewer than eight million individuals, learning disabilities are a lifelong impairment.
   D. Poor reading may be a learning disability related to auditory processing skills.
   E. Eight million individuals in the United States experience difficulty in learning to read.

43. The primary purpose of the passage is to

   A. explain the process of language control.
   B. assure readers that a great number of individuals are not learning disabled.
   C. discuss relationships among learning disability, reading difficulty, and the sensorimotor system.
   D. relate the history of auditory processing.
   E. explain the criteria used to decide whether or not a child can spell.

44. If the final statement of the passage is true, which of the following must also be true?

   A. Reading difficulty may not have a simple cause.
   B. Five and only five separate abilities comprise auditory processing.
   C. An intact sensorimotor system has five components.
   D. Children may acquire different auditory processing skills at different ages.
   E. More research into auditory processing remains to be done.

45. Which of the following conclusions is implied by the first sentence in the passage?

   A. Childhood disorders are the most serious type of human psychological or physiological disorder.
   B. Childhood disorders other than learning disabilities also exist.
   C. Learning disabilities are the only childhood disorders that occur with any frequency.
   D. The only handicapping childhood disorders are those that occur with some frequency.
   E. Learning disabilities are almost always reading disabilities.

Read the passage below and answer the question that follows.

In recent years, teachers in elementary schools have received modest pay raises regularly, but considering economic trends, their salaries have decreased 23 percent.

46. Which of the following best expresses the point of the preceding statement?

   A. Being a teacher means living at or below the poverty line.
   B. Many teachers must hold second jobs.
   C. The effects of the economy can negate the benefits of a pay raise.
   D. Teachers' salaries are not adequate.
   E. Those who teach in elementary schools can live on less than those who teach in high schools.

Read the passage below and answer the question that follows.

For some preschool children, television cartoons can stimulate the childrens' creative drawings if their parents provide the graphic materials and indispensable encouragement.

47. The author of the statement would probably agree with which of the following?

   A. A decision to ban television cartoons as useless is not wise.
   B. Television cartoons are the preschooler's primary source of creative inspiration.
   C. For older children, cartoons have no educational value.
   D. Cartoons are a viable substitute for parents when they are not available.
   E. Cartoons accelerate a young child's learning of new words.

GO ON TO THE NEXT PAGE

Read the passage below and answer the question that follows.

It is clear that the first four or five years of a child's life are the period of most rapid change in physical and mental characteristics and greatest susceptibility to environmental influences. Attitudes are formed, values are learned, habits are developed, and innate abilities are fostered or retarded by conditions the child encounters during these early years.

48. Which of the following, if true, would most weaken the author's argument?

   A. Many young children possess attitudes and habits similar to those of their peers.
   B. There are significant, basic differences between a five-year-old from Samoa and one from New York.
   C. "Midlife crisis" provokes many adults to change their entire personality structures within only a few months.
   D. The environment continues to influence personal characteristics in adolescents.
   E. Environmental influences can have either positive or negative effects on human development.

Read the passage below and answer the two questions that follow.

Integrating sports into the elementary curriculum can have a far more beneficial effect than merely allowing students to "blow off steam" or providing an opportunity for physical exercise. The inclusion of a physical rather than a mental skill will allow those students less adept in the classroom to ____49____ their physical proficiencies to their peers and to their teachers, thus allowing ego-enhancing experiences which they might not otherwise get sitting at their desks. The teachers' overall knowledge of their students will also be enhanced, and thus they will have more to draw upon when relating to their students and the students' ____50____.

49. The word that best completes ____49____ is

   A. boast.
   B. display.
   C. give.
   D. relate.
   E. explain.

50. The word that best completes ____50____ is

   A. grades.
   B. sports.
   C. work.
   D. exercise.
   E. games.

Section II: Mathematics

50 Questions

Directions: In the following questions or incomplete statements, select the one *best* answer or completion of the five choices given. Make sure that you mark your answers for this section on the Mathematics section of the answer sheet.

1. What is the value of 342,499 rounded to the nearest thousand?

   A. 342,000
   B. 342,400
   C. 342,500
   D. 343,000
   E. 343,400

2. Of the following, which is the largest in value?

   A. .09
   B. $\frac{1}{11}$
   C. $8\frac{1}{2}\%$
   D. .084
   E. $\frac{1}{13}$

Use the table given below to answer the question that follows.

Ball Park Snacks Menu	
Soda	$1.00
Popcorn	$ .60
Licorice	$ .35

3. The ball team purchased the following: 3-dozen sodas, 23 bags of popcorn, and 27 pieces of licorice. Which answer represents this purchase?

   A. 36($1.00) + 23($.35) + 27($.60)
   B. 3($1.00) + 23($.35) + 27($.60)
   C. (36 + 23 + 27) + ($1.00 + $.35 + $.60)
   D. 36($1.00) + 27($.35) + 23($.60)
   E. (3 × 12) + $1.00 + 23($.60) + 27($.35)

4. The track team walked the following distances in April: $4\frac{3}{4}$ miles, $5\frac{1}{2}$ miles, 6 miles, and $5\frac{3}{4}$ miles. What was the average distance they walked in miles?

   A. $4\frac{1}{2}$
   B. 5
   C. $5\frac{1}{2}$
   D. 6
   E. 22

5. A square 4 inches on a side is cut up into smaller squares 1 inch on a side. What is the maximum number of squares that can be formed?

   A. 4
   B. 8
   C. 16
   D. 36
   E. 64

Use the table below to answer the following question.

Monday	Tuesday	Wednesday	Thursday	Friday
10°	13°	−5°	−12°	22°

6. Students at Cleveland High School recorded outdoor temperatures at 2:00 p.m. for five afternoons. What is the difference between the week's highest and lowest temperatures?

   A. −34
   B. −17
   C. −7
   D. 17
   E. 34

7. The length of a rectangle is 6*l* and the width is 4*w*. Which of the following is an expression that represents the perimeter of the rectangle?

   A. 24*lw*
   B. 10*lw*
   C. 6*l* + 4*w*
   D. 20*lw*
   E. 12*l* + 8*w*

GO ON TO THE NEXT PAGE

Use the information below to answer the question that follows.

> Amir was given the expression $9x^2 + 3y - 5$ to evaluate. Although he was given the values of −3 for x and −2 for y, he was unsure of his method for evaluating.

8. If Amir evaluated the expression correctly, what value should he have?

    A. −92
    B. −65
    C. 70
    D. 80
    E. 82

Use the figure below to answer the question that follows.

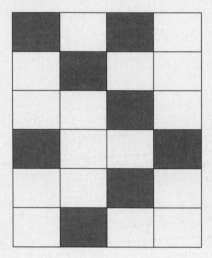

9. Which answer best represents the shaded part of the preceding box?

    A. $\frac{1}{8}$

    B. $\frac{1}{4}$

    C. $\frac{1}{3}$

    D. $\frac{2}{5}$

    E. $\frac{2}{3}$

10. If x is between 0 and 1, which of the following statements is (are) true?

    I. $x^2 > 1$
    II. $x^2 > 0$
    III. $x^2 > x$

    A. I only
    B. II only
    C. III only
    D. I and II only
    E. II and III only

11. Armand is making a salad from the following ingredients: three different kinds of lettuce, three different kinds of tomatoes, and four different kinds of beans. If he wants to use only one kind of lettuce, one kind of tomato, and one kind of bean, how many different combinations of salads can he possibly make?

    A. 3
    B. 6
    C. 10
    D. 15
    E. 36

Read the information below and then answer the question that follows.

> Sandra's weekly wage is $30 less than three times David's weekly wage.
>
> If Sandra's weekly wage is $270, what is David's weekly wage?

12. If t represents David's weekly wage, which of the following equations can be used to solve the preceding problem?

    A. $\$270 = 3t - 30$
    B. $\$270 - 30 = 3t$
    C. $3t - t - 30 = \$270$
    D. $t - \$30 = 3(\$270)$
    E. $3t + t = \$270$

13. If 3 divided by a number y is 18, then what is the value of the number y plus 2?

   A. $2\frac{1}{6}$

   B. $4\frac{1}{6}$

   C. $6\frac{1}{6}$

   D. $8\frac{1}{6}$

   E. $12\frac{1}{6}$

14. An art class has 30 students. Each student needs a piece of ribbon 2 feet, 6 inches in length. What is the total length of ribbon needed?

   A.   780 feet, 6 inches
   B.   240 feet
   C.   78 feet, 6 inches
   D.   78 feet
   E.   75 feet

15. A flat-screen television is marked down 20% to $320. Which of the following equations could be used to determine its original price, P?

   A. $320 - 0.20 = P$
   B. $0.20P = \$320$
   C. $P = \$320 + 20$
   D. $0.80P + 0.20P = \$320$
   E. $0.80P = \$320$

16. Paul has a bag of gumballs. The bag contains 16 yellow, 13 purple, 9 green, and 6 orange gumballs. Paul randomly takes a purple gumball from the bag and chews it. What is the probability that the next gumball Paul takes from the bag will be purple or green?

   A. $\dfrac{9}{43}$

   B. $\dfrac{21}{44}$

   C. $\dfrac{21}{43}$

   D. $\dfrac{1}{2}$

   E. $\dfrac{22}{43}$

17. Which of the following questions can be answered on the basis of the following facts?

Kim can mow 8 lawns in one day. Last year, the average number of days Kim mowed each month was 20.

   A.   How many lawns did Kim mow in the first two weeks?
   B.   What is the average number of lawns Kim mowed last year?
   C.   How many lawns can Kim mow in 3 hours?
   D.   What is the maximum number of lawns Kim could have mowed this year?
   E.   What is the minimum number of days Kim mowed each month?

18. What percent of 60 is 15?

   A.   4%
   B.   15%
   C.   25%
   D.   40%
   E.   60%

19. Travis rides the bus from home to work each day. If his bus stops four times every mile to pick up passengers, how many stops does it make in 8 miles?

   A.   2
   B.   4
   C.   8
   D.   16
   E.   32

20. Ms. Thomas can correct 3 tests in 9 minutes. At this rate, how long will it take her to grade 30 tests?

   A.   27 minutes
   B.   54 minutes
   C.   1 hour, 27 minutes
   D.   1 hour, 30 minutes
   E.   2 hours, 30 minutes

GO ON TO THE NEXT PAGE

Use the diagram below to answer the following question.

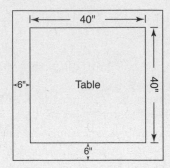

21. A table cloth covers a square table, with each side measuring 40 inches. If the table cloth is 6 inches wider than the table on each side, what is the perimeter of the table cloth?

    A. 104 inches
    B. 160 inches
    C. 184 inches
    D. 200 inches
    E. 208 inches

22. Ninety percent of 80 percent of 70 percent is approximately equal to which of the following?

    A. 25%
    B. 40%
    C. 50%
    D. 65%
    E. 80%

23. How many buses are needed to carry 98 children to the park if each bus holds 42 children?

    A. 2
    B. 2.14
    C. $2\frac{1}{3}$
    D. 3
    E. $3\frac{1}{2}$

24. If $5x$ is the average of two numbers and one of the numbers is 3, what is the other number?

    A. $5x$
    B. $10x$
    C. $10x - 7$
    D. $10x - 3$
    E. $10x + 7$

25. A school is going to build a new playground. State regulations require no more than 50 percent asphalt and no less than 20 percent grass for any school playground. If the school plans to build a playground of exactly 200 square feet, which of the following is acceptable?

    A. 50 square feet grass, 110 square feet asphalt, and the rest sand
    B. 30 square feet grass, 90 square feet asphalt, and the rest sand
    C. 20 square feet grass, 95 square feet asphalt, and the rest sand
    D. 50 square feet grass, 95 square feet asphalt, and the rest sand
    E. 45 square feet grass, 115 square feet asphalt, and the rest sand

26. If a store purchases several items for $1.80 per dozen and sells them at 3 for $.85, what is the store's profit on six dozen of these items?

    A. $ 4.20
    B. $ 5.70
    C. $ 9.60
    D. $10.60
    E. $20.40

Read the information below and then answer the question that follows.

Arnold takes 8 weekly tests in his history class, and his scores range from a low of 72% to a high of 94%.

27. From the preceding information, which of the following must be true regarding Arnold's average for all 8 tests?

    A. His average for all 8 tests is 83%.
    B. His average for all 8 tests is above 83%.
    C. His average for all 8 tests is lower than 83%.
    D. His average for all 8 tests is any score between 1% and 100%.
    E. His average for all 8 tests is between 72% and 94%.

28. Assume that inflation will increase the prices of everything at a rate of 5 percent a year over the next 10 years. In 3 years, what will be the price of a stereo that now costs $100? Round your answer to the nearest hundredth.

    A. $105
    B. $115
    C. $115.52
    D. $115.76
    E. $150

29. Using the formula $F° = \frac{9}{5}C° + 32°$, where F = Fahrenheit temperature and C = Celsius temperature, what is the temperature in Fahrenheit degrees when the temperature is 25° Celsius?

    A.   77°
    B.   57°
    C.   45°
    D.   25°
    E.   −7°

30. Daniel took a standardized math test. Use his test scores below to answer the following question.

Raw Score	Percentile	Stanine
55	82	8

    Which of the following is true regarding Daniel's test scores?

    A.   Daniel answered 55% of the questions correctly.
    B.   Forty-five percent of the test takers scored higher than Daniel.
    C.   Twenty-eight percent of the test takers scored lower than Daniel.
    D.   Daniel scored as high as or higher than 82% of the other test takers.
    E.   Daniel answered 82% of the questions correctly.

Read the information below and then answer the question that follows.

The PTA is making school banners that measure $3\frac{1}{2}$ square yards. PTA members purchase $49\frac{3}{5}$ yards of purple fabric and $7\frac{1}{2}$ yards of yellow fabric.

31. What is the total amount of fabric purchased?

    A. $60\frac{3}{5}$ yards

    B. $57\frac{1}{10}$ yards

    C. $56\frac{10}{11}$ yards

    D. $56\frac{1}{10}$ yards

    E. $42\frac{2}{3}$ yards

Use the information below to answer the question that follows.

Phil is taking a math quiz. One of the problems on his quiz requires him to add the fractions $\frac{2}{3}, \frac{1}{5},$ and $\frac{1}{6}$.

32. Which of the following methods should Phil use to answer this question most efficiently?

    A.   Use a common denominator of 90.
    B.   Use a common denominator of 15.
    C.   Use a common denominator of 30.
    D.   Use the "invert and multiply" technique.
    E.   Multiply the denominators.

33. What is the probability of rolling two dice that total 7?

    A. $\frac{1}{6}$

    B. $\frac{1}{4}$

    C. $\frac{11}{36}$

    D. $\frac{1}{3}$

    E. $\frac{1}{2}$

GO ON TO THE NEXT PAGE

Use the graph below to answer the two questions that follow.

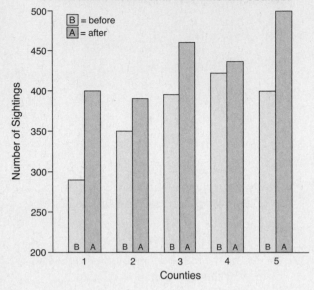

Number of Wild Bear Sightings Before and After Conservation Measures in Five Different Counties

$\boxed{B}$ = before
$\boxed{A}$ = after

Number of Sightings

Counties

34. According to the graph, which county had the most bear sightings before the conservation measures?

A. 1
B. 2
C. 3
D. 4
E. 5

35. To determine in which county the sightings increased by approximately 25 percent, one would

A. find the county that had 250 more sightings after the conservation measures.
B. find the county that had 25 more sightings after the conservation measures.
C. find the county in which the "B" bar is $\frac{1}{4}$ taller than the "A" bar.
D. find the county in which the number of sightings indicated by the "A" bar is 250 more than those indicated by the "B" bar.
E. find the county in which the number of sightings indicated by the "A" bar is $\frac{1}{4}$ more than those indicated by the "B" bar.

36. How long will it take a school bus averaging 40 miles per hour to reach its destination 10 miles away?

A. 15 minutes
B. 20 minutes
C. 30 minutes
D. 1 hour
E. 4 hours

37. The value 68 percent falls between which one of the following pairs of fractions?

A. $\frac{3}{8}$ and $\frac{2}{5}$

B. $\frac{3}{5}$ and $\frac{5}{6}$

C. $\frac{1}{2}$ and $\frac{2}{3}$

D. $\frac{7}{10}$ and $\frac{3}{4}$

E. $\frac{4}{5}$ and $\frac{9}{10}$

38. A commission of $6.80 is paid for each $50 of sales. How much did sales total if the commissions equaled $156.40?

A. $1,100
B. $1,150
C. $1,200
D. $1,250
E. $1,300

39. There are 36 students in a certain geometry class. If $\frac{2}{3}$ of the students are boys and $\frac{3}{4}$ of the boys are under 6 feet tall, how many boys in the class are under 6 feet tall?

A. 6
B. 12
C. 18
D. 24
E. 27

40. An astronaut weighing 207 pounds on Earth would weigh 182 pounds on Venus. The weight of the astronaut on Venus would be approximately what percent of his weight on Earth?

    A. 50%

    B. 60%

    C. 70%

    D. 80%

    E. 90%

Read the information below and then answer the question that follows.

Sylvia is given a worksheet by her tutor to practice dividing by fractions. The first question asks her to explain the operation of dividing some number by $\frac{2}{4}$.

41. Which of the following explanations should Sylvia give to properly explain the operation of division by fractions?

    A. Dividing some number by $\frac{2}{4}$ is the same as multiplying that number by $\frac{1}{2}$.

    B. Dividing some number by $\frac{2}{4}$ is the same as dividing that number by 2.

    C. Dividing some number by $\frac{2}{4}$ is the same as multiplying that number by 2.

    D. Dividing some number by $\frac{2}{4}$ is the same as multiplying that number by 2 and then dividing by 4.

    E. Some numbers cannot be divided by fractions.

42. At Marshall High School, 1 out of 4 seniors takes Physics. If there are 1,260 seniors, how many *do not* take Physics?

    A. 945

    B. 630

    C. 420

    D. 315

    E. 126

Use the chart and information given below to answer the question that follows.

Sequoia High School Enrollment	
Grade	**Total**
9th	267
10th	176
12th	139

As the school registrar types the enrollment roster, she notices that 11th grade has not been included. She also knows that the total enrollment for grades 9 through 12 is 688.

43. Based on the chart above and the given information, what is an accurate number of the enrolled 11th graders?

    A. 794

    B. 688

    C. 582

    D. 119

    E. 106

Use the information below to answer the question that follows.

Robert's four paychecks total $2,520, and the largest paycheck is $300 more than the average for the four paychecks and $600 more than the smallest paycheck.

44. Which of the following *cannot* be determined from the preceding information?

    A. The average of the four paychecks.

    B. The largest paycheck.

    C. The smallest paycheck.

    D. The sum of the largest and the smallest paychecks.

    E. The sum of the two largest paychecks.

GO ON TO THE NEXT PAGE

45. What number could be added to the following set of data so that the median and mode of the set are equal?

$$23, 14, 16, 19, 21$$

   A.   14
   B.   18
   C.   19
   D.   21
   E.   24

46. Judith has a purse full of coins totaling $9.15. She has at least one of every U.S. coin (dollar, half-dollar, quarter, dime, nickel, and penny). What is the largest number of quarters she can have in her purse?

   A.   25
   B.   27
   C.   28
   D.   29
   E.   30

47. Alice wants to send 400 wedding invitations. She can write about 16 per day. If she begins on January 1, when would she be expected to be finished?

   A.   January 25
   B.   February 18
   C.   March 30
   D.   April 15
   E.   May 1

48. Which of the following number phrases is *not* equivalent to 8×100?

   A. 4×200
   B. 16×50
   C. $(2 + 6) \times (25 + 75)$
   D. $(4 \times 50) + (4 \times 150)$
   E. $(2 \times 4) + (5 \times 20)$

Use the graph below to answer the two questions that follow.

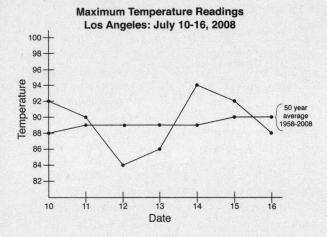

49. Of the seven days shown, on about what percent of the days did the maximum temperature exceed the average temperature?

   A.   3%
   B.   4%
   C.   43%
   D.   57%
   E.   93%

50. Between which two dates shown did the greatest increase in maximum temperature occur?

   A.   July 11–12
   B.   July 12–13
   C.   July 13–14
   D.   July 14–15
   E.   July 15–16

Section III: Writing

2 Essays

Directions: In this section, you plan and write two essays, one for each topic given. Read each topic carefully to make sure that you are properly addressing the issue or situation. *You must write on the specified topic. An essay on another topic will not be acceptable.*

Plan your time wisely. Each essay is weighted equally, so plan to spend the same amount of time on each one.

The two essay questions are designed to give you an opportunity to write clearly and effectively. Use specific examples whenever appropriate to aid in supporting your ideas. Keep in mind that the quality of your writing is much more important than the quantity.

Write each essay on the two sheets of lined paper provided. Your writing should be neat and legible. Because you have only a limited amount of space in which to write, please do *not* skip lines, do *not* write excessively large, and do *not* leave wide margins.

You may use the bottom of the topic page in the test booklet to organize and plan your essay before you begin writing.

GO ON TO THE NEXT PAGE

Topic 1

"High school is a period in life when, in addition to being given opportunities to learn, a person can master important social skills, make lifelong friends, and have carefree good times." Discuss the extent to which you agree or disagree with this opinion. Support your views with specific reasons and examples from your own experience and observations. Compare your response to the sample essays for this topic on pages 223-226.

GO ON TO THE NEXT PAGE

GO ON TO THE NEXT PAGE

GO ON TO THE NEXT PAGE

Topic 2

Some educators believe that the most important trait a teacher can have is self-acceptance. It allows the teacher to better relate to his or her students, to better deal with student problems, and to better provide a positive and constructive role model.

Present your arguments in agreement with this statement, or, if you disagree, present your viewpoints as to what you believe *is* the most important quality for a teacher to have.

GO ON TO THE NEXT PAGE

GO ON TO THE NEXT PAGE

Answer Key and Analysis for Practice Test 1

Answer Key for Practice Test 1

Section I: Reading

1. D	18. B	35. D
2. A	19. D	36. C
3. C	20. E	37. A
4. B	21. A	38. B
5. B	22. D	39. D
6. E	23. D	40. E
7. A	24. E	41. D
8. E	25. C	42. D
9. B	26. C	43. C
10. D	27. C	44. A
11. C	28. C	45. B
12. A	29. B	46. C
13. E	30. D	47. A
14. C	31. C	48. C
15. B	32. E	49. B
16. D	33. B	50. C
17. B	34. D	

Section II: Mathematics

1. A	18. C	35. E
2. B	19. E	36. A
3. D	20. D	37. B
4. C	21. E	38. B
5. C	22. C	39. C
6. E	23. D	40. E
7. E	24. D	41. C
8. C	25. D	42. A
9. C	26. C	43. E
10. B	27. E	44. E
11. E	28. D	45. C
12. A	29. A	46. D
13. A	30. D	47. A
14. E	31. B	48. E
15. E	32. C	49. D
16. C	33. A	50. C
17. B	34. D	

Scoring Your CBEST Practice Test 1

To score your CBEST Practice Test 1, total the number of correct responses for each section of the test separately. Do not subtract any points for questions attempted but missed, because there is no penalty for guessing. The score for each section is then scaled from 20 to 80. (About 70% right is a passing score.)

Analyzing Your Test Results

Use the charts on the following page to carefully analyze your results and spot your strengths and weaknesses. Complete the process of analyzing each subject area and each individual question for this Practice Test. Reexamine these results for trends in types of errors (repeated errors) or poor results in specific subject areas. This reexamination and analysis is of tremendous importance for effective test preparation.

Subject Area Analysis Sheet				
	Possible	**Completed**	**Right**	**Wrong**
Reading	50			
Mathematics	50			
TOTAL	100			

One of the most important parts of test preparation is analyzing *why* you missed a question so that you can reduce your number of mistakes. Now that you have taken Practice Test 1 and corrected your answers, carefully tally your mistakes by marking them in the proper column.

Tally Sheet for Questions Missed				
	Reason for Mistake			
	Total Missed	**Simple Mistake**	**Misread Problem**	**Lack of Knowledge**
Reading				
Mathematics				
TOTAL				

Reviewing the preceding data can help you determine *why* you are missing certain questions. Now that you have pinpointed the type of error you are most likely to make, when you take Practice Test 2, focus on avoiding those errors.

Essay Checklist

Use this checklist to evaluate your essays.

Diagnosis of Timed Writing Exercises		
A good essay:	**Essay 1**	**Essay 2**
. . . addresses the assignment		
■ stays well focused		
■ expresses a clear thesis statement on the topic		
. . . organizes points logically		
■ uses smooth transitions between paragraphs		
■ has coherent, unified paragraphs		
. . . develops ideas presented		
■ gives specific examples to support points		
■ anticipates and addresses opposing views		
. . . is grammatically sound (with only minor flaws)		
■ uses correct sentence structure		
■ uses correct punctuation		
■ uses standard written English		
. . . uses language skillfully		
■ uses a variety of sentence types		
■ uses a variety of words		
. . . is legible		
■ shows clear handwriting		
■ appears neat		

Answers and Complete Explanations for Practice Test 1

Section I: Reading

1. **D.** Information about subjective complements is listed under "complement, subjective, with linking verb, 188–190." The pages listed in Choice **A** address compound subjects; Choice **B** addresses complements (not subjective complements); Choice **C** addresses intransitive verb complements; Choice **E** addresses compound sentences.

2. **A.** The entry under "Comparison, theme based on, 54–57" is the best place to look for information about an essay that would compare the two planets. The pages listed in Choice **B** would give information only about conclusions in essays. Choices **C**, **D**, and **E** address grammatical information, not essay (theme) writing information.

3. **C.** The adjective *versatile* means accomplished in many areas, able to turn easily from one subject to another, many-sided. The word comes from the Latin verb *vertere,* to turn. This definition focuses on the multifaceted aspects of the paragraph's content—that Jackie Robinson achieved success in many areas. None of the other answer choices address this multitalented resourcefulness.

4. **B.** This is the only sentence that is consistent with the rest of the paragraph in both style and substance. The content in Choice **A** is irrelevant to the passage; additionally, you should reject **A** because it uses the first person ("I"), whereas the rest of the passage uses only the third person ("he"). Similarly, Choice **C** can be eliminated because of its use of the second person ("you"). Choice **D** can be eliminated because of its careless use of slang, "big deal," plus the fact that its information is off the topic of Jackie Robinson. Choice **E** can be eliminated because the language is far too pompous to fit the tone of the passage.

5. **B.** The passage moves forward in time, from Robinson's becoming a Major League player in 1947 to his life after baseball and his 1962 election to the Hall of Fame. The other four options are simply untrue; all of them misrepresent the true structure of the passage.

6. **E.** The first blank requires a transition indicating a contrast between the ancients and the "more modern." Of the five choices offered for this first transition, the only ones that are possible choices are **C**, "Meanwhile," and **E**, "However." On the other hand, the second transition should point to a similarity between the "more modern" and the "1990s." Thus, Choice **C** is eliminated because the second word "Consequently" does not fit well in the second space. Choice **E** is correct because "Similarly" does fit well.

7. **A.** The best of the five choices is "based on whim; capricious." The passage does not specifically suggest that modern man is lacking in judgment, Choice **B**. The definition in Choice **C**, "conveying a truth," actually contradicts the intended meaning of "arbitrary," as the passage continues with "has no special significance." The definition offered by Choice **D** is too strong for this answer. The passage does not imply that naming a date in time is totally useless; indeed, the last sentence states that names and dates were created to make "relationships easier to grasp." Finally, Choice **E** does not fit into the overall meaning of the passage; nothing alludes to "two meanings" of names.

8. **E.** The sentence in Choice **E** opens with the comparison "Like the names of the stars," which links the subject of the first paragraph (the arbitrary names people give to stars) with the useful terms called numbers. The point of the passage is that both are fictions created by humans, not eternal natural truths.

9. **B.** This author indicates that the starry constellations in Earth's skies are merely useful fictions; they are patterns created by humans that would make no sense if viewed from any other point in the universe, and that our names for them simply reflect the times in which they were created. Therefore, even if the author is an "expert" on stars, he is a skeptic overall, so it is NOT reasonable to conclude that he would "trust astrology." Rather, it is much more reasonable to infer that the author would tend to be skeptical of astrology, so Choice **B** is correct. There is no support in the passage for Choice **D**; nothing indicates whether the author approves or disapproves of comics and cartoons. Choice **C** contradicts the passage;

the author explicitly says that the millennium "has no special significance in the natural world." Finally, the claim made in Choice **E**, that people can have absolutely no influence on the events of the natural world, is not the point of this author, who merely indicates that some things, such as our dates or our names, have no effect upon nature.

10. **D.** In the Natural Sciences, the lowest percentage is in Physics; in the Social Sciences, the lowest is in Sociology; in the Humanities, the lowest is in French.

11. **C.** Choice **C** provides an accurate and comprehensive summary of the author's main point about social psychology. The ideas in choices **D** and **E**, on the other hand, address only subsidiary points. Choice **A** incorrectly focuses on the behavior of the scientist rather than the behavior of individuals, and Choice **B** does not even mention the main topic, social psychology.

12. **A.** In the closing sentence, this passage expresses approval of children talking in the classroom, thus implying that the "flip-flop" is a change from a past preference for quiet children in classrooms. In Choice **B**, the word "trivial" is simply incorrect. Choice **C** is incorrect because the passage never addresses the quality of an individual's education; rather, it deals with changes in educational philosophy. Choice **D** can be eliminated for two reasons: the passage does not indicate whether Strickland explicitly stated her opinions, and this point is irrelevant to the passage's intent anyway. The point in Choice **E**, that there are fewer quiet children now, cannot be ascertained from the information in the passage.

13. **E.** Choices **A, B,** and **D** are terms with a negative connotation that suggest *creative writing* is "underdeveloped" or "incomplete." Choice **C** is ambiguous and irrelevant. Only Choice **E** suggests the negative connotation of *precious,* which is the author's meaning in the passage.

14. **C.** Choices **A, B,** and **D** are incorrect because they either mention a secondary rather than primary point, or assign a purpose (for example, "to urge readers"); thus, they go beyond the scope of the passage. Choice **E** obviously contradicts the passage.

15. **B.** By stating that the new type of citizen will not be intimidated by ending careers, the author presumes that present citizens *are* intimidated. Choice **D** is incorrect because it states an implication rather than an assumption; remember that an assumption addresses what the author believes before writing, and an implication addresses what the reader can reasonably conclude after reading the passage. Choices **A, C,** and **E** all draw conclusions that are beyond the scope of the passage.

16. **D.** The final sentence of the passage expresses a somewhat skeptical, qualified view of the ultimate value of technology; the point in Choice **D** is too upbeat for this author. On the other hand, each of the other choices *is* consistent with the author's views about humanity.

17. **B.** To embrace the idea of abolishing grades, one must presume that there are, indeed, viable and more useful alternatives; none of the other choices correctly identifies a necessary condition for agreeing with the argument.

18. **B.** By stating that the abolition of grades will increase student interest in subject matter, the author implies that graded students are less interested in and motivated by the subject matter of their classes. Choice **A** contradicts the passage, which implies that graded students *are* motivated to attain a high grade-point average. The points in choices **C, D,** and **E** are not addressed in the passage.

19. **D.** The words "we will have students" indicate the author is a teacher who is talking to other teachers; this is also emphasized by the use of the word "us" in the third sentence.

20. **E.** Choice **D** restates one part of the author's argument, but even if the reader agrees that exams cause fatigue, this is not likely to lead to an acceptance of the overall argument, which stresses fun over study. To accept that argument, the reader has to believe that students study too much—Choice **E**.

21. **A.** The author stresses the value of "good fellowship and extracurricular activities," which are both aspects of the social scene. Choice **E** appears attractive, but "a pleasant attitude" is really not a memorable characteristic after college life; rather, it deals with one's approach while at college. Choices **B, C,** and **D** are not consistent with either the content or the tone of the passage.

22. **D.** By choosing to open with a focus on the negative aspects of studying, the author does not lead off with a strong and generally accepted example of enjoying life; a revision would strengthen the essay. On the other hand, choices **A** and **C** would weaken rather than strengthen the argument, and Choice **B** contradicts the argument. Choice **E** is too vague; by failing to identify a particular audience, one cannot tell what effect such a change might have.

23. **D.** The teacher is trying to "walk a fine line"; he does not advocate or recommend the use of steroids, but apparently he is not categorically against steroid use in all cases. Choice **D** offers a nuanced description of his statements, but choices **A**, **B**, **C**, and **E** can all be eliminated because they assign an absolute point of view that is not expressed.

24. **E.** This is the most comprehensive choice, describing the overall purpose of the passage rather than secondary purposes and implications. Choice **A** states the case too strongly; it does not really address the author's overall purpose, and a "widespread lack of self-expression" is never specifically mentioned. Addressing anxiety, Choice **B**, is not discussed in the passage. Choice **C** is irrelevant because the passage's purpose is not to place any value judgment on good literature. Encouraging creative writing, Choice **D**, may be something the author would like, but it is not his or her primary purpose in writing this passage.

25. **C.** A discussion of creative writing is relevant to English and psychology but not to technical writing.

26. **C.** The passage states that dormant tensions may be released through the revealing of a "deep, inner thought;" Choice **C** correctly restates this idea. Choice **A** is wrong because the passage does not imply that creative writing will necessarily be autobiographical. Choice **B** is an illogical response that does not follow from the question. Choices **D** and **E** are not supported by information in the passage.

27. **C.** Spelling is the one characteristic the author neither expresses nor implies as relevant to creative writing.

28. **C.** The passage explicitly states that creative writing is "above all . . . a means of self-expression." The ideas in all the other choices are included in the passage, but none of them encapsulates the most important idea.

29. **B.** The passage stresses ways of changing the social studies curriculum, thus designating its audience as those who can effect such changes—teachers.

30. **D.** "Humans have always been interested in where they are going" is preceded by a series of historical examples—that is, facts about occurrences in the past. While the examples in the passage may have affected the historical progress of science, they are not examples of scientific facts, Choice **E**.

31. **C.** By advocating the addition of futurism to the social studies curriculum, the author must assume that futurism is not adequately represented at this time. Without that assumption, the author would have no reason to make his argument. Choice **A** is too strong when it claims futuristic studies "should take precedence over *all* other school studies." The passage does not assume how much knowledge students have, which makes Choice **B** incorrect. Choice **D** may be an implication of the passage, but the argument does not require the underlying assumption that historical figures are equal to "modern fortunetellers." Choice **E** contradicts the passage, which states that some universities do teach futuristics.

32. **E.** By distinguishing global from national in the passage, the author suggests that a global society is larger and more inclusive than any national one could be. However, the passage does not go so far as to suggest that such a society necessarily includes outer space.

33. **B.** The author's argument would be weakened with the contradictory information of Choice **B**. Choices **C** and **D** would strengthen the argument for the value of futurism. Choices **A** and **E** are irrelevant to the strength or weakness of the argument.

34. **D.** The overall stress on changes in education indicates the author is an educator. Choice **A** may seem attractive because of the historical examples presented, but the passage's thrust is on the social studies curriculum, not history itself. Choice **B** is a contradiction, as futuristics is not a traditional subject. Choice **E** is unreasonable; the passage offers no support for the idea that the author would be a pacifist.

35. **D.** By relating a series of school situations in which students are discouraged from expressing themselves, the author implies that attending school may cause children to become inhibited. The other choices are not reasonable inferences that readers can draw from the passage.

36. **C.** The overall suggestion in the passage is that students are inhibited by being severely criticized or corrected; the meaning of "chopped off" given by Choice **C** is consistent with this overall view.

37. **A.** The author repeatedly addresses the reader with what are presumed to be common experiences, using phrases such as "Possibly everyone" and "Perhaps some." However, the passage offers no educational theory, so Choice **B** is incorrect. The anecdotes that the author provides, Choice **C**, are not illogical. The passage does not contain a story, Choice **D**, or any reference to the reader's *teaching* experience, Choice **E**.

38. **B.** The author cites a number of negative situations, leaving no question that he or she is critical of the practices described. The word choices in answers **A** and **D** have positive connotations, and thus they are contradicted by the author's tone. The word "skeptical," Choice **C**, means to doubt, which does not accurately specify the author's attitude. Choice **E**, "affected," means to influence or pretend, which is also inaccurate.

39. **D.** Choice **D** accurately restates the author's overall point. Choices **A**, **B**, and **C** contradict the argument of the passage. Choice **E** may contradict the implied argument; because the meaning of "assist" is not made clear, it may suggest the teacher should supply words for the student.

40. **E.** In the second sentence, the author states that approximately "eight million children in the United States can be classified as learning disabled." The third sentence adds that "many more function ineffectually throughout their entire lives." Choices **A**, **B**, and **C** are contradicted in the passage. Choice **D** is too mild because of the phrase "just over."

41. **D.** The passage explicitly addresses auditory processing and learning disabilities and is not so technical that it would be intended for practicing audiologists—Choice **E**. All the other choices are unreasonable.

42. **D.** The second paragraph generally supports this point. Choices **A** and **B** contradict the passage, and choices **C** and **E** go beyond the scope of the passage.

43. **C.** Choice **C** is the most comprehensive statement; other choices express secondary rather than primary purposes—as in Choice **B**—or are simply not in evidence in the passage.

44. **A.** The final statement of the passage explicitly stresses the complexity of auditory processing related to reading, but it does not restrict this complexity to only five causes. Therefore, choices **B** and **C** are incorrect. Choices **D** and **E** are irrelevant to the final statement.

45. **B.** The first sentence states that learning disabilities are among childhood disorders, thus implying that other disorders exist as well. Choice **A** is too strong to follow the first sentence of the passage. Choices **C**, **D**, and **E** have no backing in this sentence.

46. **C.** Choice **C** accurately expresses the primary point of the passage. Each one of the other choices goes beyond the scope of the passage.

47. **A.** Choices **C** and **E** make statements beyond the scope of the passage, Choice **D** contradicts the passage (the parents' contribution is said to be indispensable), and Choice **B** makes cartoons a primary source of inspiration. The author would agree that cartoons have some value and should not be banned.

48. **C.** Choice **C** weakens the emphasis on early childhood as a time of rapid change by saying that midlife may be a time of rapid change as well. The other choices are irrelevant; they do not weaken the argument.

49. **B.** "Display" best fits the meaning of the sentence.

50. **C.** "Work" best fits the meaning of the sentence. Choice **A** is incorrect because the passage does not deal with a teacher's ability to "relate" to a student's grades.

Section II: Mathematics

1. **A.** 500 or above rounds up to the next highest thousand. 499 or below rounds down to the previous thousand. Thus, 342,499 rounds down to 342,000. Note that choices **B**, **C**, and **E** could have been quickly eliminated, since they were rounded to nearest hundreds, not thousands.

2. **B.** Converting all the terms to decimals gives:

   A. .09, **B.** .0909, **C.** .085, **D.** .084, **E.** .077

   Note that Choice **E** can be eliminated quickly, since it is smaller than Choice **B**. Choices **C** and **D** are smaller than Choice **A** and also can be eliminated quickly.

3. **D.** Note: 3 dozen $= 3 \times 12 = 36$ sodas

   $36(\$1.00) + 27(\$.35) + 23(\$.60)$

   Sodas   Licorice Popcorn

4. **C.** Add all distances:

$$4\frac{3}{4} = 4\frac{3}{4}$$
$$5\frac{1}{2} = 5\frac{2}{4}$$
$$6 = 6$$
$$+5\frac{3}{4} = 5\frac{3}{4}$$
$$\overline{20\frac{8}{4} = 22}$$

   To find the <u>average</u>, divide the total (22) by 4 (the number of distances you added):

$$\frac{22}{1} \div \frac{4}{1} = \frac{22}{1} \times \frac{1}{4} = \frac{22}{4} = 5\frac{2}{4}$$

$$5\frac{2}{4} = 5\frac{1}{2}$$

5. **C.** The maximum number of squares, 1 inch by 1 inch, is 16.

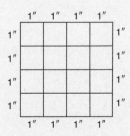

6. **E.** The highest temperature is 22°, and the lowest temperature is −12°.

   The difference is $22° - (-12°)$

   $= 22° + 12°$

   $= 34°$

7. **E.** The perimeter of a rectangle is equal to the sum of its sides. For this rectangle,

   perimeter $= 6l + 4w + 6l + 4w$

   $= 6l + 6l + 4w + 4w$

   $= 12l + 8w$

8. C. Plugging the values for x and y into the expression:

$$9x^2 + 3y - 5 =$$
$$9(-3)^2 + 3(-2) - 5 =$$
$$9(9) + (-6) - 5 =$$
$$81 - 6 - 5 = 70$$

9. C. $\dfrac{\text{Shaded}}{\text{Total}} = \dfrac{8}{24}$; Reducing gives $\dfrac{1}{3}$.

10. B. Since the square of a positive number is always a positive number, Choice **B** is the correct answer.

11. E. To find the number of different combinations possible, simply multiply the number of kinds of lettuce (3) by the number of kinds of tomatoes (3) by the number of kinds of beans (4).

$3 \times 3 \times 4 = 36$ different combinations

12. A. Change the sentence, word for word, into an equation.

$$\underbrace{\text{Sandra's weekly wage}}_{\$270} \; \underset{=}{\downarrow} \; \underbrace{\text{is}}\; \underbrace{\$30 \text{ less than}}_{-\$30} \; \underbrace{\text{three times}}\; \underbrace{\text{David's wage.}}_{3t}$$

13. A. Solving the equation:

$\dfrac{3}{y} = 18$ Cross-multiplying gives $18y = 3$

$\dfrac{3}{y} = \dfrac{18}{1}$

Divide by 18 to get $\dfrac{18y}{18} = \dfrac{3}{18}$, $y = \dfrac{3}{18}$

Therefore $y = \dfrac{1}{6}$

$$y + 2 = \frac{1}{6} + 2 = 2\frac{1}{6}$$

14. E. First change 2 feet, 6 inches to $2\frac{1}{2}$ feet. Next, since there are 30 students, multiply $2\frac{1}{2} \times 30$. If you change $2\frac{1}{2}$ to $\frac{5}{2}$, you can cancel as follows:

$$\frac{5}{\underset{1}{\cancel{2}}} \times \frac{\overset{15}{\cancel{30}}}{2} = 75 \text{ feet}$$

Note: Choices **A** and **B** are unrealistic and can be quickly eliminated.

15. E. If the flat-screen television is marked down 20%, then its current price is 80% of its original price. Thus, $0.80P = \$320$.

16. C. Use the definition of probability to determine the answer.

Probability of taking a green or purple gumball:

$$\frac{\text{\# of purple \& green gum balls}}{\text{total \# of gumballs}} = \frac{12 + 9}{16 + 12 + 9 + 6} = \frac{21}{43}$$

Remember to decrease the number of purple gumballs by one because Paul already took one purple gumball and chewed it.

17. B. Since Kim can mow eight lawns in one day, and averaged working 20 days each month, Kim mowed an average of 160 lawns each month. So the most lawns Kim could have mowed in a year is 12×160, or 1,920.

18. C. You can set the problem up as follows:

$\frac{15 \text{ Part}}{60 \text{ Whole}}$ reduce $\frac{15}{60}$ to $\frac{1}{4}$ then cancel $\frac{1}{\underset{1}{\cancel{4}}} \times \frac{\overset{25}{\cancel{100}}}{1} = 25\%$, or you can set up a proportion: $\frac{x}{100} = \frac{15}{60}$ and solve as follows:

$$\frac{x}{100} = \frac{15}{60}$$

$$\frac{x}{100} = \frac{1}{4}$$

$$4x = 100$$

$$\frac{4x}{4} = \frac{100}{4}$$

$$x = 25$$

19. E. Since the bus stops 4 times each mile, the total number of stops will equal the number of miles times 4. Thus, 8 miles multiplied by 4 stops each mile = 32 total stops.

20. D. One way to solve this problem is to set up a ratio: 3 tests is to 9 minutes as 30 tests is to how many minutes?

$$\frac{3 \text{ tests}}{9 \text{ min}} = \frac{30 \text{ tests}}{x}$$

Cross-multiplying gives:

$$3x = 9 \times 30$$

$$3x = 270$$

$$\frac{3x}{3} = \frac{270}{3}$$

$x = 90$ minutes or 1 hour, 30 minutes

Another method is to realize that 30 tests is exactly 10 times 3 tests. Therefore, the time it takes to correct 30 tests is exactly 10 times 9 minutes. Thus $10 \times 9 = 90$ minutes = 1 hour, 30 minutes

21. E. The perimeter is the sum of the lengths of the four sides of the tablecloth.

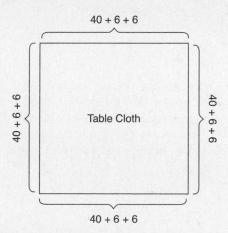

$$P = (40 + 6 + 6) + (40 + 6 + 6) + (40 + 6 + 6) + (40 + 6 + 6)$$

$$P = 52 \times 4 = 208 \text{ inches}$$

22. C. The word *of* means *multiply*. Thus, 90% of 80% of 70% is $(0.90)(0.80)(0.70) = 0.504$, or approximately 50%.

23. D. Since each bus carries a maximum of 42 children, three buses can carry all 98 children. Remember, a fractional bus (for instance, $\frac{1}{3}$ bus) is not a logical answer.

24. **D.** If two numbers average to $5x$, the sum of the two numbers must be $10x$, since $10x$ divided by the two numbers gives $5x$ for an average. Therefore,

> one number + other number = $10x$

$$3 + ? = 10x$$

Subtract 3 from both sides.

$$? = 10x - 3$$

Therefore, the other number is $10x - 3$.

25. **D.** The state requires no more than 50% asphalt. So 50% of 200 square feet is 100 square feet of asphalt *maximum*. Notice that this maximum limit eliminates choices **A** and **E**. The other requirement is no less than 20% grass. So 20% of 200 is 40 square feet of grass as a *minimum*. This eliminates choices **B** and **C**. Only Choice **D** provides no more than 50% asphalt and no less than 20% grass.

26. **C.** The selling price for a dozen at three for $0.85 is $3 \times 4 = 12$ = one dozen = $\$0.85 \times 4 = \$3.40$. Hence, six dozen will yield $\$3.40 \times 6 = \$20.40$. The cost for six dozen at $1.80 per dozen is $\$1.80 \times 6 = \$10.80$. Hence, the profit on six dozen of these items will be $20.40 - $10.80, or $9.60.

27. **E.** Since his scores were all between 72% and 94%, Arnold's average for the eight tests must fall between the highest and lowest scores. The average for all eight tests, however, does not necessarily have to be 83%, the average of only the highest and lowest scores.

28. **D.** Price today = $100

In 1 year = $100 + 5% of 100 = $105

In 2 years = $105 + 5% of 105 = $110.25

In 3 years = $110.25 + 5% of 110.25 = $115.7625

Round to nearest hundredth = $115.76

29. **A.** To change Celsius degrees to Fahrenheit degrees, simply plug into the formula and solve:

$$F° = \frac{9}{5}C + 32°$$
$$F° = \frac{9}{5}(25°) + 32°$$
$$F° = 45° + 32°$$
$$F° = 77°$$

30. **D.** Only Choice **D** uses the correct meaning of *percentile*. Choice **A** is incorrect because a score of 55% incorrectly assumes that there were a total of 100 questions. Choice **B** is incorrect because 18%, not 45% (use percentile), did better than Daniel. Choice **C** is incorrect because 82% (again, use percentile) did worse than Daniel. Choice **E** is incorrect because we don't know the percentage of correctly answered questions. Choice **D** is correct; use percentile to compare Daniel's score to that of other test takers.

31. **B.** To find the answer, add $49\frac{3}{5}$ and $7\frac{1}{2}$.

$$49\frac{3}{5} = 49\frac{6}{10}$$
$$+7\frac{1}{2} = 7\frac{5}{10}$$
$$\overline{56\frac{11}{10} = 57\frac{1}{10}}$$

The total amount of fabric purchased was $57\frac{1}{10}$ yards.

Note: The $3\frac{1}{2}$ square yards given in the original information is not needed to find the answer.

32. **C.** To solve an addition problem containing fractions with different denominators, a common denominator must be found. Both 90 (Choice **A**) and 30 (Choice **C**) are common denominators, but only 30 is the *lowest* common denominator. Using 30 for the denominator eliminates the necessity of reducing your final answer and also minimizes the size of the numbers in your computations.

33. **A.** There are 36 possible combinations of two dice. Of these 36 combinations, only 6 combinations equal 7 (1, 6; 2, 5; 3, 4; 4, 3; 5, 2; 6, 1). Thus, 6 out of 36 equals $\frac{6}{36}$, or $\frac{1}{6}$.

34. **D.** According to the graph, the tallest "B" (before) bar is county 4.

35. **E.** To determine a 25% increase, find the county in which the increase in the number of sightings equals $\frac{1}{4}$ of the original number of sightings.

$$\text{percentage change} = \frac{\text{increase or change}}{\text{original number}}$$

$$25\% \left(\text{or } \frac{1}{4}\right) = \frac{A - B}{B}$$

Note that merely approximating the size of the bars does not work because the bars do not begin at 0 (they begin at 200).

36. **A.** Problems of distance, speed, and time can be solved using $d = rt$, where d is distance; r is rate, or speed; and t is time. So

$d = rt$

10 miles = 40 miles per hour (t)

$t = \frac{10}{40}$. Thus, $t = \frac{1}{4}$ hour, or 15 minutes

37. **B.** The process of elimination will help you find the correct answer. Note that the bigger fraction in Choice **A** is only $\frac{2}{5}$, or 40%. Thus, Choice **A** is incorrect. In Choice **C**, $\frac{1}{2}$ is 50% and $\frac{2}{3}$ is $66\frac{2}{3}$%. Thus, Choice **C** is incorrect. In Choice **D**, $\frac{7}{10}$ is 70% and $\frac{3}{4}$ is 75%. Thus, Choice **D** is incorrect. And Choice **E** is between 80% and 90%. Choice **B** is correct: $\frac{3}{5}$ is 60%, and $\frac{5}{6}$ is $83\frac{1}{3}$%. Thus, 68% lies between them.

38. **B.** Dividing the amount of commission by $6.80 will give the number of $50 sales:

$$\frac{\$156.40}{\$6.80} = 23$$

Thus, $23 \times \$50 = \$1,150$.

39. **C.** Since $\frac{2}{3}$ of the students are boys, there are $\frac{2}{3}(36) = 24$ boys in the class. Out of the 24 boys in the class, $\frac{3}{4}$ are under 6 feet tall, or $\frac{3}{4}(24) = 18$ boys under 6 feet tall.

40. **E.** $\dfrac{\text{weight on Venus}}{\text{weight on Earth}} = \dfrac{182}{207} \approx 88\%$

or approximately 90%

41. **C.** Dividing by a fraction is the same as multiplying by the reciprocal of the fraction (the fraction inverted, or turned upside-down). This procedure is used in division of fraction problems; the second fraction is inverted and then multiplied. For instance,

$$\frac{3}{4} \div \frac{2}{4} = \frac{3}{4} \times \frac{4}{2} = \frac{3}{4} \times \frac{2}{1} = \frac{6}{4} = \frac{3}{2} = 1\frac{1}{2}$$

Therefore, dividing by $\frac{2}{4}$ is the same as multiplying by $\frac{4}{2}$, or multiplying by 2.

42. A. Since $\frac{1}{4}$ of the seniors take Physics, $\frac{3}{4}$ of the seniors do not take Physics.

Now multiply $\frac{3}{4}$ by the total number of seniors (you may want to do some canceling):

$$\frac{3}{\underset{1}{\cancel{4}}} \times \frac{\overset{315}{\cancel{1260}}}{1} = 945$$

43. E. To find the answer, first add up the figures given for 9th, 10th, and 12th grades.

$$
\begin{array}{ll}
\text{9th} & 267 \\
\text{10th} & 176 \\
\text{12th} & \underline{139} \\
& 582
\end{array}
$$

Next, subtract this number (582) from the *total* enrollment.

$$
\begin{array}{r}
688 \\
-582 \\
\hline
106
\end{array} = \text{11th grade enrollment}
$$

44. E. Since Robert's four paychecks total $2,520, the average of the four paychecks is $630. If the largest is $300 more than the average, the largest paycheck is $930, and if the largest is $600 more than the smallest, the smallest paycheck must be $330. However, you cannot determine the second-largest paycheck.

45. C. In order to find the median of a set of data, first list the numbers from least to greatest.

14, 16, 19, 21, 23

Before adding any number, we can see that 19 is the median (the middle number). If we add 19 to the set, it still remains the middle number. Also by adding 19, it now becomes the mode (the most occurring number) because it occurs twice.

46. D. First add the value of one of each coin:

$1.00 + $0.50 + $0.25 + $0.10 + $0.05 + $0.01 = $1.91

That leaves $9.15 – $1.91, or $7.24, for the rest of the quarters:

$$\frac{\$7.24}{0.25} = 28\frac{24}{25}, \text{ or 28 additional quarters}$$

Remember that you already counted one quarter when you added each circled coin above. Now, add the 28 additional quarters to the 1 original quarter. Thus, 29 is the largest number of quarters she can have.

47. A. You want to find how many groups of 16 it takes to make 400, so divide 16 into 400.

$$
\begin{array}{r}
25 \\
16\overline{)400} \\
\underline{32} \\
80 \\
\underline{80} \\
0
\end{array}
$$

48. E. Choice E is not equivalent to 800, since $(2 \times 4) + (5 \times 20) = (8) + (100) = 108$.

49. D. There were four days (July 10, 11, 14, and 15) on which the maximum temperature exceeded the average; thus, $\frac{4}{7}$ is approximately 57%.

50. C. The maximum temperature rose from 86° to 94° from July 13 to July 14. This was the greatest increase.

Section III: Writing

To help you evaluate your essay writing skills, listed below are examples of three different written responses for essay topic 1 (there are no examples for topic 2). Compare your essay to these three examples of a well-written essay, an average essay, and a poorly written essay. Use the checklist (p. 212) to evaluate your essays, and to help you take a closer look and understand your scoring range. Topic prompt can be found on page 204.

Essay 1: A Well-Written Essay

When I entered high school in a suburb of San Francisco, my parents told me I could expect to have the "time of my life." My father emphasized that I would make the best friends I would ever have and my mother told me that, in addition to taking aim at a future career, I would have good old-fashioned fun, with football games, proms, and parties. To some extent, they were right. I worked on the school newspaper and had a good time with the other staff members, some of who are still among my closest friends. I loved cheering at the football games and choosing a dress for my senior prom.

But the idea that high school presents "carefree good times" is, in my opinion, out of date or just too simple. With the pressure to get into a good college, I took advanced classes in several subjects and had to compete with other college-bound students, which meant that many weekends I was bent over my books or computer, feeling anything but "carefree." I took subjects I didn't like rather than ones I did (calculus rather than drama, for example) because "they would look good on my transcript." I think that in todays world, the focus on getting into a good university trumps your chances of hanging out after classes at the local pizzeria.

In addition, some of the social skills I mastered were problematic. For example, I learned how to turn down offers of alcohol and pills and yet maintain a friendly relationship with the classmate who offered them at least most of the time. Sometimes I was branded a "geek" and had to withstand bullying. And, at least twice, I had to convince suicidal friends to seek the help of a counselor. I certainly didn't feel "carefree."

To blame todays world for complicating high school life, however, is not entirely fair. I don't think that period of life has ever been as idyllic as nostalgia sometimes paints it. If pressed, even my parents would probably agree with that. (My father, for example, had to help support his family when he was in high school.) But many teenagers today are affected by strong negative forces in society—drugs and violence, for example—as well as by economic pressures and the need to succeed. Also, while access to the world through the Internet and living in a more open and tolerant society provide great possibilities for today's high school students, they provide problems and dangers as well.

My experiences in high school were a mixed bag. I had good times and bad times, probably much like most people have had. But to emphasize the idea that those years present "carefree good times" is, I think, a mistake. High school provides opportunities and challenges, happy times and sad times, but, I believe, those years are never "carefree."

Analysis of Essay 1

This is a well-written, well-organized essay. The writer's thesis statement appears in the second paragraph after an interesting introduction, which sets the scene. Since the topic asks for a discussion of "the extent to which you agree or disagree" with the statement, the writer focuses on the aspect of the quotation with which she doesn't agree: that high school presents "carefree good times." Using specific examples in paragraphs two and three, the writer supports her opinion.

In the third paragraph, the writer introduces the idea that perhaps high school has never been truly carefree; in the following paragraph, she uses her father's experience as support. However, she remains on topic, and the essay is coherent and logical. The use of transitions ("but," "in addition," "however") is helpful. The concluding paragraph restates the writer's opinion succinctly.

Throughout the essay, the writer uses varied sentence structure and makes only minor errors ("who" rather than "whom" in paragraph one, omission of an apostrophe in "today's" in paragraphs two and four). She also uses mature vocabulary ("idyllic," "problematic") but not simply to impress the reader. Words are chosen because they are appropriate. When slang ("geek") or clichés ("trumps your chances," "mixed bag") are used, they are for effect, not because the writer doesn't know better.

Essay 2: An Average Essay

In my opinion, high school is a very important time in a persons life, There are many reasons for this. Its important that you make the most of your time in high school because there will never be another time like it.

There are many opportunities to learn new subjects, such as foreign languages, advanced mathematics, and world history. Unlike in grammar school, you usually have different teachers for the different subjects and therefore you learn from people who understand their fields well. You can take not only the basic classes but you can also take classes in subjects that interest you, like art or music. For example, I took an excellent class in ceramics. Also, you can participate in outside activities like sports and clubs and learn a lot from these too.

High school helped me learn how to get along with people of all kinds. I was in classes with students of all abilities and from different walks of life. This experience was good for me in that I made friends of all types, not just people who had the same abilities and background I have. I also learned how to get along with teachers on a mature level. In playing sports I learned about the importance of teamwork and of always giving your best.

I made several lifelong friends in high school. My high school friends and I are still in close contact. We call each other and keep each other up to date on what we are doing now. I feel closer to my high school friends than to the people I met in college, even though I have many good friends from there also.

My friends and I had some very good, carefree times. When we were juniors in high school, we went on some weekend camping trips that I will never forget. We liked to fish and hike and I can remember some of the best times in my life sitting around a campfire laughing and telling stories. Also playing football and winning games was a "peak" high school experience.

To summarize, I would say that high school was an unforgettable time that helped me become an adult. Young people should make the most of the time they have in those years because they are very unique.

Analysis of Essay 2

The writer of this essay makes an attempt to organize his thoughts and to stay with the topic, but the examples used are generally sketchy and weak. In paragraph three, for example, there are general statements, but they are not illustrated with specific details. Exactly what did the writer learn from participating in outside activities, for example? Although the writer includes an introduction and a conclusion, both are mechanical and add little to the essay. The thesis statement in the first paragraph is vague. Although there are few errors in this essay, the writer uses little variety in sentence structure.

Essay 3: A Poorly Written Essay

I went to a pretty good high school, therefore my feelings about that time are positive. I had good teachers and many classmates who were good friends. I didn't like some things. Like the fact we had a closed campus and couldn't leave during lunch. Lucky for me it was a small high school, so I knew most of the people.

But some people go to big high schools in citys and don't get to know anyone. Sometimes city high schools are in bad physical shape and doesn't have very good teachers. And their may be problems with gangs. We didn't have gangs in my town. The discipline in my school was pretty tough. If someone did something bad, they usually got suspended right away.

I think small schools have a big advantage over large ones. Students get more personal attention in my opinion. Making good friends is an important part of high school, and I think it is much easier in small schools than in big schools.

The only bad experiance I had in high school was when my best friend was hurt bad in a car accident. He was in the hospital for a long time. A good thing about my school, however, was that everyone wrote him cards and letters. People visited him alot too. That is another advantage of going to a small school.

Analysis of Essay 3

This essay is poorly organized and lacks coherence. It also lacks a clear thesis statement and does not stay on the assigned topic. Notice, for example, that in paragraph three the writer begins to enumerate the advantages of a small school, which is far from the assigned topic. There is a random, not a logical, progression of thought. In the second paragraph, the writer begins by talking about the size and physical condition of city high schools and moves into the subject of gangs and how there were no gangs in his or her town. The essay also contains spelling, grammatical, and sentence structure errors throughout.

Practice Test 2

Answer Sheet for Practice Test 2

(Remove This Sheet and Use It to Mark Your Answers)

Section I: Reading

1 Ⓐ Ⓑ Ⓒ Ⓓ Ⓔ		26 Ⓐ Ⓑ Ⓒ Ⓓ Ⓔ
2 Ⓐ Ⓑ Ⓒ Ⓓ Ⓔ		27 Ⓐ Ⓑ Ⓒ Ⓓ Ⓔ
3 Ⓐ Ⓑ Ⓒ Ⓓ Ⓔ		28 Ⓐ Ⓑ Ⓒ Ⓓ Ⓔ
4 Ⓐ Ⓑ Ⓒ Ⓓ Ⓔ		29 Ⓐ Ⓑ Ⓒ Ⓓ Ⓔ
5 Ⓐ Ⓑ Ⓒ Ⓓ Ⓔ		30 Ⓐ Ⓑ Ⓒ Ⓓ Ⓔ
6 Ⓐ Ⓑ Ⓒ Ⓓ Ⓔ		31 Ⓐ Ⓑ Ⓒ Ⓓ Ⓔ
7 Ⓐ Ⓑ Ⓒ Ⓓ Ⓔ		32 Ⓐ Ⓑ Ⓒ Ⓓ Ⓔ
8 Ⓐ Ⓑ Ⓒ Ⓓ Ⓔ		33 Ⓐ Ⓑ Ⓒ Ⓓ Ⓔ
9 Ⓐ Ⓑ Ⓒ Ⓓ Ⓔ		34 Ⓐ Ⓑ Ⓒ Ⓓ Ⓔ
10 Ⓐ Ⓑ Ⓒ Ⓓ Ⓔ		35 Ⓐ Ⓑ Ⓒ Ⓓ Ⓔ
11 Ⓐ Ⓑ Ⓒ Ⓓ Ⓔ		36 Ⓐ Ⓑ Ⓒ Ⓓ Ⓔ
12 Ⓐ Ⓑ Ⓒ Ⓓ Ⓔ		37 Ⓐ Ⓑ Ⓒ Ⓓ Ⓔ
13 Ⓐ Ⓑ Ⓒ Ⓓ Ⓔ		38 Ⓐ Ⓑ Ⓒ Ⓓ Ⓔ
14 Ⓐ Ⓑ Ⓒ Ⓓ Ⓔ		39 Ⓐ Ⓑ Ⓒ Ⓓ Ⓔ
15 Ⓐ Ⓑ Ⓒ Ⓓ Ⓔ		40 Ⓐ Ⓑ Ⓒ Ⓓ Ⓔ
16 Ⓐ Ⓑ Ⓒ Ⓓ Ⓔ		41 Ⓐ Ⓑ Ⓒ Ⓓ Ⓔ
17 Ⓐ Ⓑ Ⓒ Ⓓ Ⓔ		42 Ⓐ Ⓑ Ⓒ Ⓓ Ⓔ
18 Ⓐ Ⓑ Ⓒ Ⓓ Ⓔ		43 Ⓐ Ⓑ Ⓒ Ⓓ Ⓔ
19 Ⓐ Ⓑ Ⓒ Ⓓ Ⓔ		44 Ⓐ Ⓑ Ⓒ Ⓓ Ⓔ
20 Ⓐ Ⓑ Ⓒ Ⓓ Ⓔ		45 Ⓐ Ⓑ Ⓒ Ⓓ Ⓔ
21 Ⓐ Ⓑ Ⓒ Ⓓ Ⓔ		46 Ⓐ Ⓑ Ⓒ Ⓓ Ⓔ
22 Ⓐ Ⓑ Ⓒ Ⓓ Ⓔ		47 Ⓐ Ⓑ Ⓒ Ⓓ Ⓔ
23 Ⓐ Ⓑ Ⓒ Ⓓ Ⓔ		48 Ⓐ Ⓑ Ⓒ Ⓓ Ⓔ
24 Ⓐ Ⓑ Ⓒ Ⓓ Ⓔ		49 Ⓐ Ⓑ Ⓒ Ⓓ Ⓔ
25 Ⓐ Ⓑ Ⓒ Ⓓ Ⓔ		50 Ⓐ Ⓑ Ⓒ Ⓓ Ⓔ

Section II: Mathematics

1	Ⓐ Ⓑ Ⓒ Ⓓ Ⓔ	26	Ⓐ Ⓑ Ⓒ Ⓓ Ⓔ
2	Ⓐ Ⓑ Ⓒ Ⓓ Ⓔ	27	Ⓐ Ⓑ Ⓒ Ⓓ Ⓔ
3	Ⓐ Ⓑ Ⓒ Ⓓ Ⓔ	28	Ⓐ Ⓑ Ⓒ Ⓓ Ⓔ
4	Ⓐ Ⓑ Ⓒ Ⓓ Ⓔ	29	Ⓐ Ⓑ Ⓒ Ⓓ Ⓔ
5	Ⓐ Ⓑ Ⓒ Ⓓ Ⓔ	30	Ⓐ Ⓑ Ⓒ Ⓓ Ⓔ
6	Ⓐ Ⓑ Ⓒ Ⓓ Ⓔ	31	Ⓐ Ⓑ Ⓒ Ⓓ Ⓔ
7	Ⓐ Ⓑ Ⓒ Ⓓ Ⓔ	32	Ⓐ Ⓑ Ⓒ Ⓓ Ⓔ
8	Ⓐ Ⓑ Ⓒ Ⓓ Ⓔ	33	Ⓐ Ⓑ Ⓒ Ⓓ Ⓔ
9	Ⓐ Ⓑ Ⓒ Ⓓ Ⓔ	34	Ⓐ Ⓑ Ⓒ Ⓓ Ⓔ
10	Ⓐ Ⓑ Ⓒ Ⓓ Ⓔ	35	Ⓐ Ⓑ Ⓒ Ⓓ Ⓔ
11	Ⓐ Ⓑ Ⓒ Ⓓ Ⓔ	36	Ⓐ Ⓑ Ⓒ Ⓓ Ⓔ
12	Ⓐ Ⓑ Ⓒ Ⓓ Ⓔ	37	Ⓐ Ⓑ Ⓒ Ⓓ Ⓔ
13	Ⓐ Ⓑ Ⓒ Ⓓ Ⓔ	38	Ⓐ Ⓑ Ⓒ Ⓓ Ⓔ
14	Ⓐ Ⓑ Ⓒ Ⓓ Ⓔ	39	Ⓐ Ⓑ Ⓒ Ⓓ Ⓔ
15	Ⓐ Ⓑ Ⓒ Ⓓ Ⓔ	40	Ⓐ Ⓑ Ⓒ Ⓓ Ⓔ
16	Ⓐ Ⓑ Ⓒ Ⓓ Ⓔ	41	Ⓐ Ⓑ Ⓒ Ⓓ Ⓔ
17	Ⓐ Ⓑ Ⓒ Ⓓ Ⓔ	42	Ⓐ Ⓑ Ⓒ Ⓓ Ⓔ
18	Ⓐ Ⓑ Ⓒ Ⓓ Ⓔ	43	Ⓐ Ⓑ Ⓒ Ⓓ Ⓔ
19	Ⓐ Ⓑ Ⓒ Ⓓ Ⓔ	44	Ⓐ Ⓑ Ⓒ Ⓓ Ⓔ
20	Ⓐ Ⓑ Ⓒ Ⓓ Ⓔ	45	Ⓐ Ⓑ Ⓒ Ⓓ Ⓔ
21	Ⓐ Ⓑ Ⓒ Ⓓ Ⓔ	46	Ⓐ Ⓑ Ⓒ Ⓓ Ⓔ
22	Ⓐ Ⓑ Ⓒ Ⓓ Ⓔ	47	Ⓐ Ⓑ Ⓒ Ⓓ Ⓔ
23	Ⓐ Ⓑ Ⓒ Ⓓ Ⓔ	48	Ⓐ Ⓑ Ⓒ Ⓓ Ⓔ
24	Ⓐ Ⓑ Ⓒ Ⓓ Ⓔ	49	Ⓐ Ⓑ Ⓒ Ⓓ Ⓔ
25	Ⓐ Ⓑ Ⓒ Ⓓ Ⓔ	50	Ⓐ Ⓑ Ⓒ Ⓓ Ⓔ

CUT HERE

Practice Test 2

The total testing time is 4 hours. You may work on any section of the exam during this time period.

Section I: Reading—50 Questions
Section II: Mathematics—50 Questions
Section III: Writing—2 Essays

Section I: Reading

50 Questions

Directions: A question or number of questions follows each of the statements or passages in this section. Using only the *stated* or *implied* information given in the statement or passage, answer the question or questions by choosing the *best* answer from among the five choices given. Make sure to mark your answers for this section on the Reading section of the answer sheet.

Read the passage below and answer the two questions that follow.

Parallax is a range-finding technique used to measure the distance to some nearby stars from the annual, angular displacement of a nearby star against the background of more distant, relative, fixed stars. Observe parallax by noting the apparent position of a vertical pencil in front of your face with only your right eye; the pencil shifts across the background.

1. To make this passage clear to a general audience, the author can do which of the following?

   A. Concede that parallax is not the only range-finding technique used by astronomers.

   B. Define angular displacement in nontechnical terms.

   C. Cite references in *Scientific American*.

   D. Explain that stars are never even "relatively" fixed.

   E. Eliminate the demonstration using a pencil.

2. In the second sentence, the author suggests which of the following?

   A. Most people have never really considered the position of a pencil.

   B. The perceived position of any object varies according to the point from which it is observed.

   C. Parallax is also a technique used by nonscientists.

   D. The right eye is a more reliable observer than the left eye.

   E. A pencil is very similar to a star.

Read the passage below and answer the two questions that follow.

At the outset of the Civil War, the North possessed a large population, a superior rail system, a greater industrial capacity, greater capital assets, and a larger food-production capability than did the South. Despite the North's apparent economic superiority, the South did possess a few military advantages. Among them were fighting a defensive war on their home ground and an established military tradition. Most of the leaders of the pre-war army were from the South, whereas the North had to train a new military leadership.

3. The final sentence of this passage functions in which of the following ways?

   A. To support the general contention that most of the talent in the United States was concentrated in the South.

   B. To hint that the North found many of its military leaders in the South.

   C. To argue that the North entered the war without leaders.

   D. To underscore the importance of the South's "established military tradition."

   E. To show that the South probably should have won the war.

GO ON TO THE NEXT PAGE

229

4. The author implies which of the following points in the passage?

   A. The North did not have an economic advantage at the end of the war.
   B. Prior to the beginning of the war, the South was already fighting another war and seasoning its leaders.
   C. Almost all the banks in the United States were located in the North.
   D. Military advantages are much more important than economic advantages.
   E. The North had a greater capacity for enduring a prolonged conflict.

Read the passage below and answer the question that follows.

Few opticians have recognized the value of target practice for stimulating the eyes and improving vision. The value of a day on the rifle range surpasses that of a whole crop of fresh carrots.

5. The writer assumes that his or her readers are already convinced that

   A. poor eyesight is a widespread problem.
   B. target practice is enjoyable and useful.
   C. carrots are good for the eyes.
   D. most people should own guns.
   E. the "day" mentioned is an eight-hour day.

Read the passage below and answer the three questions that follow.

The doctrine of association had been the basis for explaining memories and how one idea leads to another. Aristotle provided the basic law, association by contiguity. We remember something because of past experiences. Seeing a shotgun may remind you of a murder, or it may remind you of a hunting experience in Wyoming, depending on your history. When you hear the word *table*, you are likely to think of *chair*. *Carrots* makes you think of *peas*, *bread* makes you think *butter*, and so on. In each case, the two items have been *experienced* contiguously—in the same place or at the same time, or both. Today, the terms *stimulus* and *response* are used to describe the two units that have been associated by contiguity.

6. The author of the passage would most likely agree with which of the following statements?

   A. Many of the associations that Aristotle posited have become part of modern experience.
   B. A number of adults have had no experiences and therefore have no memories.
   C. When one smells coffee, one is not likely to think of eating a donut.
   D. No one thing is necessarily associated with any other thing in particular.
   E. Guns always remind people of an experience in which someone or something was killed.

7. Which of the following statements, if true, would most weaken the argument of the passage?

   A. Many people tend to become depressed when the weather is rainy.
   B. Only a very few researchers question the doctrine of association.
   C. More recent studies show that word-association responses are random and not determined by experience.
   D. Of 100 people tested, 96 of those given the word "bread" responded with the word "butter."
   E. Psychologists have found that people have many common associations.

8. The argument of the passage is most strengthened by which of the following statements?

   A. It is certainly possible to experience more than two items contiguously.
   B. Aristotle never used the terms *stimulus* and *response*.
   C. Those Londoners who endured the German bombings of World War II still become fearful when they hear a loud noise.
   D. Some people think of butter when they hear "carrots."
   E. Aristotle's own writing is full of very uncommon and unexplained associations.

Read the passage below and answer the question that follows.

All experts on testing and learning admit that multiple-choice tests measure knowledge only within limits. Yet the fact remains that multiple-choice tests are used, both in school and out of school, as significant indicators of intellectual ability and the capacity for learning.

9. The passage implies which of the following statements?

   A. The administration of tests is a more cost-effective measure than the exploration of other modes of measurement.

   B. Tests are appropriate only when the students tested have limited knowledge.

   C. A person's capacity for learning cannot be measured by any sort of test.

   D. Those who work first-hand with tests must know something that the experts do not.

   E. Those who use multiple-choice tests may not be experts on testing.

Read the passage below and answer the four questions that follow.

Ostensibly, punishment is used to reduce tendencies to behave in certain ways. We spank and scold children for misbehavior; we fine, lock up, or assign to hard labor adults who break laws; we threaten, censure, disapprove, ostracize, and coerce in our efforts to control social behaviors. Does punishment, in fact, do what it is supposed to do?

The effects of punishment, it has been found, are not the opposite of reward. It does not subtract responses where reinforcement adds them. Rather, it appears to temporarily suppress a behavior, and when punishment is discontinued, eventually responses will reappear. But this is only one aspect of the topic. Let us look at it in further detail.

Skinner defines punishment in two ways: first as the withdrawal of a positive reinforcer, and second as the presentation of a negative reinforcer, or aversive stimulus. We take candy away from children or we spank them. Note that the arrangement in punishment is the opposite of that in reinforcement, where a positive reinforcer is presented and a negative reinforcer is removed.

Since we remove positive reinforcers to extinguish a response and also to punish it, a distinction must be made. When a response is made and no reinforcement follows—that is, *nothing* happens—the response

gradually extinguishes. However, if we *withdraw* a reinforcer, and the withdrawal of a reinforcer is contingent on a response, responding is suppressed more rapidly. The latter is punishment. Sometimes we withdraw a privilege from children to control their behavior. For example, a teacher might keep a child in the classroom during recess or cancel a field trip as a result of misbehavior. Turning off the television when children put their thumb in their mouth may effectively suppress thumbsucking. Most punishments of this sort use conditioned or generalized reinforcers. Quite frequently, one sees adults withdraw attention or affection as punishment for misbehavior, sometimes in subtle ways.

10. The passage equates taking candy away from children with

    A. only one of many categories of punishment.

    B. the presentation of a negative reinforcer.

    C. the presentation of an aversion stimulus.

    D. withdrawal of negative reinforcement.

    E. withdrawal of positive reinforcement.

11. Which of the following may be concluded from the last paragraph of the passage?

    A. Most children regard the classroom as a prison.

    B. It is usually best to ignore whatever bothers us.

    C. The author considers recess and field trips to be privileges.

    D. The withdrawal of affection is an unconscious form of punishment.

    E. Children who do not like television are harder to punish.

12. The passage does not do which of the following?

    A. Give a definite answer to the question posed in the first paragraph.

    B. Discuss generally some of the effects of punishment.

    C. Provide examples of some common forms of punishment.

    D. Distinguish punishment from reinforcement.

    E. Mention the temporary suppression of behavior.

GO ON TO THE NEXT PAGE

13. Which of the following facts, if true, supports one of the author's contentions about punishment?

    A. Those who were spanked as children may not praise the benefits of such discipline.
    B. Imposing longer jail terms on criminals does not necessarily permanently reduce their tendency to return to crime.
    C. Any species or race that is consistently punished will eventually become extinct.
    D. The temporary suppression of a negative behavior is a fine accomplishment.
    E. People who are consistently rewarded are incapable of punishing others.

Read the passage below and answer the five questions that follow.

The question might be asked, "How can we know what is 'really' real?" Defined phenomenologically, "reality" becomes purely a hypothetical concept that accounts for the totality of all conditions imposed by the external world upon an individual. But since other individuals are included in each of our fields of experience, it does become possible to form consensus groups as we make identification of similarly perceived phenomena. In fact, we often tend to ignore and even push out of awareness those persons and their assumptions regarding what is real that do not correspond to our own. However, such a lack of consensus also affords us the opportunity of checking our hypothesis about reality. We may change our concepts about reality and thus facilitate changes in our phenomenal world of experience. Scientists, for instance, deliberately set out to gain consensus on both their procedures and conclusion. If they are successful in this quest, their consensus group considers such conclusions as constituting an addition to a factual body of sharable knowledge. This process is somewhat in contrast to mystical religious experiences, for example. By their nature, mystical experiences may not always be communicable to others. However, even a scientific researcher must finally evaluate the consequences of his or her research within a unique, personal phenomenological field. To use a cliché, truth, like beauty, exists in the eyes of the beholder.

14. Which of the following is a specific example supporting the point of the passage?

    A. Certain established scientific facts have not changed for hundreds of years.
    B. Part of the phrase in the last sentence is from a poem by Keats.
    C. Reality is a given, unique experience in an individual's phenomenal world.
    D. People think of their enemies in war as cruel and regard their own soldiers as virtuous.
    E. The fans at baseball games often see things exactly as the umpire sees them.

15. Applying the argument of the passage, one could define a political party as

    A. a political group to which few scientists belong.
    B. a consensus group whose individuals share a similar view of political reality.
    C. a consensus group whose members are deluded about what is really "real," politically.
    D. in touch with reality if it is a majority party and out of touch with reality if it is a minority party.
    E. a collection of individuals who are each fundamentally unsure about what political reality is.

16. When the author says that "reality" is a "hypothetical concept," he or she means that

    A. as for reality, there is none.
    B. one can think about reality but never really experience it.
    C. "reality" is not objective.
    D. "reality" is a figment of your imagination.
    E. only scientists know "reality."

17. According to the passage, one difference between a scientist and a mystic is that

    A. the scientist sees truth as facts; the mystic sees truth as beauty.
    B. scientists are unwilling and unable to lend importance to religious experiences.
    C. the work of the mystic does not have consequences that affect individuals.
    D. the scientist is concerned with sharable knowledge, and the mystic may not be.
    E. scientists cannot believe in anything mystical.

18. To the question, "How can we know what is 'really' real?" this author would probably answer in which of the following ways?

    A. If no one sees things our way, we are detached from reality.

    B. Whatever we are aware of can legitimately be called real.

    C. What is really real is whatever a group of individuals believe.

    D. We can, if we use the scientific method.

    E. We cannot know what is "really" real because reality varies with individual perspective.

Read the passage below and answer the five questions that follow.

He who lets the world, or his own portion of it, choose his plan of life for him has no need of any other faculty than the ape-like one of imitation. He who chooses his plan for himself employs all his faculties. He must use observation to see, reasoning and judgment to foresee, activity to gather materials for decision, discrimination to decide, and when he has decided, firmness and self-control to hold to his decision. And these qualities he requires and exercises exactly in proportion as the part of his conduct which he determines according to his own judgment and feelings is a large one. It is possible that he might be guided in some good path, and kept out of harm's way, without any of these things. But what will be his comparative worth as a human being? It really is of importance, not only what men do, but also what manner of men they are that do it. Among the works of man, which human life is rightly employed in perfecting and beautifying, the first in importance surely is man himself. Supposing it were possible to get houses built, corn grown, battles fought, causes tried, and even churches erected and prayers said, by machinery—by <u>automatons</u> in human form—it would be a considerable loss to exchange for these automatons even the men and women who at present inhabit the more civilized parts of the world, and who assuredly are but starved specimens of what nature can and will produce. Human nature is not a machine to be built after a model, and set to do exactly the work prescribed for it, but a tree, which requires to grow and develop itself on all sides, according to the tendency of the inward forces which make it a living thing.

19. One major distinction in this passage is between

    A. automatons and machines.

    B. people and machines.

    C. beauty and perfection.

    D. apes and machines.

    E. growing food and fighting battles.

20. Which of the following groups represents the type of person that the author calls an <u>automaton</u>?

    A. Comedians

    B. Botanists

    C. Workers on an assembly line

    D. A team of physicians in surgery

    E. Students who consistently ask challenging questions

21. Which of the following is an unstated assumption of the passage?

    A. Humankind will probably never improve.

    B. The essence of people themselves is more important than what people do.

    C. It is desirable to let modern technology do some of our more unpleasant tasks.

    D. Some people in the world do not select their own life plans.

    E. What man produces is really no different from man himself.

22. The author would agree that a major benefit of letting the world choose your plan of life for you is

    A. simplicity.

    B. profit.

    C. friendship.

    D. progress.

    E. happiness.

GO ON TO THE NEXT PAGE

23. The author would probably agree with each of the following statements *except:*

    A. To conform to custom, merely as custom, does not educate or develop a person.

    B. Human beings should use and interpret experience in their own way.

    C. More good may always be made of an energetic nature than of an indolent and impassive one.

    D. Persons whose desires and impulses are their own are said to have character.

    E. It makes good sense to choose the easy life of conformity.

Read the passage below and answer the two questions that follow.

Charles Darwin was both a naturalist and a scientist. Darwin's *On the Origin of Species* (1859) was based on twenty-five years of research in testing and checking his theory of evolution. "Darwinism" had a profound effect on the natural sciences, the social sciences, and the humanities. Churchmen who feared for the survival of religious institutions rushed to attack him. However, Darwin never attempted to apply his laws of evolution to human society. It was the social Darwinists who expanded the theory of evolution to include society as a whole. The social Darwinists viewed society as a "struggle for existence" with only the "fittest" members of society able to survive. They espoused basically a racist and elitist doctrine. Some people were naturally superior to others; it was in the "nature of things" for big business to take over "less fit," smaller concerns.

24. The final sentence of the passage beginning "Some people" is the author's attempt to

    A. discredit Charles Darwin's theory.
    B. voice his or her own point of view.
    C. summarize one point of view.
    D. give social Darwinism a fair shake.
    E. explain the modern prominence of big business.

25. The author's primary purpose in this passage is to

    A. warn of the dangers of having one's ideas abused.
    B. show that Darwin was unconcerned with human society.
    C. defend Darwin against modern charges of racism and elitism.

    D. explain how Darwin's theory was applied to society.
    E. give an example of Darwinian evolution.

Read this excerpt from a book index and then answer the question that follows.

Vocabulary: Vernacular, 347, 349
  African, 215
  American, 124, 188, 189, 200, 220
      Black, 211, 218–20
      Northeastern, 256–58
      Southern, 179, 181, 190–91
      Western, 263–64
  Australian, 299
      Aboriginal, 288, 290–91
      Convict "flash" language, 301
  Canadian, 233, 241
  English, 13, 17–20, 88–89, 115–19
      Cockney, 81–2
      Queen's English, 94–95, 111
  French, 25, 79
      Northern, 83, 85
      Southern, 80–81
  Greek, 65, 68

26. On which pages should one look for information about the dialect spoken by California gold miners?

    A. 124, 220
    B. 256–58
    C. 263–64
    D. 190–91
    E. 218–20

Read the passage below and answer the question that follows.

Prior to the 1980s, educational psychologists were primarily concerned with specific social, motivational, and cognitive aspects of learning. Recent comprehensive studies of early classroom learning experiences have drawn attention to the importance of multiple approaches to learning. Classroom curriculum now emphasizes activities that are sensitive to the unique abilities of individual students.

27. One of the author's points in this passage is that

    A. prior to the 1980s, no one noticed that the concerns of educational psychologists were limited.
    B. educational psychologists tend to frequently shift their interests as a group.
    C. after 1980, psychologists lost interest in the social, motivational, and cognitive aspects of learning.
    D. the academic significance of classroom activities themselves has not been the concern of educational psychologists until fairly recently.
    E. the decades preceding the 1980s were marked by poorly thought out, poorly implemented classroom activities.

Read the passage below and answer the two questions that follow.

A lesson plan is basically a tool for effective teaching. Its primary importance is to present objectives and content in a logical and systematic manner; as such, it is an <u>integral</u> part of the instructional process.

28. Which of the following is an unstated assumption made by the author of the passage?

    A. All features of the instructional process should have the same logical, systematic qualities as the lesson plan.
    B. Students learn best when material is not presented in a disorganized or unplanned manner.
    C. A teacher who is not a logical, systematic thinker has no place in the instructional process.
    D. The lesson plan is by far the most important tool for effective teaching.
    E. Teachers should not deviate from the lesson plan in any case.

29. The author uses <u>integral</u> to mean

    A. original.
    B. whole.
    C. essential.
    D. not segregated.
    E. modern.

Read the passage below and answer the four questions that follow.

In the last twenty years, tomato production in the United States has declined sharply, while imports have more than doubled. Much of the foreign crop arrives from Mexico, when the colder winters north of the Rio Grande make tomato growing difficult. _____ the seasonal imports are not the only problem for American growers. The second-leading exporter is the Netherlands, with a climate as cold as Pennsylvania's. The Dutch grow their tomatoes in greenhouses and ship gourmet varieties to markets throughout the United States.

(1) In the past, the chief worry of tomato growers was finding a fruit that could stand up to shipping and still look good. (2) The least of their concerns was taste. (3) Until recently, American seed developers concentrated on disease resistance, crop yield, and <u>shelf life</u>. (4) _____, with the competition from abroad, growers and planters are looking for flavor and color. (5) Ten years ago, most American growers offered only three kinds of tomato; now markets often stock eight to ten kinds, and specialty stores handle as many as twenty. (6) The better-looking and better-tasting tomatoes may turn out to be the answer to the competition from Mexico and Europe.

30. Which words, if inserted *in order* in the blank spaces in the first and second paragraphs, would help the reader understand the sequence of the writer's ideas?

    A. Yet; Nevertheless
    B. However; Still
    C. And; And
    D. Now; But
    E. But; Now

31. Which of the following is the best definition of the term <u>shelf life</u>, as it appears in the second paragraph of the passage?

    A. Appearance when displayed in a market
    B. Ability to last
    C. Freshness in color
    D. Texture
    E. Freedom from bacteria

GO ON TO THE NEXT PAGE

235

32. Which of the following numbered sentences is least relevant to the main idea of the second paragraph and could most easily be omitted?

    A. Sentence 1
    B. Sentence 2
    C. Sentence 3
    D. Sentence 4
    E. Sentence 5

33. From the passage, which of the following can you infer needs most to be improved by American tomato growers?

    A. Freshness
    B. Disease resistance
    C. Price
    D. Taste
    E. Distribution

Read the passage below and answer the question that follows.

Rewards tend to be more effective than punishment in controlling student behavior. Negative reinforcement often is accompanied by emotional side effects that may inhibit learning.

34. The author implies which of the following?

    A. The same student who is punished frequently may have difficulty learning.
    B. In society at large, rewards are not given nearly as often as they should be.
    C. Negative reinforcement is much more useful out of school than it is in school.
    D. The most effective punishment is that which is followed by a reward.
    E. Learning disabilities often lead to emotional problems.

Read the passage below and answer the question that follows.

Teacher salaries account for approximately 70 percent of a school budget. Any major proposal designed to reduce educational expenditures will ultimately necessitate a cut in teaching staff.

35. Neighborhood High School is staffed by fifty teachers, and its administration has just ordered a reduction in educational expenditures. According to the preceding passage, which of the following will be one result of the reduction?

    A. A reduction in both administrative and teaching salaries
    B. A teaching staff dependent on fewer educational materials
    C. A teaching staff of fewer than fifty teachers
    D. A teaching staff of only fifteen teachers
    E. A substantial change in the quality of education

Read the passage below and answer the four questions that follow.

Like many birds, the familiar orange and black monarch butterfly is <u>migratory</u>. Each year, more than one hundred million of the insects fly from their summer homes in Washington, Oregon, and northern California to areas in southern California and northern Mexico. Covering as much as sixty miles a day, the butterflies are propelled more by the seasonal winds than by the power of their wings.

How does this tiny creature find its way to a wintering place several thousand miles away? Larger migratory animals, like the species in the great herds of Africa, learn their routes from their parents or other older members of the herd. So do birds, such as the swallow, and sea animals, like the salmon or sea turtle. But because the life span of a monarch is likely to be no more than ninety days, an older generation of butterflies cannot instruct a younger one. Not one of the insects that flew north in the spring is alive to fly south in the fall.

(1) Insect ecologists have recently established that the monarchs use the position of the sun to determine their flight direction on long-distance journeys. (2) But this cannot be the whole story. (3) It may be that the butterfly can sense the force lines of the earth's magnetic field to use as a navigational aid. (4) Another theory is that the butterflies find directional clues in the changing length of the days. (5) But we still do not know how so small an insect can find its way year after year over so long a distance. (6) Parents should make a greater effort to increase their children's interest in butterflies.

36. Which of the following is the best definition of the word <u>migratory</u> in the first paragraph?

   A. Short-lived
   B. Moving periodically
   C. Susceptible to infection
   D. Able to fly
   E. Accustomed to many habitats

37. According to information presented in the passage, which of the following do butterflies use to help them find their way when they migrate?

   A. The prevailing winds
   B. One generation's teaching the next
   C. The position of the sun
   D. Force lines of the earth's magnetic field
   E. The changing length of days and nights

38. Of the following general statements, which one is best supported by the contents of this passage?

   A. Questions remain about animal behavior that scientists are unable to answer.
   B. Butterflies and other insects would be unable to navigate on cloudy days.
   C. Smaller animals like insects depend more on the wind than on their own wings for travel over long distances.
   D. Scientists will never be able to explain how butterflies can find their way over long distances.
   E. Scientists know more about the larger land and sea animals than they do about insects like the butterfly.

39. Which of the following numbered sentences in the third paragraph expresses an opinion rather than a fact?

   A. Sentence 1
   B. Sentence 3
   C. Sentence 4
   D. Sentence 5
   E. Sentence 6

Read the passage below and answer the question that follows.

Graduate students who expect to specialize in The Teaching of Writing must take English 600, either English 500 (Advanced Composition) or English 504 (Writing of Criticism), at least three literature courses concentrating on the same single century only, English 740 (Teaching of Writing), English 741 (Classical Rhetoric), and English 742 (Modern Rhetorical Theory).

40. According to the preceding statement, which of the following schedules does *not* belong to a specialist in The Teaching of Writing?

   A. English 740–42, Advanced Composition, twentieth-century drama, twentieth-century poetry, twentieth-century novels, English 600
   B. English 740–42, eighteenth-century poetry, eighteenth-century prose fiction, eighteenth-century drama, English 504, English 600
   C. English 600, Victorian poetry, Victorian prose fiction, Victorian novels, English 500, English 740, 741, and 742
   D. English 500, seventeenth-century poetry, seventeenth-century drama, Victorian novels, English 740, 741, and 742
   E. English 740, Classical Rhetoric, Modern Rhetorical Theory, English 500, English 600, Victorian poetry, Victorian prose fiction, Victorian novels

Read the passage below and answer the six questions that follow.

(1) The Morrill Act (1862) extended the principle of federal support for public education, the earliest attempt being the Northwest Ordinance of 1787. (2) The Morrill Act established land-grant colleges in each state and specified a curriculum based on agriculture and mechanical arts. (3) Land-grant colleges often were a state's first institution of public higher education. (4) Public support and public control strengthened the concept of the state-university system. (5) The Civil Rights Act of 1875 was the first federal attempt to provide equal educational opportunity. (6) The progressive theories of John Dewey <u>also</u> had a profound effect on public education. (7) Dewey believed that education included the home, shop, neighborhood,

GO ON TO THE NEXT PAGE

church, and school. (8) However, industrialization was destroying the educational functions of these institutions. (9) Dewey believed that the public schools must be society's instrument for "shaping its own destiny." (10) To do this, the schools had to be transformed to serve the interests of democracy.

41. If this passage were divided into two paragraphs, the second paragraph would begin with

   A. Sentence 3
   B. Sentence 5
   C. Sentence 6
   D. Sentence 7
   E. Sentence 8

42. The passage implies that one significant contrast between the Morrill Act and Dewey's theories was

   A. Dewey's lack of faith in land-grant colleges.
   B. the fact that the Morrill Act was not a democratic law.
   C. the neglect in the Morrill Act of education's relationship to society.
   D. Dewey's lack of knowledge about the Morrill Act.
   E. the Morrill Act's stress on a heavily agricultural and mechanical curriculum.

43. The word <u>also</u> in sentence 6 does which of the following?

   A. It opens the question concerning whether Dewey himself would have supported certain government acts concerning education.
   B. It makes clear that Dewey's theories were innovative and inconsistent with government policy.
   C. It makes the point that Dewey's theories were somewhat identical to material in the Morrill Act.
   D. It suggests that the Morrill Act, Northwest Ordinance, and Civil Rights Act had a profound effect on public education.
   E. It suggests that Dewey's theories did more than affect public education.

44. Which of the following statements, if true, would best support sentences 7 and 8?

   A. Home, shop, neighborhood, church, and school each played an ever-increasing role in the world of learning.
   B. Learning was equated exclusively with industrial progress, while moral, social, and artistic growth were undervalued.
   C. Industry was shaping the destiny of the citizens, and Dewey was a strong industrial supporter.
   D. Industry was transforming the schools so they could serve the interests of democracy.
   E. Sentence 3.

45. This passage would be *least* likely to appear in which of the following?

   A. An encyclopedia article summarizing the major legislation of the nineteenth century
   B. A brief survey of legislation and theories that significantly affected education
   C. An introduction to the theories of John Dewey
   D. An argument about the benefits of both progressive legislation and progressive educational theory
   E. A discussion of the relationship between social needs and school curriculum

46. The passage allows us to conclude which of the following?

   A. Beyond the legislation discussed in the passage, no other government acts addressed the issue of public education.
   B. Theorists always have a more significant effect on education than legislators.
   C. The framers of the Morrill Act did not appreciate the value of moral education.
   D. Dewey succeeded to some extent in transforming public education.
   E. The state-university system was a concept long before it became a reality.

Read the passage below and answer the question that follows.

Psychology is often considered a science of the mind. As an applied science, it aims to generate comprehensive theories to explain human emotions and behavior. Despite its status as a science, the "methods" of psychology sometimes seem more speculative than rational and analytical.

47. Which of the following functions does the second sentence perform?

    A. It provides a description of psychology.
    B. It provides an opinion of psychology.
    C. It denies the truth of the first sentence.
    D. It uses a metaphor.
    E. It adds an inconsistency.

Read the passage below and answer the question that follows.

In television's first decades, most programs were shown in black and white. These days, the brightly colored clothes most of us wear signal that the medium has changed.

48. The author implies which of the following in the preceding passage?

    A. People wore only black-and-white clothes when television was invented.
    B. Most people no longer will tolerate black-and-white television.
    C. Only a slight relationship exists between one's self-image and the images one sees on television.
    D. Color television is significantly responsible for our preference for brightly colored clothes.
    E. Clothing technology, like television, was relatively primitive when television was being developed.

Students Involved in Extracurricular Activities at Mercy High School				
	Music/Drama (%)	Newspaper/Yearbook (%)	Sports (%)	Miscellaneous (%)
Sophomore Girls	53	22	13	12
Sophomore Boys	62	23	10	5
Junior Girls	42	25	13	20
Junior Boys	58	20	10	12
Senior Girls	51	26	14	9
Senior Boys	63	20	10	7

Use the chart above to answer the question that follows.

49. All of the following can logically be derived from the information in the preceding chart **EXCEPT**

    A. A greater percentage of senior girls are involved in sports than are sophomore girls.
    B. A smaller percentage of junior girls are involved in the newspaper and yearbook than are senior girls.
    C. A greater percentage of sophomore girls are involved in music and drama than are senior girls.
    D. A greater percentage of junior girls are involved in the newspaper and yearbook than are sophomore girls.
    E. A greater percentage of senior boys are involved in sports than are sophomore boys.

GO ON TO THE NEXT PAGE

Read the following passage and answer the question that follows.

The political party is a voluntary association of voters whose purpose in a democracy is to control the policies of government by electing to public office persons of its membership.

50. The preceding passage would be most likely to appear in which of the following?

   A. An introductory text on political science
   B. A general interest magazine
   C. A manual of rules for legislators
   D. A piece of campaign literature
   E. A brief essay discussing the president's most recent news conference

Section II: Mathematics

50 Questions

Directions: In the following questions or incomplete statements, select the one *best* answer or completion of the five choices given. Make sure that you mark your answers for this section on the Mathematics section of the answer sheet.

1. Don shoots 80 arrows at a target, but only 15% of them actually hit the target. How many arrows actually hit the target?

    A. 11
    B. 12
    C. 15
    D. 16
    E. 18

2. Which factors do the numbers 6, 8, and 12 have in common?

    A. 1 only
    B. 2 only
    C. 1 and 2 only
    D. 1, 2, and 4 only
    E. 1, 2, 3, 4, and 6 only

3. Which of the following is the outcome when the sum of 7 and 8 is divided by $\frac{2}{3}$?

    A. $22\frac{1}{2}$

    B. $15\frac{2}{3}$

    C. 10

    D. $6\frac{1}{10}$

    E. $6\frac{1}{16}$

Use the chart below to answer the question that follows.

Company Name	Tons Shipped
Dansk	5 million
APL	7 million
SAS	9 million
Far West	12 million

4. From the preceding chart, what was the total number of tons shipped on a given workday?

    A.   33
    B.   330
    C.   33,000
    D.   330,000
    E.   33,000,000

5. Of the following fractions, which is the largest in value?

    A. $\frac{25}{52}$

    B. $\frac{31}{60}$

    C. $\frac{19}{40}$

    D. $\frac{51}{100}$

    E. $\frac{43}{90}$

6. If 7 pounds of bananas cost $4.69, at the same rate, how much do 9 pounds of bananas cost?

    A. $ 3.65
    B. $ 6.03
    C. $ 6.69
    D. $ 6.70
    E. $ 13.43

GO ON TO THE NEXT PAGE

Use the diagram below to answer the question that follows.

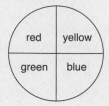

7. From the diagram of the preceding spinner, in spinning the spinner only once, what is the probability of spinning red, yellow, or blue?

   A. $\frac{1}{4}$

   B. $\frac{1}{3}$

   C. $\frac{1}{2}$

   D. $\frac{3}{4}$

   E. $\frac{3}{2}$

8. If $16\frac{1}{2}$ feet equal one rod, how many inches are there in four rods?

   A. $\frac{51}{2}$

   B. 22
   C. 66
   D. 792
   E. 2,376

9. Alex took his family out to dinner. The total cost for the meal was $47.93. He wanted to leave a 15% tip. Which of the following is the best approximation of the tip?

   A. $ 5.50
   B. $ 6.00
   C. $ 7.00
   D. $ 8.00
   E. $55.00

Use the figure below to answer the question that follows.

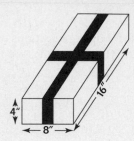

10. Sarah is wrapping a package with ribbon, as shown in the diagram below. What is the total length of ribbon needed for her present?

   A. 32 inches
   B. 64 inches
   C. 128 inches
   D. 448 square inches
   E. 512 square inches

11. Brad has written five ratios. All the ratios that Brad has written are equal except one. Which one of the following ratios is not equal to the remaining four ratios?

   A. 1 to 4
   B. 3 to 8
   C. 2 to 8
   D. 3 to 12
   E. 4 to 16

12. Which of the following statements could be expressed by the number sentence, "825.50 + 435.00 = 1,260.50"?

   A. The difference in the cost of housing in two cities, Chicago and Indianapolis
   B. The total amount of money earned in each of two months during the summer vacation
   C. The average of two months' earnings
   D. The amount of 435.00 is the result of subtracting the weight of 825.50 pounds from some unknown
   E. The total of funding received by a school district of 435 students at $825.50 per student

Use the diagram below to answer the question that follows.

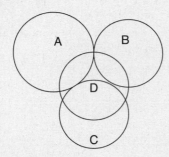

13. Which of the following is a conclusion that can be drawn from the preceding diagram of circles A, B, C, and D?

   A.   A and B have something in common.
   B.   B and C have something in common.
   C.   A and D have nothing in common.
   D.   C and D have nothing in common.
   E.   D has something in common with A, B, and C.

Use the information below to answer the question that follows.

Juan works 8 hours and receives $9.75 per hour. Mary works 24 hours and receives a total of $204.

14. Which of the following *cannot* be derived from the preceding statements?

   A.   Juan's total wages
   B.   Mary's wage per hour
   C.   The difference between the wages that Juan and Mary each receives
   D.   The average total wages received by Juan and Mary
   E.   The hours Mary worked each day

15. If 3 times *c* is equal to *d*, then *c* is equal to which of the following?

   A. $3 + d$
   B. $3d$
   C. $\dfrac{d}{3}$
   D. $\dfrac{3}{a}$
   E. $\dfrac{3}{d}$

16. On a map, 1 centimeter represents 35 kilometers. Two cities 245 kilometers apart would be separated on the map by how many centimeters?

   A.   5
   B.   7
   C.   9
   D.   210
   E.   280

17. Which of the following represents 4,316.136 rounded off to the nearest tenth?

   A.   4,320
   B.   4,316.14
   C.   4,316.13
   D.   4,316.106
   E.   4,316.1

Using the information below, answer the question that follows.

Breakfast Bill

Eggs	$5.50
Pancakes	$5.95
Orange juice	$1.25
Subtotal	$_____
Tip	$2.00
Tax	$0.76
Total	$15.46

18. What is the subtotal of the bill?

   A. $ 0.76
   B. $ 2.00
   C. $11.97
   D. $12.70
   E. $15.46

19. The fraction $\dfrac{1}{8}$ is between the numbers listed in which of the following pairs?

   A. $\dfrac{1}{10}$ and $\dfrac{2}{17}$
   B.   0.1 and 0.12
   C.   0.08 and 0.1
   D.   1 and 2
   E. $\dfrac{1}{9}$ and $\dfrac{2}{15}$

GO ON TO THE NEXT PAGE

20. A class of 30 students all together has 60 pencils. Which of the following *must* be true?

   A. Each student has 2 pencils.
   B. Every student has a pencil.
   C. Some students have only 1 pencil.
   D. Some students have more pencils than other students.
   E. The class averages 2 pencils per student.

21. Mr. Welsh is doing a project with his class of 19 students. If each student needs 8 inches of string, how much string will be left over from a spool of 5 yards?

   A. 2 feet, 4 inches
   B. 2 feet, 8 inches
   C. 3 feet
   D. 4 feet, 4 inches
   E. 28 feet

22. A man purchased 4 pounds of round steak priced at $3.89 per pound. How much change did he receive from a $20 bill?

   A. $ 4.34
   B. $ 4.44
   C. $ 4.46
   D. $15.56
   E. $44.66

Read the information given below and then answer the question that follows.

   Sara is trying to compose a logical series of numbers as an extra credit assignment for her math class. To get the extra credit, she needs six numbers in the series. So far, she has the numbers 8, 9, 12, 17, and 24.

23. From the preceding information, which of the following would have to be the next number in the series for Sara to receive the extra credit?

   A. 29
   B. 30
   C. 33
   D. 35
   E. 41

24. Sara's after-school job pays her $7.25 per hour. Which of the following expressions best represents her total earnings in dollars if she works 4 hours on Monday, 2 hours on Tuesday, 3 hours on Wednesday, 4 hours on Thursday, and 3 hours on Friday?

   A. $4 + $2 + $3 + $4 + $3
   B. $12 + $7.25
   C. $16 + $7.25
   D. 12($7.25)
   E. 16($7.25)

25. If the edges of a 4-inch by 6-inch photograph are each enlarged by 20%, what is the perimeter of the new photograph?

   A. 12 inches
   B. 16 inches
   C. 24 inches
   D. 28 inches
   E. 34.5 inches

26. Sam tries to construct a pie graph representing his classmates' eye colors. In his class of 24 students, 6 students have blue eyes, 12 students have brown eyes, 5 students have hazel eyes, and 1 student has green eyes. His teacher tells him that his graph (shown below) is not correct.

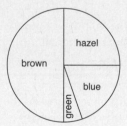

In order to fix the graph, Sam should

   A. increase the amount of green and decrease the amount of blue.
   B. increase the amount of blue and decrease the amount of hazel.
   C. decrease the amount of blue and increase the amount of brown.
   D. decrease the amount of hazel and increase the amount of brown.
   E. increase the amount of hazel and increase the amount of blue.

27. Richard can fit 36 history textbooks into one carton. How many of the same textbooks can he fit into $11\frac{1}{2}$ cartons?

    A.   432
    B.   414
    C.   396
    D.   360
    E.   240

Use the graphs below to answer the two questions that follow.

AVERAGE COLLEGE STUDENT'S EXPENSES

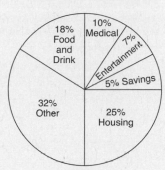

2005
Total Expenditure $30,000

2010
Total Expenditure $34,000

28. How much more money did the average college student spend on medical expenses in 2010 than in 2005?

    A. $800–$900
    B. $900–$1,000
    C. $1,000–$1,100
    D. $1,100–$1,200
    E. $1,200–$1,300

29. What was the approximate increase from 2005 to 2010 in the percentage spent on food and drink?

    A.   4%
    B.   18%
    C.   22%
    D.   40%
    E.   50%

30. The length of rectangle ABCD is twice as long as the side of square WXYZ. The width of rectangle ABCD is $\frac{2}{3}$ as long as the side of square WXYZ. If the area of the square is 36 square inches, what is the perimeter of the rectangle?

    A.   50 inches
    B.   48 inches
    C.   32 inches
    D.   24 inches
    E.   12 inches

31. How many inches are there in m yards and n feet?

    A. $m + n$
    B. $36m + 12n$
    C. $36(m + n)$
    D. $36m + n$
    E. $12(m + n)$

32. In a senior class of 800, only 240 decide to attend the senior prom. What percentage of the senior class attended the senior prom?

    A.   8%
    B.   24%
    C.   30%
    D.   33%
    E.   80%

GO ON TO THE NEXT PAGE

Practice Test 2

33. What is the probability of tossing a penny twice so that both times it lands heads up?

    A. $\frac{1}{8}$

    B. $\frac{1}{4}$

    C. $\frac{1}{3}$

    D. $\frac{1}{2}$

    E. $\frac{2}{3}$

34. Which of the statements is correct?

    A. $5\frac{5}{6} < 5\frac{2}{6} < 4\frac{5}{6}$

    B. $5\frac{5}{6} > 4\frac{5}{6} > 5\frac{5}{6}$

    C. $5\frac{1}{6} > 4\frac{1}{6} > 5\frac{2}{6}$

    D. $5\frac{1}{6} > 5\frac{4}{6} > 4\frac{4}{6}$

    E. $5\frac{5}{6} > 5\frac{4}{6} > 4\frac{4}{6}$

35. A suit that originally sold for $120 is on sale for $90. What is the rate of discount?

    A. 20%
    B. 25%
    C. 30%
    D. $33\frac{1}{3}\%$
    E. 75%

36. Alicia hiked $16\frac{1}{4}$ miles, and Melanie hiked $8\frac{3}{7}$ miles. What was the total number of miles they hiked?

    A. $24\frac{19}{28}$

    B. $24\frac{4}{11}$

    C. $8\frac{4}{11}$

    D. $8\frac{2}{3}$

    E. $5\frac{7}{8}$

Use the information below to answer the question that follows.

Elsa is having trouble changing units of measure. Her teacher has given her a practice problem requiring her to change 3 miles to inches.

37. To get the correct answer, Elsa should

    A. multiply 3 by 5,280.
    B. multiply 3 by 5,280 and then divide by 12.
    C. multiply 3 by 5,280 and then multiply by 12.
    D. divide 3 into 5,280 and then multiply by 12.
    E. divide 3 into 12 and then multiply by 5,280.

38. What is the largest integer if the sum of three consecutive even integers is 318?

    A. 100
    B. 104
    C. 106
    D. 108
    E. 111

39. In a certain classroom, girls account for 40% of the students. Also in that classroom, 1 out of every 3 boys has brown hair. If there are Q students in that classroom, the best expression for boys without brown hair would be

    A. $(0.6Q)\frac{2}{3}$

    B. $\frac{1}{3}Q - 40$

    C. $\left(\frac{1}{3}Q\right)(0.6)$

    D. $(0.4Q)\frac{2}{3}$

    E. $\left(\frac{Q}{.6}\right)2$

40. A basketball is fully inflated to 9 pounds per square inch. A football is fully inflated to 10 pounds per square inch. The air pressure in the football is what percent of the air pressure in the basketball?

    A. 33%
    B. 54%
    C. 79%
    D. 90%
    E. 111%

41. A triangle has a perimeter of 14 feet. One leg has a length of 36 inches, and another leg has a length of 60 inches. What is the length of the third leg?

 A. 6 inches
 B. 6 feet, 2 inches
 C. 72 inches
 D. 7 feet, 2 inches
 E. 72 feet

Read the information given below and then answer the question that follows.

Today is Lucy's fourteenth birthday. Last year, she was three years older than twice Charlie's age at that time.

42. Using *c* for Charlie's age now, which of the following can be used to determine Charlie's age now?

 A. $13 - 3 = 2(c - 1)$
 B. $14 - 3 = 2c$
 C. $13 - 3 = 2c$
 D. $13 + 3 = 2c$
 E. $13 + 3 = 2(c - 1)$

43. If 15 students in a class average 80% on an English exam and 10 students average 90% on the same exam, what is the average in percent for all 25 students?

 A. 83%
 B. $83\frac{1}{2}\%$
 C. 84%
 D. 85%
 E. $86\frac{2}{3}\%$

Read the information below and then answer the question that follows.

Eagle Savings and Loan pays 3% annual interest.

InterGuild Federal Credit Union pays 4% annual interest.

Simple interest is calculated as interest = principal × rate × time, or *I = Prt.*

44. What would be the difference in the amount of simple interest earned over three years on $1,200 if it were invested in the Credit Union instead of in the Savings and Loan?

 A. $ 12
 B. $ 36
 C. $300
 D. $360
 E. $432

45. Angela has nickels and dimes in her pocket. She has twice as many dimes as nickels. What is the best expression of the amount of money she has in cents if *x* equals the number of nickels she has?

 A. $25x$
 B. $10x + 5(2x)$
 C. $x + 2x$
 D. $5(3x)$
 E. $20(x + 5)$

46. If the value of *x* is between 0.0036 and 0.052, which of the following could be *x*?

 A. 0.0028
 B. 0.0481
 C. 0.0529
 D. 0.053
 E. 0.07

Use the information below to answer the question that follows.

Four construction workers build a house containing 16 rooms. The house has four floors, and the workers take exactly four months (without stopping) to build it.

47. From the preceding information, which of the following must be true?

 A. They build 4 rooms each month.
 B. Each floor has 4 rooms.
 C. No floor has fewer than 3 rooms.
 D. They build an average of one floor per month.
 E. The house averages 3 rooms per floor.

GO ON TO THE NEXT PAGE

48. Max is installing new hardwood floors in the family room. If the total floor area is 420 square feet and he has completed 45% of it, how many square feet has he covered?

   A.   19   square feet
   B.   27   square feet
   C.   153   square feet
   D.   189   square feet
   E.   231   square feet

49. If $x > -\frac{1}{2}$, which of the following could be a possible value for x?

   A. $-\frac{2}{3}$

   B. $-\frac{1}{2}$

   C. -2

   D. -1

   E. $-\frac{1}{4}$

Using the information given below, answer the question that follows.

Bob is taller than Sam. Sam is shorter than Ed. Ed is taller than Cecil but shorter than Amir. Ricardo is taller than Amir but shorter than Bob.

50. From the information given, who is the tallest?

   A.   Bob
   B.   Amir
   C.   Ricardo
   D.   Cecil
   E.   Ed

Section III: Writing

2 Essays

Directions: In this section, you plan and write two essays, one for each topic given. Read each topic carefully to make sure that you are properly addressing the issue or situation. You must write on the specified topic. An essay on another topic will not be acceptable.

Plan your time wisely. Each essay is weighted equally. Plan to spend the same amount of time on each essay.

The two essay questions are designed to give you an opportunity to write clearly and effectively. Use specific examples whenever appropriate to aid in supporting your ideas. Keep in mind that the quality of your writing is much more important than the quantity.

Write each essay on the two sheets of lined paper provided. Your writing should be neat and legible. Because you have only a limited amount of space in which to write, please do *not* skip lines, do *not* write excessively large, and do *not* leave wide margins.

You may use the bottom of the topic page in the test booklet to organize and plan your essay before you begin writing.

Topic 1

An important issue in today's world is improving our environment and preserving the planet. However, some people believe that individual efforts to combat pollution, global warming, and the depletion of natural resources are not likely to make a difference. Discuss the extent to which you agree or disagree with this opinion. Support your opinion with specific reasons. Compare your response to the sample essays for this topic on pages 269-271.

Topic 2

What particular experience had the greatest impact on your decision to enter the education field? Explain why that particular experience was so important.

Answer Key and Analysis for Practice Test 2

Answer Key for Practice Test 2

Section I: Reading			Section II: Mathematics		
1. B	18. E	35. C	1. B	18. D	35. B
2. B	19. B	36. B	2. C	19. E	36. A
3. D	20. C	37. C	3. A	20. E	37. C
4. E	21. D	38. A	4. E	21. A	38. D
5. C	22. A	39. E	5. B	22. B	39. A
6. D	23. E	40. D	6. B	23. C	40. E
7. C	24. C	41. C	7. D	24. E	41. C
8. C	25. D	42. E	8. D	25. C	42. A
9. E	26. C	43. D	9. C	26. B	43. C
10. E	27. D	44. B	10. B	27. B	44. B
11. C	28. B	45. A	11. B	28. C	45. A
12. A	29. C	46. D	12. B	29. A	46. B
13. B	30. E	47. B	13. E	30. C	47. D
14. D	31. B	48. D	14. E	31. B	48. D
15. B	32. E	49. E	15. C	32. C	49. E
16. C	33. D	50. A	16. B	33. B	50. A
17. D	34. A		17. E	34. E	

Scoring Your CBEST Practice Test 2

To score your CBEST Practice Test 2, total the number of correct responses for each section of the test separately. Do not subtract any points for questions attempted but missed, as there is no penalty for guessing. The score for each section is then scaled from 20 to 80. (About 70% right is a passing score.)

Analyzing Your Test Results

Use the charts on the following page to carefully analyze your results and spot your strengths and weaknesses. Complete the process of analyzing each subject area and each individual question for this Practice Test. Reexamine these results for trends in types of errors (repeated errors) or poor results in specific subject areas. This reexamination and analysis is of tremendous importance for effective test preparation.

Subject Area Analysis Sheet

	Possible	Completed	Right	Wrong
Reading	50			
Mathematics	50			
TOTAL	100			

One of the most important parts of test preparation is analyzing *why* you missed a question so that you can reduce your number of mistakes. Now that you have taken Practice Test 2 and corrected your answers, carefully tally your mistakes by marking them in the proper column.

Tally Sheet for Questions Missed

	Total Missed	Simple Mistake	Misread Problem	Lack of Knowledge
Reading				
Mathematics				
TOTAL				

Reviewing the preceding data can help you determine *why* you are missing certain questions. Now that you have pinpointed the type of error you are most likely to make, when you take Practice Test 3, focus on avoiding those errors.

Essay Checklist

Use this checklist to evaluate your essays.

Diagnosis of Timed Writing Exercises		
A good essay:	**Essay 1**	**Essay 2**
. . . addresses the assignment		
■ stays well focused		
■ expresses a clear thesis statement on the topic		
. . . organizes points logically		
■ uses smooth transitions between paragraphs		
■ has coherent, unified paragraphs		
. . . develops ideas presented		
■ gives specific examples to support points		
■ anticipates and addresses opposing views		
. . . is grammatically sound (with only minor flaws)		
■ uses correct sentence structure		
■ uses correct punctuation		
■ uses standard written English		
. . . uses language skillfully		
■ uses a variety of sentence types		
■ uses a variety of words		
. . . is legible		
■ shows clear handwriting		
■ appears neat		

Answers and Complete Explanations for Practice Test 2

Section I: Reading

1. **B.** Clarifying the confusing term *angular displacement* would help to make the passage clearer, especially since the question refers to clarifying the material for a "general audience." Choices **A** and **C** would not necessarily add clarity, especially for a general audience. Choice **D** would likely add to the confusion of a general reader, not lessen it. The demonstration cited in Choice **E** already helps to add clarity; deleting it would diminish understanding.

2. **B.** The position of the pencil appears to shift, depending on which eye is viewing it—that is, the apparent position is dependent on the point from which it is observed. The remaining choices are not reasonable suggestions from this passage.

3. **D.** The sentence explains that the established military tradition supplied the South with military leaders. In Choice **A**, the phrase "most of the talent" is too broad a term; this passage deals only with military leaders. Choice **B** is incorrect because the passage does not hint that the North found any military leaders in the South whatsoever. Choice **C** is unreasonable; it is not logical to jump from the final sentence of the passage to the idea that the North had no leaders at all. Choice **E** also displays an unreasonable jump of logic; the passage deals with the beginning of the Civil War, not its outcome.

4. **E.** Of the various advantages held by the North, the passage concentrates on long-term advantages, such as their food production; this ties in directly with the response "enduring a prolonged conflict." Each of the other choices posits a conclusion that is well beyond anything implied in the passage.

5. **C.** By stating that carrots are good for the eyes but not explaining the connection, the author assumes that readers already understand the connection. None of the other choices delineates an assumption the author has about the readers.

6. **D.** Choice **C** flatly contradicts the argument of the passage, and choices **A** and **B** present information not touched on in the passage. Choice **E** is weak because associations are not universal; they depend on each individual's personal experience. This point—that associations are personal rather than universal—is expressed by Choice **D**.

7. **C.** Choice **C** directly contradicts the main point of the passage, that associations are developed through experience. Choices **A**, **D**, and **E** provide examples which actually strengthen the argument in favor of association. In addition, the phrase in Choice **B** that "only a very few researchers question the doctrine" also helps to strengthen the argument because it implies that the vast majority of researchers *do* agree with the doctrine of association.

8. **C.** Choices **D** and **E** neither weaken nor strengthen the passage; they simply suggest other examples of associations without explaining the stimulus that produced them. Choices **A** and **B** are irrelevant issues. Choice **C**, though, strengthens the argument of the passage by citing an example of experience reinforcing an association—or, in other words, an example stimulating a response.

9. **E.** The passage implies that those who try to interpret multiple-choice tests as indicators of true intellectual ability are not really experts on testing and, further, that they should realize the tests are very limited measurement instruments.

10. **E.** According to paragraph 3, taking candy away is the withdrawal of a positive reinforcer, and spanking is the presentation of a negative reinforcer.

11. **C.** The mention of recess and field trips follows this sentence: "Sometimes we withdraw a privilege from children to control their behavior." Therefore, it is reasonable to conclude that the author is using recess and field trips as examples of such privileges. Choice **A** overstates the argument made in the passage by using the word "prison." Choice **B** is not consistent with the intent of the last paragraph. Choice **D** is irrelevant

because it brings up a new concept (unconscious punishment) that cannot be logically concluded from the last paragraph. Choice **E** is off the topic.

12. **A.** Choice **A** is correct because the question posed in the first paragraph—"Does punishment, in fact, do what it is supposed to do?"—is never answered definitively; the question is discussed but never actually answered. For example, the first sentence of the passage states "punishment is used to reduce tendencies to behave in certain ways," and the second paragraph continues to state that punishment "appears to temporarily suppress a behavior." This is a less-than-definite answer to the question. On the other hand, the ideas in the other choices *are* discussed in this passage, at least to some extent.

13. **B.** Choice **B** is correct because the author suggests that imposing punishment does not seem to have any permanent effect (paragraph 2). Each of the other choices can be eliminated because the conclusions they reach are beyond the scope of the passage.

14. **D.** The point of the passage is that "reality" varies according to who experiences it and what "consensus group" he or she is a member of. In these terms, a war is a conflict between two different consensus groups, and so the example given by Choice **D** is most appropriate. Choices **A** and **C** do not offer specific examples at all. Choice **B** mentions a specific example, but it is irrelevant to answering this question about the passage's main point. Choice **E** contradicts information in the passage.

15. **B.** Both choices **B** and **C** mention "consensus group," but **C** says that the members of the group are deluded about reality, which contradicts the author's argument that no view of reality is, strictly speaking, a delusion. In Choice **A**, the word "scientists" is irrelevant. Choice **D** is incorrect because "reality," as it is defined in the passage, is not related to a consensus of the majority.

16. **C.** Once again, the point of the passage is that different people or groups acquire different versions of reality based on their differing experiences. Reality is, therefore, subjective, but it is never termed a mere figment of imagination.

17. **D.** Choice **D** is validated by sentences 8 and 9 of the passage. The ideas in the other choices have no corroboration in the passage.

18. **E.** This choice correctly paraphrases the author's point about reality and our perception of it. Choice **A** does not answer this question. Choices **B**, **C**, and **D** contradict the passage.

19. **B.** The author states "human nature is not a machine" and then repeatedly stresses this point throughout the passage. Choice **A** is incorrect because the words "automatons" and "machines" may be used synonymously. The ideas in the other choices are mentioned in the passage, but they do not identify major distinctions made by this author.

20. **C.** One way in which the author describes an automaton is a human machine "set to do exactly the work prescribed for it." This description corresponds most closely to workers on an assembly line. The groups in the other choices, on the other hand, require independent thinking and decision making.

21. **D.** The author develops arguments in favor of "he who chooses his plan for himself"; therefore, the author must assume an audience that needs to hear this argument—namely, those who do not select their own life plans. The ideas in the remaining choices are not assumptions the author had to believe to write this passage.

22. **A.** Early in the passage, the author shows that those who choose their own life plans must have complex skills, whereas those whose plan of life is chosen may live simply, with "no need of any other faculty than the ape-like one of imitation." There is nothing in the passage to substantiate the other choices.

23. **E.** The passage is an extended argument *against* the easy life of conformity. Thus, Choice **E** is correct; this answer contradicts the passage, while all the other answers are consistent with its message.

24. **C.** The final sentence serves to explain and summarize the "racist and elitist doctrine" mentioned in the preceding sentence. Although the author states that social Darwinists expanded Darwin's theory to society as a whole, the author does not attempt to "discredit" Darwin at all (Choice **A**). The phrase "some people" implies that the author separates himself or herself from those who claim some people are superior to others (Choice **B**). In Choice **D**, the phrase "fair shake" is an implausible idea for the author's purpose. Choice **E** is incorrect because of the phrase "modern prominence."

25. **D.** The fourth sentence of the passage focuses on the relevance of Darwin's theory to human society, and the bulk of the passage develops this connection. Choice **A** has no evidence in the passage. Choice **B** is too strong to be the primary purpose, and the passage does not provide evidence that this answer is an accurate statement about Darwin. Choice **C** is unreasonable, especially since the author points out that Darwin did not apply his theories to society anyway. Choice **E** is inaccurate because the passage does not supply any examples of Darwinian evolution; it is not the primary purpose.

26. **C.** Because California is in the American West, it is logical to look for information about an early California dialect under "American, Western" on pages 263–64. All of the incorrect choices refer to pages concerning other locations in America, or to the general section about American vocabulary.

27. **D.** The author contrasts the early concern with social, motivational, and aptitudinal aspects of learning with the more recent interest in class activities. None of the other choices expresses an explicit point of the passage.

28. **B.** By citing the value of planning the presentation of material in an orderly way, the author must assume that such organized instruction is beneficial. Each of the other choices draws conclusions beyond the scope of the passage.

29. **C.** None of the other choices makes good sense when substituted for *integral*, and *essential* is one of the meanings of *integral*.

30. **E.** Because the third sentence includes the negative ("not the only problem"), any of the three connectives "Yet," "However," or "But" can be used. The blank in the second paragraph calls for a word to introduce a contrast with "until recently." Of the three possibilities, only "Now" fits.

31. **B.** The "shelf life" of a product is its durability—how long it will last on the shelf of the market without going stale or spoiling. This definition is further supported by the phrase, "fruit that could stand up to shipping and still look good."

32. **E.** The main idea in the second paragraph is the race to develop better-looking and better-tasting tomatoes to remain competitive in the future. However, the fifth sentence deals only with varieties available in the past and present, so it is the most expendable line. All the other sentences directly relate to the paragraph's main subject.

33. **D.** The second paragraph suggests that "better-looking and better-tasting tomatoes" are what American growers most need. By comparison, the other choices address what American tomato growers can already produce.

34. **A.** Understanding punishment to be a type of negative reinforcement, one may infer that frequent punishment "may inhibit learning." Because the passage focuses on education, one phrase used in Choice **B**, "in society at large," leads to its elimination. Choice **C** is an illogical answer; if negative reinforcement does not work well in school, it will not be "useful out of school" either. Choice **D** misstates the author's intent; reward should be used *instead* of punishment, not after it. Choice **E** is irrelevant to this passage; the point may be true, but it is not addressed by the author.

35. **C.** The passage states that budget cuts are predicated on cuts in the teaching staff, so this fact must appear in the correct answer. Only choices **C** and **D** specify a staff cut, but **D** is a weak answer; it is unnecessarily specific and possibly not accurate.

36. **B.** "Migratory" is the adjective form of the verb "to migrate," which means "to move from one place to another," or "to move from one place to another with the change of season."

37. **C.** Choice **C** is confirmed in the first sentence of the third paragraph, which states, "the monarchs use the position of the sun to determine their flight direction." The ideas in choices **D** and **E** are mentioned, but they are not presented as a certainty, as is Choice **C**. The winds may help propel the insects, as in Choice **A**, but winds do not aid in navigation. Choice **B** is contradicted in the passage with the phrase, "an older generation of butterflies cannot instruct a younger one."

38. **A.** A point underlying this passage is that scientists cannot yet fully explain how a migrating butterfly finds its way; thus **A** is the best choice. There is insufficient evidence about butterfly navigation to know whether Choice **B** is true. There is nothing in the passage to either support or refute the ideas in choices **C** and **E**. Choice **D** may or may not be true, but it is not the primary point.

39. **E.** The author's encouraging parents to increase their children's interest in butterflies is clearly a statement of opinion rather than a statement of fact, as in the other answer choices.

40. **D.** Choice **D** offers the true exception; it contradicts the passage because it includes three literature courses not within the same century.

41. **C.** Sentence 6 would be a good breaking point to begin a new paragraph because it introduces a new topic; the discussion shifts from education legislation in general to an examination of John Dewey in particular.

42. **E.** Sentence 7 stresses Dewey's belief that education is concerned with many areas and experiences; this belief contrasts with the Morrill Act's stress on agricultural and mechanical arts as primary educational areas. The passage presents no evidence that Dewey lacked faith in land-grant colleges (Choice **A**), even though he felt education should transform. Choice **B** is an unreasonable answer. Choice **C** is contradicted in the passage; the Morrill Act *did* demonstrate an understanding of the relationship between education and society. The passage offers no evidence for Choice **D**, and it is not a contrast between Dewey and the Morrill Act; therefore, it does not answer the question.

43. **D.** "Also" indicates that Dewey's theories are being discussed in addition to previous information and that reference to the previous information is included in the statement about Dewey. None of the other choices is consistent with the meaning of the word "also" or the passage's message.

44. **B.** Dewey's belief in a comprehensive education is inconsistent with a focus on industrialization, and Choice **B** explains that inconsistency, thus supporting the statement that industrialization is destructive. Choice **A** essentially restates sentence 7 and thus does not offer any additional support. Choice **C** does not support sentence 7, which presents Dewey's idea that the whole community, not just industry, needs to contribute to education. Choice **D** is a contradiction to sentence 8, which states "industrialization was *destroying* the educational functions of these institutions." Sentence 3 (Choice **E**) is irrelevant to the question.

45. **A.** The passage is about education and related legislation, but it is not about legislation in general. All other choices do correctly allude to educational issues.

46. **D.** The passage states that Dewey's theories "had a profound effect on public education." Each of the other choices draws a conclusion beyond the scope of the passage.

47. **B.** In the second sentence, the author provides an opinion that psychology is more "speculative than rational" without offering any objective facts to support the assertion. A limited description of psychology occurs in the first sentence, not the second sentence, Choice **A**. The truth of the first sentence is never denied, Choice **C**. If facts had been presented to prove that psychology "methods" were unscientific, the second sentence could be viewed as inconsistent, Choice **E**, but it only offers an opinion.

48. **D.** The author sketches parallel changes in television and clothes, implying that the medium (television) was responsible for changing taste in clothes. All other choices are unreasonable and are not implied in the passage.

49. **E.** Ten percent of senior boys are involved in sports, and 10 percent of sophomore boys are also involved in sports; therefore, an equal percentage of senior and sophomore boys participate, NOT a greater percentage of senior boys. All the other answers can be derived from the facts in the chart.

50. **A.** The definition of a political party belongs in a text that explains such organizations and systems—namely, an introductory text on political science.

Section II: Mathematics

1. **B.** "What number is 15% of 80" can be changed into an equation:

   $N = 0.15 \times 80$

   $N = 12$

2. **C.** The number 6 is divisible by 1, 2, 3, and 6. The number 8 is divisible by 1, 2, 4, and 8. And the number 12 is divisible by 1, 2, 3, 4, 6, and 12. So the common factors are 1 and 2 only.

3. **A.** $(7+8) \div \frac{2}{3}$

   $15 \div \frac{2}{3}$

   $15 \times \frac{3}{2} = \frac{45}{2} = 22\frac{1}{2}$

4. **E.** Simply add the tons shipped for each company, $5 + 7 + 9 + 12 = 33$.

   But remember that the answer must be expressed in millions: 33,000,000.

5. **B.** Only Choice **B**, $\frac{31}{60}$, is greater than $\frac{1}{2}$. All the other choices are less than $\frac{1}{2}$.

6. **B.** Set up the ratio:

   $\frac{7lbs}{\$4.69} = \frac{9lbs}{x}$

   $7x = \$42.21$

   $x = \$6.03$

   Or simply divide $4.69 by 7 and multiply this result by 9.

7. **D.** There are three chances out of four of spinning red, yellow, or blue. Thus, the correct answer is $\frac{3}{4}$.

8. **D.** 4 rods = $(4)(16\frac{1}{2}$ feet) = 66 feet

   66 feet $\times$ 12 = 792 inches

9. **C.** The easiest way to do this problem is to round $47.93 to $48 and then multiply by 15%.

   $\begin{array}{r} 48 \\ \times.15 \\ \hline 240 \\ 48 \\ \hline \$7.20 \end{array}$

   So, rounded to the nearest dollar, the tip is $7.00.

10. **B.** The total length of ribbon equals the ribbon shown plus the ribbon not shown. There are four pieces of ribbon shown. Find the length of these pieces and then multiply by two.

    Length shown = 4 inches + 16 inches + 8 inches + 4 inches

    Total length = 2×32 inches = 64 inches

11. **B.** Ratios may be expressed as fractions. Thus Choice **A**, 1 to 4, may be expressed as $\frac{1}{4}$. Notice that choices **C**, **D**, and **E** are all fractions that reduce to $\frac{1}{4}$.

    $\frac{2}{8} = \frac{1}{4}$

    $\frac{3}{12} = \frac{1}{4}$

    $\frac{4}{16} = \frac{1}{4}$

    Only Choice **B** $\left(\frac{3}{8}\right)$ does not equal $\frac{1}{4}$.

Practice Test 2

263

12. **B.** The number sentence is an addition problem (825.50 + 435.00). The only choice that expresses a problem in addition is **B**.

13. **E.** Since D intersects (overlaps) A, B, and C, it must have something in common with each one.

14. **E.** Mary worked a total of 24 hours, but you do not know in how many days. Therefore, you can't derive the number of hours she worked each day. Each of the other choices can be derived from the statements given.

15. **C.**

$$3c = d$$
$$\frac{3c}{3} = \frac{d}{3}$$
$$c = \frac{d}{3}$$

16. **B.** This question requires that you use a proportion.

$$\frac{map(cm)}{actual(km)} : \frac{1}{35} = \frac{x}{245}$$
$$35x = 245$$
$$x = 7 cm$$

17. **E.** The tenth place is the number immediately to the right of the decimal point. To round off to the nearest tenth, check the hundredth place (two places to the right of the decimal point). If the hundredth number is a 5 or higher, round the tenth up to the next number. For instance, 0.36 would round to 0.4. If the hundredth is a 4 or lower, simply drop any places after the tenth place. For instance, 0.74356 would round to 0.7. Thus, 4,316.136 rounded to the nearest tenth is 4,316.1—which is Choice **E**.

18. **D.** To find the subtotal, simply add $5.50 + $5.95 + $1.25. The subtotal equals $12.70.

19. **E.** The fraction $\frac{1}{8}$ equals 0.125. Thus, it would lie between $\frac{1}{9}$ (0.111. . .) and $\frac{2}{15}$ (0.133. . .).

20. **E.** The only statement that *must* be true is Choice **E**. The class averages 2 pencils per student. Notice that 30 students could each have 2 pencils; so choices **C** and **D** may be false. Likewise, just one of the students could have all 60 pencils; therefore choices **A** and **B** may be false. Only Choice **E** must be true.

21. **A.** First, find the total length of string by multiplying 8 inches by 19:

8 inches × 19 = 152 inches

To determine the amount of string left over from the spool, first convert 5 yards to inches by multiplying 5 by 36 inches = 180 inches. Then, subtract 152 inches from 180 inches:

180 − 152 = 28 inches = 2 feet, 4 inches

22. **B.** Four pounds of round steak at $3.89 per pound cost $15.56. Change from a $20 bill would therefore be $20.00 − $15.56, or $4.44.

23. **C.** In the series 8, 9, 12, 17, 24 . . . , note the changes, or differences, between numbers:

$$9 - 8 = 1$$
$$12 - 9 = 3$$
$$17 - 12 = 5$$
$$24 - 17 = 7$$

Hence, the difference between the next term and 24 must be 9, or $x - 24 = 9$, and $x = 33$. Therefore, the next term in the series must be 33.

24. **E.** The total hours equals:

    $4 + 2 + 3 + 4 + 3 = 16$

    Since the earnings equal the total hours times the hourly rate:

    $16\ (\$7.25)$

25. **C.** Enlarging each dimension by 20%, the new dimensions would be 4.8 inches and 7.2 inches. Therefore, the new perimeter would be 2(length) + 2(width):

    $P = 2(7.2 \text{ inches}) + 2(4.8 \text{ inches})$

    $\quad = 14.4 \text{ inches } + 9.6 \text{ inches}$

    $\quad = 24 \text{ inches}$

26. **B.** In order to have the pie graph represent blue-eyed students as 6 out of 24, the piece of the "pie" representing blue-eyed students should be $\frac{6}{24}$ or $\frac{1}{4}$. So the blue piece needs to be increased. Likewise, for hazel to represent $\frac{5}{24}$, its piece of the pie should be slightly less than $\frac{6}{24}$, so its size should be decreased.

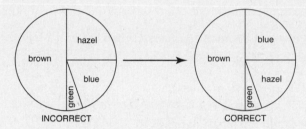

27. **B.** To answer this question, multiply 36 by $11\frac{1}{2}$. You can also change $11\frac{1}{2}$ to 11.5.

    $36 \times 11.5 = 414$

    or

    $36 \times 11\frac{1}{2}$

    $36 \times \frac{23}{2} = 414$

28. **C.** In 2005, 10% of $30,000, or $3,000, was spent on medical expenses. In 2010, 12% of $34,000, or $4,080, was spent on medical expenses. Thus, there was an increase of $1,080.

29. **A.** There was an increase from 18% to 22%, or 4%.

30. **C.** If the area of the square is 36 square inches, then the side of the square must be 6 inches. Thus, the length of the rectangle must be 12 inches (since it is twice as long as the side of the square). The width of the rectangle is 4 inches (since it is $\frac{2}{3}$ the side of the square). So the perimeter of the rectangle equals $12 + 12 + 4 + 4$, or 32 inches.

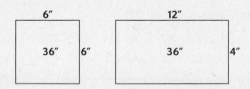

31. **B.** Since m yards = $36m$ inches, and n feet = $12n$ inches, m yards and n feet = $(36m + 12n)$ inches.

32. **C.** 240 out of 800 can be expressed as $\frac{240}{800}$, which reduces to $\frac{3}{10}$ or 30%.

33. B. The probability of throwing a head in one throw is

$$\frac{\text{chance of a head}}{\text{total chances}\,(1 \text{ head}+1 \text{ tail})} = \frac{1}{2}$$

Since you are trying to throw a head *twice*, multiply the probability for the first toss $\left(\frac{1}{2}\right)$ by the probability for the second toss (again $\frac{1}{2}$). Thus, $\frac{1}{2} \times \frac{1}{2} = \frac{1}{4}$, and $\frac{1}{4}$ is the probability of throwing heads twice in two tosses. Another way of approaching this problem is to look at the total number of possible outcomes:

	First Toss	Second Toss
1.	H	H
2.	H	T
3.	T	H
4.	T	T

Thus, there are four different possible outcomes. There is only one way to throw two heads in two tosses. Thus, the probability of tossing two heads in two tosses is 1 out of 4 total outcomes, or $\frac{1}{4}$.

34. E. This is the only true statement because $5\frac{5}{6}$ is greater than $5\frac{4}{6}$, and $5\frac{4}{6}$ is greater than $4\frac{4}{6}$.

35. B. The amount of discount was $120 - $90 = $30. The rate of discount equals

$$\frac{\text{change}}{\text{starting point}} = \frac{30}{120} = \frac{1}{4} = 25\%$$

36. A. To answer this question, add the mixed numbers $16\frac{1}{4}$ and $8\frac{3}{7}$.

First, get a common denominator:

$$16\frac{1}{4} + 8\frac{3}{7}$$

$$16\frac{7}{28} + 8\frac{12}{28} = 24\frac{19}{28}$$

37. C. To change 3 miles to feet, simply multiply 3 by 5,280 (since 5,280 is the number of feet in a mile). This gives you the number of feet in 3 miles. Then multiply this product by 12, since there are 12 inches in each foot. The resulting product is the number of inches in 3 miles.

38. D. If the first integer is x, then the next consecutive even integer must be $x + 2$. The third consecutive even integer must then be $x + 4$. Since their sum is 318,

$$(x) + (x + 2) + (x + 4) = 318$$
$$3x + 6 = 318$$
$$\underline{-6 \quad -6}$$
$$\frac{3x}{3} = \frac{312}{3}$$

The largest integer of the three is thus $x + 4$, or 108.

39. A. First, calculate the number of boys in the classroom. Since 40% of the students are girls, 60% must be boys, or $0.6Q$ (60% of the total number of students). Now, of those boys, $\frac{2}{3}$ do not have brown hair; therefore, the best expression of boys without brown hair would be $(0.6Q)\frac{2}{3}$, or Choice **A**.

40. E. To compute the percentage, simply plug into the formula:

$$\frac{\text{is}}{\text{of}} = \frac{\text{percent}}{100}$$

The problem asks: "The air pressure in the football is approximately what percent of the air pressure in the basketball?" Thus:

$$\frac{10 \ lbs}{9 \ lbs} = \frac{x}{100}$$
$$1000 = 9x$$
$$\frac{1000}{9} = \frac{9x}{9}$$
$$x = 111.11 \approx 111\%$$

(question asks for an approximate answer)

41. **C.** Use the formula for the perimeter of a triangle to determine the length of the third leg.

$$P = L_1 + L_2 + L_3$$

Since the length of one leg is 36 inches and that of the other leg is 60 inches, the equation would be:

14 feet = 36 inches + 60 inches + L_3

14 feet = 96 inches + L_3

168 inches = 96 inches + L_3

72 inches = L_3

42. **A.** If today Lucy is 14, then last year she was 13. Likewise, if Charlie's age now is c, then last year he was $c - 1$. Now put these into an equation.

$$\underbrace{\text{Lucy's age last year}}_{13} \underset{=}{\text{is}} \underbrace{\text{three years older than twice Charlie's age last year.}}_{3 + 2(c - 1)}$$

Transposing the 3 on the right side to the left side gives: $13 - 3 = 2(c - 1)$.

43. **C.** In this type of problem (weighted average), you must multiply the number of students by their respective scores and divide this total by the number of students, as follows:

$$15 \times 80 = 1200$$
$$10 \times 90 = \ \ 900$$
$$TOTAL = 2100$$

Now divide 25 into 2,100. This gives an average of 84%; therefore, the correct answer is Choice **C.**

44. **B.** The difference in the amounts invested would be 4% – 3%, or 1% of the principal ($1,200) over three years.

$$I = Prt$$
$$I = (\$1,200)(0.01)(3)$$
$$I = \$36$$

45. **A.** The number of nickels that Angela has is x. Thus, the total value of those nickels (in cents) is $5x$. Angela also has twice as many dimes as nickels, or $2x$. The total value in cents of those dimes is $2x(10)$, or $20x$. Adding together the value of the nickels and dimes gives $5x + 20x$, or $25x$.

46. **B.** Use elimination to determine the correct answer. Choice **A** (0.0028) is less than 0.0036. Choices **C, D,** and **E** are all larger than .052. Therefore, only Choice **B,** .0481, is between .0036 and .052.

47. **D.** Since there are four floors, and the construction workers take four months to build the house, the average is one floor per month. The workers may build more or less than four rooms each month. Building four rooms each month, Choice **A,** is only the average. The same is true for how many rooms are on each floor. Having four rooms per floor, Choice **B,** is also an average. Choice **C** is not necessarily true. Choice **E** is wrong; the house averages four rooms per floor.

Practice Test 2

267

48. D. To answer this question, multiply the total floor area by the percentage covered.

(Total area) × (part covered)

$420 \times 45\%$

$420 \times 0.45 = 189$ square feet

49. E. The problem states "if x is greater than $-\frac{1}{2}$." This means that it cannot equal $-\frac{1}{2}$. You are looking for an answer <u>greater</u> than $-\frac{1}{2}$. The answer must be to the <u>right</u> of $-\frac{1}{2}$ on a number line. (Numbers increase going to the right on a number line and <u>decrease</u> going to the left.)

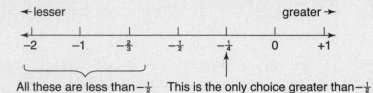

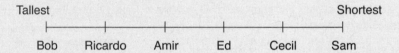

50. A. Bob is the tallest. Amir is taller than Ed, who is taller than Sam and Cecil. Since Ricardo is taller than Amir but shorter than Bob, Bob is the tallest.

It is sometimes helpful to arrange names on a line from tallest to shortest.

Tallest   Shortest

Bob   Ricardo   Amir   Ed   Cecil   Sam

Section III: Writing

To help you evaluate your essay writing skills, listed below are examples of three different written responses for essay topic one (there are no examples for topic two). Compare your essay to these three examples and the analysis of a well-written essay, an average essay, and a poorly written essay. Use the suggested analysis sheet (p. 257) and checklist (p. 258) to evaluate your essays, and to help you take a closer look and understand your scoring range. Topic prompt can be found on page 250.

Essay 1: A Well-Written Essay

Does each of us have a responsibility to the environment and the planet, or are our individual efforts negligible? I believe that although it is essential for governments to take action to save the planet, each of us can make a difference in the way we live our lives. Governments must agree to strict regulations regarding emissions, waste disposal, and preserving resources, but we ourselves must not only adhere to regulations but also go a step further. Our personal behavior may seem unimportant in terms of the total problem, but just our commitment to a better world will influence legislators and corporation executives who are in a position to make major environmental decisions.

When we buy environmentally friendly products, manufacturers will respond by making more of them. For example, if we choose a hybrid car, such as the Prius, then car manufacturers will see the value in making such cars and make more of them. This is true with a variety of products, from paper towels to kitchen appliances. Supermarket shelves now reflect the consumer's interest in buying environmentally friendly products, and advertising includes claims relating to a product's environmental benefits. These developments would not have occurred without individuals demanding that companies pay more attention to saving the planet. The truth is that the marketplace responds when we as consumers choose to buy "green" products.

In addition, when we choose to support and elect representatives who place environmental issues high on their agendas, we increase the chances that governing bodies will make decisions that favor conservation of resources and preservation of the planet. Groups that work to elect "green" candidates are made up of individuals, after all. Each of us is responsible for being informed about issues such as global warming so that we can make our decisions about candidates based on facts, not propaganda or campaign slogans.

On another level, one individual's actions can make a significant difference when joined with other individuals' actions. My not using an aerosol spray will have little effect on global warming perhaps, but if tens of thousands of people like me give up aerosol sprays, who knows what the result will be? The point is that our individual actions

Practice Test 2

may become part of a movement, and the more of us who make a commitment, the greater the effects will be. Recycling, which has increased in the last several years, has already had an effect on the size of landfills.

It is too easy to decide that our individual actions won't make much difference when it comes to saving the planet. It's what I would call a "cop-out." In fact, most things of general value to the world are a result of many individual actions joined together, and this is certainly true when considering the preservation of our planet and the improvement of our environment. With the information we have today, it is irresponsible, in my opinion, to ignore the importance of our actions.

Analysis of Essay 1

The opening paragraph includes a thesis statement and is a well-developed introduction. The three following paragraphs support the writer's thesis, explaining specifically how an individual's actions can make a difference. Each paragraph is logically and coherently developed, and the writer uses transitions from one point to another. The writing is clear and free of errors, and the concluding paragraph reiterates the writer's point of view throughout the essay.

Essay 2: An Average Essay

There are many ways a person can work on the environment. First, one can join organizations that are devoted to environmental issues. Second, one can save energy and conserve other resources in his everyday life. Third, one can vote for candidates who support the environment.

Many groups exist that work on environmental issues, for example, one can join the Sierra Club, the Natural Resources Defense Council and similar groups that put pressure on Washington D.C. to do things such as prevent drilling in the Arctic, preserve old forests, and research alternative energy ideas.

Secondly, in their daily lives people can buy products made from recycled materials. And they can themselves recycle paper, cans, and bottles. Don't rely on disposable products but instead on reusable products. Drive a vehicle that doesn't use too much gas. Consider riding your bike to work rather than driving a car. Remember to turn off your lights and unplug your appliances when you leave home.

Vote for candidates who take a stand on matters such as global warning, auto emissions, and for seeking new ways to preserve resources. Write letters to your congressman to let him or her know that you want attention paid to environmental issues.

It is up to all of us to make sure that the earth remains a livable place. Not just for humans but for all species. Remember that the actions of human beings effects all life on earth and also determines the future of the planet.

Analysis of Essay 2

The topic asks a question: Are individual efforts negligible? If they are, why? If they are not, why not? This essay lists ways in which an individual can address environmental problems but doesn't discuss their effectiveness. The organization of the essay is adequate and some specific details are used, but the paragraphs are not fully developed. The writer also sometimes uses "a person" or "one" and sometimes addresses "you" (see paragraph three). Consistency should be maintained. There are a few minor errors (a run-on sentence in paragraph two, a fragment in paragraph five, and a subject-verb agreement problem in the last sentence).

Essay 3: A Poorly Written Essay

I completely disagree with the opinion that our actions don't make a difference when it comes to the enviroment, if we don't save the earth, who will? We need to do everything we can, to make sure that our natural resources will last and that massive pollution will not cover the world. We should try to find alternative energy sources. We will run out of fossel fuels at some time, and besides we also should realize that they create terrible smog problems, especially in the big cities. Developing solar power is important. As well as further investigating the possibilities of hydrogen fuel cells. Right now the idea seems to be to finding more places to get oil, but this isn't the answer. What is especially stupid is that we are ready to dig for oil in places that endanger species and our oceans.

Strickter regulations on emissions are necessary. It is true this may mean we will pay more for our cars, but what is more money for cars when compared to the future of the world.

We as individuals must work for a better future, lets not leave a world on the brink of disaster for our children and our childrens children to inherit.

Analysis of Essay 3

This is a poorly written essay in several ways. It doesn't address the topic, and the points it does include are not presented in a coherent way. For example, in the first paragraph, sentences aren't logically connected. The writer simply skips from one point to another. Overall, this essay is disorganized. It should include a clear introduction with a thesis statement, which is then developed in the following paragraphs. Sentence errors—as well as spelling, punctuation, and grammatical errors—occur throughout.

Practice Test 3

Answer Sheet for Practice Test 3

(Remove This Sheet and Use It to Mark Your Answers)

Section I: Reading

1	Ⓐ Ⓑ Ⓒ Ⓓ Ⓔ		26	Ⓐ Ⓑ Ⓒ Ⓓ Ⓔ
2	Ⓐ Ⓑ Ⓒ Ⓓ Ⓔ		27	Ⓐ Ⓑ Ⓒ Ⓓ Ⓔ
3	Ⓐ Ⓑ Ⓒ Ⓓ Ⓔ		28	Ⓐ Ⓑ Ⓒ Ⓓ Ⓔ
4	Ⓐ Ⓑ Ⓒ Ⓓ Ⓔ		29	Ⓐ Ⓑ Ⓒ Ⓓ Ⓔ
5	Ⓐ Ⓑ Ⓒ Ⓓ Ⓔ		30	Ⓐ Ⓑ Ⓒ Ⓓ Ⓔ
6	Ⓐ Ⓑ Ⓒ Ⓓ Ⓔ		31	Ⓐ Ⓑ Ⓒ Ⓓ Ⓔ
7	Ⓐ Ⓑ Ⓒ Ⓓ Ⓔ		32	Ⓐ Ⓑ Ⓒ Ⓓ Ⓔ
8	Ⓐ Ⓑ Ⓒ Ⓓ Ⓔ		33	Ⓐ Ⓑ Ⓒ Ⓓ Ⓔ
9	Ⓐ Ⓑ Ⓒ Ⓓ Ⓔ		34	Ⓐ Ⓑ Ⓒ Ⓓ Ⓔ
10	Ⓐ Ⓑ Ⓒ Ⓓ Ⓔ		35	Ⓐ Ⓑ Ⓒ Ⓓ Ⓔ
11	Ⓐ Ⓑ Ⓒ Ⓓ Ⓔ		36	Ⓐ Ⓑ Ⓒ Ⓓ Ⓔ
12	Ⓐ Ⓑ Ⓒ Ⓓ Ⓔ		37	Ⓐ Ⓑ Ⓒ Ⓓ Ⓔ
13	Ⓐ Ⓑ Ⓒ Ⓓ Ⓔ		38	Ⓐ Ⓑ Ⓒ Ⓓ Ⓔ
14	Ⓐ Ⓑ Ⓒ Ⓓ Ⓔ		39	Ⓐ Ⓑ Ⓒ Ⓓ Ⓔ
15	Ⓐ Ⓑ Ⓒ Ⓓ Ⓔ		40	Ⓐ Ⓑ Ⓒ Ⓓ Ⓔ
16	Ⓐ Ⓑ Ⓒ Ⓓ Ⓔ		41	Ⓐ Ⓑ Ⓒ Ⓓ Ⓔ
17	Ⓐ Ⓑ Ⓒ Ⓓ Ⓔ		42	Ⓐ Ⓑ Ⓒ Ⓓ Ⓔ
18	Ⓐ Ⓑ Ⓒ Ⓓ Ⓔ		43	Ⓐ Ⓑ Ⓒ Ⓓ Ⓔ
19	Ⓐ Ⓑ Ⓒ Ⓓ Ⓔ		44	Ⓐ Ⓑ Ⓒ Ⓓ Ⓔ
20	Ⓐ Ⓑ Ⓒ Ⓓ Ⓔ		45	Ⓐ Ⓑ Ⓒ Ⓓ Ⓔ
21	Ⓐ Ⓑ Ⓒ Ⓓ Ⓔ		46	Ⓐ Ⓑ Ⓒ Ⓓ Ⓔ
22	Ⓐ Ⓑ Ⓒ Ⓓ Ⓔ		47	Ⓐ Ⓑ Ⓒ Ⓓ Ⓔ
23	Ⓐ Ⓑ Ⓒ Ⓓ Ⓔ		48	Ⓐ Ⓑ Ⓒ Ⓓ Ⓔ
24	Ⓐ Ⓑ Ⓒ Ⓓ Ⓔ		49	Ⓐ Ⓑ Ⓒ Ⓓ Ⓔ
25	Ⓐ Ⓑ Ⓒ Ⓓ Ⓔ		50	Ⓐ Ⓑ Ⓒ Ⓓ Ⓔ

Section II: Mathematics

1 Ⓐ Ⓑ Ⓒ Ⓓ Ⓔ	26 Ⓐ Ⓑ Ⓒ Ⓓ Ⓔ
2 Ⓐ Ⓑ Ⓒ Ⓓ Ⓔ	27 Ⓐ Ⓑ Ⓒ Ⓓ Ⓔ
3 Ⓐ Ⓑ Ⓒ Ⓓ Ⓔ	28 Ⓐ Ⓑ Ⓒ Ⓓ Ⓔ
4 Ⓐ Ⓑ Ⓒ Ⓓ Ⓔ	29 Ⓐ Ⓑ Ⓒ Ⓓ Ⓔ
5 Ⓐ Ⓑ Ⓒ Ⓓ Ⓔ	30 Ⓐ Ⓑ Ⓒ Ⓓ Ⓔ
6 Ⓐ Ⓑ Ⓒ Ⓓ Ⓔ	31 Ⓐ Ⓑ Ⓒ Ⓓ Ⓔ
7 Ⓐ Ⓑ Ⓒ Ⓓ Ⓔ	32 Ⓐ Ⓑ Ⓒ Ⓓ Ⓔ
8 Ⓐ Ⓑ Ⓒ Ⓓ Ⓔ	33 Ⓐ Ⓑ Ⓒ Ⓓ Ⓔ
9 Ⓐ Ⓑ Ⓒ Ⓓ Ⓔ	34 Ⓐ Ⓑ Ⓒ Ⓓ Ⓔ
10 Ⓐ Ⓑ Ⓒ Ⓓ Ⓔ	35 Ⓐ Ⓑ Ⓒ Ⓓ Ⓔ
11 Ⓐ Ⓑ Ⓒ Ⓓ Ⓔ	36 Ⓐ Ⓑ Ⓒ Ⓓ Ⓔ
12 Ⓐ Ⓑ Ⓒ Ⓓ Ⓔ	37 Ⓐ Ⓑ Ⓒ Ⓓ Ⓔ
13 Ⓐ Ⓑ Ⓒ Ⓓ Ⓔ	38 Ⓐ Ⓑ Ⓒ Ⓓ Ⓔ
14 Ⓐ Ⓑ Ⓒ Ⓓ Ⓔ	39 Ⓐ Ⓑ Ⓒ Ⓓ Ⓔ
15 Ⓐ Ⓑ Ⓒ Ⓓ Ⓔ	40 Ⓐ Ⓑ Ⓒ Ⓓ Ⓔ
16 Ⓐ Ⓑ Ⓒ Ⓓ Ⓔ	41 Ⓐ Ⓑ Ⓒ Ⓓ Ⓔ
17 Ⓐ Ⓑ Ⓒ Ⓓ Ⓔ	42 Ⓐ Ⓑ Ⓒ Ⓓ Ⓔ
18 Ⓐ Ⓑ Ⓒ Ⓓ Ⓔ	43 Ⓐ Ⓑ Ⓒ Ⓓ Ⓔ
19 Ⓐ Ⓑ Ⓒ Ⓓ Ⓔ	44 Ⓐ Ⓑ Ⓒ Ⓓ Ⓔ
20 Ⓐ Ⓑ Ⓒ Ⓓ Ⓔ	45 Ⓐ Ⓑ Ⓒ Ⓓ Ⓔ
21 Ⓐ Ⓑ Ⓒ Ⓓ Ⓔ	46 Ⓐ Ⓑ Ⓒ Ⓓ Ⓔ
22 Ⓐ Ⓑ Ⓒ Ⓓ Ⓔ	47 Ⓐ Ⓑ Ⓒ Ⓓ Ⓔ
23 Ⓐ Ⓑ Ⓒ Ⓓ Ⓔ	48 Ⓐ Ⓑ Ⓒ Ⓓ Ⓔ
24 Ⓐ Ⓑ Ⓒ Ⓓ Ⓔ	49 Ⓐ Ⓑ Ⓒ Ⓓ Ⓔ
25 Ⓐ Ⓑ Ⓒ Ⓓ Ⓔ	50 Ⓐ Ⓑ Ⓒ Ⓓ Ⓔ

CUT HERE

Practice Test 3

The total testing time is 4 hours. You may work on any section of the exam during this time period.

> Section I: Reading—50 Questions
> Section II: Mathematics—50 Questions
> Section III: Writing—2 Essays

Section I: Reading

50 Questions

Directions: A question or number of questions follows each of the statements or passages in this section. Using only the *stated* or *implied* information given in the statement or passage, answer the question or questions by choosing the *best* answer from among the five choices given. Make sure to mark your answers for this section on the Reading section of the answer sheet.

Use the excerpt from the index below to answer the two questions that follow.

> if clauses, 152
>
> ignorance, verbs expressing, 139
>
> Imperative, 91–93; formation in irregular verbs, 154; negative, 94; third person of, 150
>
> Impersonal construction, 128
>
> Impersonal verbs, 141; auxiliary used with, 135
>
> Imprecations, 150
>
> in, 39, 116; after a superlative, 126; auxiliary used with, 135
>
> Indefinite antecedent of a relative pronoun, 147
>
> Indefinite article: forms, 19; before possessives, 53; omitted, 151
>
> Indefinite pronoun, 147
>
> Independent clauses, subjunctive in, 150
>
> Indicative. *See* Tenses
>
> Infinitive, 22; contracted, 154; dependent, 159–60; in noun clauses, 140; used as a noun, 148; used as a stem, 48; used as an imperative, 94; used as the object of a preposition, 148; without preposition, 162
>
> Irregular verbs, 169; formation, 154; regular forms of, 153–54

1. All the following are possible uses of the infinitive, except:

   A. as the object of the preposition.
   B. as a noun.
   C. in a noun clause.
   D. as a subjunctive.
   E. as a stem.

2. On what page would you look for information about the use of the preposition *in* a phrase like *the best in the world* or *the worst in the state*?

   A. Page 39
   B. Page 116
   C. Page 126
   D. Page 135
   E. Page 150

Read the passage below and answer the question that follows.

   Recent studies show that aptitude test scores are declining because of lack of family stability and students' preoccupation with out-of-school activities. Therefore, not only the student's attitude but also his or her home environment must be changed to stop this downward trend.

GO ON TO THE NEXT PAGE

3. Which of the following is one assumption of the preceding argument?

   A. Recent studies have refuted previous studies.
   B. Heredity is more important than environment.
   C. Aptitude test scores should stop declining soon.
   D. The accuracy of the recent studies cited is not an issue.
   E. More out-of-school activities are available than ever before.

Read the passage below and answer the question that follows.

Once again, our City Council has shown all the firmness of a <u>bowl of oatmeal</u> in deciding to seek a "compromise" on sheep grazing in the city. As it is wont to do more often than not, the council overturned a Planning Commission recommendation, this time to ban sheep grazing in the city.

4. The preceding passage uses the phrase <u>bowl of oatmeal</u> to

   A. condemn the actions taken by the City Council.
   B. add levity to the otherwise tragic situation.
   C. imply that grazing sheep would prefer oats.
   D. praise the City Council for its recent vote.
   E. urge the City Council to overturn the Planning Commission.

Read the passage below and answer the four questions that follow.

(1) Herbs and other natural medicines are no longer found only in health-food stores. (2) They are now sold in supermarkets, discount stores, by mail, and over the Internet. (3) The Internet is rapidly becoming America's favorite place to buy. (4) One in three Americans uses medicinal herbs, and sales exceed three billion dollars each year. (5) Several reasons are behind this phenomenon. (6) One is that the Food and Drug Administration no longer has regulatory power over dietary supplements, so the marketing of these products has increased. (7) _____ .

The rise in the consumption of herbal remedies has raised some questions in the medical community. One is the unsupported claims for herbal remedies by manufacturers. Another is that quality and purity can vary greatly among herbal preparations. Some physicians remain skeptical of their effectiveness and argue that the reported benefits are based more on imagined effects than on science. _____, studies in Europe have shown that the herb known as Saint-John's-wort worked as a remedy for depressed moods; _____ an extract of the ginkgo tree has been shown to modestly improve other ailments such as forgetfulness.

5. Which of the following numbered sentences is the *least* relevant to the ideas of the first paragraph?

   A. Sentence 2
   B. Sentence 3
   C. Sentence 4
   D. Sentence 5
   E. Sentence 6

6. Which sentence, if inserted into the blank line in the first paragraph, would be most consistent with the writer's purpose in this passage?

   A. More and more people have been turned on to herbs and herbal compounds.
   B. You could also say that more doctors have told their patients to take herbs.
   C. A second is that more doctors are recommending herbal remedies to their patients.
   D. The fact that herbs are being recommended by doctors and medical practitioners in larger and greater numbers is also a factor.
   E. And is expected to increase even more.

7. Which words or phrases, if inserted *in order* into the blanks in the second paragraph, would help the reader understand the sequence of the writer's ideas?

   A. Also; on the other hand
   B. Thus; conversely
   C. In addition; nevertheless
   D. However; furthermore
   E. On the other hand; however

8. Which of the following best reflects the content of the two paragraphs of the passage?

    A.   I. The increased consumption of herbal remedies
           II. The concerns of doctors and potential benefits of herbs

    B.   I. The growth of herbal medicines in the American marketplace
           II. How to guard against ineffective herbal medicines

    C.   I. The use of herbal remedies
           II. Comparing herbal and traditional medicines

    D.   I. The popularity of herbal medicines
           II. The dangers of herbal medicines

    E.   I. Herbal remedies and the Food and Drug Administration
           II. Successful testing of herbal remedies

Read the passage below and answer the three questions that follow.

From the U.S. Supreme Court now comes an extraordinary decision permitting inquiries into the "state of mind" of journalists and the editorial process of news organizations. This is perhaps the most alarming evidence so far of a determination by the nation's highest court to weaken the protection of the First Amendment for those who gather and report the news.

The Court last year upheld the right of police to invade newspaper offices in search of evidence, and reporters in other cases have gone to jail to protect the confidentiality of their notebooks. Under the recent 6 to 3 ruling in a libel case, they now face a challenge to the privacy of their minds.

Few would argue that the First Amendment guarantees absolute freedom of speech or freedom of the press. Slander and libel laws stand to the contrary as a protection of an individual's reputation against the irresponsible dissemination of falsehoods. The effect of this latest decision, however, is to make the libel suit, or the threat of one, a clear invasion by the courts into the private decision making that constitutes news and editorial judgment.

In landmark decisions of 1964 and 1967, the Supreme Court established that public officials or public figures bringing libel actions must prove that a damaging falsehood was published with "actual malice"—that is, with knowledge that the statements were false, or with reckless disregard of whether they were true or not.

Justice Byron R. White, writing for the new majority in the new ruling, says it is not enough to examine all the circumstances of publication that would indicate whether there was malicious intent. It is proper and constitutional, he says, for "state-of-mind evidence" to be introduced. The court is thus ordering a CBS television producer to answer questions about the thought processes that went into the preparation and airing of a segment of *60 Minutes*.

That six justices of the Supreme Court fail to see this as a breach of the First Amendment is frightening. The novelist George Orwell may have been mistaken only in the timing of his vision of a Big Brother government practicing mind control.

9. This article deals principally with

    A.   the U.S. Supreme Court's decisions.
    B.   explaining the First Amendment to the Constitution.
    C.   an attack on the freedom of the press.
    D.   slander and libel laws.
    E.   Big Brother in government.

10. How many justices would have to change their minds to reverse this decision?

    A.   One
    B.   Two
    C.   Three
    D.   Four
    E.   Five

11. This writer thinks the Supreme Court is wrong in this case because

    A.   newspapers were unsophisticated when the First Amendment was written.
    B.   reporters are entitled to special rights.
    C.   it challenges the privacy of a journalist's mind.
    D.   Judge White has himself been accused of slander and libel.
    E.   the Supreme Court is capable of malicious intent.

GO ON TO THE NEXT PAGE

Read the passage below and answer the two questions that follow.

Sometimes the U.S. government goes out of its way to prove it can be an absolute nuisance. Take the case of Southern Clay, Inc., which has a factory at Paris, Tennessee, putting out a clay product for cat boxes best known as "Kitty Litter."

It's a simple enough process, but the federal Mine Safety and Health Administration insists that since clay comes from the ground—an excavation half a mile from the Kitty Litter plant—the company actually is engaged in mining and milling. Therefore, says MSHA, Southern Clay is subject to all the rules that govern, say, coal mines working in shafts several hundred feet down.

The company has been told to devise an escape system and fire-fighting procedure in case there is a fire in its "mine." Southern Clay estimates it will lose six thousand hours in production time giving its 250 factory workers special training in how to escape from a mine disaster.

One thing that has always impressed us about cats, in addition to their tidiness, is that they seem to watch the human world with a sense of wise and detached superiority, as though they wonder what all the hustle and bustle is about. If they grin from time to time, as some people insist, it's no wonder.

12. The author's purpose in writing this article is to

    A. explain how Kitty Litter is produced.
    B. describe the Mine Safety and Health Administration.
    C. show how tidy cats are.
    D. show that the government can sometimes be a nuisance.
    E. describe how to prevent fires in mines.

13. What does the author mean by the article's last sentence?

    A. Cats sometimes laugh at their own tidiness.
    B. Cats sometimes seem to be amused by human antics.
    C. People sometimes appear to be laughing at the antics of cats.
    D. Some people think cats are laughing at the Kitty Litter plant.
    E. Some people think cats are laughing at the futility of fire-fighting procedures.

Read the passage below and answer the three questions that follow.

Plant identification requires little paraphernalia. Only two items are essential: a field guide or manual and a hand lens. Some progress can be made without the lens, but a good magnifying glass is especially helpful in ascertaining twig characteristics. Lenses for general use should magnify six to ten times. Whenever possible, identifications should be made in the field, where additional specimens and supplementary data are available. When there is a need for collecting specimens, however, one can secure a vasculum (a metal container to keep specimens fresh) and a plant press. One can substitute any fairly airtight bag or box for the vasculum and make a press of scrap wood and blotters held together by straps. A roll of newspaper or even a large magazine often does as well as a carrier of specimens that are merely being carried for early identification.

14. Which of the following is the best definition of paraphernalia as it is used in the first sentence?

    A. Technical knowledge
    B. Experience
    C. Manual skill
    D. Equipment
    E. Stamina

15. According to the passage, why is it preferable to make identifications in the field?

    A. To avoid having to transport specimens.
    B. To have more specimens at hand.
    C. To prevent the deterioration of specimens.
    D. To take advantage of natural light.
    E. To eliminate carrying heavy equipment.

16. A plastic bag is a suitable replacement for a vasculum because it is

    A. lightweight.
    B. easy to see through.
    C. inexpensive.
    D. disposable.
    E. airtight.

Read the passage below and answer the question that follows.

The Jesuit Antonio Vieira—missionary, diplomat, and voluminous writer—repeated the triumphs he had gained in Bahia and Lisbon in Rome, which proclaimed him the prince of Catholic orators. His two hundred sermons are a mine of learning and experience, and they stand out from all others by their imaginative power, originality of view, variety of treatment, and audacity of expression.

17. The author's attitude toward Vieira may be described as

    A. spiritual.

    B. idolatrous.

    C. indifferent.

    D. admiring.

    E. critical.

Read the passage below and answer the question that follows.

The 65-mile-per-hour speed limit has not only lowered the number of accidents, but it has also saved many lives. Yet, auto insurance rates have not reflected this decrease. Therefore, insurance companies are making profits rather than lowering premiums.

18. This argument implies that

    A. the 65-mile-per-hour limit is unfair.

    B. auto manufacturers agree with insurance companies' policies.

    C. insurance companies are taking advantage of drivers.

    D. saving lives is of more importance than lowering premiums.

    E. driving skills have improved greatly since the 65-mile-per-hour limit has been in effect.

Read the passage below and answer the two questions that follow.

It may be true that there are two sides to every question, but it is also true that there are two sides to a sheet of flypaper, and it makes a big difference to the fly which side he chooses.

19. This statement suggests that

    A. every question has only one answer.

    B. the choice of questions is very important.

    C. flypaper is not useful.

    D. every question may be interpreted in more than one way.

    E. every question is answered.

20. Which of the following is true?

    I. The statement uses an analogy to make a point.

    II. The statement emphasizes the importance of choice.

    III. The statement points out the ways of getting stuck on a question.

    A. I only

    B. II only

    C. III only

    D. I and III only

    E. I and II only

GO ON TO THE NEXT PAGE

Use the chart below to answer the two questions that follow.

Super Sale on Mattresses				
	Original Price	Sale Price	Bonus Discount	Final Cost with Bonus
Regal:				
Twin, each piece	$299.95	$149.00	$15.00	$134.00
Full, each piece	$399.95	$199.00	$20.00	$179.00
Queen, 2-piece set	$949.95	$499.00	$50.00	$449.00
King, 3-piece set	$1,199.95	$699.00	$70.00	$629.00
Extra Firm:				
Twin, each piece	$329.95	$179.95	$18.00	$161.95
Full, each piece	$429.95	$249.95	$25.00	$224.95
Queen, 2-piece set	$999.95	$549.95	$55.00	$494.95
King, 3-piece set	$1,249.95	$749.95	$75.00	$674.95
Royal Satin:				
Twin, each piece	$329.95	$219.95	$22.00	$197.95
Full, each piece	$399.95	$279.95	$28.00	$251.95
Queen, 2-piece set	$1,019.95	$699.00	$70.00	$629.00
King, 3-piece set	$1,339.95	$899.95	$90.00	$809.95

21. As shown in the chart, the largest bonus discount for Extra Firm mattresses is

    A. $55.00
    B. $75.00
    C. $90.00
    D. $674.95
    E. $809.95

22. According to the chart, for which two items was the sale price the same?

    A. Regal Full and Royal Satin Full
    B. Extra Firm Twin and Royal Satin Twin
    C. Regal King and Royal Satin Queen
    D. Extra Firm King and Regal King
    E. Extra Firm Queen and Regal Queen

Read the passage below and answer the five questions that follow.

Some parents, teachers, and educators have tried to spoil the centennial celebration of one of America's greatest novels, *The Adventures of Huckleberry Finn*, by claiming that it and author Mark Twain were racist.

Most readers over the years have viewed this masterpiece as anything but offensive to blacks. Beneath the surface of a darn good yarn, it is one of several major writings by Twain that condemn the brutality of slavery. For some who suddenly find the novel offensive, the misunderstanding may lie in Twain's unmatched use of irony and the crude vernacular of river folk to tell the story of the friendship between a runaway Negro slave and young Huck—through the eyes of the uneducated boy.

Any doubts about Mr. Twain's views on slavery should have been dispelled by an even later work published in 1894, *Pudd'nhead Wilson*. The story of the murder trial shows how slavery damages the human personality. But silly detractors apparently need more than the unspoiled and color-blind innocence of Huck or the eccentric but clever lawyer Wilson. For them, we have a letter from Mr. Twain himself, or rather Samuel L. Clemens, the writer's real name.

Written the same year as *The Adventures of Huckleberry Finn*, the letter details Twain's offer to pay the expenses of one of the first black students at Yale Law School. The student Twain befriended and financially assisted, Warner T. McGuinn, was the commencement orator at his graduation and went on to a distinguished legal and political career in Baltimore.

"I do not believe I would very cheerfully help a white student who would ask a benevolence of a stranger, but I do not feel so about the other color. We have ground the manhood out of them and the shame is ours, not theirs; and we should pay for it," Mr. Clemens wrote Francis Wayland, the law school dean.

In addition to being a critic of slavery, Mark Twain was fascinated with the subject of transmogrification. On this 100th anniversary of his death, Twain might find ironic delight in the timing of the publication of a letter vindicating his commitment to racial progress.

23. The preceding passage was written

    A. to promote the sale of *The Adventures of Huckleberry Finn.*
    B. 100 years after Mark Twain's death.
    C. to exonerate those who claim Twain's writing was racist.
    D. to explain the misunderstandings in Twain's philosophy.
    E. as a condemnation of the principle of transmogrification.

24. Mark Twain offered to pay the expenses of a Yale Law School student because the student

    A. was commencement orator at his graduation.
    B. would go on to a distinguished law career.
    C. was rightfully owed the assistance of whites.
    D. was very needy and couldn't afford the tuition.
    E. was also a severe critic of slavery.

25. The *irony* referred to in the second paragraph appears to have

    A. confused some readers about Twain's intentions.
    B. made the language of the river folk difficult to understand.
    C. convinced most readers that Twain's work was actually racist.
    D. provided detractors with valid reason to condemn *Pudd'nhead Wilson.*
    E. appeased Twain's critics about the author's feelings regarding slavery.

26. The term centennial celebration in the first sentence is used to indicate

    A. a party held in Mark Twain's honor.
    B. an anniversary of Twain's *Pudd'nhead Wilson.*
    C. the one hundredth anniversary of Mark Twain's birth.
    D. the one hundredth publication of *The Adventures of Huckleberry Finn.*
    E. the one hundredth anniversary of the publication of *The Adventures of Huckleberry Finn.*

27. According to the passage, Pudd'nhead Wilson was

    A. the student Twain befriended and financially assisted.
    B. a runaway slave in one of Twain's works.
    C. the dean of the Yale Law School.
    D. the runaway slave in *The Adventures of Huckleberry Finn.*
    E. a clever but somewhat bizarre fictional character.

Read the passage below and answer the five questions that follow.

A painter with seven fingers sits at his easel, the Eiffel Tower shining outside the window, a Jewish village hovering in a cloud above his head.

This is how Marc Chagall painted himself in Paris in 1912. Three-quarters of a century later, the painting lives. But Chagall is dead, at 97.

Don't hang crepe, but strew flowers in his memory. A Jew from a Russian *shtetl* who revolutionized modern art by imposing his naive vision of beauty on a world that was consumed in the flames of the Holocaust, Chagall rescued images of a world that has largely vanished. There is life, not death, in his palate of bright colors; love, not bitterness, in the paintings of cartwheeling lovers and rooftop fiddlers. And the enduring themes of Judaism glow in Chagall's stained glass windows in the Hadassah clinic in Jerusalem.

Chagall captures realism through the language of dream. A bearded peddler floats above the village of Vitebsk. A green violinist wearing a long purple coat plays an orange fiddle. Lovers astride a white horse embrace, while the horse holds a bouquet of flowers and a violin under its head. What do these paintings mean? That is like asking a bearded Hasid to explain the mysteries of the Kabala or asking history to explain why millions of simple Jews, who dreamed of births and weddings and bar mitzvahs, awoke to a nightmare of death in the concentration camps. Chagall left the interpretation to the art historians and critics. He painted the images that came to him, springing from his paintbrush to the canvas. But a closer look reveals a technical mastery and control of symbols that belies the primitive.

Chagall left his native Russian village of Vitebsk for Paris, and then returned to Russia after the Bolshevik Revolution. He joined other artists in trying to paint the new vision, but the Russian revolution was not interested in the revolution of modern art. The

GO ON TO THE NEXT PAGE

Kremlin wanted socialist realism, not visionary painting. Chagall left, disillusioned, and returned to France. There he gained fame and wealth, only to be threatened as a Jew by the Nazis, and he fled to New York. He returned to France after the war, settling in Cote d'Azur. Though he remained sequestered, he left his imprint on the Paris Opera, Lincoln Center in New York, and other public buildings.

Chagall painted a Jewish village cemetery in 1917. Hebrew inscriptions mark the peeling plaster gate. Crooked tombstones carved with the Star of David retreat up a green hill. The sky is alive with color.

The Nazis expanded the graveyard to include all of Europe. Now the artist who evoked the village Jews' lives has joined them in death. Through Chagall's paintings, their dreams survive the Holocaust—alive as the melody of a green violinist.

28. According to the passage, Chagall's paintings were

    A.   not meant to be interpreted.
    B.   unfathomable, even by the painter.
    C.   primitive in style and technical mastery.
    D.   optimistic and uplifting.
    E.   disillusioned and embittered.

29. All the following are true about the "village cemetery" mentioned in the passage, *except:*

    A.   Chagall is now buried there.
    B.   it contains tombstones with Jewish markings.
    C.   Hebrew inscriptions are on the entranceway.
    D.   the sky above it is colored brightly.
    E.   it exists in a painting by Chagall.

30. Which of the following is implied by the passage?

    A.   The Russians should never have exiled Chagall to France.
    B.   Chagall's paintings are now more popular and valuable than ever before.
    C.   Chagall's brilliant and enduring paintings will live long after his death.
    D.   Artists, like Chagall, should paint only the uplifting experiences of life.
    E.   Chagall's dreamlike paintings have never received a popular acceptance.

31. According to the passage, Chagall's self-portrait suggests that Chagall

    A.   had only one hand.
    B.   was a bearded peddler.
    C.   also played the violin.
    D.   once lived in France.
    E.   could paint only Jewish themes.

32. The phrase <u>don't hang crepe</u> in the passage is used to

    A.   urge others not to attend Chagall's funeral.
    B.   remind mourners that flowers were requested by the family.
    C.   emphasize Chagall's focus on life, not death.
    D.   commemorate the death of a great painter.
    E.   admonish those who caused a great painter to suffer.

Use the graph below to answer the question that follows.

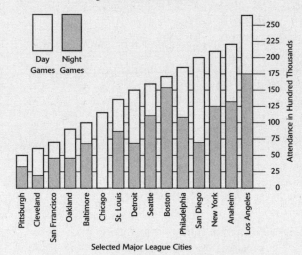

ATTENDANCE: SELECTED MAJOR LEAGUE BALL PARKS
Highest Annual, 1975-2010

33. According to the graph, which of the following cities had the highest night-game attendance compared to its day-game attendance?

    A.   Los Angeles
    B.   New York
    C.   Cleveland
    D.   Chicago
    E.   Boston

Read the passage below and answer the question that follows.

We all know life originated in the ocean. Science tells us so. Perhaps a bolt of lightning struck through the ammonia and methane gases of a volcanic planet, igniting some form of life in the primordial soup of the storm-tormented sea. But no scientific theory is sacrosanct. Now a group of scientists says we have it all wrong: Life originated in clay.

34. The preceding passage

    A. suggests that the earth began as clay, not water.
    B. argues that science has been wrong about a certain theory.
    C. implies that scientists are usually proven wrong.
    D. presents an alternative theory about the creation of life.
    E. denies the existence of life in the primordial ocean.

Read the passage below and answer the three questions that follow.

Our planet Earth has a tail and, although the appendage is invisible, it must be somewhat similar to those of comets and other heavenly bodies. Earth's tail is an egg-shaped zone of electrically charged particles positioned about 400,000 miles from us—always on the side away from the sun.

Physicist Lou Frank of the University of Iowa says researchers recently calculated the tail's existence and position by examining Explorer I satellite photos of the northern and southern lights. These natural displays—the aurora borealis and the aurora australis—glow and flicker in the night sky of the northern and southern hemispheres.

The auroras occur because the solar wind racing from the sun pushes against the Earth's magnetic field and creates an electric power supply in our planet's newly discovered tail. The displays are seen frequently at times of sunspot activity, especially in the months of March and April, and again in September and October. Their colors are mostly green, sometimes red. They have been observed in the continental United States and in Mexico.

35. According to the passage, which of the following can be inferred about the aurora borealis and aurora australis?

    A. They are unnatural phenomena caused by solar wind.
    B. They are caused by sunspot activity in March, April, September, and October.
    C. They are electrical phenomena caused by solar wind and magnetism.
    D. They are egg shaped and occur about four hundred thousand miles away.
    E. They were first photographed by Lou Frank of the University of Iowa.

36. All of the following are true about Earth's tail *except* that it

    A. is egg shaped.
    B. contains charged particles.
    C. remains on the side always away from the sun.
    D. is invisible.
    E. occurs during March, April, September, and October.

37. It can be inferred from the passage that

    A. the aurora borealis and aurora australis probably occur at the equator.
    B. the Earth's magnetic field will someday probably transform this planet into a comet.
    C. astronomers will probably now be observing Earth's tail through high-powered telescopes.
    D. the tails of comets are probably composed of electrically charged particles.
    E. the auroras race from the sun and push against the Earth's magnetic field.

GO ON TO THE NEXT PAGE

Read the passage below and answer the three questions that follow.

Homework overload has always been a complaint of school children, especially but not exclusively during the teenage years. Today, parents are becoming increasingly concerned about their children's burden, complaining that the children need more sleep and more free time and that families need more time to spend together.

The fact is that homework has been controversial in the United States since the beginning of the twentieth century. In a *Ladies Home Journal* article of 1900, editor Edward Bok referred to night study as a "fearful evil," and just a year later the California Legislature banned homework for students under age fifteen and for older children limited the time for homework to thirty minutes. In 1997, however, that law was taken off the books.

When the Soviets launched Sputnik in 1957, there was a scramble in American education to "get us back on top," and more homework in schools was a by-product. Then again in the 1980s, Japan's growing power in the business world spurred another resurgence of homework assignments. In recent years, children of very young ages have been assigned school work to take home.

Some parents are now yelling "Enough!" Some school districts are responding to their concerns by limiting the amount of homework teachers can assign. Parents and others point out that in addition to kids needing free time, many colleges require that a student be "well rounded," which encourages students to participate more in sports, clubs, and other activities.

But along with that argument comes another that is significant. Too many times, according to its critics, homework isn't meaningful but rather "busywork" that accomplishes little other than taking up a young person's valuable time. Among teachers, however, there is disagreement about what constitutes busywork and what constitutes practice. According to one mathematics teacher, "Even if a student gets three problems correct in class, he needs to do forty more at home so that the concept becomes second nature to him."

38. Which of the following would be the best title for this passage?

   A. "A Crisis in the Classroom"
   B. "Modern Theories of the Value of Homework"
   C. "Teachers versus Students: The Homework Wars"
   D. "Too Much Homework?"
   E. "The History of Homework in America"

39. According to the passage, homework assignments increased in the 1980s because

   A. Japanese success in business increased interest in improving U.S. education.
   B. students had begun slipping in academic achievement tests.
   C. parents wanted their children to get into better colleges.
   D. the United States wanted to model public schools after Japanese schools.
   E. U.S. productivity was in decline and schools were blamed.

40. The last sentence of paragraph 2 implies that

   A. the homework law was deemed unconstitutional.
   B. school districts and teachers opposed the law.
   C. attitudes toward homework had undergone changes since 1901.
   D. the homework law was seen as frivolous and completely unnecessary.
   E. most school districts did not conform to the requirements of the law.

Read the passage below and answer the two questions that follow.

California once prided itself on being the state with the finest roads in the nation. That is no longer true. Our gas taxes took care of California's highway needs for years, but they are no longer adequate. One reason the present tax no longer covers the bill is that modern cars are using less fuel. The main factor, though, is that the cost of building and maintaining highways has gone way up while the tax has not kept up with inflation.

Certainly, California streets, roads, and highways need help. Two-thirds of city streets and 77 percent of country roads are substandard. Ruts and potholes can be found almost everywhere, and the longer they go without repair, the more they will cost.

41. Which of the following best summarizes the passage?

    A. Deterioration of California's roads has resulted from increased costs and decreased funds.
    B. The quality of California roads is now second in the nation.
    C. Fuel-efficient cars cause more wear and tear on the roads than did cars of the past.
    D. Every road in the state is marred with potholes.
    E. Over three-quarters of California's roads are substandard.

42. Which of the following is *not* a problem stated by the passage?

    A. Inadequate tax revenue
    B. Ruts and potholes
    C. Increased cost of building highways
    D. Inflation
    E. Demand for new highways

Read the passage below and answer the question that follows.

Adam Smith, the founder of political economy, treated economic existence as the true human life, treated money making as the meaning of history, and was wont to describe statesmen as dangerous animals. Yet this very England became the foremost country, economically speaking, in the world.

43. The meaning of wont in this passage is

    A. desired
    B. did not
    C. accustomed
    D. unlikely
    E. unable

Read the passage below, which was written in the 1980s, and answer the two questions that follow.

The $5 million in state funds earmarked for advertising California's attractiveness as a tourist destination is an investment well worth making. Perhaps because California has long taken it for granted that everyone wants to come here, and maybe because for many years Hollywood was California's most powerful publicist, the state has never spent a dime promoting itself to potential visitors. And that may be at least partly responsible for the decline in tourism, including a 10-percent drop in spending. Since tourism is a $28-billion industry employing 1.6 million Californians, perhaps this new advertising was too long in coming.

44. Which of the following is an assumption of the passage?

    A. California will never spend funds to promote tourism.
    B. A proposed advertising campaign will decrease the competition from other states.
    C. California tax revenues are only a result of tourism.
    D. Increased tourism will result in higher state and local tax revenues as well as added state income.
    E. More Californians are visiting other states than ever before.

45. Which of the following is implied by the passage?

    A. If the advertising campaign works, the $5-million price tag will be a bargain.
    B. Advertising campaigns should be carefully and slowly monitored.
    C. Few Californians oppose the proposed advertising campaign.
    D. Hollywood should not continue to be a drawing card to attract tourists.
    E. The $28 billion is not enough to employ 1.6 million Californians.

GO ON TO THE NEXT PAGE

Read the passage below and answer the five questions that follow.

Before one begins to read an unfamiliar work of literature, it is often helpful to know what kind of work it is—that is, what genre it belongs to. If we know what expectations we should have, we are less likely to misunderstand what the author is trying to accomplish. *The Lord of the Rings* is a work of fiction written in the middle of this century about a world that greatly resembles medieval times in Europe. It is unmistakably a novel, yet the real significance of the events and the characters will be clearer to readers who know something about the literary tradition, or genre, called the epic, and who have read, for example, *The Odyssey* or *Beowulf.* Moreover, there is a special kind of pleasure in the recognition of familiar patterns of events and characterization, which are varied and even deliberately reversed. The skillful interplay of the familiar and the surprising is one of the marks of a great storyteller like Tolkien.

No one, of course, knows exactly what the Middle Ages were really like, but readers get an illusion in *The Lord of the Rings* of being in an ancient world which is in some mysterious way part of the history of our own world. Then, after the fashion of the epic tradition, they will expect that the story will follow the movements of a particular person who is of heroic stature (physically and mentally) and who embodies the ideals and values of a particular people. Readers feel sure that the hero will, like the heroes in *The Odyssey* and *Beowulf*, go on a journey and experience a variety of adventures, which he will survive after many hardships and will then return to his own home and people.

46. Which of the following is probably the intended audience for this passage?

    A. Students of the Middle Ages
    B. Those preparing to read *The Odyssey*
    C. Those who have never enjoyed *The Lord of the Rings*
    D. Those preparing to read *The Lord of the Rings*
    E. Those preparing to read *Beowulf*

47. The central point of the passage is best summarized as follows:

    A. The heroes in Tolkien's story are identical to those in *The Odyssey* or *Beowulf.*
    B. One should read familiar works of literature before reading an unfamiliar one.
    C. The history of the ancient world is related to the history of our own world.
    D. *The Lord of the Rings* is not only a novel.
    E. Fully appreciating *The Lord of the Rings* involves familiarity with the epic tradition.

48. The author implies which of the following about the conclusion of *The Lord of the Rings*?

    A. It is a happy one.
    B. It is a unique one.
    C. It has been plagiarized.
    D. It is very much like the opening of the novel.
    E. It contains explicit references to *The Odyssey* and *Beowulf.*

49. Which of the following is a basic assumption about the readers of this passage?

    A. They find Tolkien's heroes especially fascinating.
    B. They know very little about the Middle Ages.
    C. They will find *The Lord of the Rings* surprising.
    D. They will be reading *The Lord of the Rings*.
    E. They like to create illusions.

50. It may be inferred that readers who expect *The Lord of the Rings* to contain elements of the epic tradition will

    A. have a background that the author of this passage does not share.
    B. have ignored this passage.
    C. have misread this passage.
    D. have their expectations fulfilled.
    E. have their expectations disappointed.

Section II: Mathematics

50 Questions

Directions: In the following questions or incomplete statements, select the one *best* answer or completion of the five choices given. Make sure that you mark your answers for this section on the Mathematics section of the answer sheet.

1. If 10 kilometers equal 6.2 miles, then how many miles are in 45 kilometers?

   A. 4.5
   B. 7.25
   C. 27.9
   D. 29.7
   E. 62

2. After selling their home, the Sullivan family paid their agent $21,360 and were left with a profit of $334,460 from the sale. What was the sale price of the Sullivan's home? Disregard any other costs.

   A. $313,280
   B. $336,776
   C. $355,820
   D. $456,000
   E. $545,000

Use the table below to answer the question that follows.

Bill for Purchases	
Science Textbooks	$840
Lab Equipment	$460
Formaldehyde	$320
Teacher's Manuals	$120
TOTAL	$2,220

3. Scholastic Supplies Inc. sends the bill above to Zither Junior High School. Although the bill includes the cost of science lab workbooks, Scholastic Supplies forgot to list them on the bill. How much did the science lab workbooks cost Zither Junior High School?

   A. $480
   B. $500
   C. $520
   D. $560
   E. $620

4. Given that the proportion $\frac{2}{9}$ is equal to $\frac{3}{q}$, what is the value of q?

   A. 3
   B. $\frac{7}{2}$
   C. $\frac{21}{2}$
   D. $\frac{27}{2}$
   E. 18

5. Springfield High School's average state test scores over a five-year period were:

	Math	Verbal
2006	520	540
2007	515	532
2008	518	528
2009	510	525
2010	507	510

   What was the mean (average) of the verbal state test scores for the five-year period 2006 through 2010?

   A. 512
   B. 514
   C. 521
   D. 527
   E. 528

6. The numbers 6, 9, and 12 have which common factors?

   A. 1 only
   B. 2 only
   C. 3 only
   D. 1 and 3 only
   E. 1, 3, 6, 9, and 12

GO ON TO THE NEXT PAGE

7. Which of the following calculations is equivalent to 51×10?

    A. 50×11
    B. 49×12
    C. $50(10) + 1(10)$
    D. $(50 + 10) \times (1 + 10)$
    E. $(50 + 1) + (6 + 4)$

8. In the equation $y = x^2 + 1$, if x is 5, which of the following is the value of y?

    A.   1
    B.   5
    C.   25
    D.   26
    E.   36

Use the graph below to answer the question that follows.

Lopez Family Income

Expenditure Breakdown

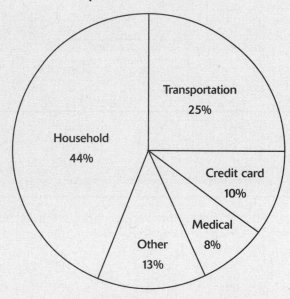

9. The preceding figure shows how the Lopez family income was spent in a given year. According to the figure, what percent of the family's income was left after household and credit card expenditures?

    A.   119%
    B.   54%
    C.   46%
    D.   21%
    E.   3%

Read the information below and then answer the question that follows.

Rosanna knows that a geometric figure is a rectangle and that it has sides of 18 and 22.

10. How can Rosanna compute the area of a square that has the same *perimeter* as the preceding rectangle?

    A.   Add 18 and 22, double this sum, divide by 4, and then multiply by 2.
    B.   Add 18 and 22, double this sum, divide by 4, and then multiply by 4.
    C.   Add 18 and 22, double this sum, divide by 4, and then square the quotient.
    D.   Add 18 and 22, double this sum, and then multiply by 4.
    E.   Add twice 18 to twice 22, divide by 2, and then square the quotient.

11. Arnold purchased one pair of slacks, a dress shirt, a tie, and a sports coat. The shirt and slacks each cost three times what the tie cost. The sports coat cost twice what the shirt cost. If Arnold paid a total of $156 for all four items, what was the price of the pair of slacks?

    A. $12
    B. $36
    C. $48
    D. $78
    E. $84

12. How many fifths are in 13?

    A. $\dfrac{13}{5}$
    B. $\dfrac{65}{5}$
    C. $13\dfrac{1}{5}$
    D.   65
    E. $65\dfrac{5}{13}$

13. Sam walks $2\frac{1}{2}$ miles twice each day. At this rate, if he walks 5 days each week, how many miles will he walk in 5 weeks?

A. $\frac{121}{2}$

B. 25

C. $\frac{621}{2}$

D. 125

E. 175

Use the information below to answer the question that follows.

Tom is just 4 years older than Emily. The total of their ages is 24 years.

14. From the preceding information, which of the following is the equation for finding Emily's age?

A. $x + 4x = 24$
B. $x + 4 = 24$
C. $4x + x = 24$
D. $x + (x + 4) = 24$
E. $4x + 1 = 24$

Use the information below to answer the question that follows.

The 2005 graduating class of Oakdale High School totaled 250 students. Of those 250 students, 20% graduated with honors.

15. Which of the following is a method that could be used to calculate the actual number of students graduating from Oakdale High School with honors?

A. 20×250

B. $250 \div 20$

C. $250 \div \frac{1}{5}$

D. $250 \times \frac{1}{5}$

E. $250 \div .20$

Use the diagram below to answer the question that follows.

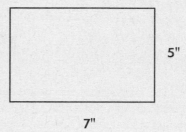

5"

7"

16. If the dimensions of the rectangle above are increased by 3 inches, what is the new perimeter of the rectangle?

A. 18 inches
B. 24 inches
C. 30 inches
D. 36 inches
E. 72 inches

17. If a package of two blank compact discs costs $2.98, how much change will Roy receive from a $20 bill if he purchases 12 discs?

A. $2.02
B. $2.12
C. $2.18
D. $2.22
E. $3.02

18. All the following are equal to the equation $2x + 4 = 3x + 3$ *except:*

A. $4 = x + 3$
B. $-x + 4 = 3$
C. $2x + 1 = 3x$
D. $x = -1$
E. $2x = 3x - 1$

19. Of the following fractions, which is the smallest?

A. $\frac{3}{5}$

B. $\frac{4}{9}$

C. $\frac{7}{13}$

D. $\frac{23}{44}$

E. $\frac{2}{3}$

GO ON TO THE NEXT PAGE

20. Which of the following is equivalent to 210,000?

   A. $(2 \times 10^4) + (1 \times 10^3)$
   B. $(2 \times 10^5) + (1 \times 10^4)$
   C. $(2 \times 10^6) + (1 \times 10^5)$
   D. $(2 \times 10^7) + (1 \times 10^6)$
   E. $(2 \times 10^8) + (1 \times 10^7)$

21. The product of two numbers is greater than 0 and equals one of the numbers. Which of the following *must* be one of the numbers?

   A. -1
   B. 0
   C. 1
   D. A prime number
   E. A reciprocal

22. Which one of the diagrams below has the greatest perimeter? The length of the side of the square is the same length for each diagram.

A.

B.    C.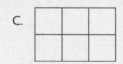

D.    E.

Read the information below and then answer the question that follows.

Holiday cards cost the Key Club $2.00 each. The Key Club sells them for $4.75 each.

23. Based on the preceding information, how could Clark determine how many cards must be sold (Q) to make a profit of $82.50?

   A. $Q = \$82.50 \div \$2.00$
   B. $Q = \$82.50 - \$2.00$
   C. $Q = \$4.75 - \$2.00(Q)$
   D. $Q = \$82.50 \div \$4.75 - \$2.00$
   E. $Q = \$82.50 \div \$2.75$

24. Which of the following represents .14739 rounded off to the nearest thousandth?

   A. .1472
   B. .1474
   C. .147
   D. .148
   E. .15

Use the information below to answer the question that follows.

Shawn purchased 12 pounds of apples at $1.60 per pound. To compute the total price he paid, Shawn used $12 \times \$1.60 = \$19.20$.

25. Which of the following is another simple method that Shawn could have used to compute the total price he paid?

   A. $10(1.60) + 2(1.60)$
   B. $13(1.60) - 1.00$
   C. $(6 \times 0.80) + (6 \times 0.80)$
   D. $10(1.00) + 2(0.60)$
   E. $12(1.00) - 12(0.60)$

Read the information below and then answer the question that follows.

Juan approximated 35×45 by rounding off each number. He then multiplied 40×50, but the answer he got was much too large.

26. Which of the following multiplications would have gotten Juan a better approximation?

    A. 50×50
    B. 45×50
    C. 30×50
    D. 30×40
    E. 20×30

27. If 16 out of 400 dentists polled recommended Smile Bright toothpaste, what percent recommended Smile Bright?

    A. 4%
    B. 8%
    C. 16%
    D. 25%
    E. 40%

Using the information below, answer the question that follows.

Sign on Laundromat Door	
Soap	50¢
Washer	$1.00
Dryer	$1.25

28. Sara brought her own soap. How much would it cost her to wash and dry seven loads of laundry?

    A. $7.00
    B. $8.75
    C. $15.75
    D. $18.25
    E. $21.50

29. Teachers will be assigned special camp duty one day of the week during a seven-day camping trip. If all the days of the week (Monday through Sunday) are tossed into a cap and each teacher chooses one day of the week, what is the probability that the first teacher will randomly select a weekday (Monday through Friday)?

    A. $\frac{1}{7}$
    B. $\frac{2}{7}$
    C. $\frac{1}{5}$
    D. $\frac{5}{7}$
    E. $\frac{5}{2}$

Use the number line below to answer the question that follows.

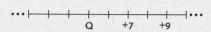

30. On the preceding number line, what is the point 15 units to the left of point Q?

    A. 10
    B. 5
    C. 0
    D. −9
    E. −10

31. If the product of two numbers is 5 more than the sum of the two numbers, which of the following equations could represent the relationship?

    A. $AB + 5 = A + B$
    B. $5AB = A + B$
    C. $AB = A + B + 5$
    D. $A/B = 5 + A + B$
    E. $A(B) + 5 = A + B + 5$

GO ON TO THE NEXT PAGE

32. Which of the following is determined by division?

    I.   The price of car *A* if it costs six times the price of car *B*

    II.   The difference in temperature between two cities

    III.   The number of yards in 39 feet

    A. I only
    B. II only
    C. III only
    D. I and II only
    E. I and III only

Use the graph below to answer the question that follows.

Stars on Hollywood and Vine

```
**  **  **  **  **  **  **  **  **  *
**  **  **  **  **  **  **  **  **
```

33. According to the preceding graph, how many stars are on the pavements of Hollywood Boulevard and Vine Street? (*Key:* Each group of 4 asterisks = 10 stars.)

    A. 45
    B. 47.5
    C. 90
    D. 92
    E. 95

34. A nearly new motocross motorcycle is selling at a 30% discount off its sticker price. Its sticker price is $8,000. What is its new selling price?

    A. $2,400
    B. $5,600
    C. $6,600
    D. $7,970
    E. $7,976

35. Harmon's new hybrid car averages 35 miles per gallon of gasoline. Assuming Harmon is able to maintain his average miles per gallon, how far can he drive on 12 gallons of gas?

    A. Almost 3 miles
    B. 42 miles
    C. 350 miles
    D. 420 miles
    E. 700 miles

36. A parallelogram has two sides of dimensions 9 and 7. What would be the side of a square with the same perimeter?

    A. 32
    B. 18
    C. 14
    D. 8
    E. 4

37. It is estimated that at a picnic, each adult will drink $\frac{1}{5}$ gallon of lemonade. How many gallons of lemonade should be brought to the picnic if 28 people, all adults, are expected to attend?

    A. 3
    B. Between 3 and 4
    C. 5
    D. Between 5 and 6
    E. More than 6

38. If 150 family members attend the annual open house and there are more adults than children, which of the following could be the number of children?

    A. 72.5
    B. 74
    C. 75
    D. 75.5
    E. 77

39. If it costs 82¢ to make a dry erase marker, how many such markers can be made for $75?

    A. 9
    B. 90
    C. 91
    D. 92
    E. 100

40. In a school of 280, only 35 students did not attend graduation. What percent of the school population did not attend graduation?

    A. 12.5%
    B. 18.5%
    C. 22.5%
    D. 25.0%
    E. 32.5%

41. If John can proofread 20 pages in 4 hours, how many hours will it take him to proofread 50 pages?

   A.   5
   B.   6
   C.   8
   D.   9
   E.   10

Read the information below and then answer the question that follows.

   Eli purchased 20 goldfish at 85¢ each and then bought eight bags of goldfish food, also at 85¢ each.

42. Given the preceding information, what would be the simplest way to compute the total amount spent by Eli?

   A. $20 \times 85¢ + 4 \times 85¢ + 2 \times 85¢ + 2 \times 85¢$
   B. $28 \times 85¢$
   C. $8 \times 20 \times 85¢$
   D. $20 \times 85¢$
   E. $850¢ \times 2$

43. In Summerville's Little League, team A has twice as many victories as team B, team C has 5 fewer victories than team A, and team D has 4 more victories than team B. If total victories of all 4 teams equal 29, how many victories does team D have?

   A.   5
   B.   9
   C.   10
   D.   12
   E.   14

Use the information below to answer the question that follows.

   Ernie cut a yardstick into two pieces. The longer piece was 6 inches longer than the shorter piece.

44. How could Ernie compute the length of the shorter piece, x?

   A. $x + 6 = 36$
   B. $2x = 36$
   C. $x + x + 6 = 36$
   D. $2x - 6 = 36$
   E. $2x + 3 = 36$

45. If 9 is added to $7p$, the outcome is 24. What is the value of p?

   A. $\dfrac{13}{7}$
   B. $\dfrac{15}{7}$
   C. $\dfrac{24}{9}$
   D.   6
   E.   8

46. It takes a student 12 minutes to make 5 milk shakes. At this rate, how long will it take this same student to make 45 milk shakes?

   A.   1 hour, 2 minutes
   B.   1 hour, 8 minutes
   C.   1 hour, 28 minutes
   D.   1 hour, 30 minutes
   E.   1 hour, 48 minutes

Use the graph below to answer the question that follows.

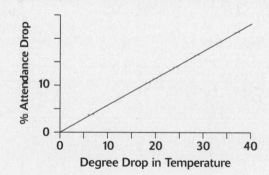

47. According to the graph, if the temperature falls 35 degrees, by what percentage will school attendance drop?

   A.   10
   B.   20
   C.   30
   D.   40
   E.   50

GO ON TO THE NEXT PAGE

48. George scored an average of 80% on three tests. What score must he get on the fourth test to bring his average to 85%?

   A.   85%
   B.   88%
   C.   90%
   D.   95%
   E.   100%

49. Maria needs to compute 30% of 50. To get a correct answer, all of the following will work *except:*

   A. $.30 \times 50$
   B. $.50 \times 30$
   C. $\frac{3}{10} \times 50$
   D. $50 \div \frac{10}{3}$
   E. $50 \div \frac{3}{10}$

50. What additional information is needed to find a solution to the problem below?

   Thelma reads eight magazines each week. How many magazines does she average each day that she reads?

   A.   The days she reads two magazines
   B.   The days she reads one magazine in the morning
   C.   The days she reads three magazines
   D.   The days she reads more than one magazine
   E.   The days she reads no magazines

Section III: Writing

2 Essays

Directions: In this section you plan and write two essays, one for each topic given. Read each topic carefully to make sure that you are properly addressing the issue or situation. You must write on the specified topic. An essay on another topic will not be acceptable.

Plan your time wisely. Each essay is weighted equally. Plan to spend the same amount of time on each essay.

The two essay questions are designed to give you an opportunity to write clearly and effectively. Use specific examples whenever appropriate to aid in supporting your ideas. Keep in mind that the quality of your writing is much more important than the quantity.

Write each essay on the two lined sheets of paper provided. Your writing should be neat and legible. Because you have only a limited amount of space in which to write, please do *not* skip lines, do *not* write excessively large, and do *not* leave wide margins.

You may use the bottom of the topic page in the test booklet to organize and plan your essay before you begin writing.

Topic 1

Some American public schools have removed the "A" to "F" grading system and substituted "Pass-Fail" grading, with the instructor adding a written statement about the student's progress. Comment on the pros and cons of such a system. Compare your response to the sample essays for this topic on pages 317-320.

Topic 2

Some people believe that the United States places more importance on the sight and sound media (film, television, radio, and so on) than on the printed word.

Present your views, either agreeing or disagreeing that reading has become less significant to Americans.

Answer Key and Analysis for Practice Test 3

Answer Key for Practice Test 3

Section I: Reading

1. D	18. C	35. C
2. C	19. D	36. E
3. D	20. E	37. D
4. A	21. B	38. D
5. B	22. C	39. A
6. C	23. B	40. C
7. D	24. C	41. A
8. A	25. A	42. E
9. C	26. E	43. C
10. B	27. E	44. D
11. C	28. D	45. A
12. D	29. A	46. D
13. B	30. C	47. E
14. D	31. D	48. A
15. B	32. C	49. D
16. E	33. E	50. D
17. D	34. D	

Section II: Mathematics

1. C	18. D	35. D
2. C	19. B	36. D
3. A	20. B	37. D
4. D	21. C	38. B
5. D	22. E	39. C
6. D	23. E	40. A
7. C	24. C	41. E
8. D	25. A	42. B
9. C	26. C	43. B
10. C	27. A	44. C
11. B	28. C	45. B
12. D	29. D	46. E
13. D	30. E	47. B
14. D	31. C	48. E
15. D	32. C	49. E
16. D	33. E	50. E
17. B	34. B	

Scoring Your CBEST Practice Test 3

To score your CBEST Practice Test 3, total the number of correct responses for each section of the test separately. Do not subtract any points for questions attempted but missed, as there is no penalty for guessing. The score for each section is then scaled from 20 to 80. (About 70% right is a passing score.)

Analyzing Your Test Results

Use the charts on the following page to carefully analyze your results and spot your strengths and weaknesses. Complete the process of analyzing each subject area and each individual question for this Practice Test. Reexamine these results for trends in types of errors (repeated errors) or poor results in specific subject areas. This reexamination and analysis is of tremendous importance for effective test preparation.

Subject Area Analysis Sheet				
	Possible	Completed	Right	Wrong
Reading	50			
Mathematics	50			
TOTAL	100			

One of the most important parts of test preparation is analyzing *why* you missed a question so that you can reduce your number of mistakes. Now that you have taken Practice Test 3 and corrected your answers, carefully tally your mistakes by marking them in the proper column.

Tally Sheet for Questions Missed				
	Reason for Mistake			
	Total Missed	Simple Mistake	Misread Problem	Lack of Knowledge
Reading				
Mathematics				
TOTAL				

Reviewing the preceding data can help you determine *why* you are missing certain questions. Now that you have pinpointed the type of error you are most likely to make, when you take Practice Test 4, focus on avoiding those errors.

Essay Checklist

Use this checklist to evaluate your essays.

Diagnosis of Timed Writing Exercises		
A good essay:	**Essay 1**	**Essay 2**
. . . addresses the assignment		
■ stays well focused		
■ expresses a clear thesis statement on the topic		
. . . organizes points logically		
■ uses smooth transitions between paragraphs		
■ has coherent, unified paragraphs		
. . . develops ideas presented		
■ gives specific examples to support points		
■ anticipates and addresses opposing views		
. . . is grammatically sound (with only minor flaws)		
■ uses correct sentence structure		
■ uses correct punctuation		
■ uses standard written English		
. . . uses language skillfully		
■ uses a variety of sentence types		
■ uses a variety of words		
. . . is legible		
■ shows clear handwriting		
■ appears neat		

Answers and Complete Explanations for Practice Test 3

Section I: Reading

1. **D.** If you read the entry for "Infinitive," you find the phrase *used as* for all of these answers except *subjunctive*.

2. **C.** Under the word *in*, you find a reference to its use "after a superlative." Since words like *best* and *worst* are superlatives, the correct choice is **C**, page 126.

3. **D.** The author's entire argument and conclusion are based on recent studies indicating a downward trend in aptitude test scores. The author must assume these test scores are accurate to have faith in the conclusion that a student needs changes in both home environment and attitude. Choice **A** does not offer an assumption; rather, it offers a new "fact" (that previous studies were overturned), which is irrelevant to this question. Choice **B** offers an assumption, but it relates to heredity and thus is irrelevant to an argument about environment and attitude. Choice **C** is unreasonable; the argument offers no rationale to believe that the ongoing decline in test scores will abruptly cease anytime "soon." Choice **E** is simply inaccurate; the argument offers nothing to indicate that "*more* out-of-school activities are available."

4. **A.** The phrase "bowl of oatmeal" is used sarcastically to condemn the actions of the City Council. Choice **B** is not accurate, as the situation is certainly not tragic. Choice **C** misreads the passage. Choice **D** contradicts the intent of the passage. Choice **E** is too much of an extension; the passage comments upon and criticizes the City Council, but it does not go so far as to urge any action.

5. **B.** Choice **B** correctly identifies sentence 3 as the least important line because the overall subject of the paragraph is the increased availability of herbs, not the increased popularity of the Internet. This third sentence could be deleted without diminishing the message. In contrast, all the other sentences *are* relevant and focused on the topic.

6. **C.** Because the fifth sentence introduces the idea of "several reasons" and the sixth sentence begins with the phrase "One is," it is logical to expect the seventh sentence to begin with a phrase like "A second is" or "And another is." The four other choices do not fit in nearly as well. In addition, each one has stylistic flaws or inconsistencies. Choice **A** uses the slang phrase "turned on"; Choice **B** introduces the pronoun "You," which has not been used elsewhere in the paragraph. Choice **D** is redundant terminology ("doctors" = "medical practitioners," and "larger" = "greater"). Choice **E** is a sentence fragment; it lacks a subject.

7. **D.** The first sentence should begin with a word that signals a contrast, since the passage is moving to the other side of the argument, the case in favor of herbs. The next sentence gives a second example, so it should begin with a word or phrase like "Furthermore" or "Additionally." Choices **A**, **B**, and **C** all begin with an incorrect transition, one that shows continuation of an idea, not a contrast. Choice **E** begins with a transition that will work in the first blank, but its second, the word "however," is the opposite of the word needed in the second blank.

8. **A.** Choice **A** and Choice **D** each give an adequate summary of the first paragraph, but only Choice **A** correctly refers to both the pros and cons of herbs given in the second paragraph. In Choice **B**, it is also item II that is incorrect; the second paragraph does not address guarding against ineffective herbal medicines. In Choice **C**, the first statement is too vague, and the second is inaccurate; the second paragraph does not discuss traditional medicines. In Choice **E**, the first idea is too vague and the second is not addressed.

9. **C.** In both the introductory and final paragraphs, the writer is concerned with attacks on the First Amendment and throughout the article emphasizes this with a detailed look at what he or she thinks is an attack on a particular group, the press, that is guaranteed a certain amount of freedom by that amendment. Because of this, choices **A** and **B** are much too broad, and choices **D** and **E** are supporting ideas rather than principal ideas; "slander and libel laws" and "Big Brother in government" are mentioned only briefly.

10. **B.** The second paragraph says a "6 to 3 ruling." So if two justices change their minds, there would be a 4 to 5 ruling for the other side.

11. **C.** The last sentence of the second paragraph says that reporters "now face a challenge to the privacy of their minds," and the last sentence in the passage is a statement against "mind control." All other choices are not explicitly supported by material in the passage.

12. **D.** As is often the case, the first sentence states the main idea of the passage. Choice **A** is incorrect, both because it is too narrow and because the passage tells the reader only that Kitty Litter is made from clay and does not tell how it is produced. Choice **B** is also too narrow and does not address the author's *purpose*. Choice **C** is incorrect because only one sentence mentions this fact; it cannot be the overall purpose. Choice **E** is incorrect because the article does not describe a method for preventing fires.

13. **B.** The word "they" in the final paragraph's last sentence refers to "cats" used in the first sentence of the paragraph. That first sentence describes cats watching the "hustle and bustle" with a sense of "superiority." Given this information, you may infer that the grin described in the last sentence comes from watching the "hustle and bustle" of human antics, in this case the antics of the U.S. government making itself a nuisance. Notice that all choices except **B** may be eliminated, if only because each describes cats "laughing" instead of grinning.

14. **D.** The best definition is "equipment." The rest of the passage describes the two pieces of equipment that are needed.

15. **B.** The passage recommends identification in the field "where additional specimens . . . are available." While it may be reasonable to assume that one would prefer to avoid transporting specimens (**A**) and possibly exposing them to deterioration (**C**), these objections are not the *main* reason it is preferable to make identifications in the field. Choices **D** and **E** are unreasonable ideas that are not supported in the passage.

16. **E.** The passage states that if one uses a substitute for a vasculum, it needs to be "fairly airtight," which is an attribute of a plastic bag. None of the ideas in the other choices are stated in the passage.

17. **D.** The tone of the author concerning Vieira is certainly positive but not so much as to be *spiritual* (**A**) or *idolatrous* (**B**). Therefore, *admiring* (**D**) is the best choice. Choice **C** is too bland, and Choice **E** has a negative, not a positive, tone.

18. **C.** Since the lower number of accidents has not resulted in lower premiums, one suggestion of the passage is that the insurance companies are pocketing the savings rather than passing them on to the consumer. Thus, the author implies that insurance companies are taking advantage of drivers. Choice **A** confuses two ideas from the passage; the passage implies that the insurance companies are being unfair, not that the 65-mile-per-hour speed limit is somehow unfair. Choice **B** cannot reasonably be concluded, because the argument does not mention auto manufacturers at all. The passage implies no greater or lesser importance to saving lives or lowering premiums, so Choice **D** cannot be accurate. Choice **E** can be eliminated because there is nothing in the argument implying that "driving skills have improved greatly."

19. **D.** The statement initially posits, "it may be true that there are two sides to every question," which can be interpreted as "every question may be interpreted in more than one way." All other answers are unreasonable suggestions, based on this passage.

20. **E.** Both statements I and II are true. The stated example of flypaper uses an analogy, and the comment that it makes a big difference which side the fly chooses indicates the importance of choice. The statement does not, however, point out different ways of getting stuck on a question.

21. **B.** According to the chart, the largest "bonus discount" for Extra Firm mattresses is $75.00. Do not be fooled by Choice **C**; while a $90.00 discount is larger, it applies to a Royal Satin mattress set, not the Extra Firm mattress specified in this question.

22. **C.** According to the chart, the sale price of both the Regal King and the Royal Satin Queen is $629.00.

23. **B.** The passage states, "On this 100th anniversary of his death, Twain . . .," so Choice **B** is correct. Remember to always read the question carefully and then select the choice that addresses it most directly. In this case, do not trick yourself by choosing **A**, **C** or **D**, which might be accurate if the question asked about the *purpose* of the passage. Choice **E** is wrong for this reason, in addition to being unsupported by the passage.

24. **C.** The passage supports Choice **C** with Twain's own words: "We have ground the manhood out of them and the shame is ours, not theirs; and we should pay for it." Choices **A** and **B** are actions the student took <u>after</u> Twain gave him financial assistance; therefore these ideas cannot be the reason for the offer in the first place. The passage offers no evidence for choices **D** or **E**.

25. **A.** The irony and vernacular in *The Adventures of Huckleberry Finn* may have confused some readers and led to a misunderstanding of Twain's feelings about slavery and issues of race. The passage offers no evidence that Twain's irony made the character's language difficult to understand (**B**). Choice **C** is wrong for two reasons: first, the phrase "most readers" is inaccurate since the passage states that "most readers" find the novel "anything <u>but</u> offensive"; second, the idea that the novel is racist contradicts the passage. Choice **D** is irrelevant because the irony mentioned refers to Huck Finn and not Pudd'nhead Wilson. Choice **E** can be eliminated; Twain's critics should be appeased by the information in paragraphs 3, 4, and 5, not the irony of the novel itself.

26. **E.** The word "centennial" means one hundredth, and in this case it refers to the celebration one hundred years after the novel's original publication. Choice **C** is incorrect because, according to the last paragraph in the passage, this is the 100th anniversary of his death. All other answers misread the passage or the question.

27. **E.** According to the passage, Pudd'nhead Wilson was "eccentric but clever." Choices **A**, **B**, **C**, and **D** all confuse or misstate the facts in the passage.

28. **D.** The idea in Choice **D**, "optimistic and uplifting," is backed up by the sentence, "There is life, not death . . . love, not bitterness in the paintings." Choices **A** and **C** contradict the passage; Chagall "left the interpretations to the art historians and critics" and he painted with "technical mastery," not with primitive skill. Choice **B** is unreasonable; the passage does explain how Chagall's work can be understood and offers no evidence that the artist himself did not understand his own work. The tone in Choice **E** contradicts the positive interpretation of Chagall's works.

29. **A.** The next-to-last paragraph includes the ideas in all of the choices except Choice **A**.

30. **C.** The phrases, "enduring themes [in his paintings]" (paragraph 3) and "through Chagall's paintings . . . dreams survive" (paragraph 7), indicate Choice **C**. The passage states that Chagall left Russia on his own account, "disillusioned," which contradicts Choice **A**. The passage offers no information about any increase (or decrease) in the value and popularity of Chagall's work, making Choice **B** incorrect. Choice **D** is unreasonable and contradicts the thrust of the passage's praise for Chagall's art. Choice **E** is contradicted by the phrase that Chagall "gained fame and wealth" in France.

31. **D.** The Eiffel Tower in the painting indicates the artist once lived in Paris. All other choices misread the description of Chagall's self-portrait in the first paragraph or misinterpret information found elsewhere in the passage.

32. **C.** Black crepe was traditionally hung in the doorway of families in mourning, so the phrase, "Don't hang crepe, but strew flowers," means don't mourn, but celebrate his life. This can be understood in context, since the phrase occurs immediately after the announcement of Chagall's death and is followed with the phrase, "but strew [i.e., spread] flowers in his memory." The passage never mentions Chagall's family, making Choice **B** wrong. Choice **D** is incorrect because it misreads the point of strewing flowers instead of hanging crepe; this passage is about celebrating his life, not remembering (commemorating) his death. Choice **E** is unreasonable for this question.

33. **E.** According to the graph, Boston had almost all night-game attendance (about 90%) compared with very small day-game attendance (about 10%).

34. **D.** The brief passage introduces the possibility that life may have begun in clay instead of water as scientists have believed. Choices **B**, **C**, and **E** are much too strong to be supported by the passage, and Choice **A** refers to the earth instead of to life.

35. **C.** According to the passage, the auroras occur because of solar wind pushing against Earth's magnetic field, causing an electrical power supply. In Choice **B**, the phrase "caused by" makes the choice incorrect. The word "unnatural" in Choice **A** is inaccurate. Choice **D** confuses Earth's "tail" with the aurora borealis and aurora australis. Choice **E** is inaccurate because physicist Lou Frank studied recent satellite photos of the auroras; he was not the first to photograph them.

36. **E.** The auroras occur during the months of March, April, September, and October; Earth's tail is always present. The other choices can all be confirmed with information found in the first paragraph.

37. **D.** Because Earth's tail must be "similar to those of comets," they are probably also composed of electrically charged particles (paragraph 1). Choice **A** is a complete misread; the passage states that the auroras are visible in the northern and southern hemispheres, not at the equator. Choice **B** is an illogical and far-fetched conclusion to draw from the passage. Choice **C** is also unreasonable, especially since the passage claims the tail is invisible and never mentions high-powered telescopes. Choice **E** also misreads the passage; the auroras do not "race from the sun"; rather, it is the solar wind that does.

38. **D.** Of the choices given, Choice **D** is the one that best covers the subject of the passage. The passage refers to events that influenced the assigning of homework, but these are not the main idea, Choice **E**. The passage doesn't present theories, Choice **B**, nor does it suggest that the problem is teacher versus student, Choice **C**. The word "crisis" in Choice **A** is too strong, and, in addition, the passage concerns homework, not the classroom.

39. **A.** In paragraph 2, the Japanese success in business is given credit for the drive to improve U.S. education and a resulting resurgence in the amount of homework assigned. Choices **B**, **C**, **D**, and **E**, while they may or may not be true, are not covered in the passage.

40. **C.** According to the passage, the law against homework was passed in 1901 and taken off the books in 1997. The implication is that attitudes toward homework changed. Choices **B**, **D**, and **E** may be true, but none of them is specifically cited as the reason for repeal of the law. Constitutionality, Choice **A**, is not an issue.

41. **A.** Choice **A** best summarizes the passage, citing two supporting points for the main idea—that California's roads have deteriorated. Choice **E** is incomplete and the "over three-quarters" phrase is correct only in reference to the state's country roads. Choice **B** has no support in the passage for its phrase, "second in the nation," and is too narrow a choice to summarize the entire passage. Choice **C** presents an idea that is not in the passage at all, the concept of how much wear and tear fuel-efficient cars cause to roads; this makes the answer incorrect. Choice **D** is not a summarization of the passage and exaggerates the passage's point with the absolute word "every."

42. **E.** The facts cited in all the other choices are mentioned in the passage, with the only exception being the demand for new highways.

43. **C.** The passage suggests that Adam Smith considered statesmen in a negative way; thus, you can determine from context that *wont* is probably used to mean "accustomed." Notice that choices **A** and **B** are verbs, words that cannot be substituted for the adjective "wont" in the sentence. Choices **D** and **E** are contradictions to the context of the sentence.

44. **D.** In promoting the spending of state funds to advertise California's tourist attractions, the author assumes such tourism will result in more income for the state. Choice **B** is incorrect because, while increased tourism may increase revenue, it cannot be assumed that such an increase will decrease the competition from other states. Choice **A** is unreasonable because of the word "never." Choice **C** cannot be assumed by the author; tax revenues could never come from tourism alone. Choice **E** is irrelevant.

45. **A.** Implied by the passage is the belief that the campaign, if effective, will bring in many times the tourist revenue than what the advertising initially cost. Nothing in the passage suggests Choice **B**, about monitoring advertising campaigns, or Choice **C**, about opposing any campaign. Choice **D** is contradicted in the passage, which implies that Hollywood is no longer the tourist draw it once was. Choice **E** is illogical and certainly not implied in the passage.

46. **D.** The passage is probably intended for those about to read *The Lord of the Rings.* The first sentences of the passage reinforce this idea. "Students of the Middle Ages," Choice **A**, are more likely to study history, not literary archetypes, making this choice irrelevant. Choices **B** and **E** are wrong for the same reason; the passage uses both *The Odyssey* and *Beowulf* as examples of other epics readers might be familiar with. Choice **C** makes no sense; readers who have read *The Lord of the Rings* are familiar with the work, and whether or not they enjoyed it is irrelevant to this question.

47. **E.** To fully appreciate a work such as *The Lord of the Rings,* one should be familiar with its historical underpinnings and the epic tradition, a prescribed path that the story will follow. Choice **A** is inaccurate because of the word "identical." The characters are similar but not identical. Choice **B** confuses the passage's main point: that knowing characteristics of the epic genre will give greater appreciation when reading another work in the same genre, not that readers "should read" familiar works before unfamiliar ones. Choice **C** confuses literature with history, and while it may be a true idea, it is not a summary of the passage's point. Choice **D** is unreasonable and contradicts the passage.

48. **A.** As does the hero in other epics, the heroes in *The Lord of the Rings* will return home after surviving many hardships. Choice **B** is contradicted in the passage with its analogies to *The Odyssey* and *Beowulf.* Nothing in the passage, however, implies the ending is a plagiarized one (**C**). Choice **D** has no evidence in the passage. The phrase "explicit references" in Choice **E** makes it wrong; the passage discusses only similarities between epics, not references.

49. **D.** Because the passage is written for people about to read *The Lord of the Rings,* it is therefore assumed that they will go on to read the epic. The entire passage is designed to enhance the audience's appreciation of the upcoming reading.

50. **D.** Since *The Lord of the Rings* satisfies the requirements of the epic tradition, a reader anticipating such elements will not be disappointed. All the other choices are unreasonable.

Section II: Mathematics

1. **C.** One way to solve this problem is to set up a ratio: 10 kilometers is to 6.2 miles as 45 kilometers is to how many miles? This is expressed in mathematical terms as:

$$\frac{10 \text{ km}}{6.2 \text{ mi}} = \frac{45 \text{ km}}{x}$$

Cross-multiplying gives:

$$10x = 6.2 \times 45$$

$$10x = 279$$

Dividing both sides by 10 gives:

$$\frac{10x}{10} = \frac{279}{10}$$

$$x = 27.9 \text{ miles}$$

Another method is to realize that 45 kilometers is exactly $4\frac{1}{2}$ times 10 kilometers. Therefore, the number of miles in 45 kilometers must be $4\frac{1}{2}$ times the number of miles in 10 kilometers, or $4\frac{1}{2}$ times 6.2. Thus, $4.5 \times 6.2 = 27.9$.

2. **C.** Add the amount paid to the real estate agent and the amount the family received to arrive at the sale price:

$$\begin{array}{r} \$334,460 \\ +21,360 \\ \hline \$355,820 \end{array}$$

3. **A.** The four listed items total $1,740. Therefore, by subtracting from the listed total of $2,220, you can see that the missing item must have cost $480:

$$\$2,220 - \$1,740 = \$480$$

4. **D.** $\frac{2}{9} = \frac{3}{q}$. Cross-multiplying gives $2q = 27$. Dividing both sides by 2 gives:

$$\frac{2q}{2} = \frac{27}{2}$$

$$q = \frac{27}{2}$$

Remember to check for this answer (in improper fraction form) in the choices before automatically changing to a mixed number $\left(13\frac{1}{2}\right)$.

5. **D.** The total of the five verbal state test scores is 2,635. Dividing that total by 5 (the number of scores) gives 527 as the average.

6. **D.** The only numbers that divide evenly into 6, 9, and 12 are 1 and 3.

7. **C.** Using the distributive property, since $51 = 50 + 1$, then $50(10) + 1(10)$ is equivalent to 51×10. Or by simply working it out, each calculation equals 510.

8. **D.** By plugging in the value of 5 for x, into the equation, you can find y.

$$y = x^2 + 1$$

$$y = (5)^2 + 1$$

$$y = 25 + 1$$

$$y = 26$$

9. **C.** To determine what percent was *left* after household and credit card expenditures, add up these two expenditures and subtract the total from 100% (because the chart represents 100%).

$$\begin{array}{r} \text{Household} = \quad 44\% \\ \text{Credit Card} = \underline{+10\%} \\ 54\% \end{array}$$

Now subtracting gives:

$$\begin{array}{r} 100\%\,(\text{total}) \\ \underline{-54\%}\,(\text{Household and Credit Card}) \\ 46\% \end{array}$$

So 46% was left.

10. **C.** Since the figure is a rectangle, its opposite sides are equal. To find its perimeter, first add the two sides and then double the sum (or double each of the sides and add the results).

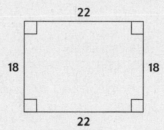

Now, to determine the side of a square with the same perimeter, simply divide by 4, since the side of a square is $\frac{1}{4}$ its perimeter. Finally, to find the area of the square, multiply its side by itself (square it).

11. **B.** If you call the price of the tie x, then the price of the shirt is $3x$, the price of the slacks is $3x$, and the price of the coat is twice that of the shirt, or $6x$. Totaling the x's, you get $13x$. Since the total spent was $156, $13x = 156$. Dividing both sides by 13 gives:

$$\frac{13x}{13} = \frac{\$156}{13}$$
$$x = \$12 \text{ (the price of the tie)}$$

Therefore, the price of the pair of slacks, $3x$, is $3(\$12) = \$36$.

12. **D.**

$$13 \div \frac{1}{5} =$$
$$\frac{13}{1} \times \frac{5}{1} = 65$$

13. **D.** Sam walks 5 miles each day. Since he walks five days each week, he walks 25 miles each week. In five weeks, he would walk 5×25, or 125 miles.

14. **D.** If Tom is 4 years older than Emily, and if you call Emily's age x, then Tom's age must be $x + 4$. Also, since the total of their ages is 24, Emily's age + Tom's age = 24. Therefore,

$$x + (x + 4) = 24$$

15. **D.** Twenty percent of 250 may be written as $.20 \times 250$ or $\left(\frac{20}{100}\right) \times 250$. Note that $\frac{20}{100}$ is reduced to $\frac{1}{5}$, which is Choice **D** $\left(250 \times \frac{1}{5}\right)$.

16. D. The new dimensions are:

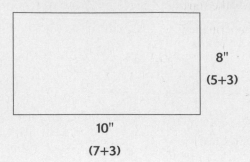

8"

(5+3)

10"

(7+3)

Note: Perimeter is the distance around. Think pe*rim*eter (*rim*). Simply add the sides (10 + 8 + 10 + 8) = 36 inches.

Or apply the perimeter formula:

2(length) + 2(width) = perimeter

2(10) + 2(8) = 20 + 16 = 36 inches

17. B. To purchase 12 blank compact discs, Roy must buy six packages. At $2.98 per package, he spends $17.88. His change from a $20 bill will be $20.00 – $17.88 = $2.12.

18. D. Solving the equation $2x + 4 = 3x + 3$, first subtract $2x$ from each side:

$2x + 4 - 2x = 3x + 3 - 2x$

$4 = x + 3$

Now subtract 3 from both sides:

$4 - 3 = x + 3 - 3$

$1 = x$

By plugging in the value of x (that is, 1) for each of the choices, you find that 1 satisfies all the equations *except* Choice **D.**

Does $x = -1$? No.

$1 \neq -1$

Therefore, **D** is the correct answer.

19. B. Note that all choices except **B** are larger than $\frac{1}{2}$. Choice **B**, $\frac{4}{9}$, is smaller than $\frac{1}{2}$.

20. B. 210,000 is equivalent to $(2 \times 10^5) + (1 \times 10^4)$. A fast way of figuring this is to count the number of places to the right of each digit that is not 0. For instance,

2̲10,000   Note that there are five places to the right of the 2, thus 2×10^5.

21̲0,000   There are four places to the right of the 1, thus 1×10^4.

So 210,000 may also be written $(2 \times 10^5) + (1 \times 10^4)$.

21. C. If the product of two numbers equals one of the numbers, then $(x)(y) = x$. If this product is more than 0, neither of the numbers may be 0. Therefore, y must be 1:$(x)(1) = x$.

22. **E.** Assume that the length of each side of each square is 1. To determine the perimeter of each diagram, add up all of the sides. Mark off the starting point.

The diagram in Choice **A** has a perimeter of 14.

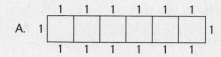

The diagram in Choice **B** has a perimeter of 10.

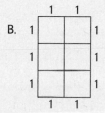

The diagram in Choice **C** has a perimeter of 10.

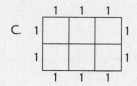

The diagram in Choice **D** has a perimeter of 14.

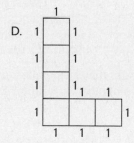

The diagram in Choice **E** has a perimeter of 24; diagram **E** has the greatest perimeter.

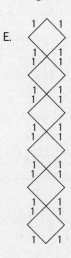

23. **E.** The sale of each card yields a profit of $2.75 (since each costs $2.00 and is sold for $4.75). Therefore, the number of cards that the Key Club needs to sell to yield a total of $82.50 can be determined by dividing $82.50 by the profit from each sale, $2.75. Choice **D** is incorrect because in the order of operations, division takes precedence over subtraction (is performed first).

24. **C.** Rounding 0.14739 to the nearest thousandth means first looking at the digit one place to the right of the thousandths place: 0.147<u>3</u>9. Since that digit is 4 or less, simply drop it. (There is no need to replace it with zeros because they are not required to the right of a decimal point.)

25. **A.** Note that 12 can be expressed as (10 + 2). Another way to compute 12×1.60 is $10(1.60) + 2(1.60)$.

26. **C.** Note that only Choice **C** raises one of the numbers by 5 while it lowers the other number by 5. This gives the best approximation of the five choices.

27. **A.** Sixteen out of 400 may be expressed as a percent, as $\frac{16}{400}$. Dividing 16 by 400 gives 0.04, or 4%.

28. **C.** You could multiply 7 by $1.00 and 7 by $1.25 and then add the results:

$$7 \times \$1.00 = \$7.00$$
$$\underline{7 \times \$1.25 = \$8.75}$$
$$\$15.75$$

or you could add the washer and dryer costs together and then multiply the total by 7.

$$\$1.00 + \$1.25 = \$2.25$$
$$7 \times \$2.25 = \$15.75$$

29. **D.** Using the probability formula,

$$\text{probability} = \frac{\text{number of lucky chances}}{\text{total number of chances}}$$

The chance of choosing a weekday = 5 weekdays / 7 total days = $\frac{5}{7}$.

30. **E.** Note that since there is a mark between +7 and +9, that mark must equal +8. Thus, each mark equals 1. Counting back, point Q is at +5. Therefore, 15 units to the left of +5 would be $+5 - 15 = -10$.

31. **C.** The "product of two numbers" indicates that the numbers must be multiplied together. The "sum" means *add*. Therefore, the product of two numbers equaling 5 more than their sum can be written as:

$$(A)(B) = A + B + 5$$

32. **C.** Only III is determined by division: $39 \div 3$. The others are determined by multiplication ($6 \times B$) and subtraction, respectively.

33. **E.** Since each cluster of symbols represents 10 stars, $9\frac{1}{2}$ clusters must equal 95 stars.

34. **B.** Thirty percent off the original price equals a discount of $(0.30)(\$8,000) = \$2,400$. Therefore, the new selling price is $\$8,000 - \$2,400 = \$5,600$.

35. **D.** Since Harmon's hybrid car averages 35 miles for each gallon of gas, on 12 gallons he'll be able to drive 12×35, or 420 miles.

36. **D.** Remember that a parallelogram has equal opposite sides. Therefore, its sides are 9, 7, 9, and 7. Its perimeter is then 32. If a square has the same perimeter, one of its sides must be $\frac{1}{4}$ its perimeter (since the four sides of a square are equal). One-fourth of 32 is 8.

37. **D.** If each adult drinks $\frac{1}{5}$ gallon of lemonade, then 5 adults consume 1 gallon. Since 28 adults attend the picnic, $\frac{28}{5}$ = slightly over 5 gallons.

38. **B.** Note that if there were an equal number of adults and children, then there would be 75 of each. Since there are more adults than children, the number of children must be lower than 75. Since **A,** a decimal number, is a ridiculous answer, of the choices given, only **B** could be the number of children.

39. C. To determine the number of dry erase markers costing 82¢ each that can be made for $75, simply divide:

$$\$75.00 \div .82 = 91.4$$

Note that since you cannot have a fractional answer in this case, 91 is the answer.

40. A. To determine the percent of the school population that *does not* attend graduation:

$$\frac{\text{part}}{\text{total}} = \frac{35}{280}$$

Dividing 35 by 280 gives 0.125, or 12.5%.

41. E. There are several quick methods of solving this problem. As in question 1, a ratio can be set up.

$$\frac{20 \text{ pgs}}{4 \text{ hours}} = \frac{50 \text{ pages}}{x \text{ hours}} \qquad 20x = 200 \qquad \frac{^1\cancel{20}x}{_1\cancel{20}} = \frac{\cancel{200}^{10}}{\cancel{20}_1} \qquad x = 10 \text{ hours}$$

Cross-multiplying gives 10 hours for the answer. Alternatively, determining John's hourly rate (5 pages per hour) tells you that he will need 10 hours to type 50 pages.

$$\frac{20 \text{ pgs}}{4 \text{ hours per page}} = 5 \text{ pages per hour} \qquad \frac{50 \text{ total pgs}}{5 \text{ pgs}} = 10 \text{ hours}$$

42. B. Note that a total of 28 items were purchased, each costing 85¢. Therefore, the simplest way to compute the total amount spent is 28×85¢.

43. B. If team B's victories are called x, then team A must have $2x$ victories, team C must have $(2x - 5)$ victories, and team D must have $(x + 4)$ victories. All together, these total $6x - 1$. The problem states that the total equals 29 victories. Thus,

$$6x - 1 = 29$$
$$6x = 30$$
$$x = 5$$

Therefore, team D has $(x + 4)$ victories, or $(5 + 4) = 9$.

44. C. If you call the smaller piece x, then the larger piece (6 inches bigger) must be $x + 6$. Since the two pieces together equal a yardstick,

$$x + (x + 6) = 36$$
$$x + x + 6 = 36$$

45. B. Solving for p, first subtract 9 from both sides.

$$7p + 9 = 24$$
$$7p + 9 - 9 = 24 - 9$$
$$7p = 15$$

Now divide both sides by 7:

$$\frac{7p}{7} = \frac{15}{7}$$
$$p = \frac{15}{7}$$

46. **E.** $\dfrac{5(\text{milkshakes})}{12(\text{time})} = \dfrac{45(\text{milkshakes})}{x(\text{time})}$ (You don't know this, so represent it as x.)

Shortcut—These are equivalent fractions.

Since $5 \times 9 = 45$

then $12 \times 9 = 108$ (which is x)

Now divide by 60:

$\dfrac{108 \text{ minutes}}{60 \text{ (minutes in one hour)}}$

$= 1$ hour, 48 minutes

You can also solve this mathematically as follows, by first cross-multiplying:

$\dfrac{5}{12} = \dfrac{45}{x}$

$(5x) = (12)(45)$

$5x = 540$

To solve for x, divide both sides by 5.

$\dfrac{5x}{5} = \dfrac{540}{5}$

$x = 108$ minutes (divide by 60 to convert to hours and minutes)

$\dfrac{108}{60} = 1\dfrac{48}{60} = 1$ hour, 48 minutes

47. **B.** Note that, on the graph, a 35-degree drop in temperature on the line correlates with a 20% attendance drop (the fourth slash up the graph).

48. **E.** So far, George has averaged 80% on each of three tests. Therefore, his *total* points scored equal 3 times 80, or 240 points. In order to average 85% for four tests, George needs a total point score of 4 times 85, or 340 points. Since George presently is 100 points short of 340, he needs to get 100 points, or 100%, on the fourth test.

49. **E.** Note that 30% of 50 may be expressed in several ways: for example, 0.30×50 or $\dfrac{3}{10} \times 50$. Whichever way it is expressed, it still totals 15. The only choice that does not total 15 is Choice **E**, which totals $166\dfrac{2}{3}$.

50. **E.** If you know the days when Thelma doesn't read, then simply divide the number of days she does read into the number of magazines for an average.

Section III: Writing

To help you evaluate your essay writing skills, listed below are examples of three different written responses for essay topic one (there are no examples for topic two). Compare your essay to these three examples and the analysis of a well-written essay, an average essay, and a poorly written essay. Use the checklist (pg. 304) to evaluate your essays, and to help you take a closer look and understand your scoring range. Topic prompt can be found on page 296.

Essay 1: A Well-Written Essay

Evaluating a student's progress is one of a teacher's major concerns. Although it would be nice to say that a grade "doesn't matter" as much as the student's experience in a class, that simply isn't true. Most People want some measurement of how well they are doing. Traditionally, the measurement has been a letter grade, but for many years some public schools have chosen the "pass-fail" method, which includes a written statement describing the student's progress.

Using a letter grade is more definitive than the "pass-fail" option. If a student receives a "C," he knows that he is ranked as average in a class. If he receives an "A," he knows he is among the top students. And if he receives a "D," he knows that he is behind his fellow students and perhaps in danger of failing a class. The "pass-fail" system, on the other hand, is always open to question. If he passes, the student doesn't know precisely where he falls in terms of the other students. Even a teacher's comment may not make it clear. A student may choose to interpret a teacher's comment as favorable when the teacher actually meant that the student's progress was simply adequate. Letter grades are also universally understood by schools, so that when a student with strong "B" average is applying to a university or moving to a different school, the school knows clearly where that student stands in relation to others.

On the other hand, letter grades are not as clear cut as they may seem. Different teachers and different schools will likely have different standards for a specific grade. For example, a teacher in my high school was notorious for giving nothing higher than a B, no matter how brilliantly a student might perform. Experiments have shown that the same student can be ranked differently by different teachers of the same subject. Another problem with evaluating students with letter grades is that a student may feel pigeon-holed, for example, and this may influence his effort or his attitude. When no comment is included with a letter grade, a student may not have a clear idea of his performance or abilities.

With a "pass-fail" system, however, students may have a clearer picture of their strengths and weaknesses. A teacher's statement, along with the pass-fail designation, can be very helpful in motivating a student. Another advantage of the pass-fail system is that students are more likely to focus on the material being taught than the letter grade they will receive. Too often students struggle more to get a certain grade than to understand what is being taught. This is perhaps the best argument for a "pass-fail" system: the emphasis is on learning, not on "getting an 'A.'" The best argument against it is that it can be too vague and can make it difficult for a student to understand where he stands in relation to his peers. Also, some colleges do not accept the "pass-fail" designation for applicants.

Each system has its good points and its bad points. What may occur is that a student, or an institution, may simply translate what is said in a "pass-fail" statement to an equivalent letter grade. In my opinion, the better option for evaluation might be a combination of the letter grade system with a written statement such as is used in the "pass-fail" system.

Analysis of Essay 1

This essay is well organized and logically developed. The writer stays with the topic, which is to "comment on the pros and cons" of the two systems. Notice that the topic does not require the writer to take a stand on which system is better, though this writer does offer an opinion in the last paragraph. The opinion doesn't come out of the blue, however; the reader has been prepared for it in the essay as a whole. A particular strength of this essay is that the paragraphs are well developed (except perhaps for the last one), and the writing is smooth and without errors. The writer uses varied sentence structure and good transitions (for example, "on the other hand," "however").

Essay 2: An Average Essay

The advantages of a letter grade system are (1) everyone understands what the letter grade means; (2) it can be used to distinguish levels of student achievement (3) provides students with clear targets to aim for, and (4) is an efficient way for colleges to evaluate students. The disadvantages of the letter grade system are (1) it doesn't explain details of performance to a student; (2) it can intimmidate a student; and (3) sometimes it makes students more interested in the grade than in the material.

The biggest advantages of a "pass-fail" system is (1) it tends to make students relax and pay more attention to the class itself and (2) the teacher is able to make a verbal evaluation that could be helpful to the student.

In looking at the letter grade system, it is obvious that it will be more easily understood and it will help a student know more exactly where he stands. If a student gets a "D" for example he may work harder than he would if he merely got a "pass" with a few negative comments. Letter grades are important when a student is transfering to another school or applying to a college, since everyone is clear on what the letter grade means, however it is also true that grades don't let students know exactly where their weaknesses are, they provide no detailed explanation. Also some students become more interested in their grade average than in the classes they are taking.

The "pass-fail" system is good because it takes pressure off the student. It allows you to focus on the class and not what grade you will get. You can also get some good pointers from the teacher that may improve future performance. At the same time, the student might want to know where he stands in relationship to his fellow students, and the pass-fail system doesn't help as much here as the letter grade system.

Both systems can be used well and both systems can be used poorly. It depends on the teacher and the school. Also, some students may acheive more under one system than they do under the other, depending on personality. Both systems have advantages and disadvantages.

Analysis of Essay 2

Although this essay does address the topic, its organization and paragraph development need work. The first paragraph uses a numbered list to cover the "A" to "F" grading system. The second paragraph covering the advantages of a "pass-fail" system doesn't stand well on its own. (Note that the list items are not parallel in either paragraph.) A solution might be an introductory paragraph that mentions the main advantages of both systems. The following two paragraphs need more development, and the concluding paragraph is sketchy. Grammatical and spelling errors also detract from the essay. Notice that the writer uses "students" in the first three paragraphs and "you" (as well as "student") in the fourth paragraph. There is also a run-on sentence in the third paragraph.

Essay 3: A Poorly Written Essay

I believe that the pass-fail grading system is better than the "A" to "F" grading system because it takes more into account. For example, in a class a student may participate a lot in discussion but he may not do so well on exams. With the pass-fail system the teacher will probably take the class discussion into more account than just the letter grades on tests.

When a student is very concerned about a grade, he doesn't pay so much attention to what he is studying. Which means he is not really learning. Letter grades make students feel very competetive with other students and this also means they spend too much time worrying about the letter grade.

With the pass-fail system, a student feels more confident. I think the comments that the teacher makes with a pass-fail grade will mean much more than just an A, B, C, D, or F. This seems to me to be much more personal. I have never been in a pass-fail situation, but have been told that it improves the atmosphere in a class.

Sometimes you might need a letter grade rather than just "pass" or "fail." But usually it isn't too hard for a teacher to tell you what grade you would get; if the teacher were assigning grades. I don't think that not having a letter grade on a transcript will keep anyone out of college.,

You really have to ask yourself what a grade means. Does it say how you are doing or does it say this is what the teacher thinks of you. Sometimes a student gets an A just because the teacher likes him or her. I think in the long run the pass-fail system proves to be a much more fair way to evaluate students because a teachers prejudices will not matter so much.

In summing up, it is clear that grades probably do more harm than good, whereas pass-fail probably gives students more opportunity to succeed.

Analysis of Essay 3

This essay doesn't really address the topic, which concerns the pros and cons of each system. It is not coherent; one idea (and one paragraph) doesn't lead clearly to the next. Paragraph development is very weak, and some points are not logical (for example, why would a letter-grade system favor teacher prejudice more than a pass-fail system, and why would the pass-fail system mean the teacher will take class discussion more into account?). The concluding paragraph is only a sentence, and it makes a point that hasn't been explained.

Practice Test 4

Answer Sheet for Practice Test 4

(Remove This Sheet and Use It to Mark Your Answers)

Section I: Reading

1 ⒶⒷⒸⒹⒺ	26 ⒶⒷⒸⒹⒺ
2 ⒶⒷⒸⒹⒺ	27 ⒶⒷⒸⒹⒺ
3 ⒶⒷⒸⒹⒺ	28 ⒶⒷⒸⒹⒺ
4 ⒶⒷⒸⒹⒺ	29 ⒶⒷⒸⒹⒺ
5 ⒶⒷⒸⒹⒺ	30 ⒶⒷⒸⒹⒺ
6 ⒶⒷⒸⒹⒺ	31 ⒶⒷⒸⒹⒺ
7 ⒶⒷⒸⒹⒺ	32 ⒶⒷⒸⒹⒺ
8 ⒶⒷⒸⒹⒺ	33 ⒶⒷⒸⒹⒺ
9 ⒶⒷⒸⒹⒺ	34 ⒶⒷⒸⒹⒺ
10 ⒶⒷⒸⒹⒺ	35 ⒶⒷⒸⒹⒺ
11 ⒶⒷⒸⒹⒺ	36 ⒶⒷⒸⒹⒺ
12 ⒶⒷⒸⒹⒺ	37 ⒶⒷⒸⒹⒺ
13 ⒶⒷⒸⒹⒺ	38 ⒶⒷⒸⒹⒺ
14 ⒶⒷⒸⒹⒺ	39 ⒶⒷⒸⒹⒺ
15 ⒶⒷⒸⒹⒺ	40 ⒶⒷⒸⒹⒺ
16 ⒶⒷⒸⒹⒺ	41 ⒶⒷⒸⒹⒺ
17 ⒶⒷⒸⒹⒺ	42 ⒶⒷⒸⒹⒺ
18 ⒶⒷⒸⒹⒺ	43 ⒶⒷⒸⒹⒺ
19 ⒶⒷⒸⒹⒺ	44 ⒶⒷⒸⒹⒺ
20 ⒶⒷⒸⒹⒺ	45 ⒶⒷⒸⒹⒺ
21 ⒶⒷⒸⒹⒺ	46 ⒶⒷⒸⒹⒺ
22 ⒶⒷⒸⒹⒺ	47 ⒶⒷⒸⒹⒺ
23 ⒶⒷⒸⒹⒺ	48 ⒶⒷⒸⒹⒺ
24 ⒶⒷⒸⒹⒺ	49 ⒶⒷⒸⒹⒺ
25 ⒶⒷⒸⒹⒺ	50 ⒶⒷⒸⒹⒺ

Section II: Mathematics

1 Ⓐ Ⓑ Ⓒ Ⓓ Ⓔ	26 Ⓐ Ⓑ Ⓒ Ⓓ Ⓔ
2 Ⓐ Ⓑ Ⓒ Ⓓ Ⓔ	27 Ⓐ Ⓑ Ⓒ Ⓓ Ⓔ
3 Ⓐ Ⓑ Ⓒ Ⓓ Ⓔ	28 Ⓐ Ⓑ Ⓒ Ⓓ Ⓔ
4 Ⓐ Ⓑ Ⓒ Ⓓ Ⓔ	29 Ⓐ Ⓑ Ⓒ Ⓓ Ⓔ
5 Ⓐ Ⓑ Ⓒ Ⓓ Ⓔ	30 Ⓐ Ⓑ Ⓒ Ⓓ Ⓔ
6 Ⓐ Ⓑ Ⓒ Ⓓ Ⓔ	31 Ⓐ Ⓑ Ⓒ Ⓓ Ⓔ
7 Ⓐ Ⓑ Ⓒ Ⓓ Ⓔ	32 Ⓐ Ⓑ Ⓒ Ⓓ Ⓔ
8 Ⓐ Ⓑ Ⓒ Ⓓ Ⓔ	33 Ⓐ Ⓑ Ⓒ Ⓓ Ⓔ
9 Ⓐ Ⓑ Ⓒ Ⓓ Ⓔ	34 Ⓐ Ⓑ Ⓒ Ⓓ Ⓔ
10 Ⓐ Ⓑ Ⓒ Ⓓ Ⓔ	35 Ⓐ Ⓑ Ⓒ Ⓓ Ⓔ
11 Ⓐ Ⓑ Ⓒ Ⓓ Ⓔ	36 Ⓐ Ⓑ Ⓒ Ⓓ Ⓔ
12 Ⓐ Ⓑ Ⓒ Ⓓ Ⓔ	37 Ⓐ Ⓑ Ⓒ Ⓓ Ⓔ
13 Ⓐ Ⓑ Ⓒ Ⓓ Ⓔ	38 Ⓐ Ⓑ Ⓒ Ⓓ Ⓔ
14 Ⓐ Ⓑ Ⓒ Ⓓ Ⓔ	39 Ⓐ Ⓑ Ⓒ Ⓓ Ⓔ
15 Ⓐ Ⓑ Ⓒ Ⓓ Ⓔ	40 Ⓐ Ⓑ Ⓒ Ⓓ Ⓔ
16 Ⓐ Ⓑ Ⓒ Ⓓ Ⓔ	41 Ⓐ Ⓑ Ⓒ Ⓓ Ⓔ
17 Ⓐ Ⓑ Ⓒ Ⓓ Ⓔ	42 Ⓐ Ⓑ Ⓒ Ⓓ Ⓔ
18 Ⓐ Ⓑ Ⓒ Ⓓ Ⓔ	43 Ⓐ Ⓑ Ⓒ Ⓓ Ⓔ
19 Ⓐ Ⓑ Ⓒ Ⓓ Ⓔ	44 Ⓐ Ⓑ Ⓒ Ⓓ Ⓔ
20 Ⓐ Ⓑ Ⓒ Ⓓ Ⓔ	45 Ⓐ Ⓑ Ⓒ Ⓓ Ⓔ
21 Ⓐ Ⓑ Ⓒ Ⓓ Ⓔ	46 Ⓐ Ⓑ Ⓒ Ⓓ Ⓔ
22 Ⓐ Ⓑ Ⓒ Ⓓ Ⓔ	47 Ⓐ Ⓑ Ⓒ Ⓓ Ⓔ
23 Ⓐ Ⓑ Ⓒ Ⓓ Ⓔ	48 Ⓐ Ⓑ Ⓒ Ⓓ Ⓔ
24 Ⓐ Ⓑ Ⓒ Ⓓ Ⓔ	49 Ⓐ Ⓑ Ⓒ Ⓓ Ⓔ
25 Ⓐ Ⓑ Ⓒ Ⓓ Ⓔ	50 Ⓐ Ⓑ Ⓒ Ⓓ Ⓔ

CUT HERE

Practice Test 4

The total testing time is four hours. You may work on any section of the exam during this time period.

    Section I: Reading—50 Questions
    Section II: Mathematics—50 Questions
    Section III: Writing—2 Essays

Section I: Reading

50 Questions

Directions: A question or number of questions follows each of the statements or passages in this section. Using only the *stated* or *implied* information given in the statement or passage, answer the question or questions by choosing the *best* answer from among the five choices given. Make sure to mark your answers for this section on the Reading section of the answer sheet.

Read the passage below and answer the two questions that follow.

The concentration of harmful ozone pollution in the lower atmosphere has more than doubled in the last one hundred years, and it will likely rise at an even faster rate during the next thirty years, researchers claim. Recent measurements of ground-level ozone indicate that levels of the gas are, on average, twice as high as those recorded by French researchers in Paris in the late 1800s.

Ozone is not emitted directly into the air but is formed through complex reactions between nitrogen oxide and other chemicals found in automobile and industrial emissions which contain nitrogen oxide. When it is in the upper atmosphere, ozone shields Earth from the sun's ultraviolet rays, which can cause skin cancer and other health problems. But when found near ground level, this highly corrosive form of oxygen can cause respiratory distress.

Based on projected increases in nitrogen oxide emissions, researchers have used computer simulations to show that between now and 2020, concentrations of ground-level, or "tropospheric," ozone will rise "at a rate faster than during the past hundred years." In fact, the increase in tropospheric ozone during the next thirty years could equal that for the entire last century.

1. The predicted increase in tropospheric ozone will not result in a decrease in skin cancers because

    A. ozone in the upper atmosphere cannot protect against the harmful rays of the sun.
    B. tropospheric ozone can cause respiratory diseases.
    C. ozone is not emitted directly into the air.
    D. the ozone at ground level does not protect against the harmful rays of the sun.
    E. ozone is a corrosive form of oxygen.

2. From the passage, it can be inferred that in thirty years there will be

    A. an increase in the number of skin cancers.
    B. an increase in the number of respiratory diseases.
    C. a decrease in the amount of ozone in the upper atmosphere.
    D. a decrease in the amount of nitrogen oxide emissions.
    E. a decrease in the amount of automobile and industrial emissions.

GO ON TO THE NEXT PAGE

Use the excerpt from the outline below to answer the three questions that follow.

I. Elements of Music
   A. Pitch
      1. High or low and may repeat
      2. Creates melody
   B. Rhythm
      1. Measured by units of time
      2. "Beats" can be organized in sets
   C. Harmony
      1. Two or more simultaneous tones
      2. Three or more simultaneous tones make a chord
   D. Form
      1. "Design" or music created by interaction of elements
      2. "Phrases" can be similar or different
      3. Repetition of elements creates unity
      4. Contrasting elements create variety
   E. Texture
      1. Total sound—thick, thin, opaque, and transparent
      2. Motifs' textures—legato (smooth sounding) and staccato (detached)
   F. Tempo
      1. Speed
      2. Terms—examples, lento (slow) and presto (quick)
   G. Dynamics
      1. Loudness and softness of music
      2. Terms—examples, piano (soft) and forte (loud)
   H. Timbre
      1. Unique tonal quality
      2. Each instrument family has characteristic sound
   I. Notation
      1. Written form
      2. Composed of symbols for notes, rests, pitch, and so on.

3. Where should the term *fortissimo* (very loud) be placed in the outline?

   A. B.2
   B. C.2
   C. D.1
   D. F.1
   E. G.2

4. From the information given in the outline, repetition of elements could create which of the following?

   A. Rests
   B. Unity
   C. Chords
   D. Variety
   E. Notes

5. The outline indicates that the unique tonal sound created by the woodwind family would be called which of the following?

   A. Timbre
   B. Pitch
   C. Harmony
   D. Tempo
   E. Rhythm

Read the passage below and answer the question that follows.

The Celtic story of Queen Maeve tells of a powerful goddess warrior. It is possible that the aggressive goddess, a surprising figure in a patriarchal culture, may reflect a preceding matriarchal age when women were the dominant sex.

6. The author of the preceding quotation makes all the following assumptions, *except:*

   A. The culture of an age will be reflected in its myth.
   B. Celtic myths are different from the myths of other cultures.
   C. A culture may be either matriarchal or patriarchal.
   D. A myth may reflect the culture of an earlier age.
   E. A patriarchal culture is likely to create myths of powerful men.

Read the passage below and answer the six questions that follow.

According to a recent set of calculations by Frank D. Drake, a University of California, Santa Cruz astronomer, between ten thousand and one hundred thousand "advanced" civilizations (this, dubiously, includes us) exist in our own Milky Way galaxy alone. He explains that it's a simple matter of estimating the rate of formation of stars and then multiplying by the fraction with planets around them, and the average number of planets per star suitable for life to evolve. This figure is then adjusted downward on the assumption that only some will actually have evolved life, that only some of those have ended up with intelligent life, and that only a fraction of *those* have developed advanced civilizations. Drake even takes into account the fact that such civilizations will be only temporary.

So the question is not "Are there more advanced creatures out there?" but "What will they do to us when they find us?" To answer, consider what we have done to chimpanzees and gorillas, creatures that stand in a relationship to us that may parallel the relationship we could have to the extraterrestrials. We steal their habitats, experiment on them, cage them in zoos to satisfy our curiosity, train them to do tricks in circuses, kill them to display their body parts, eat them, and attempt to have them do useful work—slave labor. L. S. Shklovskii and Carl Sagan's five-hundred-page book *Intelligent Life in the Universe* devotes only four sentences to the possibility that anything bad might result from letting extraterrestrial civilizations know of our existence and location, and astronomers today are equally nonpessimistic.

This is naive both philosophically and scientifically. Contrary to the fantasy of advanced extraterrestrials helping us in our own progress, the likely result of contact would be the most grotesque disaster that has ever befallen our species, so instead of spending a hundred million dollars searching for them, we should hide for at least a few centuries—until we can protect ourselves from creatures that are likely to treat us as well as we've treated rhesus monkeys, cows, dogs, and dodos.

7. One of the author's purposes of the second paragraph is to

   A. encourage increased expenditure on space exploration.
   B. argue for the existence of UFOs.
   C. comment on humans' treatment of animals.
   D. assert the probability of life on other planets.
   E. question the likelihood of extraterrestrial life.

8. Which of the following words in the first paragraph of the passage reveals the author's attitude toward the present inhabitants of the Earth?

   A. "Advanced"
   B. Dubiously
   C. Intelligent
   D. Simple
   E. Temporary

9. In the second paragraph, the author suggests that the question, "Are there more advanced creatures out there?" should not be asked because

   A. the answer is clearly "yes."
   B. the answer is clearly "no."
   C. the answer can never be known.
   D. the answer is irrelevant to contemporary human concerns.
   E. the question is unscientific.

10. The author assumes all the following about the inhabitants of "advanced" civilizations in the Milky Way, *except* that

   A. the number of civilizations is a small fraction of the number of stars in the galaxy.
   B. they exist in large numbers.
   C. they will find Earth.
   D. they are essentially benevolent.
   E. they will be aided in finding us by our search for them.

11. The author assumes that the relation of extraterrestrials to humans would resemble that of

   A. humans to religiously worshipped beings.
   B. women to men.
   C. children to parents.
   D. slaves to free people.
   E. humans to animals.

12. This passage would most appropriately appear in a(n)

   A. book on astronomy.
   B. book on astrology.
   C. collection of science fiction stories.
   D. collection of satirical essays.
   E. introductory science textbook.

GO ON TO THE NEXT PAGE

Read the passage below and answer the three questions that follow.

Styles of domestic architecture come and go, but one that has continued to interest a small number of <u>discerning</u> homeowners is 1950s modernism. The houses are usually described with such words as "clean" or "uncluttered." Most fifties modern houses have an open plan with as few interior walls as possible and an enclosing structural skeleton of wood or steel. Floor-to-ceiling glass doors link the interior with a courtyard or garden. Above all, the lines are clean and simple. As a rule, the roof is flat.

Many of the fifties modern houses are situated in wooded areas. Some are built around a tree that grows through the flat roof. Others may have a pool that is part of the living room. The most spectacular example of this impulse is probably Frank Lloyd Wright's Pennsylvania house, built on a waterfall. Within ten years, the fifties modern style was altogether out of fashion. In the 1960s, the simplicity that had once attracted buyers was condemned as cold and unwelcoming.

13. The word <u>discerning</u>, as it is used in the first paragraph, can be best defined as

   A. affluent.
   B. perceptive.
   C. artistic.
   D. confident.
   E. inquisitive.

14. This passage is an example of which of the following kinds of writing?

   A. Prose fiction
   B. Logical argument
   C. Expository prose
   D. Personal essay
   E. Dialogue

15. Which of the following is the best choice as a final sentence for the second paragraph?

   A. As I said at the beginning, there are still a number of buyers for these houses.
   B. Consequently, there are still some buyers for these houses now.
   C. But fifty years later, a small but enthusiastic group is eager to buy these houses and willing to pay very high prices for them.
   D. "Are there buyers for them out there nowadays?" is a question real estate agents are asking themselves today.
   E. However, the market for these houses dried up in the sixties but has shown a new life some fifty years after the houses were first built.

Read the passage below and answer the three questions that follow.

The following are the guidelines governing medical expense deductions on state income taxes.

1. Self-employed taxpayers may deduct twenty-five percent (25%) of their health insurance costs, regardless of whether or not they itemize their deductions.

2. Self-employed taxpayers may deduct medical, dental, and pharmaceutical expenses only if they itemize their deductions.

3. All taxpayers who itemize their deductions may deduct fifty percent (50%) of their health insurance costs up to a total deduction of $2,000.

4. All taxpayers who itemize deductions are ineligible for the $1,000 exemption awarded to all taxpayers who do not itemize deductions.

16. According to the guidelines, a self-employed taxpayer with health insurance costs of $4,000 and medical, dental, and pharmaceutical bills of $500 each would have the largest deduction if he or she

   A. did not itemize deductions.
   B. itemized only deductions for medical and dental purposes.
   C. itemized only deductions for pharmaceuticals.
   D. did not itemize health insurance costs.
   E. itemized deductions for health insurance, medical, dental, and pharmaceutical expenses.

17. A taxpayer who earned his or her living as a substitute high school teacher and part-time consultant for publishers of high school textbooks would probably want clarification on which of the following terms in the guidelines?

- **A.** Self-employed
- **B.** Taxpayer
- **C.** Deduction
- **D.** Pharmaceuticals
- **E.** Exemption

18. According to the guidelines, a taxpayer who is not self-employed would be certain to save money by itemizing deductions if his or her

- **A.** income was more than $50,000.
- **B.** health insurance costs were more than $2,000.
- **C.** health insurance costs were more than $1,400.
- **D.** dental costs were more than $500.
- **E.** doctors' costs were more than $800.

Read the passage below and answer the question that follows.

A television spot depicts a group of executives sitting at a conference table in a smoke-filled office. "We're not in this business for our health," says one of the group.

19. This spot is probably a commercial for which of the following?

- **A.** Cigarettes
- **B.** An antismoking campaign
- **C.** A room freshener
- **D.** A business school
- **E.** A political campaign

Read the passage below and answer the three questions that follow.

(1) The new Florida Gulf Coast University is offering its students a wide choice of new kinds of classes. (2) Some are given on weekends, some in off-campus locations, some on videotape, and some over the Internet. (3) Almost 10 percent of this term's courses will be conducted electronically, and many students will never see the campus. (4) The school has elected to eliminate many things people expect to find at a university. (5) There are no dorms, no football stadium, no intercollegiate athletics. (6) The average freshman is not an 18-year-old just out of high school

but a 33-year-old with fifteen years of work experience. (7) The president of the student body is a grandmother.

Unlike the other state universities, Florida Gulf Coast will focus on the education of an older generation of students. About 80 percent of the students will be part-time. More than half the classes will be offered at night. Career-oriented fields like health care and real estate will be taught at several off-campus sites. In a cyberspace age, this university will test how well "distance learning" can work.

20. Which of the following best describes the relation of the first and second sentences of the first paragraph?

- **A.** The first sentence is literal; the second sentence is figurative.
- **B.** The first sentence raises a question; the second sentence answers it.
- **C.** The first sentence is general; the second sentence is specific.
- **D.** The first sentence is factual; the second sentence is an opinion.
- **E.** The first sentence refers to a primary source; the second sentence refers to a secondary source.

21. Which *two* sentences in the first paragraph best sum up the first paragraph?

- **A.** Sentences 1 and 3
- **B.** Sentences 1 and 4
- **C.** Sentences 2 and 5
- **D.** Sentences 3 and 6
- **E.** Sentences 3 and 7

22. From the passage as a whole, you can infer that the phrase "distance learning" in the final sentence refers to

- **A.** instruction in a college classroom.
- **B.** instruction using visual aids.
- **C.** classes in which no grades are awarded.
- **D.** classes in nonacademic subjects such as real estate.
- **E.** instruction apart from a central campus.

Read the passage below and answer the five questions that follow.

Just over a year ago, University of Utah electro-chemists B. Stanley Pons and Martin Fleischmann announced to a stunned world that they had discovered a simple desktop reaction, carried out at room

GO ON TO THE NEXT PAGE

temperatures, that produced energy in the same way as does the fiery furnace of the sun. When they applied a small electric current to platinum and palladium electrodes immersed in deuterium oxide, a "heavy" form of water, the deuterium atoms fused together, they said, forming helium atoms and releasing large amounts of energy. Their announcement promised something that researchers have been dreaming of and seeking for decades—an inexpensive source of energy that is produced from highly abundant materials and that produces no polluting by-products. But, despite subsequent reports of partial successes elsewhere, most chemists and physicists around the world were unsuccessful in their hurried efforts to reproduce the unexpected results. Within four months, the unorthodox concept had seemingly been relegated to the dustbin of history. At the end of March, however, more than two hundred staunch advocates of cold fusion from the United States, Italy, Japan, India, and Taiwan gathered here for the First Annual Conference on Cold Fusion to compare notes on their research, encourage one another in their lonely quest, and generally shout their defiance to the physics community at large.

The physics community, for its part, took little public notice of the affair—except for Robert Parks of the American Physical Society, who derisively termed the meeting a "séance of true believers." After three days of presentations and debate, an independent observer was left with several conclusions:

- That some new evidence has accumulated during the last year supporting the reality of cold fusion, particularly from the prestigious U.S. Department of Energy laboratories.

- That most observers outside the field are still not ready to accept that evidence.

- And that another year or two is going to be necessary for cold fusion to be either vindicated or finally discredited.

23. The alleged success of the Pons/Fleischmann cold fusion experiment was remarkable because it seemed to promise all the following, *except:*

    A. a low-cost source of energy.
    B. an energy source that was not dependent on fossil fuels.
    C. an energy source based on materials in large supply.
    D. an energy source that could be produced only in the United States.
    E. an energy source with no dangerous side effects.

24. According to the passage, most experiments that attempted to reproduce the results claimed by Pons and Fleischmann were

    A. wholly successful.
    B. partially successful.
    C. unsuccessful.
    D. not exact reproductions of the Pons/Fleischmann experiment.
    E. the source of unexpected developments in cold fusion theory.

25. Which of the following best describes the judgment of most chemists and physicists on the Pons/Fleischmann cold fusion claims four months after their announcement?

    A. They supported the Pons/Fleischmann claims.
    B. The were guardedly skeptical about the Pons/Fleischmann claims.
    C. They were sharply divided in their response to the Pons/Fleischmann claims.
    D. They rejected the Pons/Fleischmann claims.
    E. They had no opinion on the Pons/Fleischmann claims.

26. Robert Parks's reference to the meeting of cold fusion advocates as a "séance of true believers" suggests that his view of the supporters of cold fusion is that they are

    A. dedicated scientists.
    B. unscientific zealots.
    C. disinterested observers.
    D. religious scholars.
    E. defiant researchers.

27. Which of the following is the most appropriate title for the passage?

    A. The Fraud of Cold Fusion
    B. Cold Fusion: The Hope of the Future
    C. Cold Fusion: An Unanswered Question
    D. Scientific Breakthrough: Cold Fusion
    E. New Evidence to Support Cold Fusion

Read the passage below and answer the two questions that follow.

Politicians who stay in office longest are usually risk averse, and those who speak out for change, for what is necessary but unpopular or costly, are generally regarded as politically naive. To speak freely, one must have one foot out the door.

28. Which of the following is the best description of an enduring politician as implied by this statement?

   A. One who encourages change
   B. One who understands what is necessary
   C. One who avoids the unpopular stand
   D. One who supports the taking of risks
   E. One who speaks honestly

29. Which of the following best restates the meaning of the second sentence?

   A. Politicians who tell the truth must do so with an eye to the future.
   B. Dishonest politicians are likely to be voted out of office.
   C. Only the politician about to leave politics can tell the truth.
   D. Politicians who speak freely must be able to think fast.
   E. Freedom of speech is a privilege free people do not value sufficiently.

Use the graph below to answer the three questions that follow.

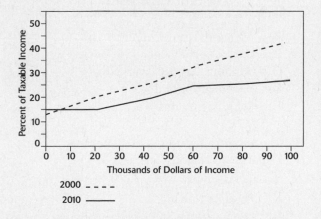

INDIVIDUAL INCOME TAX
Married Couple with Two Children

2000 – – – –
2010 ———

30. According to the graph, a married couple that had two children and earned a taxable income of $70,000 in 2010 would have paid

   A. a higher percentage of income as income tax than in 2000.
   B. a lower percentage of income as income tax than in 2000.
   C. approximately the same percentage of income as income tax in 2000.
   D. a higher dollar amount than in 2000.
   E. approximately the same dollar amount as in 2000.

31. According to the graph, the percentage of taxable income of the individual income tax in 2010 would be closest to that of 2000 if a married couple with two children were earning approximately

   A. $ 5,000
   B. $15,000
   C. $25,000
   D. $65,000
   E. $95,000

32. According to the graph, approximately what percentage of their taxable income would a married couple that had two children and earned $55,000 have paid in taxes in 2000?

   A. 22%
   B. 25%
   C. 30%
   D. 35%
   E. 40%

Read the passage below and answer the question that follows.

Students who are bilingual and majoring in Spanish regard literary censorship very differently from bilingual students majoring in other languages and from students who know no second language.

33. From this statement, which of the following can be most reliably inferred?

   A. Attitudes toward literary censorship are not influenced by knowledge of foreign languages.
   B. There is no single bilingual students' attitude toward literary censorship.
   C. Bilingual students' attitude toward literary censorship is different from that of students who speak only one language.
   D. Students who speak only one language have a similar attitude toward literary censorship.
   E. There can be no subject on which all people will agree.

GO ON TO THE NEXT PAGE

Read the passage below and answer the two questions that follow.

In July 1847, a manuscript of a novel, bearing the crossed-out addresses of three other publishing houses, reached my office. The parcel contained "The Professor" by "Currer Bell," which was eventually published after Charlotte Brontë's death. After reading the work, we decided to write "Currer Bell" a letter of appreciative criticism, but we declined to publish this work. In reply had come a brief note from "Currer Bell" expressing grateful appreciation of the attention that had been given to the manuscript and saying that the author was about to finish a second novel. The second novel would become *Jane Eyre.*

34. From details of this passage, one can infer that its author is a

    A. novelist.
    B. publisher.
    C. newspaper editor.
    D. drama critic.
    E. broker.

35. The passage puts the name "Currer Bell" in quotation marks because it

    A. wants to emphasize the name.
    B. is repeated three times in the passage.
    C. is a pseudonym for Charlotte Brontë.
    D. indicates respect.
    E. is an unusual first name for a woman.

Read the passage below and answer the six questions that follow.

To the dismay of geography teachers, the Mercator remains the most common world map sold in American bookstores. When a spokesperson at the U.S. State Department in Washington, D.C., takes the podium, the Mercator map is the backdrop. "The Mercator is something people have burned inside their minds. For them it is the way the world is supposed to look," says John Garver of the National Geographic Society. "But the Mercator map was never intended to be used as a world political map." Mercator's remarkable invention solved the problem of long-distance travel. Navigators can draw a straight line in any direction on his map and it will represent a constant compass heading. But to manage that, the farther a point is from the equator, the more Mercator stretched and exaggerated the land masses. In the 1700s, as European nations expanded their empires by sea power, the Mercator was such an essential navigational tool that it slowly became accepted as the view of the world.

The National Geographic Society, which distributes 11 million world maps each year, does its best to make people forget the Mercator by endorsing other designs. In 1922 the society picked a pumpkin-shaped map by a Chicago engineer, Alphons van der Grinten, who lessened some of Mercator's distortions. Two years ago the society settled on a more "realistic" world map developed by Arthur Robinson, a retired cartographer from the University of Wisconsin. His map is elliptic, "to give the impression it's a round Earth we live on," Robinson says. He drastically shrank the Soviet Union, which appears more than twice its relative size on van der Grinten's map. On Robinson's map, the country is a mere 18% bigger than its proportional size. But he was democratic in his tailoring: he also shrank the United States so it appears smaller than its "true" size.

The National Geographic Society hailed the Robinson map as a great step forward, and the Pentagon keeps a Robinson map in its briefing room. But despite the Society's underline, the map has not caught on everywhere. In Scotland, John Bartholomew & Sons decided to stick with its world map, saying the Robinson makes no great improvement.

36. The world map that most Americans assume represents the way the world looks is

    A. Mercator's.
    B. the National Geographic Society's.
    C. Alphons van der Grinten's.
    D. Arthur Robinson's.
    E. John Bartholomew's.

37. The author refers to the Mercator map at State Department briefings in order to

    A. show how important maps are in political decision making.
    B. show that the State Department must be as well informed about geography as the Pentagon.
    C. show how pervasive is the influence of the Mercator map.
    D. criticize the geographical knowledge of the State Department.
    E. show how maps may be used in a medium like television.

38. From information in the passage, you can infer that a northern European country on a Mercator map of the world would appear to be

   A. the same size as a larger country located to its north.
   B. larger than a larger country located to its east.
   C. smaller than a smaller country located to its south.
   D. larger than a country of the same size located to its north.
   E. larger than a country of the same size located to its south.

39. According to the passage, which of the following could be used to support the continued use of the Mercator map of the world?

   A. It accurately represents the comparative size of the United States and the Soviet Union.
   B. It enables the navigator of a ship to find a compass heading.
   C. It is the most familiar and most accurate representation of the actual size and shape of the world's land masses.
   D. It represents more accurately than other maps the shape of the polar lands.
   E. Its representation of equatorial lands is more accurate than that of other maps.

40. Which of the following best represents the author's view of the Mercator map?

   A. It is the best of the competing world maps but is not perfect.
   B. It is a world map that has never been useful.
   C. It represents the world more accurately than van der Grinten's map but less accurately than Robinson's.
   D. It represents the world more accurately than Robinson's map but less accurately than van der Grinten's.
   E. It is a map that has largely outlived its usefulness.

41. The word imprimatur can best be defined as

   A. printing error.
   B. stamp of approval.
   C. criticism.
   D. question of validity.
   E. printed copies.

Read the passage below and answer the question that follows.

A magazine article on the works of a prominent writer of fiction concluded with the remark, "He can cut a Colossus from a rock, but he cannot carve heads upon cherry stones."

42. From this comment, it can be inferred that

   A. the writer is also an accomplished sculptor.
   B. the writer's short works are superior to his longer works.
   C. the writer writes both fiction and nonfiction.
   D. the writer is weakest in scenes requiring subtlety.
   E. the writer's works are too long.

Read the passage below and answer the four questions that follow.

Ostrich eggshells are among the most commonly found objects at archeological sites in Africa. Primitive humans used the eggs as food and the shells for water containers, bowls, and beads. Now archeologists may find them even more valuable for understanding the history of early humans. A team of paleoanthropologists reported recently in the journal *Science* that the slow decomposition of proteins in the eggshells can be used to date the archeological sites, particularly in the range of forty thousand to one hundred thousand years ago—a period for which there are few usable dating techniques.

One particular advantage of the new technique is that it is inexpensive, so that a large number of objects at a site can be dated to determine whether artifacts from different time periods have been jumbled together by weather, flooding, or excavations—a problem that occurs frequently. In the tropics, the technique can be used to date objects as old as two hundred thousand years. In cooler climates, such as in China, it can be used on objects one million years old.

Although ostriches are most common in Africa, ostrich eggs have also been found in China and Mongolia and would be useful for dating there. Moreover, the research team has found that every other type of bird egg they have studied gives similar results, so those types of shells can be used as well. They are now beginning to study owl eggs, which are found at many archeological sites in northern Europe.

GO ON TO THE NEXT PAGE

43. From the information in the passage, it can be inferred that ostrich eggshells

   A. last longer in cold climates than in warm.
   B. are different in composition from other birds' eggshells.
   C. are rarely found in areas that contain human remains.
   D. are unable to survive floods.
   E. are no longer used as water containers by humans.

44. An ostrich egg in which the protein has decomposed almost completely is probably

   A. recently discovered.
   B. not useful in dating.
   C. extremely old.
   D. a costly means of dating.
   E. Chinese in origin.

45. According to the passage, ostrich eggs are useful in dating archeological sites in all the following places, *except:*

   A. China.
   B. the tropics.
   C. Africa.
   D. northern Europe.
   E. Mongolia.

46. The study of owl eggs referred to in the final paragraph is probably intended to

   A. throw light on the habits of the owl in ancient times.
   B. throw light on the habits of humans in ancient times.
   C. enable anthropologists to date northern European sites.
   D. enable anthropologists to date sites in Africa and Asia more accurately.
   E. assist the study of the development of modern birds from ancient species.

Read the passage below and answer the question that follows.

According to a recent study, 60 percent of the men and women called for jury duty in Middlesex County believe that a person should be presumed innocent until proven guilty. Sixty-five percent of the same group said that if a person has been indicted by a grand jury, that person is likely to be guilty.

47. This information could be best used to support an argument that

   A. the jury system is the fairest way of dealing with people accused of crimes.
   B. either the grand jury system or the jury system should be discontinued.
   C. accused persons can depend upon the jury's presuming them to be innocent at the outset of their trials.
   D. juries are prejudiced by a grand jury's indictments.
   E. trial before a judge without a jury is fairer to the accused than trial before a jury.

Read the passage below and answer the three questions that follow.

A unicorn is a mythical beast, you say. Oh, no, it isn't. There's one on display right now in New York, during the Madison Square Garden appearance of the Ringling Brothers and Barnum & Bailey Circus. This circus unicorn is a billy goat with one polished black horn growing straight from the center of his forehead. It appears the goat's horns were fused together in infancy. The operation is said to be painless. The unicorn is really getting the goat of officials from the American Society for the Prevention of Cruelty to Animals. They want to know where he came from so they can stop any future "creations."

Actually, the ASPCA arrives to the rescue rather late. Unicorns have been in the news for several years, appearing at carnivals and festivals. One of the first modern-day unicorns was created in 1933 by Dr. W. Franklin Dove at the University of Maine. Dr. Dove transplanted the horn buds of a day-old Ayrshire bull calf from the side of its head to the center. In later life, the horn proved to be a great weapon, and the dairy bull became the leader of the herd.

Powdered unicorn horns were valued in ancient times as an antidote to poison. The powder also was considered a cure for epilepsy, plague, hydrophobia, drunkenness, and worms. Julius Caesar believed in unicorns, as did Pliny and Aristotle. In ancient days, hunters were convinced that unicorns were suckers for purity and beauty. They would station a young virgin in the center of a forest glen. Soon a unicorn would approach and put his head meekly in her lap. That was the way they captured unicorns in the old days. It must have worked, because one doesn't see too many unicorns around.

48. Which of the following can be inferred from the preceding passage?

   A. Unicorns were proven to have existed many years ago.
   B. The ASPCA wants to protect unicorns.
   C. Mythical creatures may occasionally be the product of another species.
   D. Only billy goats can pass for the mythical unicorn.
   E. Many circuses and carnivals will soon have their own unicorns.

49. According to the preceding passage, unicorns could be captured by

   A. transplanting the horn buds of a day-old bull calf.
   B. fusing together an infant goat's horns.
   C. performing a painless operation.
   D. enticing the creature with a beautiful virgin.
   E. using an antidote for poison.

50. All the following are believed to be attributes of the unicorn's horn, *except:*

   A. a cure for epilepsy.
   B. a great weapon.
   C. a beauty aid.
   D. an antidote to poison.
   E. a cure for worms.

GO ON TO THE NEXT PAGE

Section II: Mathematics

50 Questions

Directions: In the following questions or incomplete statements, select the one *best* answer or completion of the five choices given. Make sure that you mark your answers for this section in the Mathematics section on the answer sheet.

1. Jesse needs to wash five loads of clothes. Each load takes 15 minutes to wash. If Jesse begins the first load at 3:20 p.m. and washes continuously, what time will all of the loads be finished?

   A. 1:15 p.m.
   B. 3:35 p.m.
   C. 4:35 p.m.
   D. 5:35 p.m.
   E. 6:15 p.m.

2. What is $\frac{3}{8}$ expressed as a decimal? Round your answer to the nearest hundredth.

   A. .25
   B. .38
   C. .46
   D. .50
   E. .83

3. Which of the following is the best estimate for $6.23 \times .83$?

   A. .5
   B. 5
   C. 6
   D. 50
   E. 60

Read the information below and then answer the question that follows.

> Suzanne worked 47 hours at $9.25 per hour. How much did Suzanne earn?

4. Which of the following is the most appropriate way to estimate Suzanne's total earnings for the time worked above?

   A. 40×9
   B. 50×9
   C. $50 \div 9$
   D. 92×47
   E. $40 \div 9$

5. If Tina was born on December 2, 1963, how old was she in 2008?

   A. 43 or 44
   B. 44
   C. 44 or 45
   D. 45
   E. 45 or 46

6. The Faculty Club's bank balance showed a deficit of $2,800 in March. If additional debts in April totaled $1,300 and there was no income during that month, what did the Faculty Club's balance book show?

   A. −$4,100
   B. −$1,500
   C. −$1,300
   D. $1,500
   E. $4,100

Use the graph below to answer the question that follows.

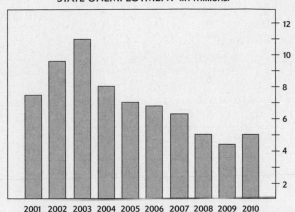

STATE UNEMPLOYMENT (in millions)

2001 2002 2003 2004 2005 2006 2007 2008 2009 2010

7. According to the preceding graph, approximately how many more people were unemployed in 2003 than in 2010?

A. 10.5 million
B. 8 million
C. 6 million
D. 4.5 million
E. 4 million

8. Rounded to the nearest hundredth, 294.3549 would be expressed as

A. .35
B. .36
C. 294.35
D. 294.36
E. 300.00

Read the information below and then answer the question that follows.

On six tests, Franklin averaged 85%. Although he failed to achieve a passing score on just one test (on which he received a 56%), he also scored 100% twice.

9. Which of the following can be determined from the preceding information?

A. His two lowest percentage scores
B. His three highest percentage scores
C. The sum of all six percentage scores
D. The sum of the three lowest percentage scores
E. The average of the three highest percentage scores

10. Nine hundred head of cattle must be transported from Wichita to Chicago. If each cattle car can hold a maximum of 80 head, what is the lowest number of cattle cars required to transport all the cattle?

A. 11
B. $11\frac{1}{4}$
C. 12
D. $12\frac{3}{4}$
E. 13

11. The length of a rectangle is 3 feet less than two times the width. If the perimeter of the rectangle is 48 feet, what is the length of the rectangle?

A. 9 feet
B. 15 feet
C. 17 feet
D. 24 feet
E. 31 feet

12. What is the greatest common factor of the numbers 18, 24, and 30?

A. 2
B. 3
C. 4
D. 6
E. 12

13. If .8 gallons of heating oil are required to heat three rooms, how many gallons of heating oil are needed to heat 42 rooms?

A. $11\frac{1}{5}$
B. 14
C. $14\frac{2}{5}$
D. 18
E. 24

GO ON TO THE NEXT PAGE

335

14. Cindy's Algebra teacher wrote the following expression on the board: $3y^3 - 4y^2 + y - 6$. The teacher asked Cindy to solve the problem if $y = -3$. Cindy correctly solved the value of the expression to be

    A. −126
    B. −90
    C. −54
    D.   90
    E.   126

15. Helen purchased 3 times as many carnations as roses. If roses cost $1 each, carnations cost 50¢ each, and she spent a total of $7.50 for the flowers, how many roses did she purchase?

    A. 2
    B. 3
    C. 4
    D. 5
    E. 6

16. If $\frac{3}{10}$ of a person's gross earnings are paid to taxes and last week Joshua paid $15,000 in taxes, what were Joshua's gross earnings last year?

    A. $45,000
    B. $50,000
    C. $65,000
    D. $70,000
    E. $105,000

17. A teacher purchased 39 bottles of water for a field trip. If each bottle cost 78¢, how much did he spend for the water? (Disregard any sales tax.)

    A. $11.70
    B. $17.11
    C. $28.39
    D. $30.42
    E. $42.30

18. Which of the following decimals is equivalent to $\frac{1}{8}$?

    A. .125
    B. .25
    C. .33
    D. .375
    E. .38

19. A regular pentagon has a perimeter of 90 feet. What is the length of each side?

    A. 9 feet
    B. 10 feet
    C. 15 feet
    D. 18 feet
    E. 22.5 feet

Use the chart below to answer the question that follows.

Net Films	Prices
New Releases	$3.99
Educational Releases	$1.99
All Other Releases	$2.99

20. Mark rented 3 DVDs from Net Films. Disregarding sales tax, what type(s) of DVD did he rent if his total bill was $11.97?

    A. 3 educational releases
    B. 3 new releases
    C. 1 new, 1 educational, and 1 other release
    D. 2 new and 1 other release
    E. 2 other and 1 new release

Use the graph below to answer the question that follows.

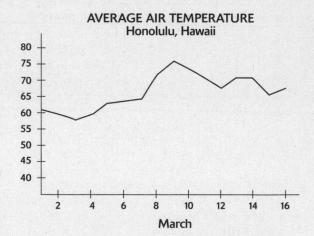

21. Approximately how much greater was the highest average daily air temperature than the lowest average daily air temperature during the dates shown on the preceding chart?

    A. 75°
    B. 58°
    C. 28°
    D. 18°
    E. 6°

22. Maria plans to make sandwiches for a picnic. She has 3 types of bread from which to choose (rye, sourdough, and white), 4 types of meat from which to choose (turkey, roast beef, salami, and pastrami), and 3 types of cheese from which to choose (Swiss, cheddar, and jack). If Maria will only use 1 type of bread, 1 type of meat, and 1 type of cheese on each sandwich, how many different kinds of sandwiches can Maria make?

    A.   3
    B.   4
    C.   10
    D.   17
    E.   36

23. The scores, percentile ranks, and stanines of three students are shown below for a test.

Student	Score	Percentile Rank	Stanine
Samantha	70	82	8
Isabella	57	60	6
Tony	83	93	9

    Which of the following is true regarding the chart above?

    A.   Samantha got 70% of the test questions correct.
    B.   Samantha scored just as high or higher than 82% of the students who took the test.
    C.   Tony got 93% of the test questions correct.
    D.   17% of the students who took the test did better than Tony.
    E.   60% of the students who took the test scored higher than Isabella.

Read the information below and then answer the question that follows.

A painting crew painted 3 rooms on Monday, 5 rooms on Tuesday, 2 rooms on Wednesday, and 4 rooms on Thursday. How many gallons of paint did the crew use?

24. What other information must be provided to solve the above problem?

    A.   The average number of rooms in the house
    B.   The average number of rooms painted per day
    C.   The cost per gallon of paint
    D.   The total number of rooms painted in the house
    E.   The average number of gallons of paint used per room

25. Theo walked $6\frac{1}{4}$ miles on Wednesday. Shalla walked $4\frac{3}{4}$ miles on Thursday. What is the difference between the distance Theo walked on Wednesday and the distance Shalla walked on Thursday?

    A.   11 miles
    B. $2\frac{1}{2}$ miles
    C. $2\frac{1}{4}$ miles
    D. $1\frac{3}{4}$ miles
    E. $1\frac{1}{2}$ miles

26. The interest, I, that results when a certain principal, P, is invested at rate r over a period of t years is found by the equation $I = Prt$. What is the value of t if $I = \$500$, $P = \$2,000$, and $r = 10\%$?

    A.   .25
    B.   .40
    C.   2.5
    D.   4.0
    E.   25

GO ON TO THE NEXT PAGE

Use the graph below to answer the question that follows.

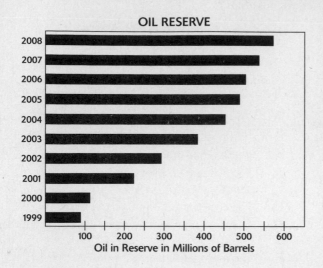

27. According to the preceding graph, approximately how many more barrels of oil were in reserve in 2006 than in 2000?

A.   400
B.   500
C.   300,000,000
D.   400,000,000
E.   500,000,000

Use the figure below to answer the question that follows.

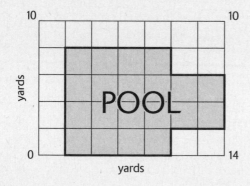

28. What is the total perimeter of the pool in the above diagram?

A.   20 yards
B.   25 yards
C.   30 yards
D.   40 yards
E.   45 yards

29. A fair spinner at a bazaar has 12 equal sections, numbered 1 through 12. If the spinner is spun twice, what is the probability that the second spin will come up an odd number?

A. $\frac{1}{12}$

B. $\frac{1}{6}$

C. $\frac{1}{2}$

D. $\frac{1}{1}$

E. $\frac{2}{1}$

30. If a square carpet, 8 feet on a side, is cut up into smaller squares each 2 feet on a side, what is the largest number of smaller squares that can be formed?

A.   8
B.   16
C.   32
D.   64
E.   128

31. What is $\frac{3}{5}$ of $\frac{30}{7}$?

A. $\frac{33}{12}$

B. $\frac{18}{7}$

C. $\frac{29}{12}$

D. $\frac{7}{50}$

E. $\frac{1}{65}$

Use the table below to answer the question that follows.

Chart of an Adult ESL Class	
Ethnic Background	**Number of Students**
Hispanic	15
Cambodian	12
Russian	8
Arabic	5

32. What is the probability of teaching a student who is Arabic or Hispanic?

 A. $\dfrac{3}{40}$

 B. $\dfrac{1}{8}$

 C. $\dfrac{3}{8}$

 D. $\dfrac{1}{2}$

 E. $\dfrac{27}{40}$

33. Below are the measures of rainfall for five consecutive days during the winter.

 6" 2" 10" 2" 5"

 For the measure of those five days, which of the following is true?

 I. The median equals the mode.
 II. The median equals the arithmetic mean.
 III. The range equals the median.

 A. I only
 B. II only
 C. III only
 D. I and II only
 E. I and III only

Using the information below, answer the question that follows.

A gumball machine contains 7 white gumballs and 5 red gumballs. Each gumball costs 1¢.

34. What is the lowest amount of money that must be deposited in the machine to ensure getting two gumballs of the same color?

 A. 2¢
 B. 3¢
 C. 4¢
 D. 5¢
 E. 7¢

Use the figure below to answer the question that follows.

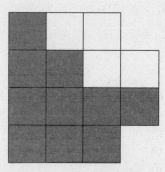

35. In the figure, if each small square is 3 inches in length, what is the perimeter of the shaded area?

 A. 30 inches
 B. 36 inches
 C. 39 inches
 D. 48 inches
 E. 51 inches

36. If a number q is divided by 5, the outcome is 10. What is 2 more than the value of q?

 A. 4
 B. 6
 C. 48
 D. 50
 E. 52

GO ON TO THE NEXT PAGE

37. Ms. Ferguson purchased a new car for $18,600 with an additional upgrade charge of $1,800. If the state sales tax requires an additional 8% of all charges, what is the total price Ms. Ferguson paid?

    A. $16,800
    B. $18,144
    C. $20,400
    D. $21,400
    E. $22,032

38. Which of the following polygons appears to contain two pairs of parallel sides?

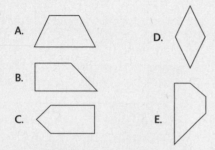

39. Of the five people mentioned below, who is the shortest?

    Tom is shorter than Lebron, Lebron is taller than Anthony. Kobe is taller than Tom but shorter than Jordan. Jordan is shorter than Anthony.

    A.   Tom
    B.   Lebron
    C.   Anthony
    D.   Kobe
    E.   Jordan

40. If 12 cups of flour are needed to make 5 cakes, how many cakes can be made with 30 cups of flour?

    A.   2.5
    B.   6
    C.   10
    D.   12.5
    E.   60

41. A random poll of 2,500 moviegoers throughout California found that 1,500 preferred comedies, 500 preferred adventure films, and 500 preferred dramas. Of the 8,000,000 moviegoers in California, which of the following is (are) the most reasonable estimate(s) drawn from the poll?

    I.   1,500,000 prefer comedies.
    II.   500,000 prefer dramas.
    III. 1,600,000 prefer dramas.

    A.   I only
    B.   II only
    C.   III only
    D.   I and II only
    E.   I and III only

42. Mrs. Solis purchased a refrigerator at a 30% discount off the retail price. If the retail price was $800, how much did Mrs. Solis pay for the refrigerator?

    A. $2,400
    B. $ 770
    C. $ 660
    D. $ 560
    E. $ 240

43. Which equation can be used to find the perimeter, P, of a rectangle that has a length of 18 feet and a width of 15 feet?

    A. $P = (18)(15)$
    B. $P = 18 + 15$
    C. $P = 2(15)(18)$
    D. $P = (2)15 + 18$
    E. $P = 2(15 + 18)$

Use the graph below to answer the question that follows.

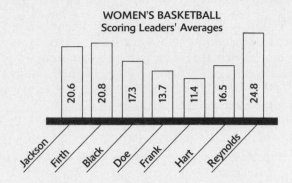

WOMEN'S BASKETBALL
Scoring Leaders' Averages

20.6 | 20.8 | 17.3 | 13.7 | 11.4 | 16.5 | 24.8

Jackson | Firth | Black | Doe | Frank | Hart | Reynolds

44. According to the bar graph, Reynolds's average score exceeds Doe's average score by how many points?

A. 13.4
B. 11.1
C. 8.3
D. 7.4
E. 2.3

45. If 240 miles can be driven using 9 gallons of gasoline, how many miles can be driven using 12 gallons of gasoline?

A. 80
B. 270
C. 320
D. 370
E. 480

Use the chart below to answer the question that follows.

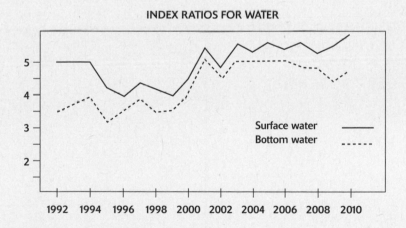

INDEX RATIOS FOR WATER

Surface water ———
Bottom water - - - - -

1992 1994 1996 1998 2000 2002 2004 2006 2008 2010

46. For which of the years shown on the chart was the difference between index ratios of bottom water and surface water the greatest?

A. 1992
B. 1997
C. 2000
D. 2007
E. 2010

GO ON TO THE NEXT PAGE

Read the information below and then answer the question that follows.

Jerran's age is 3 years less than half Sue's age. If Jerran is 9 years old, how old is Sue?

47. Suppose S represents Sue's age. Which of the following equations can be used to find Sue's age?

A. $9 = \left(\frac{1}{2}\right)(S) - 3$

B. $9 - 3 = \left(\frac{1}{2}\right)(S)$

C. $9 = 3 - \left(\frac{1}{2}\right)(S)$

D. $3 - 9 = \left(\frac{1}{2}\right)(S)$

E. $\left(\frac{1}{2}\right)(9) = S - 3$

48. A hat costs $29.54. Which of the following answers reflects this cost to the nearest dollar? (Disregard any sales tax.)

A. $31.00
B. $30.00
C. $29.50
D. $29.00
E. $28.00

49. What is the sum of $6x + 2y + x + y$?

A. $x^7 + y^3$
B. $7x + 3y$
C. $62 + xy$
D. $8x + 4y$
E. $6x + 3y$

Read the information below and then answer the question that follows.

Tickets to the county fair sell for $2 per adult, $1 per senior citizen, and 50¢ per child. Three times as many senior citizen tickets were sold than adult tickets, and 10 more adult tickets were sold than children's tickets. If 450 tickets were sold in all for a total of $501, how many of each ticket were sold?

50. Having read the preceding information, Arnold tried solving the problem by using 150 tickets of each kind. Having done that and assessed his results, he could correctly say that

A. more than 150 adult tickets were sold.
B. fewer than 150 adult tickets were sold.
C. exactly 150 adult tickets were sold.
D. more than 400 children's tickets were sold.
E. exactly 300 children's tickets were sold.

Section III: Writing

2 Essays

Directions: In this section you plan and write two essays, one for each topic given. Read each topic carefully to make sure that you are properly addressing the issue or situation. You must write on the specified topic. An essay on another topic will not be acceptable.

Plan your time wisely. Each essay is weighted equally. Plan to spend the same amount of time on each essay.

The two essay questions included in this section are designed to give you an opportunity to write clearly and effectively. Use specific examples whenever appropriate to aid in supporting your ideas. Keep in mind that the quality of your writing is much more important than the quantity.

Write each essay on the two lined sheets of paper provided. Your writing should be neat and legible. Because you have only a limited amount of space in which to write, please do *not* skip lines, do *not* write excessively large, and do *not* leave wide margins.

You may use the bottom of the topic page in the test booklet to organize and plan your essay before you begin writing.

Topic 1

Reflect upon a good friend and select the one character trait that you feel to be the most important. Describe and explain why that particular trait is more important than any other. Compare your response to the sample essays for this topic on pages 364-366.

Topic 2

Some educators maintain that an all-male or all-female environment is beneficial to learning. Compare and contrast the advantages of such an academic environment to those of a coeducational atmosphere.

Answer Key and Analysis for Practice Test 4

Answer Key for Practice Test 4

Section I: Reading

1. D	18. B	35. C
2. B	19. B	36. A
3. E	20. C	37. C
4. B	21. B	38. E
5. A	22. E	39. B
6. B	23. D	40. E
7. C	24. C	41. B
8. B	25. D	42. D
9. A	26. B	43. A
10. D	27. C	44. C
11. E	28. C	45. D
12. D	29. C	46. C
13. B	30. B	47. D
14. C	31. A	48. C
15. C	32. C	49. D
16. E	33. B	50. C
17. A	34. B	

Section II: Mathematics

1. C	18. A	35. D
2. B	19. D	36. E
3. C	20. B	37. E
4. B	21. D	38. D
5. C	22. E	39. A
6. A	23. B	40. D
7. C	24. E	41. C
8. C	25. E	42. D
9. C	26. C	43. E
10. C	27. D	44. B
11. B	28. D	45. C
12. D	29. C	46. A
13. A	30. B	47. A
14. A	31. B	48. B
15. B	32. D	49. B
16. B	33. B	50. B
17. D	34. B	

Scoring Your CBEST Practice Test 4

To score your CBEST Practice Test 4, total the number of correct responses for each section of the test separately. Do not subtract any points for questions attempted but missed because there is no penalty for guessing. The score for each section is then scaled from 20 to 80. (About 70% right is a passing score.)

Analyzing Your Test Results

Use the charts on the following page to carefully analyze your results and spot your strengths and weaknesses. Complete the process of analyzing each subject area and each individual question for this Practice Test. Reexamine these results for trends in types of errors (repeated errors) or poor results in specific subject areas. This reexamination and analysis is of tremendous importance for effective test preparation.

Subject Area Analysis Sheet				
	Possible	Completed	Right	Wrong
Reading	50			
Mathematics	50			
TOTAL	100			

One of the most important parts of test preparation is analyzing *why* you missed a question so that you can reduce your number of mistakes. Now that you have taken Practice Test 4 and corrected your answers, carefully tally your mistakes by marking them in the proper column.

Tally Sheet for Questions Missed				
	Reason for Mistake			
	Total Missed	Simple Mistake	Misread Problem	Lack of Knowledge
Reading				
Mathematics				
TOTAL				

Reviewing the above data can help you determine *why* you are missing certain questions. Now that you have pinpointed the type of error you are most likely to make, focus on avoiding those errors.

Essay Checklist

Use this checklist to evaluate your essays.

Diagnosis of Timed Writing Exercises		
A good essay:	**Essay 1**	**Essay 2**
. . . addresses the assignment		
■ stays well focused		
■ expresses a clear thesis statement on the topic		
. . . organizes points logically		
■ uses smooth transitions between paragraphs		
■ has coherent, unified paragraphs		
. . . develops ideas presented		
■ gives specific examples to support points		
■ anticipates and addresses opposing views		
. . . is grammatically sound (with only minor flaws)		
■ uses correct sentence structure		
■ uses correct punctuation		
■ uses standard written English		
. . . uses language skillfully		
■ uses a variety of sentence types		
■ uses a variety of words		
. . . is legible		
■ shows clear handwriting		
■ appears neat		

Answers and Complete Explanations for Practice Test 4

Section I: Reading

1. **D.** Choice **D** is correct because tropospheric ozone is ground-level ozone and, unlike ozone in the upper atmosphere, ground-level ozone does not provide protection from the sun's ultraviolet rays. Choices **B**, **C**, and **E** may appear tempting because they restate facts from the passage; however, those facts are irrelevant to answering this particular question. Choice **A** contradicts the passage; ozone *does* provide UV protection if it is in the upper atmosphere.

2. **B.** In the last sentence of paragraph 2, the passage states that ground-level ozone "can cause respiratory distress," and in the closing line, the passage predicts a large increase in tropospheric ozone during the next thirty years. Choice **B** correctly brings these two ideas together; based on this passage, it *is* likely that an increase in respiratory disorders over the next thirty years will occur. The ideas in the other choices are not supported by the information in the passage.

3. **E.** Since *fortissimo* (very loud) refers to the dynamics of music, and "Dynamics" is section G, the correct answer must begin with the letter "G." Next, when considering the two items in section G, it may be tempting to stop at G.1 (loudness or softness), but the correct answer is G.2, because it is more specific, containing the "terms" for loud or soft music. (Note, however, that only one answer begins with the letter "G," so Choice **E** must be the correct answer, regardless of any difference between sections G.1 and G.2.)

4. **B.** From the information given in the outline, the repetition of elements in form creates unity (see section D.3). While the other choices bring up key words that appear in the outline, they are irrelevant to answering this particular question.

5. **A.** In section H, the outline considers two aspects of "Timbre," first as a unique tonal quality and second as the characteristic sound produced by each instrument family. The question refers to woodwinds, but the two defining elements of timbre are included: "the unique tonal sound" and "woodwind *family*." So, Choice **A** must be the correct answer.

6. **B.** The ideas in choices **A**, **C**, **D**, and **E** appear to be assumptions underlying the ideas in this passage. However, the passage provides no information regarding how Celtic myths do or do not differ from the myths of other cultures, so Choice **B** is the exception, the correct answer.

7. **C.** The second paragraph shifts the focus from other civilizations in the universe to a critical comment on humans' treatment of the nonhuman creatures on Earth. The ideas in choices **A**, **B**, and **E** are not consistent with the passage. Choice **D**, while an underlying idea of the second paragraph, is not its purpose.

8. **B.** The author uses the word "dubiously" as a sarcastic parenthetical aside, implying that he or she questions the accuracy of including our present human civilization on any list of "advanced" civilizations in the universe. The author's attitude toward human civilization, jaded and somewhat cynical, is revealed even more clearly in the second and third paragraphs of the essay.

9. **A.** Throughout this passage, the author repeatedly asserts that the existence of more advanced cultures elsewhere in the universe is a fact. Thus, Choice **A** is correct; the author's answer to the question he or she poses in the second paragraph is clearly "Yes." The other choices do not accurately reflect the author's position on that question.

10. **D.** All the ideas enunciated in choices **A**, **B**, **C**, and **E** underlie the author's argument in this passage. However, the author certainly does not assume that other civilizations are likely to be benevolent to humans; rather, he or she repeatedly draws a parallel with the way humans have mistreated animals throughout history and, thus, assumes that humans will in turn be mistreated by extraterrestrial civilizations.

11. **E.** Choice **E** correctly restates the author's main concern; the passage is a warning that extraterrestrials may treat humans no better than humans have treated animals. None of the ideas stated in the other choices actually appears in the passage. Do not be tricked by Choice **D**, which reverses the nature of the relationship.

12. **D.** The passage contains repeated references to extraterrestrials and to outer space, but that is mere "window dressing." The central theme of this passage actually relates to "civilized" humans' uncivilized cruelty to animals. Thus, this passage may be best understood if it is read not as science nor as science fiction but rather as a satire critical of human nature.

13. **B.** As it is used in this passage, the best definition of <u>discerning</u> is *perceptive*; thus, Choice **B** is correct. Some of the other choices offer tempting alternatives, such as "artistic" and "inquisitive," but none are as accurate as Choice **B**.

14. **C.** The passage is an example of expository prose; that is, it provides an explanation, a setting forth of fact in paragraph form. Choice **A** is incorrect because of the word "fiction"; the passage is prose but not fiction. It does not contain an argument, which makes Choice **B** inaccurate. Choice **D**, "personal essay," can be eliminated because the passage is not personal; it is written in third person, not the first person ("I," "me," "we," and so on) that accompanies personal essays. The passage contains absolutely no dialogue, a quoted conversation between speakers, thus making Choice **E** wrong.

15. **C.** Choice **C** is by far the best choice; this is the only sentence that is consistent in style and content with the rest of the passage, bringing in information from both paragraphs. Choice **A** incorrectly uses a first-person pronoun and does so in a phrase that is unnecessary. The use of the word "Consequently" to begin Choice **B** makes no sense. Choice **D** is wordy, awkwardly phrased, and at odds with the content of the first paragraph. Choice **E** is redundant because of its repetition of information from the previous sentence, "the market for these houses dried up in the sixties," and does not contain the comment in Choice **C** about a small number of enthusiastic buyers. Thus, Choice **C** is the best response.

16. **E.** Under Choice **A**, the savings is $2,000; under Choice **B**, it is $2,000; under Choice **C**, it is $1,500; under Choice **D**, it is $2,000. But under Choice **E**, the taxpayer saves $3,500—$2,000 for itemizing his or her health insurance (50% of the total costs) and $500 each for itemizing his or her medical, dental, and pharmaceutical expenses.

17. **A.** The term this taxpayer would most likely need clarified by the tax guidelines is a definition of "self-employed," because it can be a somewhat nebulous concept. The other choices are mostly straightforward terms for which the taxpayer is unlikely to need clarification; Choice **B**, "taxpayer" = individual filing tax return; Choice **C**, "deduction" = a nontaxable item; Choice **E**, "exemption" = a deduction for an individual, such as the taxpayer or a dependent. Finally, Choice **D** introduces the subject of pharmaceuticals, which is completely off the topic.

18. **B.** This question deals only with non-self-employed taxpayers, so you can disregard guidelines 1 and 2 and base your response only on guidelines 3 and 4. For taxpayers who do not itemize, the automatic credit is $1,000, but for those taxpayers who do itemize, the deductible portion of medical expenses is 50 percent. So, for a taxpayer to be certain that he or she is saving money by itemizing, he or she must have spent in excess of $2,000 on medical expenses that year, so that the 50 percent deduction will exceed the $1,000 automatic deduction.

19. **B.** The passage describes the juxtaposition of two ideas, a smoke-filled room and the phrase, "We're not in this business for our health." Only Choice **B** answers why these ideas are related; this spot is most likely designed to be part of an antismoking campaign.

20. **C.** Choice **C** correctly describes the relationship of these two sentences. The first sentence is general ("a wide choice of new kinds of classes"), whereas the second sentence is much more specific (classes given "on weekends," "in off-campus locations," "on videotape"). The other choices all contain specific factual errors; both sentences are literal and factual (so **A** and **D** can be eliminated), and neither raises a question or refers to primary or secondary sources (so **B** and **E** cannot be correct).

21. **B.** Choice **B** is correct because sentences 1 and 4 are both general statements, describing the varied choice of classes and the elimination of some things one might expect to find at a college. The other choices are all too specific to appropriately sum up the entire paragraph. Sentences 2 and 3 merely give examples of the first idea, and sentences 5, 6, and 7 illustrate the fourth idea. The meaning of the paragraph would still be clear if these examples were not used.

22. **E.** Choice **E** is correct; the phrase "distance learning" refers to learning outside of a conventional campus classroom. The passage provides several examples, including classes on the Internet, off-campus, or on videotape. Choice **A** contradicts the definition from the passage, and choices **B**, **C**, and **D** are all irrelevant to answering this question.

23. **D.** Choices **A**, **B**, **C**, and **E** all promise benefits that the initial experiment seemed to confirm. The potential benefits in choices **A**, **C**, and **E** all appear in one sentence in the first paragraph, "an inexpensive source of energy that is produced from highly abundant materials and that produces no polluting by-products." This sentence also implies the benefit in Choice **B**, that the new technology is not dependent on fossil fuels. However, the passage never asserts that this new energy source was to be limited to a single geographical area, the United States, so Choice **D** is the correct exception.

24. **C.** The passage cites early reports of follow-up studies that seemed to provide partial corroboration of the initial experiment, but then it concludes that these initial replications were illusory and all other attempts to reproduce the findings have been unsuccessful. Thus, Choice **C** is the only answer that correctly states the facts in the passage.

25. **D.** According to the passage, only four months after the exciting results were announced, most chemists and physicists had already rejected the Pons/Fleischmann claims (Choice **D**). Or, as the passage phrased it, "[the] unorthodox concept had seemingly been relegated to the dustbin of history."

26. **B.** By choosing to use the term "séance," Parks suggests that the convention is more a gathering of spiritualists than a meeting of scientists. His use of the term "true believers" further emphasizes his view of their commitment to belief, regardless of the evidence.

27. **C.** While the passage does provide some arguments in favor of Choice **A** (cold fusion as fraud), the final paragraphs suggest that the question has not yet been answered definitively, either in the affirmative or negative, "and that another year or two is going to be necessary." Thus, Choice **C** is the better title overall.

28. **C.** The passage suggests that the best way to prolong a political career is not to anger voters, for example, by avoiding risk-taking and spending and by refusing to defend unpopular causes. Choices **A**, **D**, and **E** all contradict the passage, and Choice **B** misstates the author's point. Understanding what is necessary and actually doing what is necessary are two very different things.

29. **C.** Choice **C** provides the best restatement of the idea in the second sentence, namely, that any politician who wants to continue in politics cannot afford to tell the truth. The statement in Choice **A** is close in meaning to the second sentence, but it is not as accurate as Choice **C**. The ideas in choices **B**, **D**, and **E** are not supported by this passage.

30. **B.** Choice **B** is correct; the percentage rate of taxes in 2010 (the solid line) is about 10 percent lower than the tax rate in 2000 (the dashed line). Choices **A** and **C** both misstate this percentage relationship; the tax rate in 2010 was neither higher than nor equal to the rate in 2000. Choices **D** and **E** refer to dollar amounts, but they make the same mistake; the dollar amount paid in 2010 was not higher than in 2000, nor was it about the same.

31. **A.** The correct answer will be found where the solid line for 2010 and the dashed line for 2000 come together and then cross one another—at approximately $5,000.

32. **C.** The correct answer (30 percent) is found using a three-step process. First, find the spot for $55,000 on the bottom line, the "Dollars of Income" scale. Next, go straight up to find a point on the dashed 2000 line (directly above the point for $55,000). Finally, go to the left, to the "Percentage of Taxable Income" vertical scale, and you see that the percentage rate is approximately 30 percent for $55,000 in 2010.

33. **B.** Because the passage clearly states that the attitude of bilingual Spanish-speaking students differs from the attitude of other bilingual students, one can be certain there is "no single bilingual students' attitude" (**B**). Choices **A** and **C** both contradict the passage; apparently, attitudes *are* affected by knowledge of foreign languages. Insufficient information is available to know whether Choice **D** is correct. Choice **E** is irrelevant to answering this question.

34. **B.** The details in the passage clearly point to its author being a publisher; the clues about publishing begin in the very first sentence with the phrase, "a manuscript of a novel, bearing the crossed-out addresses of three other publishing houses." In actual fact, this passage was written by the publisher of Charlotte Brontë's famous novel *Jane Eyre*.

35. **C.** Charlotte Brontë's name did not originally appear on *Jane Eyre*; rather, as published, the novel bore the pseudonym "Currer Bell." Apparently, however, the publisher must have realized early on that the name on the letter was not genuine; thus, he placed it in quotation marks to make this point. Choice **A** does not make sense; placing the pseudonym in quotation marks does not emphasize it. Choices **B** and **E** are irrelevant and do not state a logical reason for using quotation marks. Choice **D** contradicts common usage because quotation marks are placed around phrasing that is considered inaccurate; therefore, their use here is certainly not to show respect.

36. **A.** Choice **A** is correct; Mercator's map of the world is deeply ingrained in the American psyche, much more so than the other examples. The passage affirms this point repeatedly, beginning in the first sentence with "the Mercator remains the most common world map sold in American bookstores."

37. **C.** Choice **C** correctly identifies the reason the author mentions the Mercator map always appearing behind every State Department spokesperson; namely, that the Mercator map is ubiquitous and used everywhere, even by people who should know better.

38. **E.** Mercator maps consistently exaggerate the size of countries in direct proportion to their distance from the equator; that is, the closer any country is to the North Pole or South Pole, the larger its size on a Mercator map. Thus, Choice **E** posits a correct relationship; on a Mercator map, a northern European country would appear larger than a country of the same size that is located to its south.

39. **B.** Choice **B** correctly identifies the only major advantage of a Mercator map; while it makes no claim of accurately showing the comparative size of countries, a Mercator map does allow a navigator to find a compass heading accurately. All the other choices make the same mistake; each one contains a false claim that the Mercator map is more accurate than other maps.

40. **E.** This author's negative view of the Mercator map is conveyed by his tone throughout the passage. His opinion is that, despite its past usefulness and the current popularity of the iconic map style, the Mercator map is largely no longer useful. Choice **B** is contradicted in the passage; the word "never" makes it wrong.

41. **B.** The word <u>imprimatur</u>, which is Latin for *let it be printed,* means to sanction (to allow), to license, or to provide a stamp of approval. This can be inferred from the context of its use in this passage, wherein it is used as shorthand to invoke the grandeur and prestige of the National Geographic Society in its approval of the new Robinson map.

42. **D.** The metaphor of the rock and the cherry stones suggests the fiction writer is skilled at handling large tasks but is less successful in dealing with more delicate requirements; Choice **D** correctly identifies his lack of subtlety. Choice **B** reverses the relationship intended by the metaphor, and Choice **E** makes the same mistake. Choice **C** is irrelevant, and Choice **A** is simply off the topic.

43. **A.** To draw a valid inference, one often must find a connection between two different parts of the passage. In this case, the first paragraph indicates that the new age-dating technique is based on the examination of eggshells. The second paragraph states that a new technique is effective in dating objects in the tropics that are up to two hundred thousand years old, but in colder climates the new technique is good for objects up to one million years old. By putting these two facts together, one can reasonably infer that the eggshells that are being tested must last longer in cooler climates.

44. **C.** The passage states that the new age-dating technique relies on the consistent decomposition of protein in eggshells over a long time period. So, if the protein in a given specimen has decomposed almost completely, a very long time has presumably passed and it is likely that the egg is very old. The information in the passage does not support the conclusions in the other choices.

45. **D.** The passage specifically mentions the testing of eggshells found in the tropics, China, Africa, and Mongolia. Thus, Choice **D** correctly identifies the exception; the passage never mentions eggshells from northern Europe being tested in this way.

46. **C.** Since owl eggs are found in northern European archeological sites, anthropologists hope to use them to age-date objects in the same way ostrich eggshells have been used to age-date objects in warmer climates. The idea in Choice **B**, learning more about ancient humans, does appear in the passage, but it is not related to the example of owl eggs. There is no support in the passage for Choice **D**, about the sites in Africa and Asia, and both choices **A** and **E** are off the topic.

47. **D.** If 65 percent of the prospective jurors do, indeed, believe that a person indicted by a grand jury is likely to be guilty, then Choice **D** is certainly correct; almost two-thirds of a jury is prejudiced by a grand jury's indictment. Two other choices contradict the passage; Choice **A** states that juries are the fairest system, which is not supported by the passage. Choice **C** incorrectly states that juries have a presumption of innocence. The other two choices, **B** and **E**, both posit conclusions that are not warranted by the information in the passage.

48. **C.** Choice **C** states that a so-called "mythical" creature may actually be the product of another species, an idea that follows directly from the information in the passage. One cited example is Dr. Dove transplanting the horn of a calf from the side of its head to the center to "produce" a mythical creature (unicorn) from another species (Ayrshire dairy bull). Choice **A** is inaccurate because unicorns were *not* proven to have existed. Choice **B** can be eliminated because the ASPCA wants to stop supposedly "painless" animal creations. Choice **D** wrongly uses the absolute term "only." Choice **E** is unreasonable.

49. **D.** The third paragraph states that unicorns could be *captured* by using a virgin's beauty to lure the creature from its forest home. All the other choices mention ideas that are included in the passage, but none of them accurately identifies the specific information to answer this question about *capturing* a unicorn.

50. **C.** The third paragraph states that a unicorn's horn was used as a cure for epilepsy, Choice **A**, an antidote to poison, Choice **D**, and a cure for worms, Choice **E**. The second paragraph illustrates how the horn was used as a "great weapon," Choice **B**. However, "a beauty aid" was never mentioned as a possible attribute of a unicorn's horn.

Section II: Mathematics

1. **C.** Five wash loads at 15 minutes per load equals 1 hour and 15 minutes. If the washing commences at 3:20 p.m., adding 1:15 results in the work being finished at 4:35 p.m.

2. **B.** The decimal equivalent of the fraction $\frac{3}{8}$ may be found by dividing the numerator by the denominator, or 3 divided by 8:

$$
\begin{array}{r}
.375 \\
8\overline{)3.000} \\
\underline{24} \\
60 \\
\underline{56} \\
40 \\
\underline{40}
\end{array}
$$

The closest answer is .38.

3. **C.** Round 6.23 to 6 and round .83 to 1. Then multiply 6 by 1 to get 6.

4. **B.** Round the hours Suzanne worked, 47, to 50 hours. Round $9.25 to $9.00. Then, to determine Suzanne's total earnings, multiply the rounded number of hours, 50, by her rounded hourly wage, $9.00.

$$= 50 \times \$9.00$$

5. **C.** Depending on the date in 2008, Tina could be 44 or 45. If the date is before December 2, she was 44; if it is on or past December 2, then Tina was 45.

6. **A.** Combining debts of $1,300 with a deficit of $2,800 gives a much bigger deficit: –$2,800 combined with –$1,300 = –$4,100.

7. **C.** In 2003, approximately 11 million people were unemployed. In 2010, approximately 5 million people were unemployed. So 11 million – 5 million = 6 million.

8. **C.** Evaluate the digit that is one place to the right of the hundredths place. Since that digit (thousandths place) is less than 5, that digit and all digits to its right are dropped:

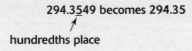

294.3549 becomes 294.35

hundredths place

9. **C.** If six tests average 85%, then their total must be 6 x 85, or 510 total percentage points. None of the other choices can be determined from the information given.

10. **C.** Nine hundred cattle divided evenly into 80 cars gives a quotient of $11\frac{1}{4}$ cars. However, since cattle cars cannot be divided into fractions, rounding up to the nearest whole number, 12, gives the smallest number of cars required.

11. **B.** Draw a diagram and label it accordingly.

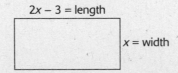

Use the formula $P = 2l + 2w$ to determine the width of the rectangle.

Replace with the correct dimensions to get:

$$48 = 2(2x - 3) + 2(x)$$
$$48 = 4x - 6 + 2x$$
$$48 = 6x - 6$$
$$54 = 6x$$
$$x = 9 \text{ feet (width)}$$
$$l \text{ (length)} = 2x - 3$$
$$l = 2(9) - 3 \text{ (replace } x \text{ with 9)}$$
$$l = 15 \text{ feet}$$

12. **D.** The largest number that divides evenly into 18, 24, and 30 is 6. You could work from the answers.

13. **A.** Set up a ratio: $\frac{.8}{3} = \frac{x}{42}$

Cross-multiplying produces $3x = 33.6$

Dividing each side of the equation by 3 results in:

$x = 11.2$ or $11\frac{1}{5}$ gallons of heating oil required to heat 42 rooms. The correct answer is **A.**

14. **A.** Substitute -3 for each y:

$$3y^3 - 4y^2 + y - 6 =$$
$$3(-3)^3 - 4(-3)^2 + (-3) - 6 =$$
$$3(-27) - 4(9) - 3 - 6 =$$
$$-81 - 36 - 3 - 6 = -126$$

15. **B.** Algebraically: Let x equal number of roses; then $3x$ equals number of carnations. So,

$$(x)(1.00) + (3x)(.50) = 7.50$$
$$x + 1.5x = 7.50$$
$$2.5x = 7.50$$
$$x = 3 \text{ roses}$$

Working up from the choices may be easier. Notice that only Choice **B**, 3 roses, gives a total of $7.50, since 3 roses purchased means 9 carnations purchased (triple the number of roses). Three roses at $1 each plus 9 carnations at $0.50 each equals $3 + $4.50 = $7.50. Only Choice **B** results in $7.50 being spent on all the flowers.

16. **B.** Set up an equation:

$\frac{3}{10}$ of gross is 15,000

$$\frac{3}{10}x = 15,000$$

Multiply both sides by $\frac{10}{3}$:

$$\left(\frac{10}{3}\right) \times \left(\frac{3}{10}\right)x = \frac{\overset{5,000}{\cancel{15,000}}}{1}\left[\frac{10}{\cancel{3}_1}\right]$$
$$x = 5,000(10)$$
$$x = 50,000$$

Or, realizing that $\frac{3}{10}x = 15,000$, divide by 3 to get $\frac{1}{10}x = 5,000$. Multiply by 10 to get $x = \$50,000$.

17. **D.** To answer this question, multiply 78¢ by 39.

$$.78 \times 39 = \$30.42$$

Because of the range in choices, you can approximate by rounding both numbers up and multiplying.

$$.80 \times 40 = \$32.00$$

Because you rounded up, your answer will be slightly less than \$32.00. Choice **D** is the closest.

18. **A.** To change any fraction to a decimal, divide the denominator (bottom number) into the numerator (top number):

$$
\begin{array}{r}
.125 \\
8\overline{)1.000} \\
\underline{8} \\
20 \\
\underline{16} \\
40 \\
\underline{40} \\
0
\end{array}
$$

19. **D.** A regular pentagon has five equal sides. To determine the length of each side, divide:

$$90 \text{ feet} \div 5 = 18 \text{ feet}$$

20. **B.** A careful look tells you that the only answer possible is

$$3 \times 3.99 = \$11.97.$$

A quick way to approach this is to round prices up one cent.

$$3 \times 4.00 = \$12.00$$

21. **D.** The highest average daily temperature during the dates shown was approximately 76°. The lowest was approximately 58°. Therefore,

$$76° - 58° = 18°.$$

22. **E.** The total number of different combinations ("how many different kinds") is found by multiplying the number of ways for each item. Therefore, 3 different breads times 4 different meats times 3 different cheeses = $3 \times 4 \times 3 = 36$.

23. **B.** The percentile score of each student shows how he or she did compared to the other students. Samantha's score of 70 is the same as or better than 82% of the other students' scores. Choice **A** is incorrect because a score of 70% incorrectly assumes that there were 100 questions on the test. Choice **C** is incorrect because Tony's percentile score of 93% shows how he did in regard to the other students. Choice **D** is incorrect because 7% of the students did better than Tony. Choice **E** is incorrect because 60% of the students did worse than Isabella.

24. **E.** To determine the amount of paint used, you need to know the number of rooms painted and how many gallons were used in each room. Since the question itself provides the number of rooms painted, Choice **E** provides the necessary information: number of rooms x number of gallons used = total number of gallons used.

25. **E.** To answer this question, subtract the distance Shalla walked from the distance Theo walked:

$$
\begin{array}{r}
6\frac{1}{4} = \ 5\frac{5}{4} \\
-4\frac{3}{4} = -4\frac{3}{4} \\
\hline
\frac{6}{4} = 1\frac{2}{4} = 1\frac{1}{2}
\end{array}
$$

Another way to approach this is to change each mixed fraction to an improper fraction, then subtract and reduce your answer.

$$6\frac{1}{4} = \frac{25}{4}$$
$$-4\frac{3}{4} = -\frac{19}{4}$$
$$\frac{6}{4} = 1\frac{2}{4} = 1\frac{1}{2}$$

26. **C.** Substituting the given values into the equation:

$$I = Prt$$
$$\$500 = (2000)(0.10)(t)$$
$$500 = (200)(t)$$
$$500 \div 200 = t$$
$$2.5 = t$$

27. **D.** In 2006, *approximately* 500 million barrels were in reserve. In 2000, approximately 100 million barrels were in reserve. Therefore, there were approximately 400 million, or 400,000,000, more barrels in reserve in 2006 than in 2000.

28. **D.** To find the perimeter of the pool, add together the lengths of its sides. The length of the side of each square on the grid is equal to 2 yards. The perimeter of the pool consists of 20 lengths of the squares. Therefore, the total perimeter is 20 × 2 yards = 40 yards.

29. **C.** Simple probability is computed by the number of possible "winners" out of the total number of possibilities. Since there are 6 odd numbers from 1 to 12 (1, 3, 5, 7, 9, 11), out of a total of 12 numbers, the probability of getting an odd number is $\frac{6}{12}$ or $\frac{1}{2}$.

30. **B.** The large carpet, 8' by 8', equals 64 square feet. A small square, 2' by 2', equals 4 square feet. Dividing the large area of 64 by 4 equals 16 small squares.

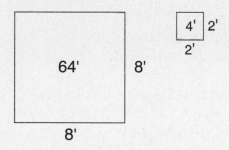

31. **B.**

$$\frac{3}{5} \times \frac{30}{7} =$$

Canceling gives:

$$\frac{3}{\underset{1}{5}} \times \frac{\overset{6}{30}}{7} = \frac{18}{7}$$

32. **D.** Since you are looking for the probability of teaching an Arabic or Hispanic student, you must first add:

Hispanic	+	Arabic	=
15	+	5	=	20

Then get the total population: And finally set up a fraction:

$$15 + 12 + 8 + 5 = 40$$ $$\frac{20}{40} = \frac{1}{2}$$

33. **B.** II only. The arithmetic mean is the average (sum divided by number of items), or $6 + 2 + 10 + 2 + 5 = 25$ divided by $5 = 5$.

The median is the middle number after the numbers have been ordered: 2, 2, <u>5</u>, 6, 10. The median is 5.

The mode is the most frequently appearing number: 2.

The range is the highest minus the lowest, or $10 - 2 = 8$.

Therefore, only II is true: The median (5) equals the mean (5).

34. **B.** If you deposit 2¢, you could get 1 white and 1 red gumball. But if you deposit 3¢, you will have to get 2 gumballs of the same color, either white or red. So the least amount to ensure 2 of the same color is 3¢.

35. **D.** Starting from the lower left-hand corner and simply counting the number of sides around the outside of the shaded area gives 16 sides. Now multiply $16 \times 3 = 48$, since each side is 3 inches.

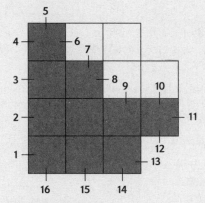

36. **E.** First solve the equation: $\frac{q}{5} = 10$

Multiply each side by 5. Therefore, $q + 2 = 50 + 2$

$$5\left(\frac{q}{5}\right) = 5(10)$$ $$q = 52$$

$$q = 50$$

37. **E.** The total charges (without tax) equal $18,600 + $1,800 = $20,400. To determine 8% of $20,400, multiply .08 by $20,400 = $1,632. The total price = $20,400 + $1,632 = $22,032.

38. **D.** Parallel lines are always the same distance apart. Only the figure in Choice **D** appears to contain two pairs of parallel lines.

39. **A.** Since Tom is shorter than Lebron and Kobe, and since Kobe is shorter than Jordan, who is shorter than Anthony, Tom is the shortest.

40. D. Since 30 cups is $2\frac{1}{2}$ times 12 cups, multiply 5 cakes by 2.5:

$$5 \times 2.5 = 12.5$$

or $\frac{12}{5} = \frac{30}{x}$

Cross-multiplying gives $\qquad 12x = 150$

Dividing by 12: $\qquad x = \frac{150}{12} = 12.5$

41. C. III only. The random sample indicates that 1,500 out of 2,500 California moviegoers, or 60% of those polled, prefer comedies. Of those polled, 500 out of 2,500, or 20%, prefer dramas; the same number prefer adventure films. Therefore, out of 8,000,000 total California moviegoers, 60% (4,800,000) prefer comedies, and 20% (1,600,000) prefer dramas. Only III accurately reflects one of these estimates.

42. D. Since Mrs. Solis received a 30% discount, she paid 70% of the retail price: (.70)($800) = $560. Mrs. Solis paid $560.

43. E. Find the perimeter of a rectangle by adding the length to the width and doubling this sum: $P = 2(15 + 18)$.

44. B. From the graph, Reynold's average score is 24.8 and Doe's average score is 13.7. The difference between 24.8 and 13.7 is obtained by subtraction.

$$\begin{array}{r} 24.8 \\ -13.7 \\ \hline 11.1 \end{array}$$

45. C. Twelve gallons is one-third more than 9 gallons. Therefore, the number of miles will be one-third more than 240, or 240 + 80 = 320. Or $\frac{240}{9} = \frac{x}{12}$

Cross-multiplying gives: $\qquad 9x = 2,880$

Divide by 9: $\qquad x = \frac{2,880}{9} = 320$

46. A. In 1992, the difference between index ratios of bottom water and surface water was the greatest, 3.5 to 5.

47. A. Change the word sentence into a number sentence (equation):

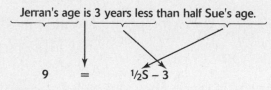

48. B. To answer this question, simply round off $29.54 to the nearest dollar. $29.54 is closest to $30.00.

49. B. Combine all x's and then all y's:

$6x + x = 7x$ (remember $x = 1x$) $\qquad$ The answer is $7x + 3y$

$2y + y = 3y$ (and $y = 1y$)

Note: You can't combine $7x$ and $3y$ because the letters are different. You can only combine like terms.

50. B. Using 150 of each kind of ticket assumes that an equal number of each kind were sold: 150 + 150 + 150 = 450. But since you know that three times as many senior citizen tickets were sold as adult tickets, if 150 adult tickets were sold, that would mean 450 senior citizen tickets were sold, for a total of 600 for the adults and senior citizens. Therefore, you know—since the total of all the tickets is 450—that the adult tickets sold must be fewer than 150.

Section III: Writing

To help you evaluate your essay writing skills, listed below are examples of three different written responses for essay topic one (there are no examples for topic two). Compare your essay to these three examples of a well-written essay, an average essay, and a poorly written essay. Use the checklist (pg. 352) to evaluate your essays, and to help you take a closer look and understand your scoring range. Topic prompt can be found on page 344.

Essay 1: A Well-Written Essay

When forming a friendship, I don't consciously evaluate the possible friend's character traits. It is usually a case of something that simply clicks. Over the long run, however, when I reflect on my best friend, Mike, I realize that the character trait most important to me in a friend is loyalty. By loyalty I mean a staunch support of me through thick and thin, regardless of whether or not the friend agrees with me.

Loyalty can be tricky. Should a friend support you, even when he doesn't actually approve of what you are doing or planning to do? This is a situation that arose between Mike and me. I wanted to quit school for a year and work to save money to help my mother, who had recently lost her job. Mike disagreed with my plan completely. He told me that it would be better for me to finish college and to borrow money from other relatives to help my mother. We argued about it, but our conversations never became angry. In fact, I appreciated the points he made, even though I chose to leave school temporarily. Mike's loyalty to me, once I'd made my decision, was invaluable. He helped me investigate job possibilities, gave me some good leads, and sympathyzed when the job hunt led to disappointments. This is the kind of loyalty that counts: a truly loyal friend is able to disagree with you and speak his mind and then remain your supporter when you make your own choices.

Mike has other great character traits, of course, like a sense of humor, an easy-going manner with me and my family, self-confidence, and integrity. When I place his loyalty at the top of the list, it isn't to suggest that Mike is basically like a "good dog." Far from it. He has much more to offer. But unlike some of my other friends, it is Mike I can go to when things go wrong. He has loaned me money, loaned me his car, loaned me his ear, and even when I know that helping me has been an imposition on him, he has never made me feel that it is. Basically, he is there for me, and this kind of loyalty is more important to me than any of his other traits.

Analysis of Essay 1

This essay does what the topic calls for. The writer defines loyalty in the first paragraph, and in the following paragraph gives particular examples of why this trait is important to him. Although he could have included other examples as well, his idea is presented fully and gracefully, and his conclusion is effective. The only error is the spelling of "sympathyzed" (should be "sympathized").

Essay 2: An Average Essay

The trait I think is most important in a good friend is a sense of adventure. I like someone who helps me try things I wouldn't try by myself.

My friend Celia is like that. She is afraid of hardly anything. It was Celia who got me interested in learning to fly a plane, which I wouldn't have done without her convincing me to try it. Flying is now my favorite thing to do, and I owe this to Celia's sense of adventure.

She also got me to go with her on a trip to South America. I have always been nervous about traveling, so this was a big step for me. That trip had its share of problems, but with her along to cheer me on I did fine. And the memories I have are wonderful. Celia sometimes takes big chances that don't work out so well, but she is never boring to be around.

The third example of Celia's trait is maybe the most important, which is that she helped me decide to move away from my hometown and try life in the "big city." I never thought I'd like living in a city, it was a frightning idea. I guess I didn't think I could make it on my own. But when Celia moved and got a good job in Chicago, I said to myself "maybe I can make it too." So with her sense of adventure, she became important as a role model, not just a friend.

Celia's sense of adventure is, to me, the most important trait she has as my friend. Without her help and without her as an example, my life would be much different.

Analysis of Essay 2

The writer addresses the topic, but writes short, choppy paragraphs. They could be developed with more details. For example, the introductory paragraph could explain in more detail why this trait in Celia is particularly important to the writer's own personality. The essay could also be improved with more details in the third paragraph and with a better concluding paragraph. There is one run-on sentence in the fourth paragraph and a spelling error, but the choppy paragraphs and lack of developed points are the biggest problems.

Essay 3: A Poorly Written Essay

A good friend has many important traits. Among them are honesty, loyalty, and bravery. I think honesty is the most important.

When a friend is honest, you can trust what he says and does. If he says you did a good job on something, you can trust that he means it, he isn't just flattering you. And if he tells you he will help you with something you have to do, he will do what he says he will, not make a lot of excuses. Honesty is at the top of my list of character traits in a friend which doesn't mean I don't also think loyalty and bravery are important.

How can you be a good friend with somebody who is dishonest? For example, one of my father's best friends talked him into investing money in a project that he knew was not on the up and up. My dad lost thousands of dollars. All because his friend was so dishonest.

My best friend is a very honest person. I don't think he has ever told me a lie. Even on little things. Once we were playing a tennis game and the score was tied. I returned his serve and another friend of his said my ball was outside. (This friend of his doesn't like me very well and has a tendancy to try to cause trouble between me and my best friend.) I wasn't sure whether my ball was in or out. But my best friend told the other guy that he was wrong, my ball wasn't outside. And I won the point. This is just a small example of how much I can trust my friend.

People have good and bad traits as friends. But in my opinion the most important trait a friend can have is to always be honest.

Analysis of Essay 3

The introduction is very weak. The second paragraph explains what the writer means by honesty, but it is clumsily written and contains a run-on sentence and punctuation error. The last sentence in that paragraph is tacked on; it doesn't lead anywhere. The third paragraph contains a specific example of the importance of honesty but again is poorly developed and contains a fragment. In the fourth paragraph, the writer does address the subject of honesty in his own friend, but the example he uses is confusing and includes irrelevancies ("This friend of his doesn't like me very well"). This paragraph also includes a fragment and spelling error. The concluding paragraph, like the introduction, is very weak. Generally, this essay lacks logical development and coherence.

PART IV

FINAL PREPARATION

The Final Touches

1. Make sure that you are familiar with the testing center location and nearby parking facilities.

2. Spend the last week of preparation on a general review of key concepts and test-taking strategies and techniques.

3. Don't cram the night before the exam. It is a waste of time!

4. Arrive at the testing center in plenty of time.

5. Remember to bring the proper materials: identification and admission ticket. For paper-based test takers, five or six sharpened Number 2 pencils, an eraser, and a watch.

6. Start off crisply, working the questions you know first, then going back and trying to answer the others.

7. Try to eliminate one or more choices before you guess, but make sure that you fill in all the answers. There is no penalty for guessing.

8. Mark in reading passages, underline or write down key words, write out important information, and make notations on diagrams. For paper-based test takers, take advantage of being permitted to write in the test booklet.

9. Make sure that you answer what is being asked and that your answer is reasonable.

10. Cross out or write down incorrect choices immediately: This can keep you from reconsidering a choice that you have already eliminated.

11. Using the information in the "Three Successful Approaches to the Multiple-Choice Questions" section (see page 4) is the key to getting the questions right that you should get right — resulting in a good score on the CBEST exam.